Footprints of a Twentieth Century Educator:
Lawrie Shears

# Footprints of a
Twentieth Century Educator

# Lawrie Shears

Eleanor Peeler

Published by Hybrid Publishers
Melbourne Victoria Australia
©Eleanor Peeler 2014

This publication is copyright. Apart from any use as permitted under the *Copyright Act* 1968, no part may be reproduced by any process without prior written permission from the publisher. Requests and inquiries concerning reproduction should be addressed to the Publisher, Hybrid Publishers,
PO Box 52, Ormond 3204.

First published 2014

Reprinted 2017

National Library of Australia Cataloguing-in-Publication data:
Author: Peeler, Eleanor, author.
Title: Footprints of a twentieth century educator: Lawrie Shears / Eleanor Peeler.

ISBN: 9781925000535 (paperback)

Subjects: Shears, L. W. (Lawrie William), 1921–
Educators–Victoria–Biography.
Education–Victoria–History–20th century.

Dewey Number: 370.92

Cover design: Art on Order
Cover image: Peter Lamb, Fairfax Syndication

The photo (opposite) of Dr Lawrie Shears appeared originally in *Parabo*, the annual magazine of Burwood Teachers College. Written across the top left hand corner are the words: 'To Eleanor, with all my best wishes for a happy future. L W Shears, 11/12/1962.'

This book is the outcome of a research project carried out by Dr Eleanor Peeler with the support of Professor Field Rickards of the Melbourne Graduate School of Education (MGSE), University of Melbourne, and in collaboration with Dr Lawrie Shears. The project has the approval of the MGSE Human Ethics Advisory Group (Ethics ID 0709570).

Publication of the book is supported by a Theodore Fink Publication Award, presented to members of the Melbourne Graduate School of Education community to promote dissemination of their research.

Dr Lawrie Shears

### For Dr Lawrie Shears

My principal
My friend
*This is your life*

### For my family

Thank you for your support in this task,
which seemed like a never-ending story.

### For those who have helped me

Professor Field Rickards
Emeritus Professor Richard Selleck
Dr Colin Moyle
Robyn Whiteley
and many others,
named and unnamed,
across the nation and across the seas,
who took part in interviews,
provided books, significant papers and photos,
personal writing and draft research
or dug through their archives
to provide unique insights
that have been woven together
to form the stories contained in this book.

You trusted my capacity when I had doubts,
boosted my morale when it ebbed to a low.
You saw value in the task and
encouraged me to persist.

Thank you for your trust.

# CONTENTS

| | |
|---|---|
| Illustrations | ix |
| Tables | xii |
| Abbreviations | xiii |
| Enquiries, inquiries and reports | xv |
| Preface | xvii |

## Introduction     1

## Section 1: FOUNDATIONS     5

| | | |
|---|---|---|
| Family Tree | | 6 |
| Chapter 1 | Origins | 7 |
| Chapter 2 | Childhood (1921–27) | 21 |
| Chapter 3 | Schooling (1927–38) | 35 |

## Section 2: A TEACHING CAREER     51

| | | |
|---|---|---|
| Chapter 4 | Student teacher: Fitzroy (Miller Street) State School (1939–40) | 53 |
| Chapter 5 | Training to teach: Melbourne Teachers College (1941–42) | 59 |
| Chapter 6 | Country teacher (1943–46) | 74 |
| Chapter 7 | Re-establishing lives: Rural Training Centre (1947–50) | 89 |

## Section 3: STEPPING OUT     105

| | | |
|---|---|---|
| Chapter 8 | London calling: Doctoral studies (1950–52) | 107 |
| Chapter 9 | Trainer of Teachers (1952–54) | 124 |

## Section 4: LAYING FOUNDATIONS — 139

Chapter 10  Surveying and planning the professional realm (1954–59) — 141
Chapter 11  A Harkness Fellow (1959–61) — 171
Chapter 12  The golden years at Burwood Teachers College (1961–69) — 189

## Section 5: LEADING THE FLOCK — 213

Chapter 13  In the wings (1969–72) — 215
Chapter 14  In the chair (1973–75) — 244
Chapter 15  In the hot seat (1976–79) — 273

## Section 6: NEW ERA — 309

Chapter 16  Turbulent times (1980–81) — 311
Chapter 17  Coordination (1982–84) — 341
Chapter 18  Beyond (1984– ) — 379

**ENDNOTES** — 393

**SELECT BIBLIOGRAPHY** — 429

**INDEX** — 457

# ILLUSTRATIONS

NB Where a source is credited the image is used with permission of that person or organisation. Many photos (in the illustration section) have come from personal albums or collections, not only from professional sources. Every effort has been made to trace copyright holders.

### 1. FAMILY
- 1.1 Shears' family tree
- 1.2 Annie and Robert Shears [Shears family album]
- 1.3 Ernest William Shears [Shears family album]
- 1.4 Dorothy Irene Brand [Shears family album]
- 1.5 Victoria Madeline and Josiah Brand [Shears family album]

### 2. CHILDHOOD
- 2.1 Lawrie as a baby [Shears family album]
- 2.2 Lawrie and Ernie outside the Governor's quarters, Beechworth Gaol [Shears family album]

### 3. SCHOOLING
- 3.1 The Duke of Gloucester's visit [*The Argus, 20.10.1934*]
- 3.2 Soccer team, University High School [*The Record* 1939]
- 3.3 Athletics team, University High School [*The Record* 1939]

### 4. TEACHING
- 4.1 Blackboard preparation [Lawrie Shears Notes of Lessons book, personal collection]
- 4.2 Fitzroy (Miller Street) State School/Merri Primary School [Barbara Brand]
- 4.3 Shears on stage [*The Trainee* 1942]
- 4.4 College hockey team [*The Trainee* 1942]
- 4.5 Shears with students from Form 3B at Bairnsdale High School in 1946 [East Gippsland Historical Society]
- 4.6 Staff at Bairnsdale High School 1946 [Graham Stuart]
- 4.7 Holiday work at the Myrtleford Mill [Shears family album]

### 5. RURAL TRAINING CENTRE
- 5.1 Shears' wedding to Mavis Redman [Lawrie Shears]
- 5.2 The Huffam Hut that was home to the Shears at Dookie

[Shears family album]
5.3 RTC football team, 1948 Premiers [Dookie Museum, The University of Melbourne]
5.4 Pete's Carrying Service [Peter Gemmell]

**6. 1950s**

6.1 Graduation Lawrence Shears, TPTC, BA, BCom, BEd [Shears personal collection]
6.2 Senate House, London [Institute of Education, University of London, archive]
6.3 Toorak TC trainee, on Topper, dressed as Lady Godiva [Denis Cunningham]
6.4 Shears with students at Oxford Hall
6.5 Shears with same students in recent times
6.6 Shears with Toorak TC staff [Deakin University archive]
6.7 Development of Burwood TC 1954 [Deakin University archive]
6.8 Founders of the Australian College of Education at the ACE 25th anniversary at Geelong Grammar School 1974 [Australian College of Educators archive]

**7. 1960s**

7.1 Harkness Fellow and family on tour in the USA [Unidentified source, Shears personal collection]
7.2 Shears with Mr and Mrs Waller at a Burwood TC party [Beth Chittenden]
7.3 Fun and games on sports day
7.4 Burwood TC student representative council members 1963 ['Parabo' 1963]
7.5 Shears and students on a New Guinea trip ['Parabo' 1964]
7.6 The house in Hopetoun Road [Eleanor Peeler]

**8. 1970s**

8.1 Directors General at the AEC Standing Committee meeting [DEECD]
8.2 Regional Director Ron Ginger and Lawrie Shears unveil the plaque at the Official Opening of the Western Metropolitan

Regional Office July 1974 [DEECD]
8.3 Japanese school, Commercial Road Primary School, Morwell 1989 [Roylanie School Photos, Morwell]
8.4 Tweedledum and Tweedledee [John Spooner]
8.5 The 'wedding' of the Drama Resource Centre bus to the DRC staff [Denis Gill, originally published in *News Exchange*]
8.6 Motorcycle driver training introduced, Thompson and Shears [DEECD]

**9.  1980s**

9.1 Lawrie Shears and Colin Moyle at the site for the IEA [DEECD]
9.2 Lawrie Shears, CGE [Fairfax Syndication]
9.3 Cricket field at Miller Street [Peter Lamb, Fairfax Syndication]
9.4 Miller St classroom [Peter Lamb, Fairfax Syndication]

**10.  POST-1980s**

10.1 Celebrating 50 years of marriage at the Melbourne Club [Shears family album]
10.2 Shears with Ted Liefman and Geoff Stevens [Shears family album]
10.3 Shears with Field Rickards, Dean, Melbourne Graduate School of Education [Eleanor Peeler]
10.4 Shears at a retired officers' function: Norman Curry, Kevin Collins, Geoff Spring, Lawrie Shears, Fred Brooks [DEECD]
10.5 Frank Tate (1864–1939) and Lawrie Shears [The portrait of Frank Tate that appears in this photograph was painted by the Australian artist McInnes, W. B. (1889–1939). Details are: oil on board, 79.4 x 67.0, The University of Melbourne Art Collection, gift of Dr Frank Tate, 1970. 1970.0237.000.000]
10.6 Shears with Joan and Lindsay Thompson [Eleanor Peeler]
10.7 Shears with Doreen Falk at the 30th Len Falk Memorial Lecture, August 2013 [John Duncan]
10.8 Presentation of the Sir James Darling Medal to founding member Lawrie Shears during 50th anniversary celebrations of the Australian College of Educators held at Geelong Grammar School, May 2009 [Eleanor Peeler]

10.9 ITF Farewell 2013: Government reception for outgoing International Teaching Fellows with patron Lawrie Shears and Minister for Higher Education and Skills, Peter Hall [Les O'Rourke, DEECD]

10.10 Family gathered to celebrate the inaugural Lawrie Shears Lecture, April 2013 [Les O'Rourke, DEECD]

## TABLES

Table 1.  Shears' teaching timetable for his first teaching round in Miss Hutson's Grade 3a at Coburg East State School, No. 4260

Table 2.  The changing face of education, classification of schools and enrolments 1954–60

Table 3.  Demographics of Victorian schools and their populations

Table 4.  Development of teacher education institutions in Victoria 1872–1972

Table 5.  Residential seminar series 1951–61

Table 6.  Regional seminar program 1956–60

Table 7.  People and institutions in the USA that influenced Shears' thinking

Table 8.  Secondary and technical enrolments in Education Department schools 1960–70

Table 9.  Schools and expenditure

Table 10. Regional Directors: new appointments

Table 11. Inaugural Council of the Institute of Educational Administration

Table 12. Executive staff of the Institute of Educational Administration

Table 13. Presenters at IEA Program 1

Table 14. Presenters at IEA Program 2

Table 15. Victoria's four recognised TAFE providers

Table 16. Institutional mergers from 1981 and Shears' connections

Table 17. Secondary teachers' working conditions: Analysis of State, national and international practices

Table 18. Analysis of class size

## ABBREVIATIONS

| | |
|---|---|
| AARE | Australian Association for Research in Education |
| ABC | Australian Broadcasting Corporation/Commission |
| ABV2 | Australian Broadcasting Commission/Corporation television, channel 2 |
| ACER | Australian Council for Educational Research |
| ADGE | Assistant Director-General of Education |
| ADPE | Assistant Director of Primary Education |
| ADSE | Assistant Director of Secondary Education |
| ADTE | Assistant Director of Technical Education |
| AEC | Australian Education Council |
| AUC | Australian Universities Commission |
| BA | Bachelor of Arts |
| BCom | Bachelor of Commerce |
| BEd | Bachelor of Education |
| CBD | Central Business District |
| CCEA | Commonwealth Council of Educational Administration |
| CEGGS | Church of England Girls' Grammar School |
| CMEP | Child Migrant Education Program |
| CMG | Corporate Management Group |
| CEO | Catholic Education Office |
| CRB | Country Roads Board |
| CRTS | Commonwealth Reconstruction Training Scheme |
| CSHE | Centre for the Study of Higher Education |
| CTCSA(V) | Council of Teachers' College Staff Association (Victoria) |
| DDA | Dookie Diploma of Agriculture |
| DDTE | Deputy Director of Technical Education |
| DEECD | Department of Education and Early Childhood Development |
| DGE | Director-General of Education |
| DPE | Director of Primary Education |
| DPS | Director of Planning Services |
| DRC | Drama Resource Centre |
| DSE | Director of Secondary Education |

| | |
|---|---|
| EAQ | Educational Administration Quarterly |
| ESL | English as a Second Language |
| HES | Higher elementary school |
| IEA | Institute of Educational Administration |
| ITF | International Teaching Fellow(ship) |
| LOTE | Languages Other Than English |
| LTC | Light timber construction |
| MCG | Melbourne Cricket Ground |
| NITE | National Inquiry into Teacher Education |
| OECD | Organisation for Economic Cooperation and Development |
| PAAP | Principal Aptitude Assessment Panel |
| RTC | Rural Training Centre |
| SAAP | School Aptitude Assessment Panel |
| SBS | Special Broadcasting Service |
| SCV | State College of Victoria |
| SPC | Shepparton Preserving Company |
| TAB | Totalizator Agency Board |
| TAFE | Technical and Further Education |
| TC | Teachers College |
| TEAS | Tertiary Education Assistance Scheme |
| TPTC | Trained Primary Teachers Certificate |
| TSTC | Trained Secondary Teachers Certificate |
| TTAV | Technical Teachers Association of Victoria |
| UHS | University High School |
| UNESCO | United Nations Educational, Scientific and Cultural Organization |
| UNIS | United Nations International School |
| VFSSPC | Victorian Federation of State Schools Parents' Clubs |
| VIC | Victoria Institute of Colleges |
| VIER | Victorian Institute of Educational Research |
| VPSEC | Victorian Post-Secondary Education Commission |
| VSTA | Victorian Secondary Teachers' Association |
| VTSP | Victorian Teacher Selection Program |
| VTU | Victorian Teachers' Union |

## ENQUIRIES, INQUIRIES AND REPORTS

1899–1901 Fink Royal Commission

1923–33 Hadow Report(s) (United Kingdom) on education in England by various consultative committees chaired by Sir William Henry Hadow

1929 Pike Report on soldier land settlement–report to the Federal Government

1944 McNair Report (United Kingdom). Report of the Committee appointed by the President of the Board of Education to consider the Supply, Recruitment and Training of Teachers and Youth Leaders

1945 Report on Educational Reform and Development in Victoria by the Council of Public Education Victoria

1947 Strayer Report (California)

1957 Murray Report on Australian Universities

1960 Report to the Committee on State Education in Victoria (Ramsay Report)

1963 Robbins Report (United Kingdom)

1964 Martin Report. Tertiary Education in Australia: Report of the Committee on the Future of Tertiary Education in Australia to the Australian Universities Commission 1964–65, 3 vols, chairman: L Martin

1967 Plowden Report (United Kingdom)

1971 Southwell Report

1963 Report of the Fourth University Committee, Victoria (Ramsay Report)

1972 Draft Statement of Roles and Responsibilities of Regional Directors (Dobell, Falk and Moyle)

1972 Faure Report

1973 Scott Report

1973 Karmel Report

1973 Cohen Report

1973–74 Kangan Committee

| | |
|---|---|
| 1973–75 | Swanson Committee of Inquiry into Teacher Education, 1973–75, produced the Cohen Report |
| 1974 | Bland Board of Inquiry into the Victorian Public Service |
| 1974 | First Report of the Board of Inquiry into the Victorian Public Service |
| 1974 | Second Report of the Board of Inquiry into the Victorian Public Service |
| 1974 | Kangan Report |
| 1975 | Third Report of the Board of Inquiry into the Victorian Public Service |
| 1975 | Curriculum Services Enquiry |
| 1976–79 | Committee of Enquiry into Education and Training (Williams Committee) |
| 1976 | Final Report of the Board of Inquiry into the Victorian Public Service |
| 1978 | Galbally Report |
| 1979 | Williams Report, 3 vols |
| 1980 | National Inquiry into Teacher Education (Auchmuty Inquiry) |
| 1980 | Auchmuty Report or NITE Report |
| 1980 | Victorian Enquiry into Teacher Education (Asche Enquiry) |
| 1980 | Interim Report of the Committee of the Victorian Enquiry into Teacher Education (Asche Report) |
| 1981 | PA Report |
| 1981 | Final Report of the Committee of the Victorian Enquiry into Teacher Education (Asche Report) |
| 1985 | Blackburn Report |
| 1985 | Quality of Education in Australia Review |

# PREFACE

The Lawrie Shears story records an important history of education in Victoria during the twentieth century. To begin with the roots it explores his family background and traces the evolution of public education since the *Education Act* of 1872.

Two world wars and the Great Depression affected the nation and the life of Lawrie Shears. The highs and lows of the era shaped social change and bred young people keen to express their views. Post-WWII immigration, nation building and an increasingly outspoken public challenged administrators to cope with rising demands. They wanted more teachers, more schools, and better conditions. Young people and old sought opportunities for continued learning in high schools, colleges and universities. Aligning with demands and perpetual growth were increasing calls for accountability in professional, political and public realms.

During a time of unprecedented growth, the stories told in this book address emerging trends, educational philosophies and administrative practice. They explore these in relation to Shears: how they informed his performance; how they directed his endeavours; how they influenced his philosophies and shaped his policies in each of the roles he filled.

The book tells the story of schools and classrooms, teachers and students and the people who worked in the system. It traces the influence of transnational flows of knowledge, philosophies and policy. Paying homage to the contributions of Shears and other key players, it records a significant social history, identifies the roots of today's education system and presents a platform for further research.

The work was supported by the Melbourne Graduate School of Education. As I completed it, the latest QS World University Rankings put the Melbourne Graduate School of Education at No. 2 in the world in 2014. (The Institute of Education in London is ranked No 1.) For me, that appropriately reflects the quality of the colleagues that I have had the privilege to work with.

Eleanor Hemphill Peeler<br>Melbourne, March 2014

# INTRODUCTION

The book is presented in six sections, each of which focuses on a particular era or aspect of the subject's career. Section 1 addresses Lawrie Shears' family background, childhood and schooling. Immigrant folk from Britain and Europe, his forebears ventured south in the mid-nineteenth century. The Brands and Shears left the familiar to seek a new life. Country folk with broad rural experience, they eventually migrated to suburban Melbourne. The nucleus of family played an important role in young Lawrie's life, particularly through the Great Depression.

As was required in Victoria after a child's sixth birthday, Lawrie was sent to school. An enthusiastic student, he did well academically and excelled in sport. After eight years of primary schooling he was ready for work but a neighbour suggested to his father that Lawrie sit the entrance exam for University High School. During this new phase of his life he made lifelong friends and a name for himself on the sporting field. Influenced by teachers who experimented with New Education ideals, Shears developed self-responsibility, and healthy attitudes to learning in and beyond the classroom.

Section 2 follows Shears' pathway to the teaching profession. Typical of the time, he served as a student teacher before entering teachers college. From the moment he entered the classroom he was smitten with the craft of teaching, experienced wonder in the relationship between teacher and child and became aware of the responsibility he held. Experiences as a student and trainee teacher, opportunities grasped at teachers college, and the philosophies of learning and friendships made, had a profound and lifelong effect. Equipped with the fundamentals of his career, Shears was ready to enter the classroom to teach. In country school settings he was highly regarded by colleagues and pupils, and received encouraging critique from district inspectors who noted his sound teaching and leadership skills.

Identified thus, he was plucked from the classroom with a mission to instruct at the Rural Training Centre, annexed to Dookie Agricultural College in country Victoria. Students at the Rural Training Centre were returned servicemen. Their average age was 26; Shears was 27. Though about to be married and keen to continue university studies, he accepted the challenge and during the next three years made a remarkable impact on his students' wellbeing. War-torn and broken, the men were able to re-establish their lives and make the transition from service to civilian life.

In Section 3 the story of Shears follows his career advancement. Aged 39 and equipped with three degrees, he embarked on doctoral studies in London. Staff members at the Institute of Education were forward thinkers and leaders in educational psychology. Welcomed into their ranks, Shears benefited from the experience personally as well as professionally. His philosophies of teaching and learning flourished, and his observation of youth activity in schools alerted him to the value of small-group interaction and the development of leadership qualities.

Not content to stay still, Shears travelled Britain from north to south and east to west, and visited the Continent and Scandinavia. Aware of the knowledge gleaned through these experiences, he was alerted to the value of travel for teachers who were generally cocooned in the system from their own schooling, through their training and to their teaching. On his return to Australia the 'little doctor' as he was known secured tenure as a teachers college lecturer. He left his mark on staff and students who appreciated his educational philosophies and lectures and his willingness to offer personal support.

Career advancement was significant for Shears who next stepped into administration, which is the focus of Section 4. The 1950s were challenging years for education departments nationwide, not only Victoria. He was involved in the purchase and development of sites for schools and teachers colleges, and pre-service and in-service training of teachers. In the position of Survey and Planning Officer he worked closely with the Director of Education and gained first-hand knowledge of the intricacies of administration and the education system statewide.

The opportunity to travel arose again when he was awarded a Harkness Fellowship in 1960 to broaden his knowledge in the United States. With his wife and family of four, Shears established himself at the University of California from where he observed the structure of tertiary education and the State College system. As in Britain, he toured the country with the family to understand the American people or on his own to meet the nation's leading educators, visit their universities and be present at special events. Teacher training was under review throughout the USA and he observed various models of the apprenticeship practice. The benefits of experience and observation were put to the test the following year at Burwood Teachers College where he was appointed its second principal. Shears built on Burwood's foundations, implemented liaison between schools and the college, and was at the fore among other college principals to promote the standard of courses and the status of the teaching profession.

Beyond the 'golden years' at Burwood, as they became known, Shears was promoted to senior administration in 1969. The three chapters in Section 5 deal with particular periods during the next twelve years. Assistant Director-General (Planning) and Deputy during Director-General Brooks' absence, Shears readied himself for the next career move. From the wings he worked closely with Brooks and gained further insight into Departmental operations. Times were tough for administrators and union angst was rife. Responsibilities of the Education Department had grown with the ongoing growth and increasing demands of unions and the public for more schools, more teachers and better conditions. These inherent tensions were conveyed to Shears upon his appointment as Director-General in May 1973.

Director-General for the succeeding nine years, the next two chapters address his role 'in the chair' when he established policies, and 'in the hot seat' which exposes some of the highs and lows of the period. While in the chair he created the Department he had envisaged, restructured administration, designated a Planning Services Division, and extended the Department's regional structure. He spread the power base, and in an evolutionary manner central administration began to shift laterally through the regions to schools. The school and the community movement and the training of those who sought leadership positions came to fruition. He worked in close liaison with the Minister of Education and educational directors in other states, was involved in numerous organisations and made time to visit teachers and students in Victorian schools.

Despite his effort to soothe unrest, tough times continued and were exacerbated when new Ministers were appointed. Newcomers to education, the Ministers were unaware of the nuances of the system, disregarded the steps Shears was taking towards power dissemination and, under a new guise, claimed the Department as their own. The hot seat was an uncomfortable time for Shears as the Ministers slowly eroded the Director-General's power. They reshuffled administration and ruffled the feathers of senior staff. Times were unpleasant for Shears but he survived disrepute and accepted a new senior role. Section 6 gives the reader insight into the turbulent times he and others experienced and, while Shears came through, others were broken men. Appointed Coordinator-General, ostensibly the most senior Departmental post, Shears worked with a new Minister when a new government formed, travelled abroad and wrote four Ministerial reports.

Seemingly unscathed though deeply sad that he was unable to finish his task, it was time to retire at 63. After a grand farewell he moved into a new phase of his life in which he worked in positions allied to education and attended conferences of bodies to which he belonged and where his contributions were acknowledged with patron status, several honorary Fellowships, life memberships and an annual lecture series. As age caught up he became less active, and the shift to the country removed him from the city and major activity. He suffered loss with the death of his wife, many lifelong friends and his son. The writing of this biography has stimulated a new interest in life and in friendships.

# Section 1:

# FOUNDATIONS

# Family Tree

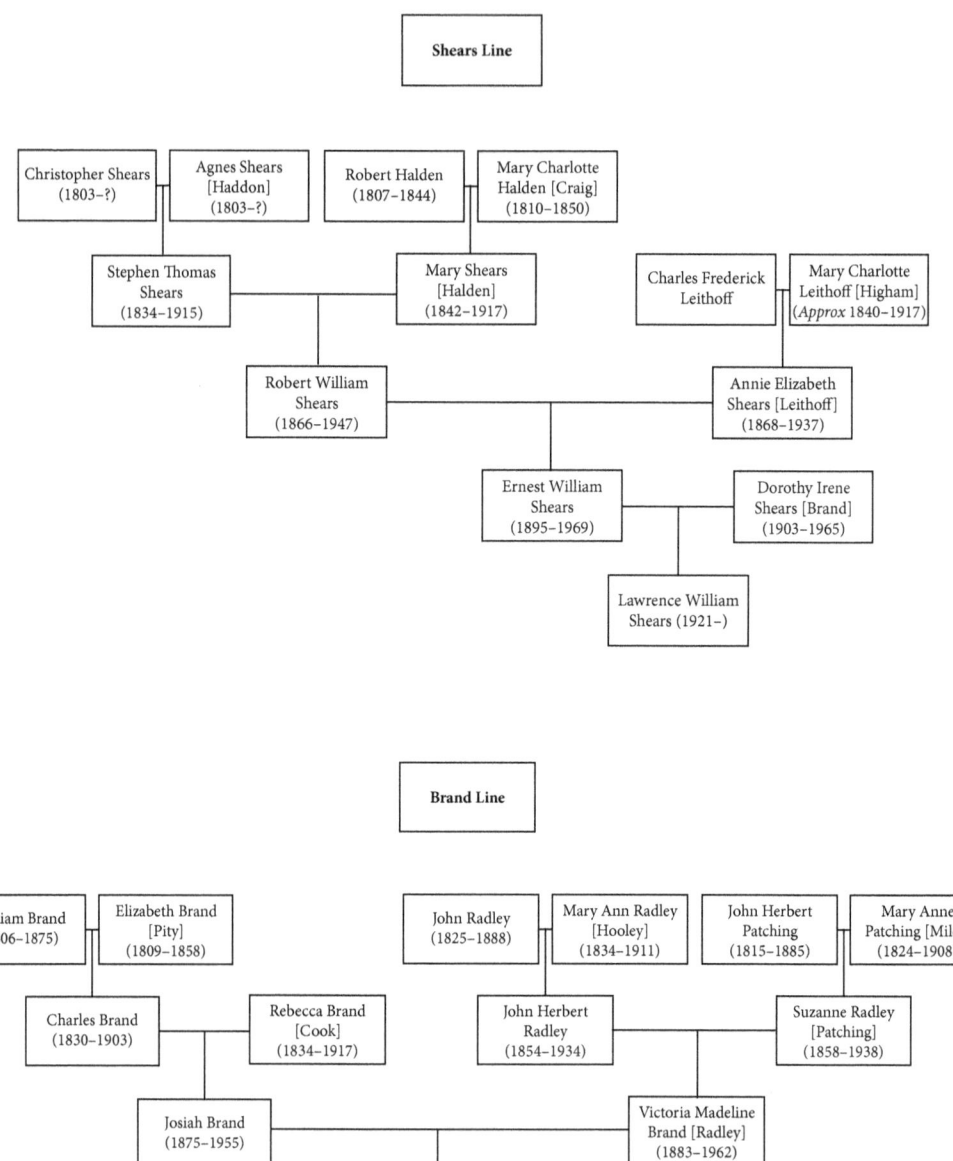

CHAPTER 1

# ORIGINS

*Let's start at the very beginning, a very good place to start;*
*When you read you begin with ABC*
*When you sing you begin with do-re-mi ...*

Oscar Hammerstein II

Winter in Melbourne; it is overcast, cold and damp. Three women wait in a simple suburban dwelling. A baby is due. In the kitchen steam rises from the boiling kettle on the gas stove. The flame flickers orange and yellow, tinged with blue. Sheets and towels are stacked on the table; some soiled linen spills from the basket on the floor.

It is Dorothy's eighteenth year when Lawrie is born. We can only imagine the scene. Three women alone: Dorothy; Annie Elizabeth her mother-in-law and a midwife who bore eleven; and Annie's sixth child, Florrie. Annie Elizabeth, wise and experienced, gives advice. Dorothy awaits the birth, uncertain what to expect. As crescendos of pain shoot through her body she tenses with each contraction. The contractions become stronger, closer and more intense. She breathes uneasily, seethes and groans. Florrie's cool hands gently calm the mother-to-be as she heaves on the bed, pushing her baby into the world. Dorothy's cries drown words of advice.

'It was a difficult birth,' Dorothy later told Lawrie. In 1920, Dorothy Brand, from Victoria's rich grazing midwest, had married Ernest William Shears, eight years her elder and born in Yalca in the State's northeast. Lawrie was their only child.

Lawrence William is the product of two pioneering families, the Shears and the Brands. The guts and courage of these early settlers typifies many families who celebrate four or five generations of Australian life. Lawrie is a legacy of ancestral journeys, dilemmas encountered en route and the character of the settlement when the settlers arrived. Some ancestors came to Sydney Cove and moved on to Van Diemen's Land while others journeyed to Port Phillip and continued into Victoria's Central Highlands. Yet others landed in Portland and ventured inland to Byaduk. Ancestral lines interwove as family members criss-crossed the nation to build a future for themselves and their descendants. Histories of the Shears and the Brands detail their perils at sea, their struggles through depression and drought, and their perseverance to establish a home and raise a family while adapting to an evolving social world. Both Shears and Brands contributed to building a new nation and adapted to the changing constructs of work as mechanisation replaced manpower. The courage of grandparents, Ernie and Annie Shears and Josiah and Madeline Brand, to journey into unknown frontiers to establish new beginnings, shines in the lives of Lawrie's parents Ernie and Dorothy and, in turn, in the life of Lawrie.

Lawrie's ancestry has links to England, Scotland, Ireland and Germany. Earliest arrivals in the Shears line came from Scotland in 1841. Robert Halden and Mary Craig became his great-great-grandparents through their daughter's marriage to Stephen Thomas Shears. The Brand line stems from settlers who arrived in Australia from England in the 1840s. Grandfather Josiah Brand married Victoria Madeline of the Radley line whose forebears came from England in 1813.

## The Shears line

We think of Aussie pluck as part of our Australian ethos. It embraces the heritage of our ancestors, their culture and courage. Lawrie's forebears were typical of many early immigrants. Great-great-grandparents hailed from Paisley, Scotland, likely victims of industrialisation – weavers of Scotland whose skills were replaced by machines, or farm workers whose knowledge of the land would hold them in good stead in the new nation. Robert Halden, his wife Mary Craig and two children arrived in Port Phillip on 30 November 1841. The barque *Alan Kerr*[1] left Greenock, Scotland, on 14 August with a crew of five, several fare-paying passengers and a load of immigrant settlers. The average journey in 1840 took 111 days and the shortest 83 days. One in every 51 adults and one in every 24 children died en route.[2]

On *Alan Kerr*'s voyage, the ship's doctor recorded deaths of nine children, three babies and a mother and child during childbirth. Three babies were born. The barque was captained by Archibald McKecknie with a First, Second and Third Mate. It had three passenger and a dozen steerage class cabins and carried 250 immigrants, mostly assisted as part of the bounty scheme. To encourage migration, settlers coming to Australia were reimbursed at set levels: £38 for married couples, £19 for single adults, £5–£15 for children according to their age. Eligibility for the bounty depended on having skills necessary for a budding agricultural economy using horse-drawn vehicles. For those employable as agricultural labourers, shepherds, carpenters or wheelwrights the bounty scheme held attraction. Bounty applicants required references to prove their sobriety and industrious nature. It was necessary for single adults to be under 30 but married couples were eligible up to the age of 40.[3]

The Halden family was among 43 married couples who shared the 81 offspring aboard. The Haldens travelled steerage and though it is unclear whether they were bounty or fare-paying passengers, shipboard conditions would have been trying. Georgiana McCrae, who travelled on the barque *Argyle*, from Plymouth in November 1840 to Port Phillip in March 1841, with four children, to join her husband Andrew in Melbourne, described being encased in a dark gloomy den, damp and comfortless, with children ill.[4]

Today we groan as we pack our bags to traverse the country or globe. We count the hours by air or road. One can only imagine the journeys of the past. Mary and Robert spent four months at sea, timeless, ever in motion from persistent winds. Each port was a respite from perpetual movement, the cramp of the cabin and the damp of the sea, day after day, day after day, rocking, pitching through the ocean's swell. On the new horizon lay the land of promise: the new Scotland for which emigrants endured their journey, trading the harsh winters of the hills and glens for scorching summers on the forested plateau of Victoria's Central Highlands.

The tall ochre and pink cliffs of Victoria's southern coast welcomed travellers who at last reached the end of the long sea voyage. Point Lonsdale heralded the narrow entrance to Port Phillip Bay where submerged rocks hindered entry. Melbourne Town, founded in 1835 by John Batman and officially named in 1836, was taking shape when Robert and Mary arrived in 1841. Hoddle's grid of broad streets and lanes named after royals and early explorers marked the city north of the river. Its rough streets were dust-ground in summer, mud-slurred in winter, '... so slushy and sticky that often to cross from any portion of the now flagged and fashionable "block" one required to be equipped in a pair of leggings or long mud boots'.[5] The city hosted the elegant, refined and unruly. In the early years of becoming established Port Phillip boasted hotels and inns, stores for supplies, haberdashers, coffee houses and an undertaker. In Collins Street West the Lamb Inn drew crowds and nearby the infant Melbourne Club became home to the horseback hoons of the Western District squattocracy. Prominent sites were the flagstaff on Lonsdale Street hill, a guide to shipping; the Bank of Australasia on a Collins Street corner; and the police station and two-roomed watchtower on Market Square used as the gaol. In 1841 construction began on the new sandstone gaol in Russell Street; St James, now known as the Old Cathedral, was a mere stone edifice; and at St Francis Church the foundation stone was laid. Shops were wooden, stilted structures; homes were weatherboard cottages with verandas overhanging the street. From ti-tree scrub in Flinders Street Watt's punt crossed the Yarra Yarra or 'Flowing Flowing' River to the southern bank where a tent city at Johnny Fawkner's farm housed new arrivals.[6] In 1831, five years before the Haldens' arrival, Port Phillip consisted of thirteen dwellings inhabited by 142 males and 35 females. By 1834 it was a collection of small, run-down brick buildings, small huts and tents scattered over the block bordered by Collins, Spencer, Bourke and King Streets. According to the *Port Phillip Gazette* the population of Melbourne Town had grown to 4,479 by 1841.[7]

Such was Melbourne, in the Port Phillip District in the colony of New South Wales, when Robert and Mary Halden arrived with their children Thomas and Jennat. It was a hot day, 74 degrees Fahrenheit, with a northerly wind. A storm was brewing and the roll of distant thunder echoed.[8] Dust-filled air rising from the unpaved streets had a propensity to dishearten the new settlers. Ashore at last and making arrangements for their onward journey, the Haldens found themselves amongst the crack of whips and the chink of chains, the whinny of horses and the crush of gravel under carriage wheels. After almost four months at sea they faced more travels, overland and inland. The growth of the woollen and pastoral industries attracted them. Stirred by British investment, Australian wool commanded high prices; land was readily gained by squatting and returns on investment were good. The family travelled 75 miles inland and northward to the Central Highlands. Day-by-day the bullocks trudged, their drays piled with supplies with barely space for families, their trunks and belongings; shantytowns with shanty pubs marked intervals along the way.

The Halden family settled at Glenlyon, seven miles northeast of Daylesford, known then as Wombat Forest. Glen Lyon Station, named after the town in the Scottish hills,[9] was the land of the Jajawurrungs, a people displaced by British settlement and disease. In 1839 James David Lyon Campbell (1809–44) grazed sheep on the Jumcra run near Mt Franklin. A later land acquisition closer to Melbourne became known as Campbellfield. 'Young' Mary Halden was born at Glenlyon in 1842. Images of McCubbin's settlers represent many like Robert and Mary, who eked a living from the bush and lived in a shingle-roofed slab shack. Though they did it hard, they cut and crafted a life. Wombat Forest timber supported a budding sawmilling industry that provided structure for mines; land cleared for grazing sustained sheep and promoted the woollen industry, with mills established in Castlemaine. Cropping complemented grazing in the pastoral region and flour mills supported the promise of a thriving wheat industry. Wages for pastoral workers averaged £25 per annum, with rations and lodging free. Skilled workers received £40 a year and during the season payment for shearers was £15 a season. The rest of the year they could undertake other work.

Squatters, shepherds, shearers and sawyers occupied Glenlyon and neighbouring runs. Robert surely found work on the land, caring for sheep, shearing or shepherding, performing pastoral duties or labouring tasks.[10] New industries in nearby towns offered alternative work. Fine wool from the Central Highlands was shipped to mills in Yorkshire, where local supplies in England had failed to keep pace with industrial change. Exports grew and squatter farmers accrued wealth but over-speculation would soon limit ready access to credit, and the 1840s drought triggered economic disaster. The depression years provoked seasonal and daily challenges to establish and maintain flocks and pastures to ensure supply. Wool prices fell as demand decreased. While things were tough in the bush, they were similarly difficult in the Port Phillip District. Wages fell and immigrant workers were severely distressed, many verging on destitution.[11] 'Banks were in peril, property values plummeted and fine-wool merino sheep, bought on borrowed money for fifty shillings a head, were selling to butchers for five shillings or were almost unsellable.'[12] Surplus stock was boiled down for tallow.

The situation gradually improved in the mid to late 1840s and confidence was redeemed by the 1850s. Port Phillip separated from New South Wales and in 1851 Victoria became a colony in its own right. As the decade unfolded the population grew and spread. With the discovery of gold in 1851 excitement rippled throughout the colony; Victoria's Central Highlands were no exception. People flocked to the established towns of Ballarat, Bendigo, Castlemaine, Daylesford, Dunolly and Mt Alexander and to numerous places beyond.

The impact of the depression on the wool-growing industry surely disheartened the Halden family, their employers and other immigrant rural settlers. Pressures of uncertainty possibly contributed to Robert's death in 1844, three years after arriving from England. Mary was pregnant with their fourth child when he died. The following year she married Richard Babbington of the Glenlyon squattocracy and Susannah was born. Mary and Richard had two sons of their own, Henry Charles (1847) and James Pringle (1850). Throughout these years of lows and highs the Halden/Babbington family sustained their livelihood at Glenlyon. Wool prices increased and in nearby towns manufacturing industries and commerce were booming. At sixteen, in 1858, 'Young' Mary Halden married Stephen Thomas Shears. Stephen and 'Young' Mary were to be Lawrie's great-grandparents.

Stephen Thomas of the Shears line hailed from England. Shears is an Anglo-Norman surname originating in Surrey where early members were 'Lords of the Manor of Shere'. Some of the family moved to England's southwest coast where the Shears of Devon formed an extensive clan in the early 1800s. Generally of working stock, they are listed as farmers and agricultural servants, carpenters, thatchers, butchers, bakers and tailors, but amongst them were an abbot and several scholars. Another branch of the Shears line in East Stonehouse produced shipwrights and seamen. Such was the background of Stephen Thomas Shears, who was born in 1834.

The land at Glenlyon provided a home for 'Young' Mary and Stephen Thomas, their two daughters and four sons. Susan Harriet was born in 1861 and their first son, Stephen Thomas, arrived in 1864. Robert William was born in 1866, Mary Charlotte in 1868, William Henry Charles in 1874 and Richard James Pringle in 1878. Stephen Thomas died at the age of sixteen.

By the 1860s, when the gold rush was over, seekers dispersed. The Central Highlands became a major agricultural centre that continued to attract regional immigrants who brought new knowledge and skills. Regions opened north of the Great Dividing Range – in the Goulburn Valley, the northern plains and the Wimmera district. Farm practices were changing, with mechanical means of preparing land and harvesting crops transforming the labour-intensive approach. New farming practices included irrigating the land. In the Goulburn Valley to the northwest of Glenlyon, Swiss and Italian winegrowers began to establish vineyards in newly irrigated areas released under selection and closer settlement schemes. The new settlers hoped the valley would support a viable fruit industry. German vine growers, artisans and orchardists, who migrated on religious, economic, political and social grounds, produced their food and crops communally, as they did on Melbourne's outskirts.[13] In far western Victoria, immigrant Germans fanned northward from Portland, joining those trickling eastward from South Australia's Barossa Valley to the Wimmera towns of Horsham and Dimboola, and northward to the Mallee towns like Hopetoun and Rainbow. Some Germans settled while others followed the Murray eastwards to the Goulburn region; their communities were close-knit, they maintained their religion and language.

As settlement spread and productivity increased, transport by wagon or coach became less cost-effective. In the late 1860s Victoria's rail network began to spread across the State linking major towns and facilitating transport from farms to cities and ports. From Western Victoria, the Leithoff family, of German origin, moved northward to Dunolly and then east to Strathmerton and the Goulburn Valley. It was in Dunolly that Charles Frederick Leithoff, a farmer, married Mary Higham and the couple's first two children, Charles and Annie Elizabeth, were born. The family may have faced difficult times in 1874 as the children were registered at the Industrial and Reformatory School.[14] Annie was a child of six. A legacy from 'schools of industry' in England, the Industrial Schools Bill, passed in 1862–63, instigated a charity-based network of industrial and ragged schools and reform centres across Victoria to provide education and care. Numbers of inmates rose alarmingly from 463 in 1864 to 1418 just two years later. Centres were located at Geelong, Princes Bridge, Sunbury, in the convent at Abbotsford and in the gold-mining centres of Ararat, Ballarat and Sandhurst where the Leithoffs sought fortune. Harsh conditions, long days, profuse punishment and too little food led to rapid spread of disease. Reports by district inspectors of education in 1871 revealed unsatisfactory educational standards, which may reflect poor levels of care.

Little more is known of the Leithoff family's movements except that Annie Elizabeth, domestic, aged 21, lived at Strathmerton at the time of her marriage to Robert William Shears, aged 23, labourer, whose address was Ulupna nearby. Robert and Annie, who became Lawrie's paternal grandparents, wed in Numurkah on 16 October 1889 at the Bible Christian Church, an offshoot of the Methodist Church. After their marriage they left the scattered settlement of Ulupna where sawmillers, farmers and fishermen eked livings from red gum forests, river flats and waters of the Murray River and Ulupna Creek. They moved beyond Strathmerton and Numurkah where irrigation held promise, travelling further north to the Riverina in southern New South Wales.

Today the trip to Jerilderie along the bitumen highway takes little more than an hour by car, unlike the journey for Robert and Annie, who spent long, long days on their journey northward to cross the Murray River at Tocumwal, and pass through Finley en route to Jerilderie. One can imagine their 90-mile journey with four young children, Archibald Robert (1890), Charles Stephen (1892), Lily May (1893) and Ernest William (1895), a babe in arms, who became Lawrie's father.[15] On the morning they left, Robert rose before dawn to harness his horses. Annie readied herself, woke the children and then loaded them into the wagon with their possessions. Hour after hour for several days the plod of hooves and the crunch of gravel beneath the wagon's iron-rimmed wheels marked the miles. The wagon swayed and pitched, dust choked and the sun beat down. Robert walked beside his harnessed pair. Annie rode aloft with the baby or walked beside him while older siblings ran ahead. The magnitude of such a journey can only be imagined: the preparation, the upheaval of packing the load and the children and leaving behind the known, the friendships and anything not of use.

In Jerilderie, Robert and younger brother James Pringle established a partnership in freight. With discussions complete Robert shifted the family to Tocumwal. He and Annie set up home in a weatherboard cottage, its rooms opening off a central passage from the front door. Here their fifth child Ivy was born in 1898 followed by Florence (1899) and, progressively, Norman (1901), Stanley (1903) Mary, known as Rose (1906), and Eva (1909). Annie was 48 when Edna arrived in 1915.

The need to provide for the family and the desire to work with pride satisfied Robert's stance to 'do anything but do it well'.[16] Business was tough and he was away for days at a time carting freight from Tocumwal to Finley to Albury and back, loaded with timber on return. Two horses pulled his laden dray and, tired by day's end, he sometimes rested on a shaft whilst trudging beside his horses. Such was life. Annie exhibited remarkable strength delivering babies for local women, rearing her own family and running the home. The family was largely self-sufficient with fruit trees and a vegetable patch in the backyard. Chooks and a cow provided fresh eggs and milk with cream to scoop off the top. There was room for children to play despite the spread of withering vines of ripened melons. Edna recalled the children all helped, 'you weren't bullied into it, you were just asked to do it and you did'. To polish the floor she and Eva slid on a mat up and down the passage where, family lore has it, Annie delivered the babies.

Britain's declaration of war against Germany in 1914 touched the entire nation. Young men and women enlisted with 'unself-conscious fervour' and people rallied to the patriotic cause despite plebiscites and anti-war angst. Schoolchildren supported the Education Department's War Relief Organisation and raised funds.[17] Annie's eldest son Archie joined the throng who left with great ceremony aboard troopships, but Ernie was not deemed fit. In 1918 Robert and Annie moved back to Victoria, living in East Shepparton in 1919 before moving to Elsternwick, five miles from Melbourne's GPO. Established beside the Elster Creek and heading south towards Brighton, the area's 1880s architecture reflected the opulence of earlier times. The 'pictures' were a new and exciting entertainment form that brought lightheartedness to people's lives as black-and-white images flickered across the screen. Tending the doors at the 'Renown' picture theatre Robert observed the stream of ex-service personnel from Caulfield Repatriation Hospital coming on crutches, in wheelchairs or on mobile hospital beds. An entrepreneur, he opened a confectioner's shop next door with the help of Ivy and Florrie and, in a double-fronted shop nearby, sold fresh fish while Rose sold flowers.

Ernest William was 23 when the family moved to Elsternwick. Classed as a 'traveller' he undertook work in the flour mills near Shepparton and as a grocer in Yalca. Joining Robert and Annie in Carre Street, Elsternwick, he established himself as a carpenter. In 1920, aged 25, he married 17-year-old Dorothy Irene Brand, spinster dressmaker of Hamilton. Dorothy's parents, Josiah and Victoria Madeline, lived in Bay View Road, Yarraville, so the wedding took place at St John's Church of England, Footscray.

## The Brand line

The rich volcanic plains of Western Victoria lured prospective farmers eager to seek land in the colony's early years. Portland Bay provided good access for newcomers and transport of stock and supplies. Farmland established by squatters reaped a good harvest until the depression slowed economic development and reduced the viability of new farming ventures. Despite shadows of uncertainty the land held promise for those willing to accept challenge. Over the years some collected substantial holdings, which in turn provided plenty of work. For others luck turned sour.

During the 1850s and 1860s the government attempted to break the squatters' reign, encouraging closer settlement on smaller holdings thus luring settlers anxious to select their own land. A series of Acts – *Land Sales Act* 1860 (Nicholson Act), *Land Act* 1862 (Duffy Act), *Amending Land Act* 1865 (First Grant Act) and *Land Act* 1869 (Second Grant Act) – enabled newcomers to select parcels of land up to 360 acres and purchase it after three years. Costs ranged from 10/- to £1 per acre according to location and improvements. Selectors generally lived in timber and daub dwellings and stocked their land by 'overlanding' flocks from Portland or the Southern Highlands of New South Wales. Selectors were exposed to stock loss from disease and dingoes, unpredictable weather conditions and fluctuating prices.

Among newcomers to move into Victoria's west were German settlers, some of whom, from South Australia, rolled in with their wagons to select and occupy land.[18] The major towns of Hamilton and Horsham, Colac and Coleraine lay on the Portland Harbour highways, while smaller towns sprang up at road junctions and water crossings. Byaduk, a small Wendish community established in 1853, was off the main track, 15 miles south of Hamilton. Some of its early arrivals from England were of Prussian descent. The Brand and Cook families were among Byaduk's pioneers.[19]

Byaduk, meaning stone axe, was for a time known as Neukirch, after a village in Saxony. Brand or Branke and Brandt stem from Brandenburg. According to Clyne (1991) Wendish, like other community languages, was banned as the medium of instruction during World War I.[20] It was a difficult time to be German, as the government could intern people of enemy nations. Australian attitudes were nationalistic; bonds with the British Empire were strong. The Victorian State *Education Act* was amended and many German place names were anglicised. People lacked tolerance for languages other than English, especially the language of German nationals.

Dorothy Irene, Lawrie's mother, was of the Brand–Radley line. Charles Brand, or Branke in some early records, born in 1830, arrived in 1854 from Chrishall, Essex. Later that year he married Rebecca Cook. After landing at Portland, Charles travelled 40 miles north with an immigrant group to settle in Byaduk. Charles and Rebecca would become Lawrie's great-grandparents. The couple had a large family, many of whom were Byaduk-born. Their son Josiah, born in 1875, who worked as an agent in Warrnambool, married Victoria Madeline Radley in 1902 according to the rites of the Free Christian Church in Queen Street, Melbourne.[21] Josiah and Madeline had five children: two daughters, Dorothy Irene (1903) and Clarice May (1905) born in Hamilton, two sons Norman Josiah (1907) and Harold William (1909) born in Byaduk, and Les Alfred (1914), their fifth child, born in suburban Cheltenham.

Lawrie's Radley heritage can be traced to William born in Dulverton, Somerset, in 1879. Corporal William Radley, a member of the 46th Regiment, was in charge of a shipload of convicts that sailed from the Isle of Wight to Sydney Cove on *HMS Windham*. The vessel left on 23 August 1813, sailing via Rio de Janeiro and Cape Horn, to arrive on 13 February 1814. Although he served in the 46th Regiment, William was a blacksmith by trade. In return for his service he was granted land in Tasmania. His personal history corresponded with the Napoleonic Wars (1803–15) and the capture by the French of *Windham* and *Ceylan*, both sailing ships of the East India Company, known as East Indiamen. Three years prior to William's journey, the British recaptured *Windham* from the Duperré squadron on 20 August 1810.[22]

In New South Wales William Radley formed an association with Catherine Cavanagh – aliases Kavanagh, Gaham and Dogherty – who was sentenced to seven years for stealing her mistress' handkerchief. Described as an 18-year-old, with 'ruddy' complexion, black hair and hazel eyes, Catherine was employed as a nursery maid. After arriving in Sydney Cove on 14 August 1815 Catherine worked in the government factory at Parramatta until she was granted Conditional Pardon number 993.[23] Catherine's journey to Sydney on *Francis and Eliza* was a nightmare, the journey long and eventful. *Francis and Eliza* sailed from Cork in convoy with *Canada*, leaving on 14 December 1814.[24] It had 54 male and 70 female convicts on board, six of whom died on the way. On 4 January, three weeks into the journey, the crew of *Warrior*, an American privateer, boarded *Francis and Eliza*. *Warrior*'s pirates held Captain Harrison and his crew hostage. They took his personal wealth and stole the ship's doctor's surgical instruments, medicine and clothing. They stripped the ship of its arms and munitions before leaving all aboard to an uncertain fate at sea. With the captain and crew in shock an unusual turn occurred as the nightmare journey continued. The *Sydney Gazette,* 12 August 1815, reported that the prisoners:

> ... no longer submitted to the usual restraints, but nevertheless conducted themselves with the most exemplary propriety, dividing themselves into watches and performing the duty of the vessel at a time when we are sorry to say the ship's company themselves had to an alarming number become refractory and insubordinate. The spirits and other liquors were treated as common plunder, and the most dreadful scene of riot and intemperance prevailed, until their arrival at Santa Cruz, on the Island of Tenerife, on the 10th of January and the ship having been several times set on fire.[25]

After this event, *Francis and Eliza* harboured at Tenerife for several days where disorderly passengers were disembarked and put on an alternative vessel. In convoy once more with *Canada* and the frigate *Ulysses, Frances and Eliza* continued the southward journey with a military detachment on board, finally arriving in Sydney Cove on 8 August, 246 days after she set sail.

In the course of his duty, William Radley met Catherine in the Parramatta workhouse and took her as his partner. Following the granting of Catherine's pardon, the couple left New South Wales to take up William's land in Launceston, Tasmania, where William re-established himself as a blacksmith. Although it appears the couple never married they had several children: Jane Charlotte (1817), William (1818), Joseph (1822), John (1825), Mary (1827) and Samuel (1829). Mary died as an infant and Samuel was badly burned when members of a local Aboriginal tribe set fire to the Radleys' blacksmith shop and home. Taking Samuel with her, Catherine swam the South

Esk River to get help. The tragic event was worsened by the subsequent need to send the older children to an orphanage school. Unable to cope, Catherine left William and eventually married in 1845. William died in Launceston the following year. Their sons William and John sailed to Portland in the 1850s and moved north to the Hamilton district, where they took up good farming land to produce fine wool. A number of Radleys had already settled near Penshurst on the southern fringe of the Grampians. It was here that John Radley married Mary Ann Hooley (1834–1911). The couple would become Lawrie's great-grandparents. John Junior, a son of this union, married Suzanne Patching. Their sixth child, Victoria Madeline, born in 1883, married Josiah Brand in 1902. The couple became Lawrie's grandparents.

Josiah and Madeline Brand remained in the Western District for several years. They left Byaduk prior to the birth of their fifth child, Harold William, in 1914, and ventured northeastward to the Goulburn Valley. The valley held promise; its irrigated land was bringing superior yields, the rail link minimised transport costs, and new markets were opening for dried fruit, canning and associated industries. The Shepparton Preserving Company (SPC) began operation in 1917. When it established canneries at Ardmona and Mooroopna, associated industries sprang up. Josiah and Madeline lived in the midst of this growth. Residing in Shepparton East in 1919 where the younger children attended primary school, they formed an alliance with the Pullar family who bred a golden clingstone peach ideal for canning. Little else is known of the Brands' activities in the valley or their reason for moving on. Perhaps concerns specific to fruit growing affected their stay: blighted blossoms, brown rot and seasonal challenges that affected supply and demand of soft-fleshed fruit. Perhaps the Brands' dream turned sour and the partnership simply dissolved with Josiah, Victoria Madeline and their family moving to Melbourne. They established roots in Seddon where Josiah set himself up as a traveller. Here their daughter Dorothy lived until her marriage to Ernest William Shears.

CHAPTER 2

# CHILDHOOD (1921–27)

*Wonder is the beginning of wisdom.*

Socrates

## Government education in Victoria

Education in Victoria became compulsory on 1 January 1873 with the passing of *The Education Act* 1872 (No. 447) by Attorney-General James Wilberforce Stephen. It stated:

> ... for the better carrying out of this Act an Education department shall be formed, to consist of a Minister of Public Instruction, who shall be a responsible Minister of the Crown, a Secretary, and Inspector-General, inspectors, teachers, and such other officers as may be deemed necessary, and such Secretary, Inspector-General, inspectors, teachers, and other officers shall be appointed and removed by the Governor in Council.[26]

The authority of the Crown stamped the Act, and those who carried it out were citizens of high esteem: a body of full-time professionals commissioned to govern education for all young Victorians.[27]

The Act provided free education to all children, including girls, 'of not less than six and not more than fifteen years (without some reasonable excuse) to attend school for a period of sixty days in each half year'. They would attain 'competency in reading, writing and arithmetic to the satisfaction of an Inspector of Schools'.[28] At this time of Victoria's history, Education became a government department. Teachers, as public servants, were paid a salary by the State and rewarded by results. 'Four hours secular instruction'[29] was given in every State school, although the Act made allowance for use of school buildings for other purposes providing they did not interfere with schools' secular responsibilities. The Act abolished State aid to church-funded schools, raising ire among denominational school communities dependent upon public moneys. The Catholic Bishop James Alipius Goold lamented the imminent 'godless compulsory education'.[30]

Central control was considered pivotal to reaching 'the scattered, sparse settlement of the country by early individuals and families … to maintain order, to administer justice in all serious cases and to undertake public works involving substantial expenditure'.[31] The rationale was to provide equity in student tuition, building programs and staffing extending into Victoria's remote areas. Though hierarchical, the centralised system guided courses of study and school hours and, through regular inspections, gave access to attendance patterns, characteristics of schools and teachers' records. Many educationists supported the carefully regulated system, believing that 'schooling could not be entrusted to impoverished local groups dotted thinly round a large colony, divided bitterly by religious disputes and lacking any strong sense of community'.[32] Others spoke vehemently against the monopoly that 'snuffed' individual freedoms.[33]

Reflecting on the era, Dr Barry Jones suggested the education system established under the 1872 Act prepared 'young people not only for work, even more for life, familial, social, cultural, political, aesthetic, sport and play'. He claimed some groups accused it of priming children for 'industrial-era process work, with rule by the clock, uniform delivery, pupils as raw material, teachers as process workers and schools looking like factories'. Supporting this stance, education historian Les Blake cited the aim of continuation schools, where education continued beyond Grade 6 to Grade 8, as being for children of working classes destined for manual labour.[34] This view is in line with the '*habit* of order and submission to rule' of Selleck's description of the mid-nineteenth century educational culture being stern, narrow and time regimented. Teachers were 'artists in their use of the cane'. Education per se taught Reading from the official Reader and Writing as penmanship. The keys to Arithmetic ability were calculation and accuracy. Knowledge of rules applied to Grammar.[35]

## The Education Act of 1872

The *Education Act* 1872 established the blueprint for education in Victoria and, with minor amendments, determined its basic structure for the succeeding century. Recording the history of teachers colleges, Don Garden noted that, in 1873, school enrolments increased 50 per cent, spearheading a decade of demand. Under the Act the newly formed Education Department took control of 453 Common Schools and negotiated control of 590 church schools. By 1880 it governed 1810 schools across the State. The passing of the Act caused a flurry of activity and planning to establish a system that provided basic education, and stirred the need to draft courses, write regulations, undertake an extensive building program and recruit and train new teachers.

'The fledgling Education Department had been flung into a new and urgent situation. Lacking comprehensive precedents in big school design and without adequate time for consultation or experiment, it was obliged to spend nearly all its time churning out accommodation.'[36] Buildings previously used by denominational schools were generally old, poorly constructed and no longer suitable. Economy was the key; hence minor variations to standard designs were adapted to alternative sites. Commonly used were symmetrical 'H' and 'U' shaped designs, with back-to-back classrooms. The Buninyong model of WH Ellerker formed the basic construction for at least sixteen schools. It consisted of 'two parallel sets of rooms sharing that windowless wall … two large schoolrooms of maximum size formed wings which were separated from the central block by transverse corridors that gave access to all rooms'.[37] Architect HR Bastow similarly used stock designs, adorning them with embellishments to give each a unique appearance. Large suburban schools were of solid brick with slate roofs and were set on bluestone foundations. In country regions, rural schools accommodating 40 to 60 students were mainly wooden though some were constructed of brick. Between 1873 and 1885 the prime concern was to build new schools but in the succeeding decade priority was given to additions, some of which had embellishments, ornamentation and towers varying the basic design.[38]

An unfortunate result of the years of expansion was poor training of new teachers. Under pressure imposed by demand, the Education Department's Certificate of Competence was the sole credential for would-be teachers. In addition to strict examinations, annual inspections were made:

> ... in order to enable the holder of the Certificate to accumulate evidence of his practical skill as a Teacher, provision is made on the back hereof for the Inspector to record from year to year his opinion of the said holder's ability and diligence in his profession.[39]

Blake reflected upon the enormity of the problem: in 1884 among the State's 2,563 teachers only five had degrees, twelve held first-class honours (having attained six or eight subjects towards their university degree), and 221 had matriculated.[40] The Training Institute in East Melbourne catered for small numbers of trainees so employment of pupil teachers and monitors in schools filled the shortfall. Under the monitorial scheme, senior students helped with classroom organisation and instruction and occasionally had full class responsibility. Though pupil teachers worked under similar conditions, they were encouraged to study concurrently to attain their Trained Teachers' Certificate. Head teachers and district inspectors offered tuition in a broad range of subjects but the rigour of the daily routine affected their ability to cope. Annual inspectorial examinations in theory and practice placed them under an additional pressure. Selleck describes a pupil teacher's typical day:

| | |
|---|---|
| 8.45 am–9.25 am: | Receive instruction |
| 9.30 am–12.15 pm: | Teach |
| 12.15 pm–12.45 pm: | Assist with keeping in defaulters |
| 1.30 pm–4.15 pm: | Teach |
| 4.15 pm–5.00 pm: | Receive instruction[41] |

A pupil teacher's diary displayed by his grandson gives insight into the process of becoming a teacher:

> It was common to start off as a pupil teacher at the age of 14 and work one's way through the various classes – 7/6/5 – but there was no actual training ... only Education Department

subjects – Certificates of Competence in a broad range of subjects such as Science, Horticulture and Botany, Swimming, Lifesaving and Physical Training, earn a St John Ambulance medallion or a licence to teach Singing. Primary school teachers had a whole variety of different bits and pieces, that's the way they got qualifications, doing Departmental subjects, which they normally did as pupils, learning from teachers within the school.[42]

Citizenship and personal wellbeing were important teacher qualities; hence from 1878, the Licence to Teach required applicants to provide certificates of personal health and character and to pass a literacy test. Between 1872 and 1880 the teacher workforce increased twofold from 2416 to 4215 while the population of school-aged children almost doubled from 136,055 to 229,732.[43] In 1888 the Training College in Grattan Street, Carlton, replaced the Training Institute. Superintendent at the time, Charles A Topp, an English-born graduate of Melbourne High School and the University of Melbourne and member of the Bar, guided curriculum changes in schools, raised entry levels at the College and extended the course to two years.

Children attending government schools benefited from educational growth but despite steady economic development Catholic schools were continually denied State aid. During the boom between 1873 and 1890 expenditure on educational infrastructure in the government sector was substantial. Correspondingly, primary and secondary industry increased and revenue rose. As often happens when economies boom, sudden downturns shake the nation. In the 1890s recession struck, placing a strain on Victoria's resources, especially those intended for education. Through the turbulent years of depression the population continued to grow and imposed an additional burden on the developing education system. Notwithstanding the need for more schools and teachers, the government reduced educational expenditure. Building programs slowed and, regardless of demand, severe staff cuts and closure of the training college dried up the teacher supply.

## The Tate years

An outspoken opponent of the funding dilemma was Frank Tate whose service to education embraced the spectrum from pupil teacher in 1877 to Director of Education from 1902 to 1928. During his term as inspector (1885–88) he publicly criticised the administration of education and was appalled by the training college's closure. Apart from school-based guidance of pupil teachers, the college was the sole means of teacher training. Speaking as a trainer of teachers (1889–95) he deplored the closure and amalgamation of schools, cutbacks in building and maintenance expenses, and reduction in bonuses for teaching extracurricular subjects, such as singing, drawing, drill and gymnastics. He criticised retrenchment of pupil teachers and monitors, salary slashing, dismissal of married women and employment of an 'army of inexperienced beginners'.

Appointed principal of the training college in 1900, Tate attempted to make it 'the powerhouse of educational reform' in the 'mould of the New Education'.* He was aware of trends overseas and interstate and believed Victoria's system was lagging behind.[44] He envisaged a more liberal curriculum and imaginative approaches to teaching the three Rs and opposed the practice of payment by results, which he believed encouraged a rote approach to learning, curbed the curriculum, stifled individuality and limited learning potential. Tate saw knowledge as empowering young minds in interesting, active, perceptual and interconnected learning processes. Being in touch with the needs of the system, the teachers and the children, he attempted to counter social and political sway that limited learning, supporting liberal alternatives and encouraging sensitivity, harmony and individual development.[45]

Views held by Tate tallied with the Fink Royal Commission's (1899–1901) appraisal of technical education in Victoria, its assessment extending beyond the technical to embrace the entire Education Department. The Commission recognised the economic benefit of an educated society wherein each additional year of schooling proportionately raised the standard of national efficiency and increased powers of production. It recommended freeing the Department from public service control and making provision for 'higher primary' pupils to be educated beyond Grade 6 in continuation schools.[46] The Commission advised restructuring of the Department. Rather than a Secretary, as implemented under the *Education Act* 1872, a Director of Education chosen from the ranks of its own professional officers was to be the Department's permanent head, solely responsible to the Minister of Education. Despite opposition, as a young man of 38 years, Frank Tate was appointed the first Director. His appointment on 26 February 1902 fulfilled the requirement for a professional educator/administrator to fill the position.[47]

Tate's appointment as Director of Education put him at the head of an Education Department of 1947 government schools, employing 5066 teachers to educate Victoria's 228,241 schoolchildren. He was scathing of a 'narrowly educated and ill-trained' lot; only 7 per cent of teachers had college qualifications, 41 per cent were classified as pupil-teachers, monitors or sewing mistresses, and 50 per cent had a Licence to Teach. The Licence stated satisfactory completion of the course for a pupil teacher '… in accordance to the Regulations under the *Education Act* 1890' and stipulated:

> In order to enable the holder of this Licence to accumulate evidence of her practical skills as a Teacher, provision is made on the back hereof for the Inspector to record from year to year his opinion of the said holder's ability and diligence to perform her profession.[48]

Following the 1890s depression, Tate's task was to expand the education system, provide schooling for all Victorian children and ensure that schools had suitably trained staff. On becoming Director, he 'inherited plant and personnel which were seriously deficient', a downhearted teacher workforce and a team of inspectors resentful of his appointment, many of whom used outmoded approaches and resisted change. In particular, senior departmental officers James Bagge and Alexander Stewart felt it outlandish to be under the control of a 'young man who buttressed his slight administrative experience with a strong will and a head full of untried ideas'.[49]

Victoria's dependence on its rural economy made agricultural education fundamental to sustaining the national economy.[50] Beyond the provision of agricultural education was a move towards establishing secondary education throughout the government sector and extending equity of educational access as envisaged in the Act of 1872. Pioneering schooling beyond the primary years by introducing continuation schools and agricultural high schools, Tate bypassed the nongovernment sector, traditional providers of secondary education. His affirmation that the powers of the Education Department should be enlarged to allow State-supervised continuation and secondary schools was applauded by successive generations.

## Training teachers

The rapid development of the education system meant an urgent need to train new teachers. During Tate's jurisdiction he worked in partnership with Dr John Smyth, affectionately known as the 'Doc'. Smyth took over from Tate as Principal of the Melbourne Teacher Training College (Melbourne TC) when it reopened in 1900 and served until his sudden death in Japan in 1927. Tate and Smyth were aware of trends and experimentation overseas filtering into the Victorian system. While Tate implemented policies Smyth's foremost goal was to improve teacher training. Smyth was influenced by his New Zealand experience where he served as Chief Inspector in the Wanganui District, by a visit to Scotland where he completed his DPhil in 1900 and by studies in Germany. He was passionate that teachers understand children's psychological development and explore the relationships between humans and their environment. He supported the philosophies of Johann Friederich (1776–1841) and Frederick Froebel's (1782–1852) stimulation through play. This was similarly applauded by Frederick John Gladman during his term as Superintendent of the Teacher Training Institute (1877–85) and integrated into the text of *School Method* published in 1877.[51] Though Tate questioned the success of Gladman's efforts to introduce these philosophies, his own attempts to 'vitalise and oxygenate the system' corresponded with Smyth's inclination toward the Herbartian approach. Like Gladman, Smyth applauded exploration, intellectual activity, and explanation, believing that teachers should be aware of modern technological society's needs and drop classical bookishness.

He affirmed that children absorbed knowledge into their 'circle of thinking' and that teaching practice embraced the child's all-round development.

Under Smyth's guidance the Melbourne TC produced high-calibre graduates who entered the workforce well aware of developing educational trends and equipped to use them. Principal Smyth, concerned with teachers' wellbeing, ensured a balance between 'learning' and 'being'. College life was both pleasurable and stimulating, building lifelong friendships in a family atmosphere created by the 'Doc' and Emma, his wife, whom the students affectionately called 'Mamma'. Daily routines began with assembly at 8.35 where Smyth alerted students to the world's changing nature and inspired them to excel academically and culturally. College life embraced musical evenings and concerts, debating and literary societies, organised sport and an exchange visit with Sydney Teachers College. It enriched students' social wellbeing in line with their expanding social, cultural and political worlds. Residential students, whose male and female students resided in separate wings of the College building, were to dress for dinner. Young ladies who left the College grounds wore gloves and young men were to seek Smyth's permission before inviting a young lady out.[52]

Melbourne TC was the core of new philosophies permeating teaching in government schools. Its quality staff, many of whom were former trainees, had distinguished credentials and expertise. George Browne entered as a student in 1910 and, following war service, was appointed lecturer in Master of Method (Secondary) in 1920, a position deferred for two years while he served as vice-principal of Lancaster Teachers College and then, as an Oxford Travelling Scholarship recipient, visited Germany and the USA. Appointed Vice-Principal in 1923 he became Principal a decade later, concurrently serving part-time as the University of Melbourne's first Professor of Education (1933–9). Matthew Stanton Sharman, a student in 1901, became a staff member in 1903 and later took on the principalship of University High School.[53] Both Browne and Sharman were Gladman Prize awardees as top-graduating students. From 1924 Alice Hoy lectured in Method and, after her studies abroad, accepted principalship of the Secondary Training College in 1949, holding the position until 1958. The influences of experimentation, child-centeredness and philosophies of the New Education swayed these and succeeding prominent educationists and, like ripples in a pond, each influenced others in turn. George Browne, Chris McRae and Ken Cunningham supported individualism and flexibility of student movement as in the Winnetka and Dalton plans (philosophies developed in the USA that encouraged creativity, initiative and self-reliance in children) and the project approach as influenced by John Dewey. Affirmation that education must focus on the child is reflected in the philosophies of Melbourne TC principal A J Law (1939–50) who argued, 'Give the child freedom ... retire to the background; be ready to give help and guidance when the demand for these is urgent but do nothing for the child which he can do for himself.'[54]

Education could not exist in isolation, divorced from the rest of society. While the seeds of major initiatives were forthcoming, education was not immune from social events. Frequent changes of government, drought, finance restrictions and World War I influenced the education system Lawrie experienced in his formative years. His learning journey was subject to social, economic and political transformations, divisions between good times and lean, and betwixt staid traditions and developing trends, each of which shaped his philosophies of life.

## Childhood

Australia's population topped six million in the mid-1920s; it was a nation on the move. Manufacturing and light industries that previously supported the war effort were channelled to sustain industrial growth. Mechanical advancements changed the nature of work while public works and construction of dams offered new employment options. An influx of British expatriates accelerated expansion, reduced unemployment in Britain, satisfied Prime Minister Bruce's call for 'Men, Money and Markets' and endorsed Australia's commitment to industrial growth.[55]

In Victoria State schools emphasised bonds with Britain. Stories of the Empire's heroes inculcated loyalties, patriotism and duty. Against a backdrop of the bush, pioneers and local heroes, *The School*

*Paper* reinforced the bond and commitment to the motherland. The Victorian Readers, new in 1928, similarly linked loyalties to Britain yet embraced the local scene. Images of acorns and field mice in the Second Book, Columbus in the Fourth, the Commonwealth and Federation in the Sixth, contrasted with the fate of little (yellow) dog dingo (Second Book), children lost in the bush and Simpson's donkey (Fourth Book), and the tale of Clancy of the Overflow (Sixth Book).

Visits from Royalty punctuated the decade. Victorian children at school traced the voyage of Edward, Prince of Wales, in 1920 and eagerly awaited his arrival in Melbourne in May. He was met with parades and displays of allegiance. Annie Finlay of Moreland School had her patriotic poem published in *The School Paper*:

> The sun shines, the flags wave, the Prince stands by;
> The children march with their heads held high …
> Shoulder to shoulder the young lads stand,
> The budding flower of Britain's farthest land,
> Their supple limbs the whistle's call to obey.

The arrival of Prince Albert, Duke of York, and his Duchess in 1927 was similarly celebrated, corresponding with the opening of Canberra's Parliament House.

The 'Golden Twenties' was exciting for women whose social avenues and workplace roles were expanding. Liberty was theirs in their lifestyle and clothing; skirts were shortened, bodices were lowered and stockings were silk. The world was abuzz with jazz, the foxtrot and the Charleston; smoking became popular and divorce rates rose. Edith Cowan's election to Parliament in 1921 presented a public voice for women, the radio kept them abreast of news and music, and silent films and 'talkies' brought new entertainments. Immigration continued to boost the population, forcing education systems to expand.

The war made parents increasingly aware that the future of youth lay in education. Technological advance gave new opportunities. Rising birth rates reflected a sense of social stability and suggested a promising future. Married in 1920, Ernest William Shears and Dorothy Irene Brand set up home in Horne Street, Elsternwick, where Lawrie was born in July the following year.

In 1924, when Lawrie was three, Ernie was appointed foreman of reconstruction at Beechworth Gaol. The small town of Beechworth in Victoria's northeastern highlands lay at the foot of Mt Buffalo. It was a long day's journey for Ernie, Dorothy and Lawrie, travelling by steam-powered train from Melbourne to Wangaratta Junction and via a branch line to Beechworth. Built in 1870, the line was constructed to attract holidaymakers to Mt Buffalo and the Victorian Railways chalet. Harold Winthrop Clapp, a railways administrator, conducted campaigns to promote agriculture and tourism to the region and produced the slogans 'Grow more grass – top dress your pasture' and 'Go up into the Brightness on the Buffalo Plateau'. A far-sighted leader with extensive travel experience, he gave insight into trends overseas that he adapted to suit local circumstance. He promoted passenger and freight services and recognised the potential threat of road transport; he was keen to employ a skilled workforce. He encouraged apprenticeship training and teamwork, cooperation and professional development among his employees.[56]

When work began on the gaol in 1924, rail was enticing visitors to the remote northeast. Victorians realised the area's natural beauty, winter sporting potential and cultural heritage stemming from recent histories of the gold-mining days peppered with heroes and scoundrels. The Beechworth Gaol, constructed in the 1860s at a cost of £47,000 and with additions in the 1880s, had housed Ned Kelly before his hanging in Melbourne. Behind its local granite walls, cellblocks ran off a central passage. It had a chapel wing and governor's quarters where Ernie, Dorothy and Lawrie lived for the year of reconstruction. World War I had forced the gaol's closure but when work was complete it would reopen as a reform centre. Among Lawrie's memories were the smell of pines, and the old tree on the post office corner where Beechworth residents nailed notices.

Mr Corbett, a local contractor, was commissioned to rebuild the gaol as a post-war reconstruction project. Employed as foreman of works, Ernie had major responsibility. Despite his commitment to a good day's work, he was a caring husband and father, enjoying country living, frequently walking into town with Dorothy and Lawrie for breakfast. An avenue of European trees led to the wide main street lined by substantial stone and brick buildings. Hotels had broad balconies with verandas that stretched across gravel footpaths. Built in local stone the electric telegraph office, the treasury and the gold office were evidence of the gold era's wealth. In autumn Lawrie shuffle-shuffled through leaves, kicked them high, watched them float and fall. On cold winter mornings his breath puffed white clouds. As he ran he chuff, chuff, chuffed like a train, his arms motioning the engine's wheels, and he whistled – 'whooooo'.

Horse-drawn wagons, coaches, jinkers and buggies were common sights. Rail connected the town to the Sydney–Melbourne line and cars were few. At weekends, driving Mr Corbett's canvas-topped 'tourer', Ernie took the family for picnics in a clearing beneath towering trees with a crystal-clear creek where Lawrie waded, stepped across the rocks and threw pebbles. Winter snow stretched a white blanket across Mt Buffalo but the high country summers were hot. Often fire threatened. A whiff of smoke from a distant blaze did not deter a picnic to Buckland Gap but as smoke darkened the sky and the wind whipped the flames the little family rushed home. The sight of the post office at the corner of town signalled their safety, but thousands of acres were burned.

When the Beechworth mission was complete the family moved to Melbourne's inner suburban Prahran. Though just south of the city along Punt Road, until 1850 when Princes Bridge was built, the suburb was accessed by punt. Proximity to the city enhanced its potential. Closer settlement in the 1870s led to allotments of a 'Very Eligible Size' that were situated within walking distance of Windsor and Hawksburn stations, and had frontages to Williams Road, and Newry and High Streets.[57] When the Shears took residence in 1925, milk and bread were delivered daily in horse-drawn carts, the dustman came weekly and the night cart called regularly. Ernie paid £50 deposit for Number 24 Newry Street, a red-brick single-fronted cottage close to High Street. It is still standing, with the original leadlight windows in the master bedroom. Lawrie's room was down the passage, the lounge and kitchen were at the rear and the washhouse was out the back.

The children of Newry Street played in the street and kicked footballs in the park nearby. Enjoying companionship, Lawrie organised small concert parties, charging a halfpenny for entry. On one occasion he sang 'You were meant for me', a popular song of the time. Across nearby High Street in the Victoria Gardens he rode his tricycle beneath arched branches of English trees that encircled a bandstand. Often playing with a friend on a bike, Lawrie pedalled as fast as he could to keep up. Though well known in the street he frequently played alone, sitting in the passageway of the house building Meccano[58] or listening to his crystal set. He heard the Grand National Steeplechase when Gus Powell rode Mosstrooper to victory on 5 July 1930, winning a three-penny bet with his dad. In the small backyard he drove his toy truck in the dirt. Tess the dog lay under the back steps waiting to grab his legs so he would bound up the stairs to avoid her. Swinging on the front gate to wait for his father to come home he slipped one day, catching his nose on the billy hook. He ran inside to nurse the wound under the kitchen table.[59] He was almost six when the tabletop was his hospital bed for his tonsils to be removed. The chloroform mask suffocated as it summoned sleep. His mother made cold jelly and custard to slip down his throat.

By day Dorothy visited family and friends or stayed at home to sew on her treadle machine. Her parents, Josiah and Madeline, lived ten minutes' walk away. Set on a corner block their house had two chimneys. Aunt Clarrie lived a few doors beyond with her locksmith husband. They had no children. Grandparents Robert and Annie lived in Elsternwick and had a farm at Rowville, a good destination for a Sunday drive.

As with many families of the era, the Shears and the Brands held strong Christian ties. Though Ernie and Dorothy were not church-goers, Lawrie attended Sunday school in a hall adjoining the red-brick Methodist church in High Street. He played a ghost, he sang and he read a passage in the Christmas pageant, which caused his friends to mock, 'Reading, reading in a book!' Each year children from Sunday school and their families picnicked at Ferntree Gully. They travelled the 16-mile journey in the back of a furniture van, sitting on rolls of thick felt padding. After lunch they climbed the tower on One Tree Hill to look across sparsely populated farmland to the city.

CHAPTER 3

# SCHOOLING (1927–38)

*Life isn't about finding yourself. Life is about creating yourself.*
George Bernard Shaw

## Windsor State School No. 1896

Turning six is an important event in a child's life. Christopher Robin recalls '… now I am six I'm as clever as clever …'; Lawrie started school at Windsor State School, No. 1896[60] on 1 July 1927, midway through the second term of the three-term school year.

The *Education Act* 1905 (No. 2005) was an Act to amend the *Education Act* 1901. It passed on 12 December 1905 and made attendance at school compulsory for children aged from six to fourteen. Primary schools (known generally as 'State schools') educated children to the end of Grade 8. A further amendment in 1910 introduced the Qualifying Certificate to mark the end of Grade 6 and the Merit Certificate to identify completion of eight years' schooling. Benchmarks for school leavers, these certificates guided students towards work or further educational options. For employers and parents the Merit Certificate was a significant achievement, marking students' proficiency across the spectrum of subjects.[61]

Montessori philosophies, the Dalton approach and the Winnetka plan influenced concepts of teaching, which built on the child's capacity and desire to learn. Teachers, the catalysts of learning, helped students establish personal benchmarks and develop skills to fulfil learning needs. Relationships were crucial to understanding the character of each child, their interests, abilities and potential. Ultimately they became independent learners whose enhanced social skills and sense of responsibility equipped them for project and group activities.[62] Values entrenched at Windsor State School began before Lawrie's school days commenced. Headmaster Grey's (1905–19) innovative programs gave learning a tangible air. Outlines of countries drawn on the asphalt transformed the playground to a large world map; flowerbeds and a vegetable plot roused interest in gardening and the wonders of nature. Senior boys attending sloyd classes had improved motor and social skills and greater self-confidence.[63]

Lawrie walked to school down Newry Street, along a backyard lane, across The Avenue to Hornby Street and left towards Dandenong Road. Built in 1877, the two-storey, red-brick building, typical of schools of the era, reflected Victoria's affluence. Gallery rooms at either end of the ground floor elongated its 'H-shaped' structure. One was the infant room, the other a hall-cum-classroom, and in the cross-section of the 'H' were several more classrooms and the headmaster's office. A bay window over the main office and a bell tower of 'unprecedented importance' erected in 1890 enhanced the building's façade. Due to persistent dampness the school was remodelled in 1915. According to a departmental formula each classroom measured 10 square feet per pupil capacity, or two children to each foot of classroom length. The school was built to accommodate 400 students, but due to constant overcrowding a second storey was added to replicate the original floor plan.[64] Classrooms remained crowded in the 1920s though enrolment had stabilised to about 500. Rows of children in two-seater desks filled the space between the back of the room and platform beneath the blackboard. Lawrie remembered class size increasing as children progressed through the school, swelling from around 30 in junior levels to 50 plus in higher classes. With 60 pupils in his Grade 4 class Mr Rowell patrolled the aisles with his strap at hand.

Lawrie adapted to routines, established friendships and played sport. The school ground seemed large, with space to kick the football and race friends to the back fence. The boys also played marbles, cherry-bobs, hopscotch and leapfrog or flicked cigarette cards across the asphalt. Reading his first book in Grade 1 was a milestone shared with Jackie Howe. In Miss Berry's Grade 3, he topped the class and received a copy of Grimms' Fairytales at the end of the year. Teachers at Windsor State School nurtured Lawrie's potential, noting his aptitude and giving him minor tasks. In Grade 4 he read to the class while Mr Rowell marked the roll and in more senior classes where students used ink he filled the inkwells.[65] Miss Powell's marriage midyear in 1931 caused minor disruption but the Great Depression changed lives. The economy slumped, building halted; there was no work for his father. Day after day Ernie walked the streets with his box of tools; day after day he trudged home heavy-hearted. Unable to maintain mortgage payments, the family moved from their Newry Street home to live with Dorothy's parents Josiah and Madeline in Pakington Street.

Soon moving again, they settled with Uncle Charlie, Aunt Gladys and Cousin Ellis in Head Street, Elsternwick. Despite the distance from the Windsor school Lawrie completed Grade 6, travelling by train with his lunch, pencils and books in a new Gladstone bag.[66] Unlike today's open-plan carriages with self-closing doors, the red rattlers of the time had brass handles not easily turned by a boy's small hand. Running late one morning he scrambled onto the platform at the back of the train instead of going through the gate onto the platform. Unfortunately the station master caught him and he was reprimanded. Fatty P, who sat immediately behind Lawrie at school, frequently kicked and prodded the Gladstone bag under the desk. Finally his antics became too much. Lawrie turned and jabbed the steel nib into Fatty's leg. Fatty yowled. He rushed outside. Lawrie was punished.

The nation's social quandary tainted Lawrie's sixth year at school. The economic dilemma troubled Ernie and Dorothy's relationship. Though shielding their son, money matters weighed heavily. Lawrie was alert to Ernie's downheartedness and Dorothy's broken spirit. School was a sanctuary in which to be a child, develop a network of friends and expand his horizons. For Lawrie as for other young people, the sight of out-of-work countrymen clouded their hopes. With no prospect of work they stayed on at school, swelling class sizes and increasing pressure on the impoverished education system.[67] Towards the end of Grade 6 Ernie took Lawrie to enrol for the following years at Elwood Central School, No. 3942. Looking at father and son the headmaster asked, 'Is your name on the list?' With the school filled to capacity he suggested Elsternwick State School, No. 2870, which had Grades 7 and 8, as the alternative.

## Elsternwick State School

Headmaster Anton William Rutherford Vroland was a strong leader and passionate teacher. A forward thinker, he was a 'beacon of progressive education'. He encouraged innovation throughout the school, 'pioneered the use of film as a teaching aid, set up a central library [and] taught foreign languages'. Inspectors acknowledged the 'vitality of his initiatives', inspiring the students and buoying their potential.[68] Keen to offer new knowledge to fresh young minds as they progressed through their school years, Vroland actively engaged students individually and in groups to develop 'the seeing eye, the thinking mind, and the understanding heart'.[69] Vroland's enthusiasm for horticulture nurtured interest in nature and was in tune with Dr Leach's efforts to draft a week-by-week course in nature study from Grade 1 to Grade 8 in 1911–2.[70] Vroland segregated the school ground into areas for play, cultivated garden and natural habitat. He built a hothouse and initiated a statewide essay competition, which students from Elsternwick entered. To Lawrie's surprise he won 3rd prize. Mrs Vroland supported her husband's horticultural interests. Upon her death in 1932 her collection of pot plants was bequeathed to the school. Lawrie was among senior students who carried them down the street to the school.

In Miss Nedwell's composite Grades 7 and 8 of 50 students, Lawrie expanded his circle of friends. There were the Lloyds who lived down the street, Jack Oldridge who was later killed in the war and Nancy Millis who later received an MBE and an AC for her work in microbiology. Lawrie was elected Class Chairman and conducted the election for Class Secretary and office bearers. Miss Nedwell prepared her pupils scholastically, developed strong citizenship ideals and instilled a love of literature. The pages of *The School Paper* and the Victorian Readers held tales of the Empire's heroes, mythology and folklore, Australian pioneers and classical poems. Henry Lawson's poetic drama of the 'Ballad of the Drover' and Byron's tale of 'Waterloo', where 'lamps shone o'er fair women and brave men ... when music arose with its voluptuous swell', enchanted Lawrie. Similarly he was impressed by Shelley's image of the cloud that brought fresh showers for the thirsting flowers, the sun's throne that was bound with a burning zone and the moon's with a girdle of pearl. The preface to the Eighth Book claimed the stories projected interest, academic advancement and moral wellbeing. From focus on the home environment they gradually took young readers afar to 'gain a rich heritage and acquire a well-founded pride in race'. While conveying the fundamentals of reading, the literary selections embraced 'the inculcation of sound morality … implanting of desire for world-wide toleration' and opposed 'international strife.'[71]

Though sport was not part of school activity until after WWII, facilities were integrated into new school plans. Older suburban schools had limited space and teachers had no formal sports training. May Cox and Frank Beaurepaire introduced swimming instruction and general sport, and interschool competition through the State Schools Amateur Athletics Association. In 1922 Rosalie Virtue advocated rhythmic movement, games and dance for health and growth. Foundations laid in the infant years supported ongoing physical development.[72] In 1934, Lawrie's last year at primary school, the Education Department established a Physical Education Branch. Four years later it introduced a Certificate of Competency in Physical Education. Correspondingly the University of Melbourne offered specialist training for teachers in the Diploma of Physical Education and from 1937 teachers college graduates could apply for time off from teaching to undertake university studies (called extension courses). Dr Fritz Duras taught 'the history, principles and methods of physical education, its anatomical and psychological bases, body mechanics, hygiene, diet and first aid'. Not until 1959 could secondary graduates gain extensions.[73]

Lawrie enjoyed sport. He had a straight kick and played rover in football, took a good swing with the cricket bat and was a keen tennis player. He often played with Cousin Howard at a neighbour's or at the public courts nearby using old balls and paying threepence a game. Though small in stature and bandy-legged, Lawrie 'ran like a hare' over short distances and outran most of his friends. Drill was a major physical activity and a pathway for children statewide to take part in the grand display of welcome to the Duke of Gloucester in 1934. Among thousands gathered at the Melbourne Cricket Ground was Lawrie.

Friends at Elsternwick, Barney Searle and Keith Miller, excelled at cricket. Keith was a good all-rounder and both he and Barney batted well, hitting 100 or 200 in an innings. A year older than Lawrie, Barney started work after completing Grade 8, and began to play district cricket. Keith went to Melbourne High School, and under the influence of Bill Woodfull played for the school and went on to play in the Sheffield Shield for Victoria and the test cricket team for Australia.[74] Lawrie often told this story, with its implications that schooling and the influence of some people are instrumental in the direction one takes in life.

> **N⁰ 259572**
>
> # Education Department,
> ### VICTORIA.
>
> ## MERIT CERTIFICATE
>
> ### This is to Certify
>
> that _Lawrence Shears_
>
> has completed satisfactorily the Course of Study prescribed for _Elementary Schools_
>
> Dated at _Elsternwick_ 2870 School this 16th day of _November_ A.D. 1934
>
> Head-teacher's name _A W R Ireland_
>
> _W Pukma_
> Inspector of Schools.

*Shears' Merit Certificate [Shears personal collection]*

Completing Grade 8 and attaining his Merit Certificate marked the time for leaving school and seeking a job. Lawrie's service as a telegram boy at Elsternwick impressed the postmaster, who offered him work. Immediate employment would relieve the family's financial pressures. But a neighbour, Mr Barnes, aware of Lawrie's enterprise in establishing the Southern Naturalists' Club as 'the biggest club in the world' and confident of his potential, took Ernie aside and advised him to allow Lawrie to continue his schooling, even offering to help. Ernie's own pathway from school to the Yalca flour mill typified the belief widespread in the community that 'parental occupation, ideas and aspirations' determined the child's future rather than any potential the child might show.[75] Taking Lawrie in hand Mr Barnes guided him to University High School where he sat the entrance exam and won the right to commence Form 3 (Year 9) in February 1935. Lawrie reflected that from then onwards the routine of his life during school term was 'catch the train at Elsternwick or Gardenvale and get off at Flinders Street, catch the cable tram to Story Street opposite the University of Melbourne and have four years at University High School'.[76]

## University High School

The significance of tiny acorns becoming mighty oaks is true of Victoria's secondary system. Stemming from Tate's efforts to introduce continuation and agricultural high schools, secondary education developed in bursts throughout the twentieth century. From the embryonic years in the 1900s, 35 high schools were scattered statewide by 1928 when Tate retired as Director of Education.[77] Before Tate's initiative an assortment of fee-paying colleges run by independent groups and churches catered for those progressing through secondary schooling. The size and standards of these varied, as did their buildings, values and teacher quality. The Education Department under Tate established the first State secondary school under the guise of the Melbourne Continuation School, in 1905. Carefully named to minimise objections to the State's incursion into the secondary sector, the school was located on the site of the Old Model School in Spring Street. This was the forerunner of similar schools in regional

Bendigo, Geelong and Castlemaine that evolved in the next four years. During the same period the Education Department established five agricultural high-cum-vocational schools in Warrnambool, Sale, Ballarat, Shepparton and Wangaratta, thus spreading the tentacles of secondary education across the State.[78]

The extension of schooling to postprimary levels was fraught with challenge. While the Victorian State School Teachers' Union endorsed the promise of equity, efficiency, and university access for all, not surprisingly leaders in the independent school sector were scathing of the developing secondary system. The thin edge of the wedge, it would erode their monopoly on secondary provision and lead to a statewide network of government schools. To overcome the dilemma of teaching standards the *Registration of Teachers & Schools Act* 1905 (No. 2013) provided for 'registration of efficient schools and qualified teachers' of an acceptable standard.[79] The general qualification for secondary teachers would be the Diploma of Education, involving two years' practical and theoretical educational study plus six university subjects selected from arts or sciences. Trainees required a minimum of 60 hours' teaching experience under the supervision of an approved teacher or lecturer.[80]

The *University Act* 1904 (No. 1926) supported postprimary training in schools of mines and agricultural colleges, and provided £1000 for evening classes. Education remained outside the university's domain and did not meet its academic profile. Despite Smyth's challenge, the University Council argued that the study of pedagogy better suited the nearby 'very useful institution' to which he was newly appointed principal. In discussion with Tate, the University Board reached a decision to balance academic and professional needs of education students, as with its mining and agricultural cohort. This led to university admission of the 'Diploma Twenty', selected from teachers in schools by the Minister of Education.[81]

Expansion of secondary schooling continued and growing enrolments in the Diploma of Education underpinned the need for training specific for secondary teaching practice. Alice Hoy in *A City Built to Music* claimed that discussion between the University, the Association of Secondary Teachers and the Education Department resolved:

> That a practising school for the training of secondary teachers be established in connection with the Diploma of Education and that the Education Department be approached and asked to establish this school as soon as possible. [82]

Close to the University and Training College, in Lygon Street, Carlton, the local primary school was in trouble. Its numbers had dwindled so the Department transferred the remaining students to schools nearby. The vacant building was an ideal site. The University Practising School, established in 1910, supported students enrolled in the Diploma of Education. It was renamed in 1913 when the privately operated University High School closed down. As a practising school for secondary candidates, the carefully selected staff members of the 'new' University High School undertook the school-based component of the 'Dip Ed' course. LJ Wrigley was appointed the first principal of University High School, a position he held concurrently with his lectureship in Method at the Training College. Matthew Stanton Sharman, who became the school's second principal, also lectured in Method.

At the end of 1929 University High School moved to new buildings in Story Street, Parkville. Set on the former horse and pig market site it was across Sydney Road from the University of Melbourne. The school's numbers more than doubled after the move, from 398 in 1930 to 940 in 1935.[83] The baby boom of the 1920s had caught up with the State's scant secondary system and placed pressure on existing schools, a trend that continued through succeeding decades. The Education Department's dilemma to accommodate secondary student growth was exacerbated by the onset of the Great Depression, which put a damper on development, overturning the post-war affluence and causing educational expansion to falter. Just two high schools were built between 1931 and 1954.[84]

Sharman served as Principal of University High School from 1915 to 1941. An innovative leader, he held his position with 'great distinction'. He was seen as a forward thinker who ran a forward-thinking school.[85] While he administered the school he concurrently served the Education Department as Vice-Principal (Secondary) at the Training College. Though holding dual roles, his passion was for that of principal. His travels abroad in 1925, supported by an Education Department scholarship, gave insight into developing trends, many of which became tradition at University High. Sharman maintained the traditions established by Wrigley, brought philosophies inherent from his student years at Scotch College, and acted on knowledge acquired while teaching at Wesley College and the Training College. Each week he addressed students gathered at Melba Hall assemblies and broadened their outlooks by imparting his own philosophies and listening to views expressed by guest speakers and past students.[86] Sharman introduced features of English public schools to University High School: the house system and sports days. He encouraged student elections of house and form captains and invited those elected to council meetings. Special events were church parades in North Melbourne and gatherings at the Shrine of Remembrance on Armistice Day, when students paid homage to those from the school who had served. Five of the school's six houses were named after old boys whose lives were lost during WWI.[87] House days to commemorate them were held at Melba Hall on a date close to their death. The girl house captain laid a wreath and the boy captain dipped the banner before the school community observed two minutes' silence.

Wendy Law Suart, a student from 1936, gave a snapshot of life at University High. She recalled the strict uniform code. In summer girls wore green gingham dresses, beige gloves, white straw hats with the school badge on the band, green jumpers with a tan V-neck and green blazers with the UHS logo embroidered on the breast pocket. Navy box-pleated tunics, white blouses and tan ties, navy felt hats and woollen gloves were the girls' winter attire. UHS boys wore grey serge trousers or shorts, white shirts, a green-and-white striped tie and a green cap. They carried their books and lunches in Gladstone bags. In addition to segregated classes, to cope with increasing enrolments the school created mixed-gender classes named Shell. Lawrie was placed in Shell 9. In February 1935 he joined new and returning students, proudly wearing his uniform and carrying his Gladstone bag. Each morning he caught the 8:19 train from Gardenvale or the 8:22 from Elsternwick to Flinders Street. He boarded a cable tram to travel along Elizabeth Street to Story Street. Ernie, whose newly established house-building business was doing well, gave him 10 shillings weekly for fares. Lawrie walked on occasions in order to purchase an after-school treat.

Traditions instilled in the early years of University High School were firmly established. Boys and girls had specific play areas, mostly studied in segregated classes and performed sport, music and drama in gender-specific groups. They united for assemblies, special events and sports carnivals. Club activities had become an integral part of school life and sixth form camps in the Sherbrooke bush were a tradition. Girls camped under shelter while the boys slept in tents. The Advisory Committee, Mothers' Club and Parents' Association bridged a link between home and school. Parents helped with voice and instrumental tuition and took part in school concerts. They raised funds at sporting events, selling tea and cakes for sixpence and a scoop of ice cream for a penny. They supported the students' war effort by giving, in cash and kind, and by making toys for Red Cross. Proud of their united achievements, Principal Sharman claimed, 'I doubt whether any school can show a better record and, in proportion to the numbers attending the school, I feel that no school can hope to compete.'[88]

The sense of self-worth Sharman instilled extended into the students' broader sphere.[89] He expected each to seek success and urged each to believe that 'every day in every way I'm getting better and better'. The school motto 'Strenue ac Fideliter' (with zeal and loyalty) charged them to challenge the spread of greed and selfishness. Education opened their eyes to a world requiring cooperation not competition. The youth of the day, they were obliged to contribute to a 'brighter and happier world'. Editorials in the University High School magazine *The Record* of 1935 celebrated educational opportunity to extend knowledge and highlighted the virtues of beauty, nature, poetry, music and literature. An education that merely imparted formulae and ephemeral pleasure would fail. Drawn to students' attention was the world's 'very sorry state'. Its nations were 'seething with jealousy, ready to fly at each other's throats; and nations which, while professing goodwill and amity, are steadily piling up armaments, and invoking the aid of science to invent even more diabolical methods of warfare'. The editorial cast a shadow of disarray for students to question. Generally editorials challenged students to think independently and interrogate actions of past generations, politicians and the media. Charged with confidence they must make a difference, and, as Kipling proposed, 'fill the unforgiving minute with sixty seconds' worth of distance run' and 'as long as the burning will is there, the will to set things right, the results will follow'.[90]

The student body valued its educational opportunity and hoped for equity wherein secondary studies available to all would induce a thinking society. But the late 1930s were uncertain times. Though the major impact of the Great Depression had passed, the threat of war loomed and the map of Europe changed continually. Editorials opined that 'war is terrible to the extreme, but, to preserve our priceless freedom – the renowned democracy of the British Empire – we must be prepared, if the necessity should arise, to make the greatest sacrifices'.[91] Let down by politicians greedy for self-fulfilment, and others wearied by age, it required Herculean effort to remedy the wrongs.

Throughout those uncertain times the school community supported its students. A broad range of sporting, social and club activities complemented the academic rigour. A typical year comprised eventful intra- and inter-school sports commitments, camps, excursions, social events and School Nights at the Melbourne Town Hall. Extracurricular activity in 1936 included the aero club where Mervyn Finster advanced his passion for flight, the band, and chess and draughts clubs. There were history, literature, orchestra and stamps clubs, the glee and Esperanto clubs, the dramatic club for Form Six pupils, the photography club (which interested Lawrie) and the science and wireless clubs whose students made crystal sets. Jean Muir (later Blackburn) was secretary of the debating club.[92] The school 'Council' and 'House of Representatives' extended students' social and political prowess and developed their leadership skills. Those elected met during activity periods and mid-morning recess to review and formulate school policies and recommend change.

Among staff at the school were Miss Conway, Miss McGarvie and Mr Miller who taught English, maths and science respectively. Interested in the Arts, Lawrie studied English and English literature, and British and modern histories to Leaving Honours level. Economics held interest but as it was not offered he and friend Alf Lesley received tuition at Taylors College in Flinders Lane. Lawrie made an unfortunate choice to drop French and was dismayed to learn that admission to study an arts degree at Melbourne University required a Leaving pass in a foreign language. He felt betrayed by the school but, determined to put the wrong right, picked up Latin. Guided by the text *Latin for Today* he studied vocabulary, grammar and constructions every spare moment; on the train, at mealtimes and on Sunday drives.

The heavy workload did not deter Lawrie from a busy sport schedule of football on Tuesdays and Thursdays, tennis on Mondays, soccer on Saturdays and athletics in season. He regularly competed in sprints and was in the relay team that beat major competitor Melbourne High, setting a new record of 46.4 seconds over four 100-yard legs. He ran third and Mervyn Finster ran in the final leg. University High also topped Melbourne High in athletics, cricket and football in 1935.[93] Lawrie was a good sprinter, and played rover in football and wing in soccer. He led the football team to victory in 1938 and, described as the 'ideal vice', won the Annual Football Award. He wore the 'Junior International Cap' to captain the Victorian High Schools soccer team against New Zealand at the MCG. Soccer was a fledgling sport at the time and the opponents were a team of very 'big fellas'. From 1935 he ran at Olympic Park with the school's Old Boys' Team to compete against affiliate clubs from nongovernment schools. He progressed from D to A Grade, often winning the 100- and 220-yard sprints.

Against this backdrop of success, tension at home overpowered Lawrie's last year at school. Ernie had overcome hard times and by the mid-1930s was building houses in Mitford Street, Elwood. He established an office at the Glenhuntly–Hawthorn Road Junction where a neon sign flashed 'Shears Master Builder'. Cousin Ellis took charge of accounts. Making good money, Ernie and Dorothy lived the high life, their big car matching their lifestyle. They made friends with the Mayor of Caulfield and his wife and, forming a foursome, attended mayoral functions, parties and community celebrations. The high life took a toll on the business and aggravated their relationship.

In 1938 disaster struck a double blow. Ernie was declared bankrupt and his marriage collapsed. He took Lawrie to live with Aunt

Lil and her husband in Head Street, Elsternwick, where they shared a double bed in a single room. Aunt Lil provided a small desk but Lawrie preferred the solace of the State Library to read, revise and rest. At 9 pm when the library closed he rushed down Swanston Street to catch either the 9.20 or 9.40 train home. He battled on academically and, as house captain and prefect, had access to the prefects' room. He developed lifelong friendships with Ted Liefman and Geoff Stevens and frequently visited their homes. Aware that Lawrie was not a confident swimmer, Ted and Geoff took him canoeing in the bay. They stopped a fair way out, according to Lawrie, rocked the boat and he overbalanced, thrashed and spluttered, though he later realised the water was just thigh deep.

Speech Night at the Melbourne Town Hall was the peak of the high school year. Cr Connelly and his wife represented the Lord Mayor and his lady to present certificates and sports awards. Students and parents hushed as the procession of staff entered, their academic gowns ablaze, followed by prefects, house captains and form captains. Students performed folk dances, put on physical culture displays and sang 'The best school of all'. Guided by Merv Finster, who proposed to join the Air Force, the aero club flew model planes that glided and swooped.[94] It was a night for celebration, congratulations and farewells. Saltau House, which won the cricket, football and relay events, was honoured with the Old Pupils' Association's baton. Captain Lawrie received the awards on behalf of the teams and placed them on Ernie's lap in the body of the hall.

End-of-year exams were held in the Exhibition Building. The cavernous space held large numbers of students who sat at single tables set in rows. Results for Shears, Lawrence William, were European History (1st Class Honours), British History (2nd), Economics (3rd), English (3rd). Awarded a Free Place at the University he was unable to access an arts degree due to failure in Latin by a single mark. He decided to study Law. His end-of-course profile in *The Record* stated:

> *Lawrence Shears* – Captain of Saltau House and vice-captain of the School football team. Captain of one of the Soccer teams, a member of School cricket, tennis and athletic teams. A versatile sportsman. Very short. Ambition – lawyer. A Prefect, and winner of a football award.[95]

The tendency for young people to stay on at school continued to pressure the Education Department so it actively recruited among school leavers to entice them into the teaching profession. As a stopgap measure before beginning university studies Lawrie made an appointment at North Melbourne (Errol Street) State School, No. 1402. The interviewing inspector noted his manner, voice and his ability to 'hold the class' and arranged a student teacher position at Fitzroy (Miller Street) State School, No. 3110.

As at the end of previous years, Lawrie found a holiday job. At the Myer Emporium he had worked as a sales assistant and in Shepparton he picked and packed fruit. In January 1939 he set off with Jackie Howe for a week in the Dandenongs. From Ferntree Gully they crossed the ridge and followed fire tracks through to Warburton. On Thursday, 12 January 1939 they left Warburton by train for Melbourne. On Black Friday, the following day, much of Victoria burned. A firestorm swept the State and caused 71 deaths.

In February Lawrie's teaching career began at Miller Street State School, 'an absolutely splendid experience' that set a new direction for his life.[96]

# Section 2:

# A TEACHING CAREER

CHAPTER 4

# STUDENT TEACHER: FITZROY (MILLER STREET) STATE SCHOOL (1939–40)

*If the teacher's personal influence is to be felt in the school and beyond it ... he must be able to speak the language of children.*

H R Hamley

## Teaching in Victoria

The onset of the Great Depression led the Victorian Labor government to slash funding for education by one-third between 1927–28 and 1933–34. Correspondingly, support for teacher education dropped, resulting in abandonment of courses and reduction of teachers college staff.[97] The funding dilemma had a flow-on effect. The abolition of allowances for teacher trainees intensified the fall in numbers and the decision to close teachers colleges in Ballarat and Bendigo at the end of 1931 made the Melbourne Teacher Training College Victoria's sole facility to train teachers for government schools.[98]

The preparation of teachers had reached low ebb and remained in the doldrums for seventeen years. Despite the turmoil created by funding cuts, trainees gained outstanding results, verified by 24 exhibitions and seventeen first-class honours awarded to graduates in 1931.[99] Money was tight and times were tough, with salary cuts and positions vacated unfilled. Such was the case in 1930 when Ken Cunningham resigned from the College and relinquished his research interests in psychological development, vocational guidance and training teachers for children with special needs. Discussions between the Victorian Institute of Educational Research (VIER) and supporters of the New Education Fellowship movement, and the stirrings of

George Bradshaw, had led to the founding of the Australian Council for Educational Research (ACER).[100] Against a strong field of candidates, including Chris McRae and George Browne, Cunningham was appointed Chief Executive Officer of ACER.[101]

Amid ongoing funding cuts, disruption continued among College staff. Alex McDonell (later Director of Education 1960–65) was assigned other duties and Wilfred Frederick (later Professor of Education at the University of Melbourne), Alice Hoy (who became Principal of the Secondary Teachers College) and Alan Ramsay (appointed Principal of Melbourne High School 1946–48 and Director of Education 1948–60) were transferred to University High School. Teaching quality at the school was thus boosted and Hoy and Ramsay continued to teach at the School of Education at the University.[102]

The passing of the *Teachers Act* 1933 (No. 4205) reduced expenditure on education by discontinuing 'all secondary courses – university, manual arts and domestic arts and curtailing the number of junior teachers progressing through the system'. This eased the backlog and career stalemate for those previously denied College entry or teacher classification. The intake of female assistant teachers increased, though at a rate reducing from 300 in 1934 to 150 in 1935–36 and 50 in 1937. Meanwhile the number of junior teachers, renamed 'student teachers', dropped from 600 in 1934 to 300 in 1935–36 and 100 in 1937. The influx of trainees burdened the College already denuded of staff and funds. Though existing studentship holders could work out their awards, until the end of WWII the intake of trainees was limited to those completing one-year primary or two-year infant teaching certificates and those undertaking university extensions or courses in manual and domestic arts[103] (which had been reinstated in 1936).

To accommodate the swell at the College while providing practical and theoretical knowledge, a platoon system of rotation had been introduced. Of six groups of 50 trainees, four attended College while the remaining two were placed in selected practising schools. The return of former staff, including Alex McDonell,[104] and the addition of Prue Hamono, minimally reduced the burden. To aggravate pressures, throughout the 1930s the Education Department and the College were at odds. The Department urgently needed trained teachers to flow into the system, a push reflecting Director Seitz's preference for 'teacher training' rather than 'teacher education'.[105] In contrast, the College sought excellence among its graduates and battled to maintain standards despite cramped conditions and the cream of its teaching staff skimmed for administration and university work, such as Alice Hoy. Four of five temporary replacement lecturers held only Fifth Class ranking on the Classified Roll of Teachers. The situation deteriorated during the war years when staff who enlisted in the forces were not replaced. Such was the case with Alan Ramsay, although his major obligation at the time was at the University's School of Education.[106]

## Miller Street

These matters of discontent were the background for Shears' student teacher experience at Fitzroy (Miller Street) State School. Daily he travelled by train from Elsternwick to Flinders Street then by tram to the corner of Miller Street, then did a short walk to the school. Located beside the Merri Merri Creek the school was formerly known as Brunswick East. Though numbers fell during the depression of the 1890s, by 1909 the school was overcrowded, needing more land and extensions. The two-storey extension added in 1926 gave it an air of solidarity.[11]

Headmaster Mr Little gave an introductory talk to the three student teachers – Sylvia Payne, Rita Konowal and Lawrie Shears – and assigned each to classes. After a week in Miss Pauline Knight's Grade 3 Shears felt his life was transformed. Working beside 'a brilliant little teacher who knew how to handle the class' he forgot about studying Law, his profession of choice upon leaving school. A hands-on experience, he was immediately involved and enjoyed 'the relationship with kids – there were 64 of them with their desks right up to the front platform'. He enjoyed reading stories to the class; 'I put in a lot of effort ... the kids enjoyed it', marking the roll, 'very very important', and 'I was sold'.[107]

Stories of the student teaching experience vary. While for some the school fulfilled its duty to provide training and educational knowledge, others experienced a lackadaisical approach. Phillip Law, appointed

'Junior teacher 2nd Grade on Probation' a decade before, recalled his own placement as a 'misnomer, as no classroom responsibilities were allocated'. Running errands, filing correspondence and learning to type, he developed office organisational skills rather than knowledge of schooling.[108] At the other extreme some junior or student teachers arriving at school were shown to their classroom and expected to teach.[109]

Miller Street played a vital role in the training of teachers and the College held those positioned there in high regard. Supporting its students, the school gave an insightful view of the learning process. Sixty years later Shears recalled the benefits of time spent in 'Grade 2 with Miss Sturdee; Grade 3 with Pauline Knight; Grade 4 with Miss Kennewell and Grade 5 with Mr Beckerleg. Miss Schaeffer taught Grade 6 and Mr Buchanan taught a composite Grade 7 and 8.'[110] Miss Kennewell had a long association with Miller Street. Warwick Eunson, later Principal of Melbourne Teachers College, remembered her as a daunting figure when he was a pupil in 1912. Then he was afraid of her long-frocked presence but he later considered her to be a 'kindly woman'.

Headmaster Little met the student teachers twice weekly in his office, once before school and once at lunchtime. In addition to practical training he required them to understand teaching philosophies, classroom techniques and the nuances of the education system. He drew on McRae's *Psychology and Education* to emphasise the needs of the child and stressed the teachers' duty to satisfy these needs and extend the potential of each child. In addition, student teachers attended classes on Saturday mornings. Shears studied art and music at Brighton Technical School. When he was unable to sing lower re, ti or do, Miss Irwin simply advised him to 'keep trying'. Miss Irwin's appointment as Supervisor of Music (1943–70) indicates the quality of staff involved in Saturday morning programs.

Mr Little's dedication to the student teachers endorses the commitment given at Miller Street. In addition to his instruction, they observed lessons across class levels and presented a series of 'criticism lessons'. They reviewed and appraised one another's performance, presentation and problems. Sharing the highs and lows of beginning teachers they identified common difficulties, offered advice and supported each other. They kept a 'Notes of Lessons' book to record lesson plans, objectives and proposed outcomes, which their supervising teacher appraised in terms of pupil engagement and each lesson's success.

Shears expected to enter College in 1940 but as his student teacher appointment had begun in February 1939 he had not completed the conditional calendar year. He lamented, 'because I didn't start promptly on the first day of schooling at the end of the first year I didn't get into College. I didn't have a full year of student teaching – one week short.'[111] Colleague Sylvia Payne's acceptance into College after a single year added salt to his wound. He was required to do a second year of student teaching.

During the second year Shears experienced the scope of class levels and accordingly observed the sequence of learning and skills development, and teachers' efforts to ensure both steady progression of pupils and smooth transitions. To help alleviate the staff shortage Mr Little gave Shears a class of twelve slow learners selected from Grade 6. Lessons took place in a small room beside that of Mr Buchanan. For homework Shears selected words from *The School Paper's* spelling list, expecting pupils to learn at night for testing next day. He used a ruler to punish any who made a mistake, with a smack on the hand. The sharp sound summoned Mr Buchanan who took Shears aside to advise 'you're not allowed to do that, you are a student teacher.' [112]

By the end of the year Shears believed, 'I really learned how to teach … vary things a bit, make the kids get interested … I was being nurtured along, feeling what school was about, what good teaching was'. Keen to know 'who's who' in the system, understand the process of promotion and identify career pathways, he read the *Education Gazette*. Seeing an advertisement for the Director of Education to replace Arnold Seitz he thought, 'that's an interesting career … a good job. I was only 17.'[113] Beyond education he considered war service.

The outbreak of war cast a shadow. Prime Minister Menzies' announcement declaring war on 3 September 1939 had wide-reaching effects on the community and on education nationwide. Afraid of devastating consequences on the British Empire and on Australia,

Menzies spoke of '… a great family of nations, involved in a struggle which we must at all costs win and which we believe in our hearts we will win'.[114] Throughout Victoria's educational community practising teachers and trainees left their positions to serve. Tension rose as the German invasion reached the English Channel in May 1940 and climaxed when British and Allied troops fled from Dunkirk. Miss Kennewell wept: 'This is the end,' she cried.[115] While the nation was torn apart school communities rallied to support the troops. Children sent letters to Australians serving abroad, raised funds and published poems and art in *The School Paper*. The Mothers' Club at Miller Street united the school community to support the Children's War Effort. They held a euchre party, a dance at the Northcote Town Hall and a ball at the Merri Palace.

District Inspector Norman Cartmill Heathcote paid several visits to Miller Street during 1939 and 1940 to discuss the school's particular needs and check on the progress of its student teachers. His assessment of Shears endorsed the school's level of care and undoubtedly gave Shears a boost. In June 1939 Heathcote wrote of him, 'Keen, energetic and interested. A v.g. S.T.' Visiting Miller Street in March and June 1940 his report suggests a leap in the young teacher's development. He noted, 'Energy and interest are outstanding. A very keen & capable young man. A distinctly v.g. S.T.' It identified Shears for promotion to 'First Grade' status.'[116]

Despite the rigours of life as a student teacher Shears maintained his sporting and academic pursuits. Contest nerves affected his tennis but not his athletics performance. When the starter called 'get set' tension drained and off he sprinted. Though ready to formalise his teaching career with a year at the Teachers College, with a Leaving Honours Certificate he was academically equipped for university entry. He was keen to commence his arts degree and with a pass in Leaving Latin achieved, he began his degree in 1940. He recalled that Miss Derham lectured in English A and Kathleen Fitzpatrick lectured in History. Having completed two years as a student teacher he left a satisfying past and moved towards a promising year at the Melbourne Teachers College and a teaching career beyond. He received a fond farewell but his most lingering memory was Miss Sturdee's kiss.

# CHAPTER 5

# TRAINING TO TEACH: MELBOURNE TEACHERS COLLEGE (1941–42)

*A wise man will make more opportunities than he finds.*

Francis Bacon, *The Essays*

Enrolled in the 12-month Trained Primary Teachers Certificate (TPTC), Lawrence William Shears entered Melbourne Teachers College on 4 February 1941. Like others embarking on teaching careers his independence increased with reinstatement of the trainee allowance of £30 per year as from 1 August 1941.[117] Two years prior, the College had celebrated its Jubilee. 'For fifty years it had been turning out teachers for the State of Victoria; and [proposed that] in another fifty years will probably be doing the same.'[118] The sentiments established over the years permeated its culture and traditions. These influenced 1941 trainees who were duty bound to understand that 'the old and the new will be side by side, and the tradition of old can easily pass to the new'. Buildings and people instilled a sense of atmosphere and place; hence the proposed dismantling of the gym and forthcoming completion of the Frank Tate building symbolised regret with the passing of time and the promise of new traditions.[119]

The deaths of former Directors of Education James McRae and Frank Tate in 1939 shed a sombre tone among the College community. Both men left a legacy that shaped the training of teachers which would in turn benefit the profession. Tate had served as principal from 1900 until 1902 and McRae was vice-principal from 1913 to 1922. He was among its first 'Diploma Twenty',[120] who enrolled in 1905. In 1909 he became Master of Method. His embrace of psychology influenced teaching approaches, as Mr Little had shown at Miller Street. McRae was remembered as 'a loyal and effective vice-principal ... a brilliant exponent of classroom practice and teacher of philosophy and experimental education'.[121] The College magazine, *The Trainee*, noted, 'Behind all these advances in education was Mr McRae's inspiring and encouraging personality.'[122]

Tate's death was a 'tragic loss', a reflection in *The Trainee* noted. 'He spared no effort to make up for the days when the College was closed, and so inspired many of the future inspectors and headmasters in schools.' Appointed the first Director of Education in 1902 Tate affirmed, 'It is my intention *to go* as much as I can amongst the teachers.' He fulfilled his promise by meeting and discussing educational issues with inspectors, teachers and schools across the State. Tate set a precedent for his successors. He travelled abroad to observe other educational systems and introduced best practice into Victorian schools. An obituary in *The Trainee* identified:

> ... the 'great old man of Australian education' ... Mr. Tate typified all the best in education, and education has suffered a tragic loss through his death.
>
> *Non Omnis Moriar* [123]

The acclaim of Tate and McRae pays heed to their contributions to the College and respect for their positions as Director of Education. Tate as 'the great old man' had salvaged the College from the economic and educational depression of the 1890s and invigorated it with new life. Despite his short-term principalship, a new building erected in the Jubilee year marked his contributions. 'The Ritz', as it was known, was incomplete until late 1940. Its modern rigidity stood in stark contrast to the 1888 building's ornate elegance. The functional character of 'The Ritz' facilitated new traditions as educational practice evolved. It housed a large hall, lecture rooms, facilities for music and drama with sound equipment, a projection room and study space for non-resident trainees.[124] Architects anticipated this would eliminate conditions that had angered Browne in 1935. He lamented 'the bad state of buildings and furnishings, the insufficient accommodation, the lack of a place for assemblies, the poor library accommodation, the old fashioned and inadequate toilets, the out-dated and gloomy kitchen and the small administrative office', and lack of facilities for non-resident trainees who had nowhere to keep their books or eat lunches.[125] With this in mind, planners bestowed upon trainees 'a possession of which we are justly proud, and trust that they will keep it so for those who follow in their turn.'[126]

## 1941 intake

College life in 1941 was abuzz with social and sporting events in addition to professional input. Trainees adapted to weekly routines of lectures, teaching rounds and midweek Community Wednesday activities. Meeting together in the Public Lecture Theatre of the University of Melbourne, 200–300 trainees heard Principal A J Law's addresses and announcements before they united in song. The stirring atmosphere had an enduring effect. Law's son Phillip recalled 'quite vividly the pleasure of singing with other trainees bellowing out the tunes'.[127]

Legacies of Professor Browne's principalship (1933–39) were reflected in the college curriculum. Travel abroad had alerted him to the Dalton Plan, as observed in England, and the Project Method espoused by Dewey. Aware that activity approaches were expanding abroad he argued:

> ... for an injection into Australian primary schools of an up-to-date and dynamic curriculum, better school equipment, more experimental work, freedom from external examinations, and the enlistment of the scholars' enthusiasm in activities and constructive work.[128]

Browne encouraged trainees to reach beyond their grasp and boosted their ego.[129] Alert to new classroom methods he was aware of the tensions between the familiar practices and new approaches. Such was the case with radio broadcasts and audiovisuals that some believed would broaden horizons while others perceived they would produce passive rather than active learners.[130]

In 1939, the roles of Professor of Education and Principal of the College were split. Browne continued his work at the University where he developed the first graduate teacher education course and A J Law became College principal. He followed a line of forward thinkers who influenced College courses, including Tate, McRae, Smyth, Wrigley and Browne.[131] Law is often recalled as stern and austere. Short in stature, with small wire-framed glasses, he appeared a foreboding figure. A second-generation educator, he had experienced the gamut of the education system as pupil teacher in 1903, trainee in 1906, university entrant and College lecturer. He moved from teacher training to the inspectorate before returning to the College, initially as vice-principal. He was strict, had strong moral fibre and held his senior position with dignity. He segregated men from women, imposed curfews on residential groups, insisted on a strict dress code and disliked women in slacks. But his veneer concealed a shy man. Shears observed 'A J' (as he was known) one day prepare to enter a lecture room; he paused, braced his shoulders and rested his hand on the doorknob momentarily before entering. He won respect rather than affection, although Shears, who knew him better in later life, considered him gentlemanly, a view correspondingly held by family, who knew him as loving and fair.[132] Law was aware that 'a changing world implies educationists to prepare future citizens to adjust their thinking to the needs of the day'. He argued, 'we teachers must place less emphasis on purely factual knowledge, and set ourselves to train our senior pupils in habits of clear thinking, right feeling and well-considered action … We should be actuated by a broad tolerance, a love of humanity as a whole, and an abiding faith in education as a force for uplift.'[133]

The editorial of *The Trainee* of 1941 reiterated these sentiments, questioning the 'invincible creed which has for many centuries indicated the boundary between right and wrong'. It urged teachers to commit to the task 'entrusted with the shaping of human lives … [as] at this very hour when empires are tottering, we need, more than ever before, to inculcate in the minds of children a broader understanding of our fellow creatures, and a knowledge of human nature, that is necessary in the time of crisis.'[134] Law regarded teachers' work as nationally important; 'they hold the key to the door of this better world … the nation's teachers must labour to produce for the future a higher form of citizenship – one which will banish selfishness and attain to levels of service and sacrifice hitherto unrealized.'[135]

These philosophies infiltrated College life and were endorsed at Wednesday assemblies where the principal, staff members or invited guests addressed trainees. Shears recalled the appeal of those addresses. Such occasions strengthened the esprit de corps within the group and endorsed philosophies of honesty, loyalty and zeal. Browne's presentation of the John Smyth Memorial Lecture in 1941 followed his recent study tour of area schools in Tasmania. He addressed consolidation, with transportation of pupils from small rural communities to larger schools in central locations He favoured minimal bureaucratic control, greater democracy in school organisation through cooperation of pupils, parents and teachers, and promoted curriculum designed to meet individual and local needs. Schools, he argued, belong to the district.[136]

The College year prepared trainees 'as a united body' both socially and professionally. It began with the Welcome Palais (a dance held in Melba Hall) and the Welcome Ball. These triggered a series of balls, 'palais' (dances) and concerts hosted by the College houses Tate, Wrigley and Smyth. Mrs O'Grady, teacher of 'voice and method', remarked on Shears' compering of the Tate House concert, 'You'll go a long way'.[137] The social calendar included a fancy dress night, a play, the mystery hike, the Yarra Stakes and numerous sporting events. Those interested could attend a series of films and musical interludes on Professor Browne's Carnegie Phonograph, symphony concerts arranged by Sir Bernard Heinze, opera and National Theatre Company productions. At weekends and during vacations trainees hiked to Ferntree Gully, Belgrave, the You Yangs and Bacchus Marsh. The philosophy behind these and other events was that 'College may make a good teacher ... [but it is] participation in activities outside the College that makes a man or a woman.'[138]

The single-year TPTC created a heavy workload. It melded the academic and practical program with the social side. One of the 50 men among five times as many women, Shears' sporting prowess was an attraction. He played football, tennis and athletics and took up hockey. There is little record of his individual feats though he appeared in photos of the hockey, athletics and tennis teams. The *Trainee* noted that 'L. Shears and F. Hooper performed well' in the 100 yards but 'J.

Lane [who] was outstanding in the sprints' defeated them.[139]

The TPTC comprised fourteen subjects. Its rigid timetable resembled high school days with lectures, teaching practice, sport and excursions. In an effort to churn out teachers, days were long, class size approximated 60 and the course was crammed to convey knowledge syllabus, teaching method and school organisation.[140] Offered over a 10-month period the course was described thus:

> A more indigestible meal would be difficult to find in any educational institution in Victoria. The trainees have little time to think or read, and have no opportunity to do more than skim their subjects in a superficial manner.[141]

College staff, carefully selected, were dedicated to the task. Prue Hamono and Gwen Wainwright lectured in English, and Charles Mellow headed the Art Department. Experimentation at Lee Street School led to a revised art syllabus. Len Whiteoak lectured in psychology and Alice Hoy in history method. Professor Browne addressed history and modern developments in education. Among 200–300 trainees crammed into a large university lecture theatre, Shears applauded Browne for his 'brilliant teaching ability'.[142] Principal Law presented a series of lectures in teaching practice. He used *Modern Teaching*, a small self-authored red-covered book, as a guide. The book implied the family, the school and broader community conjointly influenced the child's development, its learning and its risk-taking ability. The book also identified the stages of growth, the child's problems and needs, and the teacher's duty of care. Law's 'Law on Teaching' saw the tragedy in waste of time, and lack of opportunity to think and use sources of energy. Law advocated James' philosophy to 'perceive your pupil as a little sensitive, impulsive, associative and receptive organism, partly fated and partly free ...' Regardless of background, each deserved to be 'loved' and encouraged to foster a positive sense of self-belief.[143]

Four weeks after entering College, Shears sought to endorse such ideals in his first teaching round at Coburg East State School, No. 4260. Headmaster Mr H Tate, appointed in 1939, presided over 700 pupils spanning Grades 1 to 8. The College held Coburg East in high regard. Although many of its former staff had moved on to senior

Departmental positions, the legacy of their presence placed trainees in good hands.[144] Shears was assigned to Miss M Hutson Grade 3. Two days after his arrival on 3 March, College lecturer Mr J B Prictor observed his first lesson. Prictor identified, 'A good bright style in front of a grade. You did some definite, purposeful teaching'. He advised Shears to 'not overdo the teaching and sacrifice the testing and correction' and directed him to watch his handwriting 'as this is the model to all pupils'. He concluded, 'An excellent start with a new grade.'[145]

During that two-week teaching round Shears settled the class for the weekly religious instruction (RI) lesson taught by a visiting cleric, taught fourteen lessons and twice took the two extended sessions from 9.15 to 10.50 am. During these sessions he conducted phonics, discussion and morning talk, and administered short spelling and arithmetic tests. On a subsequent visit Prictor observed an extended teaching session. The phonics lesson introduced 'ee as in bee'; discussion related to the Red Cross Fund; and in morning talk, children reported on the growth of their wheat seed and on their individual interests. Prictor observed 'a brisk start … pupils busily employed … [and] that you believe in "doing" [though] you could call the answers occasionally to save time.' Art and craft lecturer, W Nicol, noted thorough preparation, originality, and snappy introduction to a 'delightful period' spent outdoors. Activity was not confined to Miss Hutson's Grade 3 and Shears had the chance to teach in every class. Harold E Loader, who taught Grades 7 and 8, suggested more 'hands on' activity in nature study. He was pleased to see 'the children are happy and anxious to work *with* you and not *for* you – a great difference. A very good period.'[146] The opportunity to be guided by reputable teachers was a privilege. Loader shifted to the Curriculum Research Office the following year where his expertise in teaching arithmetic was utilised. He was conscious of shortfalls in the training of secondary teachers, falling numbers due to enlistment and the deficit in trainees with maths and science proficiency.

Table 1. Shears' teaching timetable for his first teaching round in Miss Hutson's Grade 3a at Coburg East State School, No. 4260

| Date | Time | Subject, aims | Comments |
| --- | --- | --- | --- |
| **Week 1** | | | |
| 3.3.41 | 25 min | Dictation: examine a child's ability to unite a coherent series of words | A good bright style; some definite, purposeful teaching (JB Prictor)* |
| 4.3.41 | 35 min | Reading: recognize the printed and written word as a means of expressing ideas | Well treated by means of questioning, and explanation of difficult words; spend less time with spelling |
| 4.3.41 | 25 min | Drawing: practice in representing action | Cardboard figure used to advantage to explain movement; some good efforts |
| 5.3.41 | 35 min | Arithmetic: addition of tens and units | Children found out the method for themselves; everybody worked hard; facts and method were well taught |
| 6.3.41 | 20 min | Writing: study formation of a, o, d | Lesson given along correct lines; poor writers given special attention; keep stressing correct position |
| 6.3.41 | 95 min | RI; Phonics, Morning Talk, Discussion, Spelling Test, Arithmetic Test | Brisk start; pupils busily employed; call answers occasionally to save time; a profitable working period |
| 7.3.41 | 40 min | History: create interest in history stories; study and dramatise the story of King Midas | Story well told; blackboard used for difficult words without a break in the story; a good narrative style (JB Prictor)* |
| 7.3.41 | 30 min | Physical Training: Give children enjoyment while developing them physically | Lesson given in correct steps; children's enjoyment reflected your vigorous manner; discipline good |
| **Week 2** | | | |
| 10.3.41 | 30 min | Poetry: cultivate a love of poetry; read fairy poems for appreciation | Little more individual and simultaneous reciting; got down to the level of fairies and small children remarkably well |
| 10.3.41 | 35 min | Oral Composition: increase children's concentration, description and narration | Good use of BB followed Fairy Poetry; excellent words obtained; should show good results in follow-up written lesson |
| 11.3.41 | 35 min | Geography: teach about children's world; develop project on Africa | Excellent preparation; children thoroughly enjoyed this period (W Nicol)* as well as learning something |
| 11.3.41 | 35 min | Drawing: draw from outside an elevation of the school | Notes thoroughly prepared, neatly entered; showed originality; good work done; delightful period (W Nicol) |
| 12.3.41 | 35 min | Health: inculcate clean thoughts and habits; discuss care of the hair | Excellent preparation; very practical lesson; energy and enthusiasm are catching; versatile teacher |
| 13.3.41 | 30 min | Nature Study: appreciation of nature; study 3 types of roots, compile observation chart | Brisk and businesslike; allow children to handle specimens early in lesson; bright, happy personality (HE Loader) |
| 14.3.41 | 95 min | RI; Phonics, Morning Talk, Discussion, Spelling Test, Arithmetic Test | On checking the bookwork done during the morning I found much good work had been accomplished |
| 14.3.41 | | Singing: Appreciation of music; teach 'Brother John' in English and French | A most enjoyable period |

*Lessons observed by College staff are identified by names in italics.

On 20 April, five weeks later, Shears began his second teaching round, in Mr McMillan's Grade 6 at Carlton North State School, No. 1252, in Lee Street. Mr McMillan had strong ideals. He abhorred slovenly posture and expected 'very good' blackboard writing and clear speech. This aligned with Law's belief that the 'teacher's voice should be clear, distinct, low in pitch, and controlled; and his language simple, natural, and correct.'[147] Keeping control of group activities in McMillan's class helped Shears' organisational skills and demonstrated the need for lessons to maintain momentum and purpose. With a watchful eye, McMillan identified weaknesses but gave due praise. At the end of the fortnight he wrote, 'Mr Shears has done a very successful fortnight's work. He prepares well and teaches with skill and confidence. He should make a very successful teacher.'[148]

In the early 1940s, primary school education continued to Grades 7 and 8. Successful Grade 8 completion provided basic education to the school-leaving age of fourteen; it was a benchmark for the Merit Certificate and the pathway to high school. For young trainees not long out of school, teaching these upper levels was a huge leap. Shears made that leap in the June teaching round with assignment to Mr Baker's Grade 8 at Albert Park State School, No. 1181 in Nelson Street. Lessons were complex. Managing older children required different techniques. The scope of classes that covered history, geography, spelling, grammar, literature, composition, dramatisation, nature study, drawing, physical training and arithmetic reveal the breadth of skills required by primary teachers. Baker noted Shears' 'careful and methodical preparation' with 'lesson steps well set out'. He saw improvement in blackboard technique and acknowledged Shears' ability to obtain 'class co-operation by means of mixed questions and narrative'. Baker advised him to balance giving direction with eliciting knowledge. College lecturer Mr R L Miller noted Shears' 'good manner' and 'good terms with the pupils', and thorough supervision and connection with weaker pupils who 'showed no sign of slacking'. He concluded, 'I was very pleased to note the effective summarizing and clinching of chief methods used. An excellent period.' Like all trainee teachers, Shears experienced highs and lows in each of his placements. The final comments from Albert Park suggested the pupils' enthusiasm did not always match his own.¹⁴⁹ This surely raised a sense of disquiet that carried into his appointment in July to Carlton State School, No. 2605, in Rathdowne Street, where there was an annexe known as 'Rathdowne Street Rural'.

Rural schools are part of Victoria's educational heritage. The nature of the State, with vast distances between major towns and remote settlements, led the Education Department to establish a statewide network of smaller schools with as few as ten or twelve pupils. It supplied a full-time qualified teacher to teach across all subjects from Grades 1 to 8. Young teachers, fresh from College, often disdainful of their remote appointment, staffed many of the rural schools. Enthusiasm and flexibility underpinned their ability to achieve smooth working conditions in the cooperative environment characteristic of the rural classroom. Though hard work, the reward of effective learning outweighed the effort. To coordinate teaching across all class levels monitors were trained to assist. While the teacher taught a specific group they kept watch on the monitor and the work of pupils in other groups. Projects and weekly assignments (as in the Dalton approach) empowered pupils with responsibility for their progress while developing initiative and zest for learning. Although the number of rural schools had begun to decline, rural school practice remained integral to College training.¹⁵⁰ To fulfill this need, the timber building from Koonung Koonung, in which Frank Tate first taught, was relocated to the College grounds. Annexes attached to several training schools prepared trainees for rural classrooms.

On his two-week rural round Shears taught across all subjects and grade levels. His first 30-minute lesson was geography for Grades 3 and 4 while correspondingly supervising writing for Grades 8, 7, 6 and 5. The monitor read to Grades 1 and 2. It was a busy 30 minutes. At 1.15 he explained that the younger group would be read a story, at 1.16 he modelled the forming of **h** and **H** with the writing group and then progressed with the geography lesson. Miss Clapperton commended planning and preparation, and advised him to watch his position at the blackboard during correction. After observing a geography lesson College lecturer Mr Len Whiteoak wrote, 'A really excellent period – carefully prepared – very fine control exhibited throughout. Bb work of very fine quality and correction thorough and helpful. Excellent work'. On a subsequent visit the singing supervisor wrote, 'Very capable teaching … a fine young teacher'. At the end of the fortnight Shears was informed 'Very good business-like teaching manner. Your supervision is very thorough'. He was described as efficient in quickly setting classes to work. In addition to observation and preparation, trainees helped supervising teachers in numerous ways. In her final comment Miss Clapperton wrote, 'Many thanks for your helpful cooperation … you have been very keen and willing to help. I wish you every success in your College year, and in your work after. Your efficiency and keenness should take you far'.

Shears was certain of his decision to teach. He took heed of advice, made full use of every experience, and was developing a sound bank of skills. He completed his fifth teaching round in Miss M Stevenson's Grade 1a, an Infant class, at North Melbourne State School, No. 1402, in Errol Street. Miss Stevenson suggested he 'encourage children to give answers in sentence form' and later affirmed progress in that 'children were encouraged to give words in sentences'. Midway through the round Mr Clarke from College observed a lesson on fractions. He remarked, 'your work is very good indeed but you were too much in evidence – too much teaching'. He advised that teachers should 'lie in wait for the practical opportunities, be prompt to seize those as they pass, and thus at one operation get your pupils both to think, to feel, and to do.'[151]

On the sixth and last teaching round Shears was placed in Miss Gillard's Grade 5 Carlton State School, No.112, in Faraday Street, Carlton. Miss Gillard had previously taught him at Windsor State School, so Shears was thrilled to interact with her as an adult and teacher rather than teacher and child. Although he had developed sound basic skills Miss Gillard identified key teaching points. She advised, 'Do not reject wrong answers altogether – accept them for discussion. Here is your golden opportunity to do your best teaching.' Her comments on his last science lesson indicate his devotion to the task. The lesson was presented in a creative and capable manner and his leading questions explored concepts in depth. Miss Gillard wrote, 'Mr Shears spent hours in the preparation … once again he has made excellent preparation of his matter, his method, his notes and his blackboard. An excellent period – excellently prepared and excellently given.'

Graduation as a teacher with TPTC required passes in fourteen subjects, completion of six teaching rounds and satisfactory presentation of Teaching Record Books. Teaching practice was ranked as Unsatisfactory (U), Pass (P), Good (G), Very Good (VG) and Outstanding (OS). With five OSs and one VG Shears was top of the male trainees but, pipped by a girl with six OSs, he was ranked second overall. During teaching rounds the supervising teachers collaborated with College lecturers to determine results. Mr Loader willingly gave an OS when duly deserved; however Mr McMillan's top mark was VG.

Shears' teaching record identified his diverse abilities, fine personal qualities and leadership promise. It stated, 'Teaching outstanding; academic work excellent; very fine type of student with an excellent attitude; has taken a leading part in College life, including sport.' It also shows that he applied to enlist on 1 January 1942, before the new college year commenced.

## Teacher training 1942

With an extension to university for 1942 Shears continued his arts degree and moved towards the secondary ranks. The extension trainees attended university lectures and participated in College life, attending assemblies, and taking part in social and sports activities. He played the role of vicar in PG Wodehouse's *Baa Baa Black Sheep*. *The Trainee* noted:

> … performances deserving special mention being Merelyn Varcoe's Mrs Pottle, Lawrie Shears as Aubrey Wyndrum, and as the mournful Mr. Tickle, Mervyn Kydd, who shone in his short but pithy scene with Hugo. Credit is given to the whole cast for their sustained efforts in giving three performances instead of the usual two.[152]

Extension trainees were privileged. Lecture groups were smaller than those in the previous year and the timetable gave greater flexibility. Shears, Lou Barberis and Freddie Howe were given study accommodation in the basement of the art and craft building, a space known as the 'dungeon'. Shears was involved in the students' representative council and supported President Ken Mawson. These friends were among others who attended Shears' 21st birthday party on 1 July. His father, aunts, uncles and cousins decorated the body of Elsternwick Town Hall with the College's green and gold. To Shears' embarrassment his father requested friends send money so he could buy a single substantial present.

With his verve to participate in College life, it is remarkable that Shears managed his commitment to university studies in Latin, English, British history and geology. He also commenced an economics degree with accounting 1. Fascinated by geology, he learnt the characteristics and names of metals and minerals 'off pat'. He and other students tested each other with rows of pennies: 'If you got them right you got a penny'. Professor Sherbourne Hills, a great walker, took the group on excursions to the You Yangs and to Werribee and Lerderderg Gorges. A bright spot for Shears at the end of the year was a shared exhibition in geology. Puffed with pride Principal Law believed 'It was a pat on the back for the College'.[153]

The end-of-course report described Shears as 'an outstanding teacher and a very good student. Takes a prominent part in College social activities'. In *The Trainee* he appeared in several team photos.

He was instrumental in organising the swimming carnival and by way of 'reward' was photographed in the centre front of the girls swimming team.[154] His win in the 100 yards sprint against Joe Brennan gave him champion status and his tennis team reached the semi-final. The 'crowning event of a successful year's sport' was the premiership pennant won by the hockey team. For achievement in sport he wore College colours on his blazer pocket.

The war was much to the fore during the College years and Japanese activity across the Pacific roused concern. Male trainees had a grand parade decked in their military uniforms and dug trenches in the College grounds, near the hockey field. Geography lecturer Clarrie Coskell was appointed air raid warden with student councillors designated to help.[155] Rationing affected catering for resident students, but curtailment of sporting activities and interstate trips freed trainees to support the war effort. They ran a tennis tournament, three house concerts and a play that earned £95. They sold sweets and flowers, sent food parcels and copies of *The Griffin* to every 'exie' in service,[156] and established a fund for those held as prisoners of war. In an editorial the *The Trainee* noted, 'Without the cooperation of every student in College we could not have carried out this work. Thank you students of 1942.'[157]

The exodus of trainees, staff and teachers from the College and the Education Department continued. Keen to serve the country Shears applied again to enlist. At 21, a qualified teacher with a degree underway, he was ready for a new start. He recalled:

> Four of us, Lou Barberis, Freddie Howe, Jack Stephenson and myself, trotted off to the Navy in 1942. We had intelligence tests and were medically examined and they sent all of us a letter saying, 'Yes, you're accepted, but get your release from Manpower'. It was only a few months before that they'd introduced strict Manpower regulations and because we were secondary, in the sense that we had done our one-year primary and we were into our degrees in the second, they refused to give us leave.[158]

'Refused leave to enlist in the R.A.N.' on Shears' teaching record identify attempts to enlist in January and November 1942. Australian Military Forces records reveal that Private Lawrence William Shears, V159034, enlisted in Elsternwick, Area 6, VIC, and was subsequently discharged. As a member of the Melbourne University Rifles he was equipped with a uniform and sturdy boots to wear for exercises and military parades. Due to the shortage of teachers for higher elementary and secondary classes Manpower refused his release. To aggravate disappointment he recalled 'annoyance and chagrin when I was walking across Princes Bridge. Striding towards me, all in white, came a Sub-Lieutenant from the primary teachers' course'.

On graduation nights in Wilson Hall at the University staff and official guests were decked out in their finest regalia.[159] As the organ piped in the procession pride rippled amongst graduands and their guests.

On a subsequent occasion at Wilson Hall Matthew Stanton

Sharman was farewelled from the principalship at University High. Shears was involved in the night's organisation because he had been influenced by Sharman's aim 'to encourage self-control and initiative in the pupils who pass[ed] through his hands, by allowing them to develop naturally, and without being under any necessary restriction'.[160] As his life unfolded he exhibited qualities that reflected philosophies instilled at the school. Self-control in the pursuit of knowledge and initiative in his student teaching equipped him to keep a broad mind as life moved on, to show passion and persistence and not give in. He had thwarted challenges, as with problems at home, and was developing a confident poise as a teacher in the classroom and in the public realm. Unable to join the Navy he prepared to start his teaching career, aware of his duty to serve and thereby satisfy the needs of those in his care.

With his son moving on, his father Ernie also made a new start. He purchased the Myrtleford sawmill and interests in Victoria's thriving tobacco industry.

CHAPTER 6

# COUNTRY TEACHER (1943–46)

*Life is what happens to you while you're busy making other plans.*

Allen Saunders

The aftermath of the Great Depression followed by six years of war exacerbated the shortage of secondary teachers. The withdrawal of secondary studentships and the cessation of training for secondary teachers from 1933 had left a gap, while the number of teachers enlisting for war service cut a swathe through secondary ranks. Arnold Seitz, before becoming Director in 1936, expressed concern that corresponded with views held by delegates at the Ninth Annual Conference of the Victorian Teachers' Union (VTU) in 1935, who deplored lack of training of teachers for senior primary or higher elementary classes and secondary schools.[161] To alleviate the dilemma, in 1938 Education Minister Sir John Harris established that 'of 300 primary trainees taken into College each year, thirty would be selected for University studies, twenty of these would be selected for a third year, and ten for a fourth'. The outcome would be '10 very highly qualified graduates for teaching advanced classes in high schools, 10 well qualified teachers, and 10 teachers sufficiently qualified for higher elementary school teaching'.[162] These measures eased the shortfall in some subjects, but not in the fields of advanced mathematics and science.

The secondary school population rose steadily from 23,678 in 1934 to 32,754 in 1942, amply demonstrating the need for more teachers. Despite a declining birthrate between 1925 and 1934, more students stayed at school longer and the expected decrease in numbers did not occur. Reporting to the Minister in 1943, Charles Scarff, Chief

Inspector of Secondary Schools, identified a rise of 5,000 students since 1937.[163] Following Japan's entry into the war in 1941 'All female and male teachers not called up for armed service were considered to be an "essential service" and were not permitted to leave their job without authority from the Directorate of Manpower'.[164] To offset the decline in the number of teachers, the Department restricted call-up of secondary trainees, seconded 180 primary teachers, employed 126 temporary teachers, kept married women on the roll for the duration of the war and engaged trainee teachers to work under guidance in one-teacher schools.[165]

## Korong Vale (1943)

Though one of 300 College entrants of 1941 and among the 30 granted an extension in 1942, Shears was keen to start teaching. Equipped with TPTC and with several university subjects in hand, he was placed on the Classified Roll of teachers. Expecting his good trainee record to place him in a suburban school from which he could comfortably continue his studies, his appointment as 'Temporary Assistant' at Korong Vale State School, No. 1800 (with central classes),[166] in Victoria's central goldfields region, came as a shock. The appointment of Lou Barberis to Upwey Higher Elementary School, No. 4530 in the Dandenong Ranges aggravated Shears' concern but he accepted the decision. To assist the move Ernie constructed a large wooden box with a lid. Shears carefully packed it with books to place in the guard's van. He hugged his father and then boarded the train at Spencer Street Station.

The route to Korong Vale Junction was via Bendigo, 144 miles from Melbourne, and a further 53 miles northwest. It was a major rail link for shifting the annual harvest of grain to ports in Melbourne and Geelong. Rail and road connected the town to Bendigo, Inglewood, Boort and the Murray River region. In its heyday, Korong Vale had three bakeries and two butchers, two general stores, a fruit shop, draper, barber and four churches. There were three blacksmiths, an undertaker and a timber merchant. It formerly boasted two hotels, several boarding houses, a private hospital and a cinema, and printed its own newspaper. By 1943 many of these had gone.[167]

Korong Vale was like many country towns, unremarkable because of their sameness. The butcher, the baker and drapery store, the Mechanics Institute and Scully's Hotel lined the long main street. On the fringe of the Mallee, red dust storms typified summer days. On his arrival Shears walked from the station, lugging the box past wagons of wheat in the goods yards. He booked in at Scully's Hotel, where he slept and dined, had occasional beers and continued his studies at night. Though not keen to host regular guests the hotelier succumbed to Shears' payment of 30/- per week, a considerable sum from a fortnightly salary of 8 guineas. On that hot summer's day, he settled in and then walked to the school in Vernon Street.

Established in 1881 in a weatherboard classroom, the school drew its initial enrolment of 40 pupils from the town and goldfields nearby. By 1943 a conglomeration of buildings accommodated just over 40 pupils in Grades 1 to 8. The buildings comprised three main rooms and a converted house used for sloyd [a variety of woodwork] with a shelter shed attached.[168] One classroom housed the Infants, the second held Grades 3 and 4 and the third was occupied by Grades 5 and 6, the few pupils in Grades 7 and 8 and the trickle who had not reached school-leaving age. Officially the school had 'central classes'. Frank Tate believed these pupils 'deserved a more elaborate education than primary could offer', their 'course of instruction much closer to "secondary" education than was the existing course for seventh and eighth grades'.[169] This placed considerable pressure on small country schools with no local high school. Rivalry was rife between Korong Vale and nearby Wedderburn, formerly known as the Korong Goldfield, where central classes were established in 1940. Public pressure in Wedderburn pushed to extend these and from 1945 pupils from Korong Vale and other small schools travelled by bus to a central point at Wedderburn Junction.[170] Believing in 'efficient rural establishments',[171] as Director of Education, James McRae (1932–36) had supported consolidation of schools as the key to good secondary education but his successor Seitz (1936–48) pressed on to 'provide facilities to enable country children, remote from high or technical schools, to proceed to Proficiency Certificate (ninth year) level'.[172] Hence, pupils at Korong Vale and other small centres had this facility offered locally, but in Korong Vale's case, only till 1945.

Two weeks into Term 1, District Inspector (or DI) Oliver Charles Phillips visited Korong Vale, accompanied by two members of the Board of Inspectors of Secondary Schools. They stayed at Scully's Hotel and Shears dined with the group each evening. From Korong Vale they visited schools nearby and others along the Robinvale and Murrayville lines. During the next few weeks they traced Frank Tate's tracks of 1895–99 and covered the vast Charlton inspectorate of 5,400 square miles.[173] In the intervening years DI James Caldwell (1929–33) had stayed at Korong Vale where he paid 6/6 for overnight at Scully's Hotel. He paid £1/2/6 at Sealake, 16/- at Chilingollah and 8/- at Birchip. On previous inspectorial visits. Phillips had travelled by train to major towns and used 'sulky, gig, mail car or whatever' to reach the outlying schools. In contrast the current group visited remote areas by car and claimed petrol expenses of 1/8 to 2/- per gallon.[174]

On inspection of Shears, Phillips saw 'An interested worker who manages effectively and teaches confidently. Obtains good results from post-primary pupils'. He ranked him 'C (5 Asst)' (a C-level teaching assistant in the Fifth Class). By tradition teachers were graded from A highest to E lowest in each class. An F was unsatisfactory. First-year teachers were generally awarded C or C+. After a second visit in September Phillips wrote, 'A capable teacher who has won the confidence of pupils. Class management is effective and lessons are presented clearly'. He assessed Shears as C+ (5 Asst).[175] The comment on class management amused Shears who recalled continual defiance by the headmaster's son.

Shears took it in his stride to teach the composite Grades 3 and 4. Headmaster Mr Keamy, who taught composite Grades 5 to 8, regularly assigned to his assistant the three pupils in Grades 7 and 8. Shears took them for French, social studies, history and English. Miss June Coburn was assigned to the school as a student teacher. She spent time in each class and was instructed by Keamy and Shears. Twice weekly before school she met either one to discuss lesson planning, philosophies of education and the psychology of teaching. Though Miss Coburn's treatment seemed a 'slap happy arrangement' it was a useful learning experience.[176] Giving instruction and employing theories of McRae, Browne and Law in his teaching practice, Shears found the application of the Dalton Plan gaining relevance.

The position in Korong Vale was shrouded in local social issues. The school pupils were a mix of Catholics and Protestants and there was strong division between the two groups. Removal of the previous temporary assistant was controversial and stirred angst among the Catholic community, who wanted him back. Regardless of religious attachment, Shears believed in his duty to 'teach the kids'.[177] He was also aware of Browne's philosophy that 'the school belongs to the community'.[178] Overcoming dissension he encouraged community activity in the school and actively participated in local activities. The pupils' garden appealed to parents. They helped turn the soil, supplied a tap to provide water and regularly passed simply to admire.[179]

From the beginning of 1942 Japanese activity in the Pacific put Australia on the defensive. The *Wedderburn Express* alerted the community to the encroaching front. In April, Australian forces guided US marines in the Solomons campaign and women at home began training as mechanics and drivers for ambulances and trucks. 'News from the Troops', a regular column in the local paper, detailed events of the war and presented arguments to encourage decentralisation of industry to rural regions. *The School Paper* warned pupils of military action through poems, songs and stories, and was a vehicle of propaganda. It 'reflected the fears, tensions, relief and pride of the Australian people … without restraint'.[180] Socially aware of the horrors inflicted, teachers encouraged their pupils to write to prisoners of war while commercial radio contributed to children's understanding and the Australian Broadcasting Commission told how schools were helping.[181]

To support the war effort Shears guided the pupils to prepare a book of writing and drawing, which they sold to parents, friends and relatives.[182] They decorated the hall and prepared supper for their concert. The children's singing and dancing and the mothers' performance received good applause and at Shears' melodrama they booed. Afterwards the band played and everybody danced. A repeat performance at Wedderburn the following week was less successful.

Despite commitment to work, study, the book and the concert, Shears continued his sporting pursuits. The war had curtailed football so he played tennis and golf. Annual tennis club membership cost 2/6 and a nine-hole game of golf cost 5/-. When the season opened in April, club members shaped the bunkers and scraped smooth the sand on the 'putting greens'. He met fellow graduates from College on two occasions. Once he rode his bike 20 miles to Wedderburn to meet Marion Hoe who ran a one-teacher school and on another occasion he and Marion travelled by train to Charlton to share first-year experiences with Ruth Boundy.

Committed to his university studies, Shears worked towards completing Latin 1, History B and English C. Alone in his room at night he heard the rail workers playing billiards and cards. In his organised manner he kept 'a timetable that said what I would do every hour of the day. I added up all the hours and I added up what had to be done'.[183] Routinely he completed and posted assignments, had them returned and received more to complete. He learnt Latin by heart and used material sent by Lou Barberis to write a 3000-word essay on T S Eliot's poems. He recalled walking the town with book in hand and reciting from 'Preludes', which remained a lifelong favourite:

> The winter evening settles down
> With smell of steaks in passageways.
> Six o'clock.
> The burnt out ends of smoky days
> And now a gusty shower wraps
> The grimy scraps
> Of withered leaves about your feet …[184]

Granted two days' leave, Shears travelled to Boort for examinations. The Department paid his train fare, accommodation and lunch allowance and the local minister supervised. The position at Korong Vale was temporary. A positive Inspector's Report supported his application for a permanent position at Bairnsdale High School. He said his farewells to Mr Keamy, the Infant Mistress and student teacher Miss Coburn (who attended teachers college the following year) and left by train with his box of books.

## Bairnsdale (1944–46)

Summer holidays came and went. Officially duties at Bairnsdale High commenced on 1 January 1944, corresponding with the transfer of Shears' name to the Classified Roll of Secondary Teachers, but he was not required to report to the school until late January. Bairnsdale was 175 miles from Melbourne. The trip by train from Spencer Street took thirteen hours. When Shears arrived, Headmaster Gibbs took him to settle into a boarding house, where he resided until he found accommodation in the main street in a first-floor room with a balcony.

Bairnsdale had two distinct postprimary schools – a high school catering for all the girls and some of the boys, and a technical school that catered for most of the boys.[185] The majority of pupils attending the high school continued to senior classes. Educational tradition of the family influenced the choice of school. Despite community apathy and antagonism from the Education Department, Donald Clark, a former civil engineer, with a local committee, achieved their dream for a technical school. Clark was appointed its founding director. The North Gippsland School of Mines opened in 1890, was renamed the Bairnsdale School of Mines in 1896 and the Bairnsdale and District School of Mines in 1914. Its proposed mining and science classes languished; however up to 100 pupils studied painting, drawing, shorthand and telegraphy in the Church of England Sunday School Hall, leased for two years at £1 per week. The School of Mines introduced core studies in metallurgy and mining and constructed a treatment plant. These developments contributed to metallurgical know-how for treating Radium Hill uranium, East Gippsland ores, and ore from Omeo, which yielded two solid gold ingots.[186]

After seventeen years in Bairnsdale, Clark was shifted to the Bendigo School of Mines in 1907. As Director he raised the status of courses, doubled the number of full-time enrolments and began treatment plant operations. Junior technical classes introduced at Bendigo elementary school bridged the gap for pupils who moved to the School of Mines. In 1910 Clark gained a lectureship at the University of Melbourne and the following year he was appointed Victoria's first Chief Inspector of Technical Schools. Believing that skills developed in technical training led to employment in the same way that the academic focus of high schools led to university studies, Clark stirred for a statewide system of junior technical schools. Established as such under the *Education Act* 1910 (No. 2301), from 1915 courses at Bairnsdale Junior Technical School fed into further studies at the Bairnsdale and District School of Mines. In 1941 the two institutions integrated and became Bairnsdale Technical School.[187]

In his capacity as Chief Inspector of Technical Schools, Clark visited Bairnsdale in 1912 to peruse the educational needs in the town. He recommended a high school be established, and claimed, 'the Department was prepared to open a high school at Bairnsdale on 22 February provided that 50 pupils not less than twelve years of age were enrolled'. Bairnsdale High School opened in March 1912, housed in the newly named Bairnsdale School of Mines, thereby preceding the junior technical school by three years. Though provision of a high and a technical school aimed to satisfy a broad spectrum of educational needs, the two were seen as 'competing' rather than 'complementary' institutions.

'Esse Quam Videri', 'to be rather than to seem', reflected the ideals of Bairnsdale High School. Offering alternate pathways for the town's youth and foundational skills to build functional lives, poor conditions prevailed. The school had a history of overcrowding and until 1930 had no electric lighting. Initially housed in cramped conditions, high school staff and 70 students were moved to the buildings of Bairnsdale College, which had been established in 1891 but had recently closed. By 1924 enrolment reached 134 and by 1944 the number increased to 319: 159 boys and 160 girls. Of these, 64 students travelled by bus and those from remote regions boarded in town.[188]

Headmaster Gibbs, who began a 24-year reign as headmaster in 1935, welcomed Mr Shears and Mr Keillerup to his the staff of ten. Another newcomer, Miss Hall, commenced in May. The school offered up to six years of continuous secondary schooling. General courses in the first two years led to discrete domestic arts, commercial or professional courses. The facility to access university studies exacerbated tension between the high and technical schools, as 'the occupations and professions to which the high school gave access were accorded higher social prestige and better financial returns'.[189] This tendency was counter to Clark's ideals and opposed both Tate's hopes for equity in schooling and the philosophies underpinning Britain's Hadow Reports (1923–33).

Concepts presented by New Education Fellowship across Australasia in 1937 affected educational thinking. Principles presented at the Melbourne Conference complied with local objectives to 'develop the latent talent of the individual'.[190] Subsequently formed, the Educational Reform Association advocated amalgamation of Bairnsdale's high and technical schools but the schools' respective committee and council rejected this. Standing their ground, they urged for a modern high school, a girls' technical school with hostel accommodation, a new elementary school and improved conditions for primary education.[191] Despite their pleas, little was done. Staffing at the high school remained a concern: there were too few books for senior subjects and overcrowding continued. Education Minister Thomas Hollway, who visited Bairnsdale in August 1944, suggested the use of verandas to offer more space. The promise of a new primary school brought a glimmer of hope; however recommendations for high and technical school governing bodies to work in unity did not come to fruition.[192]

Local papers of 1944 illuminated public voice. The *Bairnsdale Advertiser* called for overhauling the structure of school committees with the head teacher as departmental representative and parents and friends being involved. Local newspaper *Every Week* reported that delegates at the Apex Club's educational reform meeting in March sought a boost in educational funding from preschool to adulthood. They argued for secondary schools to offer a 'broad general cultural course and practical activities which suit their [pupils'] needs in after life'. Fundamental were higher pay for teachers and policies to ensure their careful selection which would in turn bolster their worth in community welfare.[193] With Professor George Browne's visit in February the issue of consolidation was raised. The *Advertiser* argued its value for outlying districts, but not in town.[194]

Against this background of debates, Shears settled into routines at school where he taught a range of subjects across all year levels. His workload embraced two English classes; British, modern and general history; geography from Intermediate to Matriculation; and social studies at lower levels. Though challenged, he enjoyed them all but his passion lay with social studies. Reflecting his own experience at University High, he gave an introductory lesson to motivate pupils to explore the topic in depth. Presentation of individual and group projects stimulated class discussion. Influenced by Dalton and Winnetka philosophies, he guided 'observation, experiment and exercise' and encouraged students to use 'their own powers of thought, judgment and reasoning to establish truths for themselves,' as advocated in the 1934 curriculum revision.[195] This impressed the parents' committee, which provided £400 to furnish a social studies room with tables, provide display material and reference books.

As was the tendency in postprimary schools, large lower classes progressively decreased in size. Small senior classes enabled teachers to address individual needs. In the Matriculation or Form 6 year of 1944 seven pupils studied English expression, one pursued geography and three selected English and modern histories and English literature. In 1945 nineteen pupils completed Leaving, or Form 5 studies, and 23 completed Intermediate. Above teaching commitments, Shears conducted the weekly assembly at which pupils listened to Dr A E Floyd on ABC radio.

Shears was a young man in his early twenties when he went to Bairnsdale. He found that some of the older girls had more on their minds than their lessons. On a fifth form geography excursion 'of fully 100 yards to the fence bordering the morass', a 'brawny Australian who was cutting wood' attracted much comment from the girls.[196] During a music broadcast they noted 'Mr Shears, obviously thinking of other things' when he wrote on the board, 'O Lovely Piece' as the title of the composition' rather than 'O Lovely Peace'. The girls wondered, 'O Lovely Piece' of what?[197] On another occasion when they were learning 'Somewhere a Voice is Calling' Shears explained that at "Somewhere" the voice goes up'. When he emphasised 'Dearest my heart is up in the first line', it caused 'merriment among the senior girls, who were subsequently requested to put whatever they were laughing at under the desk'.[198]

The Mitchell River was the venue for learning to swim and for competition. Shears recalled he once swam across but, exhausted by this, walked back over the bridge. Mr Keillerup taught and trained the swimmers while Mr Stuart and Shears prepared non-swimmers for their Herald and Junior Certificates. Competition was rife at carnivals and, because of his position as Red House Master, Shears was involved in a tussle with rival Blue House, whether in swimming, athletics or football.

For a young teacher feeling his way, holidays offered a chance to keep in touch with others. During his time at Bairnsdale, Shears often met with his friend Lou Barberis to compare challenges and pupil results. In 1938 W C (Bill) Radford, who formerly taught at the school, expressed concern that Bairnsdale High School was 'failing because it was sending only a very occasional pupil to the University'. Almost a decade later things had changed. In 1945 and 1946 seven students matriculated in each year. Shears had prepared both groups, having initially taught them as Intermediate or Leaving pupils.[199] However the reality of Radford's concern was the trickle of pupils that completed Form 6, just 8 per cent, Shears later admitted. He retrospectively recalled Ina Francis, Brian Dahlsen and Ken Tragear who continued to university.[200]

The Board of Inspectors of Secondary Schools (BISS) paid several visits to Bairnsdale and marked Shears as a secondary teacher, but it was the local district inspector who seemed to give him most encouragement. D I Whelpton in 1944 noted 'a promising young teacher … class management shows initiative and is willing to take responsibility'. He was awarded 'B in Sec V' (i.e. Secondary Division, Class V). In 1945, showing 'initiative in the development of courses' and employing successful means of stimulating interest and response, Shears was assessed as 'B+ in Sec V'. The following year Whelpton remarked, 'good preparation', 'thoughtful planning' and 'brisk vigorous manner', noted 'skilful use of illustrative material and secures a v.g. response' and again awarded B+. Secondary inspector Ottaway, however, was not impressed with the social studies class. Unfamiliar with the learning philosophy, he observed pupils engaged in projects. He asked, 'Are you going to give a lesson?'[201]

During Shears' first two years at Bairnsdale war raged on. Local newspapers reported on funds raised for the war effort, sought support for limbless soldiers and published photos of conflict. The newspapers informed the community of events in Europe, New Guinea and the Pacific, and presented tributes to those who were lost. Parents catered at sports events, pupils made toffees, and community groups held dances, concerts, gymkhanas and garden parties to raise funds. Football clubs ran Queen competitions and a penny drive run by the Red Cross yielded £63.42. V E-Day, 8 May 1945, when conflict ended in Europe, was a day to remember. 'Thanks for Victory in Europe: Crowd throngs give prayers of thanksgiving following "unconditional surrender of Germany"' was the *Advertiser*'s headline.[202] Though townsfolk united to celebrate peace, war's shadow lingered in the islands and in the Pacific.

## Beyond the classroom

Beyond his commitment to school, Shears pursued many activities. There was a time when he was secretary or president of thirteen local organisations. He ran a gymkhana to support the hospital, and joined the historical society and the Apex Club. Keen to support youth he established the boys basketball club, helped run the Lakes Entrance youth camp and organised a cricket tournament for Youth Week, held annually in March. The high school beat the tech 118 runs to 68.[203] Seeing a need for girls' community sport, he called a meeting at St Andrew's Presbyterian Hall and founded the Girls' Winter Sports Association. As secretary, he worked with Rev Allan McMillan and a small committee to field four hockey and four basketball teams, of which St Andrew's Church fielded two. Author of a column report in *Every Week* and ardent reader of its competitor the *Bairnsdale Advertiser*, he noted, 'success of the [first] day and the keenness of the play gave promise of a good season' and named G Carmichael and M Redman from St Andrew's basketball blue team as best players.[204] He presented the 'best and fairest' prize at season's end to Mavis Redman, a 'small, slick lass'[205] whom he had first noticed at a local dance.

Bairnsdale, like many rural communities, suspended competitive football during the war. Men were either serving as troops or fulfilling duties at home. The proposal for a junior football association to provide activity for boys was augmented when community and church representatives met in St Andrew's hall in April 1944. Subsequently fielding four teams, Shears wrote:

> Senior football is out of the question at present but the game is being kept alive by the Bairnsdale Junior Football Association of which Rev Allan McMillan is president and Mr L Shears the energetic honorary secretary. The Association caters for youth to 21 ... is supported by leading businesses ... aims to make the game attractive to players and spectators ... improve the standard of play ... encourage more youths to participate in valuable outdoor exercise.'[206]

'Everybody got so keen when these young fellows were running around and enjoying a competition that we decided to have a shot at introducing football for the men,' Shears recalled. In 1945 the East Gippsland District Football Association fielded eight teams and two more joined in 1946. To revive enthusiasm after four years' break, he 'wrote off to the Victorian Football League (VFL) and Association (VFA)'. VFA Secretary Harold Snook 'sent half a dozen footballs and a set of jerseys and offered to send umpires'.[207] Shears enjoyed the organisational aspect as well as playing the game:

> I became President of the East Gippsland Football Association and at the same time captained and coached the Bairnsdale Football Team. We won the Premiership in 1945 and repeated this feat the following year.[208]

Dual roles of captain and president conflicted on the field when an opposing player was knocked out during a Bairnsdale–Bruthen match. A tribunal hearing left Shears without his captaincy, lost to a fellow teacher. The sweetness of two successive premierships outweighed the disquiet.

Country entertainment Bairnsdale-style was rich in variety. Among a range of travelling artists for ABC concerts were John Charles

Thomas, Babe Scott and George Wallace. Saturday night dancers filled the Mechanics Institute or the Catholic Church hall. People waltzed, tangoed and danced the Pride of Erin and Barn Dance to the rhythms of local musicians. Annual Red Cross, Dahlsen's Staff and Empire Day Balls, and the 1944 Leap Year Dance, were popular fundraising activities too.[209]

The lass who had caught Shears' eye at a dance was wearing a blue knitted frock. She was pretty, petite and danced like an angel. Mavis Redman became his girl and later his wife. Her father Fred's appointment to manage the State Savings Bank had brought the family to town. The elder of two daughters, Mavis worked as a secretary at the hospital. Education beyond Form 4 was for boys, not girls, Fred believed. Younger sister Betty, whom Shears had taught at school, worked in real estate.

Victoria's snowfields beckoned East Gippslanders in winter. On occasions Shears and his friends hitched a ride to the mountains. They hiked to a stockmen's hut where they camped overnight. Such was a break from lesson preparation and marking, the hustle of sporting and community commitments and university study. He often stayed back at school to study geography, philosophy, accountancy, commerce and economics in the quiet of the staffroom. He was keen to complete his degrees.

1947 would start a new beginning with his appointment to Frankston High School, 25 miles south of Melbourne. He proposed to live with his family in Elsternwick, midway between school and the university. Since 1945 Ernie had lived in Myrtleford with his second wife Lillian Russell, a florist. Work was progressing well at the mill and Ernie built a row of cottages for his workers. A promotion for Fred Redman to Essendon took Mavis to Melbourne. Shears and Mavis became engaged and would marry in May.

As they did each summer holiday break, Shears and Lou Barberis found work. Providing manpower for critical industries they had picked fruit in Shepparton, felled trees in Kinglake forest and helped in the Myrtleford mill. A job laying flax at Penshurst in Victoria's southwest offered a change. They made plans for their forthcoming weddings and to act as each other's best man. Lou was teaching at

Rainbow where he had met Mona, the girl he would marry. In late January Shears and Mavis drove to Rainbow for the wedding in the garden of Mona's family home.

# CHAPTER 7

# RE-ESTABLISHING LIVES: RURAL TRAINING CENTRE (1947–50)

*Do not go where the path may lead, go instead where there is no path and leave a trail.*

Ralph Waldo Emerson

## Commonwealth Reconstruction Training Scheme

Post-war Australia bore little resemblance to the nation that was stricken by fear of invasion. War service caused upheaval of social roles midst the turmoil of young people joining the forces, leaving gaps in family, workplace and social structures. Stories of rationing, training in new industries and working with skeletal staff are a fading part of Australian folklore, while memories of ex-service folk have remained very much their own. It is claimed that only those who served know the impact of war on their lives though the bearing on all is profound. One who undertook post-war training explains in the editorial of the 1948 *Dookie Collegian*, 'I could speak of the environment of war and its aftermath, but I do not feel confident writing on such matters. You of my number understand these things, those outside would not, perhaps, understand'.[210]

When it had become obvious to everyone that there would be a war and Australians would be heavily involved, post-war rehabilitation became a key concern for authorities aware of the traumas associated with re-establishing lives. To facilitate a smooth transition to civilian life and equip returning personnel with career pathways, the Commonwealth Government planned to support technical, industrial and vocational training and educational advancement. It established a Ministry for Post-War Reconstruction, headed by Treasurer Ben

Chifley, which initially offered training to support the war effort. When peace was proclaimed, the Ministry proposed 'a coherent, integrated plan to move Australians from war to peace' and envisaged a 'relatively smooth transition to civilian life and vocational, professional and rural training'. The proposal was geared towards men and women, particularly during the peak period, 1945–47.[211] To set technical training in motion, in 1939, E P Eltham, Chief Inspector of Technical Schools in Victoria, was appointed to head the Commonwealth Defence Technical Training Scheme by secondment to the Commonwealth Department of Supply and Development.[212]

Stirred by Eltham, the Department of Supply and Development requested him to prepare a training plan for employees in technical schools and colleges and the defence industry in the event of war. By 1941 training was geared to prepare civilians for work in war-related industries with priority given to technicians and tradesmen to work in engineering trades, munitions and aircraft production, and air training. In Western Australia the railway workshop produced munitions, performed submarine repairs and cast bronze propellers for ships. In Melbourne, railway workshops at Williamstown produced gun carriers, aircraft parts and shell components. Aircraft factories were established at Fisherman's Bend and munitions factories at Maribyrnong and Bendigo. The Melbourne Technical College tailored instruction for defence personnel and added an aeronautical school, which trained servicemen and munitions trainees.[213]

After the war, the transition of ex-service personnel focused on technical training. In preparation, the Ministry established four authorities to provide instruction under the Commonwealth Reconstruction Training Scheme (CRTS). The Industrial Training Division of the Department of Labour and National Service offered vocational and professional training in the technical colleges. Universities provided professional training under the auspices of the Universities Commission. The Repatriation Commission dealt with 'problem cases' as its Repatriation Department was skilled in dealing with the blind, maimed or limbless. The Rural Reconstruction Training Authority was responsible for those who aspired to life on the land, with agricultural colleges providing their training. Sir Robert Wallace,

Vice Chancellor of Sydney University and member of the Universities Commission, commented that 'universities would make a mess of a job like that'. Agricultural colleges, like teachers colleges, were seen to have expertise in their field for specialist training.[214]

## Rural reconstruction training

Meeting the needs of returned service personnel, repatriated or discharged from service, required specific training to reabsorb them into civilian life while correspondingly satisfying labour requirements. This was a 'mammoth task in a nation of Australia's size in 1945, occurring after the Depression of the 1930s and six years of war, and while Australia was embarking on an immigration program of major proportions'. In this social climate, Australia's post-war development of secondary industries was spurred on by the CRTS. Under the scheme, approximately 251,500 men and women benefited between 1945 and 1952. Ninety per cent attended technical schools, colleges and approved industrial establishments to complete full- or part-time courses.[215]

Lessons learned from the Great War guided the rural reconstruction programs; authorities were keen to avoid the plight suffered by those who had stuck it out or walked off their holdings. Victoria settled 11,000 ex-servicemen on the land between 1915 and 1938 but almost 7000 walked away. The Returned Sailors' and Soldiers' Imperial League of Australia (RSSILA, but colloquially the RSL) directed blame at the scheme, not the men, while the Pike Report of 1929 identified political pressure, an unreasonable timeframe and placement of untried and ill-trained men on unsuitable blocks.[216]

During the years of World War II, enrolments in agricultural courses slumped but after the war interest increased. Principal James Leslie Provan steered Dookie Agricultural College through these turbulent years. Numbers surged with new students, re-enrolments of returnees from the services and the new ex-service group. The Rural Reconstruction Committee had started negotiations with the Department of Agriculture in 1941. The proposal that the Rural Training Centre (RTC) be annexed to the main college, with CP

Denton appointed Officer in Charge, gradually took shape. To satisfy needs of students entering the college by traditional means as well as the ex-service group, the main college and the annexe had discrete facilities for learning and accommodation. Both groups studied the Dookie Diploma of Agriculture (DDA), but unlike young students coming directly from school, the RTC cohort had an average age of 25. War service had carved a slice off their lives and they were keen to move on. The DDA tailored to their needs was shortened in time but not in scope by fitting the six terms into two years.

Plans to commence the first course in January 1946 did not eventuate as those in service were not released or repatriated until June. When the course began on 1 October the men were keen to 'get cracking'.[217] Seven ex-air force huts shipped from Shepparton provided their accommodation, two to a room. The ablutions block was incomplete so sanitary arrangements were set amongst a sugar gums copse a short distance from Hut A. In the other direction was the trough in which to wash. In summer the heat was exhausting; the country was dusty and dry. In winter the country was muddied by rain and chilled by the winds. All year long either red dust or mud penetrated the men's clothing and skin.[218]

One hundred and twenty men enrolled in the first program but by January 1947 only 90 remained. The men received a repatriation allowance, ample food and accommodation, but the course lacked direction and educational input. Timetables were posted daily and there was no curriculum to guide the men, who found the disorganisation unsettling. Provision of tools, equipment and textbooks was inadequate and sourcing suitably trained staff was a major concern. Instruction in practical agricultural subjects was capably handled, but the teacher of English was said to be phony. Despite credentials of a doctorate from abroad and a commendable service record, the teacher's incompetence showed. His removal before the end of the year aggravated the staffing dilemma. At the 2008 reunion one ex-serviceman recalled, 'He taught us English – failed most of us. He was self-decorated. It was all a lot of bulldust.'[219] Another identified three distinct groups among the ex-servicemen: those who were older with educational experience, those with too little education to be at an agricultural college and others that lay between. The situation required an educator who understood individuals, could tailor teaching to their needs and talk with them rather than at them or above their heads.

The dilemma at Dookie called for urgent action. The fact that the ex-servicemen were unhappy and leaving in droves roused discussion between Alex McDonell and George Woodgate, Victoria's Superintendent of Agricultural Education, about a suitable person to teach at the RTC. McDonell[220] was Assistant Chief Inspector of Secondary Schools with major responsibility for administering the Education Department's Secondary Division. The inspectorial system enabled those in control to identify the merits and shortcomings of registered teachers statewide and it was common practice that 'the Education Department asked inspectors to recommend teachers to fill an urgent vacancy'.[221] To pluck the most suitable person from the system seemed the solution.

While McDonell was an educator who knew what was required, Woodgate was a man who also knew agriculture. He understood the organisation of agricultural education and the needs of the ex-servicemen. Woodgate's career in education began in 1905 at Yarra Park State School, No. 1406, in Richmond, as a 'monitor' teacher. In the succeeding twelve years he completed Bachelor of Arts at the University of Melbourne and Diploma of Education at Melbourne Teachers College.[222] Teaching experience at country schools, Melbourne High School and Longerenong Agricultural College broadened his educational knowledge and understanding of agricultural instruction. Woodgate moved to Dookie in 1940 and became principal in 1942. It was he who planned the RTC and asked McDonell to find the right person to uphold the course.

McDonell was aware of the stakes when he approached Shears who, although a qualified primary teacher, taught in the Secondary Division. Concurrently he was studying at the University of Melbourne to complete arts and commerce degrees and planned to commence a Diploma of Education (Secondary). It was not easy for Shears to commit again to country service. After four years at Korong Vale and Bairnsdale his appointment to Frankston High School would facilitate his university studies and give proximity to Mavis. He recalled:

> We were laying flax in the Western District, Penshurst. I had a telegram from Alex McDonell asking would I come and see him. He said, 'We have a position at the ex-servicemen's Rural Training Centre at Dookie College, they're in a bit of difficulty, would you like to go there?' I was uncertain at first as I had just come to Melbourne and was about to get married. Mr McDonell suggested, 'Go and talk to Mr Woodgate, the Superintendent of Agricultural Education.' Mr Woodgate described the difficulties: the men had plenty of food and good accommodation but they didn't have an educator to make sure the programs were running according to the Diploma of Agriculture. I understood that there were no syllabuses or regular timetables. I asked him about the conditions and when he told me the salary would be double what I was getting and promised to build me a house I agreed to start the following week.[223]

Negotiations led to Shears' secondment to the Victorian Department of Agriculture as second in command at the RTC. He was appointed senior lecturer in the educational program to teach English, rural economics and general principles of accountancy.

## The Rural Training Centre

Selection of Shears to the RTC put him on an unusual career path. Certainly he was developing sound teaching and organisational skills but this venture took him into the realm of adult education. The life experiences of the ex-service students differed vastly from his. They had entered the war as boys and exited as men whose lives were tainted by the experience of war. Shears' non-service could have ruffled the men and those keen for rehabilitation programs to be staffed by ex-servicemen. When, some years later, George Woodgate wrote a reference in support of Shears' application to do doctoral studies in London, he made it obvious that he had recognised that 'discharged men would be very restive under the tutelage, restraints and discipline of a college, and that this would be manifested particularly towards any member of the staff who was not a serviceman'.[224] He was aware of Shears' youth and his lack of experience in teaching adults and that he was new to agricultural education, but Woodgate also recognised his attributes and encouraged him to prove himself.

Shears set off for the RTC to commence duties on 4 February 1947. He took the 128-mile journey in his 1934 Wolseley Hornet. It was half a day's drive along the Hume Highway, over Pretty Sally hill, through Seymour and on to Euroa. Turning left at Violet Town, he travelled a thin gravel road. The sun shimmered on the stubble and dust billowed behind.

Shears was aware of the ex-servicemen's discontent and that he held the key to their success. Those who had stuck it out had been at Dookie for four months by the time he arrived. Apart from their educational problems, as the first group, they had no one to follow, no rituals to guide them and no structures in place. They had quickly established social and sporting routines, set up a canteen, transferred to local RSL groups and founded a news-sheet, 'the most exclusive newspaper in Australia' with restricted circulation to 'those directly concerned with the RTC'.[225] The men were a fractious group, and having been let down were keen to take this new fellow on. He was small in stature and could have been an easy target but they noted an air of humour and seeming ability to make sound judgments.

The first session was daunting. Heat from the iron roof and brick walls permeated the lecture hall. Standing behind the lectern, Shears faced a sea of men who sat motionless and blank at wooden benches that crammed the room. They were coatless, some wore ties, most had unbuttoned their collars. English had been a sour experience and this young bloke was wandering 'lonely as a cloud' midst 'a host of golden daffodils … beside the lake, beneath the trees …' in a poem by Wordsworth that most of them hadn't seen or heard since they read it in the sixth-grade Reader.[226] Why oh why did golden daffodils matter when they wanted to know about golden wheat and the appropriate time to harvest the crop? Why think about lakes when their concern was irrigation and watering systems? Despite the men's doubts about the new man and lethargy towards the subject matter, he exhibited warmth and seemed to care. A spark ignited. His energy engaged them and from that moment they united. It is an abstract concept and hard to define the qualities of a teacher to hold a class. The men saw structure in the lecture; it was brisk and carefully planned. The teacher engaged with men of diverse educational experience and seemed to understand their specific interests and needs. During that lecture the men felt the promise of success and held hope in their second chance.[227] As Shears developed the courses, listened to their cause and tightened procedures, he gained their trust and during this process disparities melded and the men and he developed a bond.

The importance of the Dookie years cannot be underestimated for a young man of 26 under scrutiny of the Education and Agriculture Departments. Concurrently he was undertaking university studies and engaged to be married in May. The first term was torrid. Like McDonell and Woodgate, he knew the stakes were high. He had a single room in the staff quarters, use of the common room, office and library where he did his work and planning. Before classes commenced Shears checked student records, learnt names and gathered personal details. He noted the men's ages, a year younger than his, their physique and personal traits. He identified the chap with the T-model Ford, the lad with red hair and the boys with motorbikes parked in the sugar gums carpark.[228] Hair colour, curls and moustaches were easily noted; more complex were their personal histories or the measure of grief for a best mate lost.

To prepare a lesson or lecture takes time, drive and resourcefulness. It takes energy to deliver, to observe the students constantly, to connect with them and to gauge the pace, input and measure of success. A successful lecture brings deep satisfaction but the teacher has no time to bask. On that hot February day, Shears felt satisfied yet agitated by the size and urgency of his task. In his few days at Dookie he observed grown men milling around the timetable. It was posted daily. He heard them curse. He knew what had to be done to bring about change. A regular timetable with course outlines that he prepared gave the men order, security and direction. When the library closed Shears worked in his room, lit by a single bulb. He wrote a complete curriculum for the DDA's courses in English, rural economics and general principles of accountancy, with objectives and week-by-week details. His model guided specialist staff. Shears recalled:

> The first term up there in 1947 – it was hot, hot! Here was

I struggling to come up with a decent timetable. They had been putting a timetable up every morning. You can imagine about 120 ex-servicemen who were having their second shot at getting some qualifications, milling around a single spot to read the daily timetable. It was ridiculous! They didn't have syllabuses and they didn't have the organisation they should have had … gradually we reduced the number of people who were leaving. They started with about 120 and they were down to 90 when I got there. The staff had excellent practical experience and quickly picked up the need for subject syllabuses. So I got them into the syllabus making, got all the staff who were quite good at their job, in terms of whether they were cattle or poultry or piggeries or pasture; given examples of possible curriculum outlines as a basis for their own subjects, in a few weeks they had each prepared the framework, a week-by-week plan and identified materials to use.[229]

Miss Winifred Burridge BSc, BEd, a young teacher of science, enhanced the program and bravely tackled the men. While they 'thought she was absolutely startling' they taunted her when she alluded to animal reproductive procedures. She countered inappropriate comments and continued in a matter-of-fact manner. Her persistence, depth of knowledge and sincerity gained their respect and she became a most important factor in the success of the total program.[230]

A second intake of ex-servicemen arrived in October. Shears prepared a new timetable, allocated staff, allotted rooms and resources and integrated newcomers into the fold. Correspondingly he evaluated the first group's feedback and strengthened alignment between theoretical knowledge and farm practice.[231] The range of subjects, specialist practices and environmental understanding proved an organisational challenge. The timetabling of building construction provided an obvious link. Rather than the 40-minute norm, practical classes filled an entire afternoon. Instructed by Harry Huffam, the men constructed three two-bedroom weatherboard houses. Known as Huffam huts, they eventually accommodated college principal Perc Denton, the medical officer and Shears and Mavis.

## Other dimensions of life at the RTC

Being second in command of the RTC fulfilled Shears' desire to serve. Initially it was tough living and working in prefabricated huts but he was warmed by the support of the men who realised his concern for their success and wellbeing. Foremost he worked to satisfy their needs while balancing them with his own. Denton was supportive and, having no children, was a father figure.

For the wedding of Shears and Mavis in May, Lou and Mona had travelled from Rainbow to Melbourne. Rev Allan McMillan of St Andrew's, Bairnsdale, performed the ceremony at Essendon's Presbyterian Church. The newlyweds honeymooned in Tasmania where they visited Port Arthur, drove northward along the coast to Launceston, and took their first-ever flight, from Launceston to Melbourne. They proposed to stay at the Benalla Hotel but the cost was excessive and the drive to and from college time-consuming. Mavis stayed with a local family for six weeks but then returned to her family home. Shears undertook numerous trips back and forth for fifteen months until their on-campus home was complete. Fortunately, on Monday mornings he was lecture free. Mavis learnt she was pregnant in October. After a lengthy labour she gave birth to Christine in May 1948. Shears drove as fast as he could – up to 40 miles per hour – to reach the hospital.

Mavis continued to live with her family and Shears continued his ritual visits until their new house was complete. With a home of their own he lifted his wife and his daughter over the threshold.

Their presence on campus brought a new dimension to college life. At 11 each morning the ex-servicemen visited Mavis with horses or tractors or on foot to share morning tea. Their day had started with breakfast at 7 before lectures at 8. At 11 there was a break before practical farming began. The men enjoyed company, attended dances and pursued sporting interests. They began a challenge for golfers to hit the ball to the top of nearby Mt Major with a minimum number of swings. They established a house system and ran competitive cricket, basketball, tennis, football, athletics, swimming and snooker. They organised dances in the lecture room (including decorations, band and catering) and invited local young ladies as guests. Mavis joined Shears at the dances and football and had drinks at the Dookie pub. In the saloon bar for ladies Christine took her first steps towards her father.

The number of vehicles in the sugar gums carpark gradually increased until it looked like a 'museum or a wrecker's backyard'.[232] Cars, bicycles and the college truck transported the men to local events, weekly picture shows in Dookie town and a drink at the local hotels. They spilled off the sides of the cars and the truck on their way to play or watch district cricket and football. For £50, Shears coached the Dookie township team in the Shepparton League in 1947 but the farm fellows were lax and disconnected as a team. The following year the RTC team joined the Benalla and District League. Shears was captain and coach. With the discipline of regular practice and supportive teamwork they reached the finals. The team defeated Goorambat 8.22(70) to 2.11(23) and won Dookie College's first premiership for 62 years.[233] Shears recalled, they 'performed magnificently in their first season together, for many, their first season for many years'. The players insisted, 'It was not our win, it belonged to everybody' at the RTC.[234]

## Short courses

When the diploma classes were functioning effectively, the Department of Agriculture planned a series of eight-week courses for ex-service personnel. Shears developed these, drew up timetables and prepared for a huge influx of students. The first 57 arrived in May 1947 not long after he settled in and just after his wedding.

The intensive course involved twelve core subjects and five specialist subjects selected by individuals. The 52 lectures allocated to farm management covered economics of farm practice, farm records and farm budgeting. There were fifteen lectures timetabled for plant production; 30 for climate, soils and manure; and ten for crops and pastures. Field trips included a visit to Mr Bullingham's farm to observe his Friesian herd on irrigated pastures at Tongala. The group visited a citrus grove at Cobram, jersey and red poll studs, the Shepparton Butter Factory, the Shepparton Preserving Company (SPC), and the Mooroopna flour mills. Principal Provan was among speakers who gave an after-dinner address. He spoke about 'The agricultural approach', GT Levick talked about 'insect pests' and Mr J Aird considered the work of the State Rivers and Water Supply Commission. Short courses ran successively. By August 1949, 642 men and women had graduated from eleven courses already run and 97 were currently enrolled.[235]

In response to students' request for practical knowledge of farm bookkeeping and financial management, Shears developed a double-entry method to prepare accounts for taxation. Praised by students and supported by Mr E Beruldsen, Superintendent of Agricultural Training, Shears published *A Short Course in Farm Bookkeeping*. Thenceforth it was a vital component of all courses and a tool that remained useful to graduates in later years.

## Thesis

In addition to professional and personal responsibilities, Shears undertook his Bachelor of Education. He was required to complete course work, practical teaching and a thesis. In 1948, he passed four subjects including Organisation and Method and was seen as 'a highly intelligent and very capable teacher'. He completed Modern Developments and Experimental Education with honours the following year.

Shears' current experience at the RTC had aroused his interest in adult education so for his BEd thesis he decided to undertake a comprehensive study of the educational needs of adults in rural areas. Colin Badger, Founding Director at the Council for Adult Education (CAE), visited the RTC frequently and a firm friendship had developed between the two men. Research into adult education would have mutual benefit, hence CAE funded questionnaire printing and distribution costs for Shears' study. Shears sought to identify how adults spent their time, which would provide insight for CAE regarding its future direction.

Writing the thesis involved fieldwork. Shears set aside three weeks in which to distribute 900 questionnaires to schools through the region's eleven shires. The Shires of Alexandra, Benalla, Broadford, Euroa, Goulburn, Kilmore, Mansfield, Pyalong, Seymour, Violet Town and Yea covered an area of 5744 square miles with a population of 33,134. There were 98 primary, six secondary and eight registered schools. The study examined the region's population; physical resources and their use; the general pattern of employment; use of services; transport systems; and facilities in schools. Mavis helped by typing the questionnaire and covering letter, which explained the aims and nature of the survey. The 900 copies were stencilled and duplicated, wrapped in brown paper packages, stamped, bundled and posted.

The study, entitled 'The educational needs of adults in rural areas', revealed that 62 per cent of the population had passed the Merit Certificate, 34 per cent had experienced four years of secondary education or more and 4 per cent had reached university standard. The thoroughness of the study gives a glimpse into the complexity of the task and Shears' effort and persistence to pursue his goals. It also foreshadows his administrative potential.

On his trip to collect responses, Shears observed schools across the region and noted their condition, facilities and limitations. Several weeks later he made a second visit to interview selected respondents at key centres to probe issues of concern. In his thesis he described a catastrophic scene that curtailed educational advancement. It identified the absence of central classes, a girls' school or technical schools across the entire region and revealed that the education system failed to address basic learning needs. Benalla's multi-purpose high school (which provided professional and technical courses), Euroa's cookery and woodwork centres, and the Yea woodwork centre offered glimmers of hope. Aware of the push towards consolidation he observed little of that:

> … although some buildings from schools which have been closed are placed in the grounds of Seymour, Alexandra, Euroa and Mansfield. They are purely emergency shelters made in an endeavour to house the present number of pupils in various towns. At Alexandra, Euroa and Mansfield they are literally stacked on top of one another in school grounds which were none too large before these additions arrived.[236]

Inspecting schools per se, Shears lamented such overcrowding and claimed 'it would be impossible to successfully proclaim an Act which lifts the school leaving age to 15.' He grieved at the 'castles', 'gaols', 'monuments' and 'makeshifts' that must be replaced. Reminded of conditions at the RTC, where a conglomerate of makeshift units assembled on Dookie College grounds accommodated the classes and housed the men, he wrote that he:

> ... saw the need to establish a long-range building program and the determined pursuit of such a plan ... if we are to make the school and its surrounding buildings the real centre of our adult education program; if we are to stretch out, grasp and hold the interest of adults in any area, and finally if in doing so we are to satisfy the educational needs of the people.[237]

## An era ends; a new day dawns

End-of-course examination graded the men's success. In September 1948 the graduation of 73 with Dookie Diplomas of Agriculture (DDA) marked a 'momentous period for authorities and instructors'. Woodgate was proud of 'the largest number of graduates to leave Dookie College and largest group of ex-service students in agriculture in Australia'.[238] He expressed 'pleasure with the results, and the high standard generally', and a staff member claimed, 'there were said to be no fools or loafers amongst them.'[239] Bruce Davidson was Dux and Mick Kent, Don Duncan, Ron Callander, Gil Harvey and Jack Farr earned first-class honours. Second-class honours went to 46 and eighteen passed. Two sat deferred exams. Denton conveyed 'congratulations to Davidson for his splendid results, and to all students'. He commended the men, the college and the scheme. By 1949 100 ex-servicemen had graduated with DDAs and over 1,200 completed short courses in agriculture under the Commonwealth Reconstruction Training Scheme.

The men appreciated their second chance. 'After five years of war service it was time for us to do something with our lives. This time of rehabilitation was our second chance and we couldn't afford to waste it.'[240] Lecture-filled days and examinations passed, it was time to 'settle down into our lifetime occupation'. Equipped with basic skills they undertook a diverse range of employment: Heinz, SPC, Department of Soil Conservation, State Rivers, a nursery, and even coffee production in Africa. Some furthered their study in veterinary science, agriculture, commerce and teaching. Others entered professional practice, and Don Duncan began his doctorate. Most moved to approved training farms and hoped to qualify for a farming block. Mick Kent recalled assessments on fencing, pest and weed extermination and building construction. He erected a shed to accommodate his wife, a Benalla girl.

Like seeds sown they scattered to the four corners of the State and further afield. The harvest was good. Shears reaped a harvest too; he had proved himself at the RTC and completed his studies with acclaim. He was awarded honours for his thesis and shared with Clive Streader the Freda Cohen Prize of the University of Melbourne. Equipped with bachelors' degrees in arts and commerce and a Bachelor of Education conferred in 1950, and 'magnificent references' from Woodgate and Professor Browne of the University of Melbourne, Lawrence Shears, TPTC, BA, BCom, BEd, took his next steps. An Imperial Relations Trust Fellowship, the John and Eric Smyth Travelling Scholarship, and an Education Department Travelling Scholarship supported his doctoral studies in the UK. He recalled:

> Professor Browne wanted me to go to London and he supported me strongly for the Imperial Relations Trust Fellowship, which was a very, very profitable, extensive award. I won the John and Eric Smyth Travelling Scholarship and the Education Department Travelling Scholarship. Putting it all together I had enough funds to take my wife and child to England. I was accepted straight into the doctoral degree because of the Cohen Prize and the first place in Bachelor of Education. It took seven weeks to get to England.[241]

# Section 3:

# STEPPING OUT

CHAPTER 8

# LONDON CALLING: DOCTORAL STUDIES (1950–52)

*Imagination is not a dangerous gift; it is the manifestation of a live and eager personality.*

Arthur A Lismer

The trend to travel and study education systems abroad was common among senior administrators. Frank Tate visited New Zealand in 1904 and presenting his opinions to his Minister led to three important pieces of legislation: the *Education Act* 1905 (No. 2005) amending protocol for school attendance; the *Teachers Act* 1905 (No. 2006) setting up the Committee of Classifiers, the Classified Roll and the promotion and salary schedule; and the *Registration of Teachers and Schools Act* 1905 (No. 2013) to establish a Registration Board and pertinent constitution.[242] In 1907 he studied education systems in the USA and Europe and represented Victoria at the first Imperial Education Conference in London. James McCrae, as recipient of the Education Department Travelling Scholarship, investigated education systems in Britain and USA with a focus on educational problems, in 1926–27. His successor, Arnold Seitz, was Advisor to the Australian Delegation to the first UNESCO Conference held in London in 1945 'for the establishment of an educational and cultural organization (ECO/CONF)'[243] among representatives from 44 countries.

The benefits of travel were far-reaching and, over the years, ideas from abroad filtered into Victorian schools. Dialogue with educationists visiting from abroad and subsequently with their institutions had similar impact. In 1923 Chris McRae, a lecturer at Melbourne TC, gained a 'Diplôme de Français' from the University of Dijon and enrolled in doctoral studies at the University of London where he worked with psychologists Charles Spearman and Sir Cyril Burt, knighted for his contributions to psychological testing. Ken Cunningham, founding director of the ACER, who completed his doctoral studies (1925–27) at the Teachers College, Columbia University, in New York (often referred to simply as Teachers College), under John Dewey and Edward Thorndike, similarly recognised the benefits of international study. Determined to set up networks and bridge links between institutions interstate and abroad, Cunningham developed connections with Jean Piaget of the International Bureau of Education in Geneva as well as the Scottish Council for Research in Education and the National Bureau of Education in South Africa where Ernest Malherbe was Director. Travelling with Tate through France, Italy and the UK in 1933, Cunningham accepted the valuable opportunity to discuss educational problems with academics of international renown. Among them were Sir Fred Clarke of McGill University and Sir Percy Nunn of the London Institute of Education, which promoted scholarship among promising men and women in each dominion of the British Commonwealth. Subsequently appointed to the Institute as overseas student advisor, Clarke visited Australia in 1935.

1937 became a landmark year in knowledge exchange when an entourage of prominent educationists from Britain, Europe, the USA and Japan promoted the ideals of the New Education Fellowship (NEF) at a series of conferences held across New Zealand and Australia. Following a successful tour in South Africa, Cunningham, Tate and Dr Clarence Beeby (who, at 38 in 1940, was appointed Director of Education of New Zealand) initiated the Australasian tour. The list of notables included Laurin Zilliacus of Finland (but former Superintendent of the Winnetka Schools in Illinois), chairman of the NEF; Beatrice Ensor, co-founder and secretary of the NEF and editor of its journal *Education for the New Era;* Emil De Brunner and Isaac Kandel from Teachers College; Harold Rugg, also from Teachers College, but as well cofounder of the National Council for Social Studies; E Salter Davies, Director of Education in Kent, chairman of the Carnegie United Kingdom Trust and editor of the Cambridge-based *Journal of Education* and Susan Isaacs, educational psychologist from the London Institute who promoted nursery school education.

Before returning to Teachers College, Kandel presented the Tenth

John Smyth Memorial Lecture, at the Melbourne Town Hall, entitled 'The strife of tongues'. [244]

While distances between Australia, the USA, Europe and the UK were vast and travel time lengthy, dialogue among educationists supported the benefits of knowledge transfer. At Melbourne Teachers College the influence of staff who travelled had a profound effect on trainees, particularly the views of Principal John Smyth (1902–27). Smyth attended the University of Heidelberg in 1895, completed his DPhil at the University of Edinburgh in 1900 and served for two years as Chief Inspector in the Wanganui District in New Zealand. Like others, personal experience underpinned his belief in the benefits of travel to expand horizons and develop links abroad. He died in Tokyo in 1927. In his will he left an amount of £4064 to fund the John and Eric Smyth Travelling Scholarship for teachers. The name was partly a memorial to his son who died accidentally in 1925. Recipient of the award in 1950, Shears, with his wife Mavis and daughter Christine, set sail for sabbatical study abroad.[245]

## Expanding horizons

With his collection of credentials and awards – the Imperial Relations Trust Fellowship,[246] the John and Eric Smyth Travelling Scholarship and an Education Department Travelling Scholarship for study in the UK – 29-year-old Shears embarked on his journey. Due to start in September 1950, he was offered direct entry to the doctoral program, unlike Tom Coates, the previous Imperial Relations Trust Fellow, who wrote his Master of Education thesis on board ship before commencing his doctorate at the Institute of Education.[247] A reference from George Browne, Professor of Education at the University of Melbourne, noted Shears' academic results 'sprinkled with Honours'. Of the recently completed BEd thesis Browne wrote:

> His general procedure was very good, particularly in relation to its statistical validity, and his recommendations are so valuable that the thesis may be published in the near future ... I think he is one of the best students we have ever sent to you.[248]

At the end of May 1950 Shears and the family packed their belongings at the RTC. Aware of severe rationing in Britain and with permission to travel with 70 pounds of food, the ex-servicemen and 'top college' staff presented Shears with a wooden box. It contained three 1-gallon tins; each held a dozen farm fresh eggs layered in fat. Shears explained that the carpentry staff supplied the box, the poultry boys supplied the eggs and the meat boys rendered the fat. The family stayed for three months with Mavis' parents, who had moved to Bay Street, North Brighton. Shears, Mavis and Christine departed in early August.

Sailing on *SS Moreton Bay*, refurbished after war service, they were among 514 passengers. Their cabin on the promenade deck gave them prestige among those aboard. Father-in-law Fred Redman joined crowds at Station Pier to wish them farewell but was unable to cope with the last goodbye. Shears' father Ernie, or Poppa, as he had become known, kissed Christine and held her close as he sang 'Go to sleep my little picaninny'. From the wharf he threw streamers as the whistle blew, the gangplanks were lifted, the ropes were unhitched and the ship set sail.

*Moreton Bay* sailed across the Great Australian Bight to Perth, stopping in Adelaide on the way. Waterfront strikes in both cities delayed its departure. By day the family swam, read or played deck games and at night Shears and Mavis danced beneath the star-sprinkled sky. Day after day, day after day, the engines turned as they headed north.

Nearing Colombo, the first foreign port, excitement stirred. Passengers lined the deck shoreward to view the city and the distant green hills rising to a peak beyond. Shears, Mavis and Christine, visited local sites and lunched at the Gold Hotel on the seafront. After yet another strike they crossed the Arabian Sea to Aden and sailed into the Red Sea passing Yemen, Eritrea, Ethiopia and Egypt. At Suez Christine was left with three young nurses while Shears and Mavis travelled 78 desert miles to Cairo. They visited the pyramids, rode camels to the Sphinx and lunched at Shepheard's Hotel. Travelling 100 miles by train to Port Said they joined Christine and the nurses who had sailed through the Suez Canal. Crossing the Mediterranean Sea the ship docked at Valetta in Malta where white houses were cut into the clifftops like a castle of cards. Reaching Southampton the Shears shared a moment of excitement as they set foot on British soil.

They headed northward to London by train to lodge with Dora M Gibbs where they had a room with a double bed and cot. They shared the bathroom. Looking every bit the well-groomed gentleman with his leather briefcase, Shears set off for the London Institute on 10 September. He caught the train from Sidcup Station to Waterloo and boarded a bus to cross the Thames. Thrilled to see London Bridge, Westminster Abbey and St Paul's Cathedral, he was saddened by the scars of war. Midst rubble and new constructions, Senate House stood tall and impressive at the heart of the University of London. Nearby was the Institute of Education where Shears would study.

## The Institute of Education: Shaping his vision

Established in 1836, the University of London had a strong tradition. The Institute of Education, founded in 1902, became fully affiliated in 1932 and moved to the north wing of Senate House in 1938. Originally known as the London Day Training Centre, it provided teachers for London's elementary and secondary schools. The Institute was evacuated to Nottingham during WWII when the Ministry of Information used Senate House as an observation point. It is believed Hitler identified it as his future British headquarters.[249] Under the auspices of a Carnegie Foundation grant of £1,000 and a matching sum from the Leverhulme Trust, the Institute established a Foundation for Educational Research in 1946, creating a key national body. Foundation board members included Cyril Burt, Herbert Hamley and Charlotte Fleming and the chair was Sir Fred Clarke.[250] Previously Clarke had served as Professor of Education at Hartley University College, Southampton (1906–11), the University of Cape Town, South Africa (1911–29) and McGill University in Montreal (1929–34). A powerful figure in teacher education, he was Director of the London Institute (1936–45) and Oversea [sic] Student Advisor (1934–36; 1946–50).[251]

The Institute was deserted when Shears arrived on 10 September. At 10 o'clock Oversea Student Advisor Kathleen Usher-Smith met him and he was welcomed later by Dr George Barker Jeffery (Clarke's successor as Director) and staff of the Oversea and Higher Degrees Departments. As a higher degree research student, Shears was invited to mingle in the Senior Staff Common Room.

The 1950s was an exciting time in Britain. Nation building and post-war reconstruction influenced Shears, shaping his thoughts and career aspirations. With teacher supply at an alarming low, a net was cast to recruit mature-aged applicants and employ married women. Efforts were made to advance teachers' professional profile and boost their salary scale. The McNair Report, in which both Clarke and Jeffery were influential, identified the need to improve facilities, buildings and amenities. The report advocated maintenance payments to ensure the economic viability of keeping children in school with the hope that some would become teachers.[252]

Shears became immersed in a university steeped in tradition. In the Senior Staff Common Room he witnessed current debates and had entrée to the Institute's notable staff. He mixed with the likes of Jeffrey and Clarke and his tutors Charlotte Fleming and Harold Ernest Oswald (HEO) James. Fleming's research centred on the social psychology of adolescence while James basked in the light of his study 'The teacher was black', which explored the experiences of Nigerian women as teachers in English schools in post-war Britain, and cross-cultural social attitudes. Among other notables present were Philip Vernon, who identified three levels of intelligence and argued inconsistencies of generalist IQ, and Arnaud Reid who 'launched philosophy of education as an academic discipline' in England.[253]

The London Institute was a meeting place for international students, academics and visiting scholars, among them T S Eliot, whose poems inspired Shears at Korong Vale, and Hans Eysenck, a German Jew who pioneered behavioral therapy. His controversial views on connections between genetic endowment and intellect stirred dissent. From Maudsley Hospital's psychiatry department, Eysenck had shifted to the University of London in 1948. He maintained links with the hospital and established the university's psychiatry institute in 1950.[254] Shears recalled occasional walks through university grounds, discussing literature with Eliot and concepts of psychology, personality, behaviour and group dynamics with Eysenck. Some of these, he believed, were applicable to his doctoral studies and he later introduced aspects into teacher education.

## The dynamics of leadership

Privileged by his status at the university, Shears attended lectures and seminars in the Department of Advanced Studies. He had twelve years' teaching experience, had completed (with distinction) several degrees and was embarking on his doctoral studies. He reflected on the twelve years of teaching, most recently with the ex-servicemen. Having lived side by side with the men, he was intrigued by the psychological, personality and behavioural traits of them as individuals. Observation of relationships and achievement of leadership in diverse social, sporting and academic situations braced his desire to explore the dynamics involved. He devised an approach to observe the emergence of leadership among members of 'social groups in society or small face-to-face school groups' to discover the nature of group dynamics and 'inter-member relationships which develop within them.'[255]

To establish his study he selected groups of Forms 3 and 5 students from Dorking County Grammar School, a non-residential school near Haslemere in Surrey, and Bedales School near Portsmouth in Hampshire, a co-educational residential school known for 'advanced' teaching method. The schools being relatively close presented commonality yet contrast in historic age and educational context. Given 'special' staff status, he observed interactions among the selected groups in learning and social situations during extended blocks of fieldwork. The study begun at Dorking in 1950 was replicated at Bedales the following year. The thesis preface reveals the complexity involved in his philosophy, rationale and psychological dimensions. He wrote:

> Alterations were made in the structure of the group at various stages, teacher and pupil rating and scaling tests of various kinds were employed and essays were obtained on each child's experience in each situation. In addition various preference tests, personality tests and an interview using guided

techniques were employed. All procedures adopted were for the purpose of obtaining a complete picture of the individual members of each group, the structure of the group, the background of the members of the group in the particular situations chosen for the study. From the information, it was possible to obtain relevant scores and assessments for each member and to use these in testing the hypotheses.[256]

The study provided a vision of leadership, its situational malleability and how this affected the functioning of groups. Shears perceived that training for leadership would equip potential leaders with the requisite skills and raise awareness of the nature of leadership. He endorsed increasing possibilities for taking responsibility within the groups but identified the 'possession of tool requirements for the situation was essential for the emergence of a person as leader in all situations at both age levels'.[257] Examination of 'functioning natural adolescent school groups' revealed:

> ... that the leaders who emerged were not the highest in intelligence, that personality adjustment was not a significant determinant in the emergence of leaders, that the leader figure cannot be profitably considered outside of the group in which he or she is called upon to function, and finally, that at the senior adolescent level, <u>the emergence of leaders was specific to the situation in which the group functioned</u>.[258]

Shears' observations drew attention to the prospect of optional leadership structures, the benefits of cooperative procedures and chances for each to contribute using his or her unique talent. Leadership was a shared activity wherein group dynamics determined intra-group relationships. He stressed 'the importance of group relationship based on friendship patterns and workmate choices'. He advocated Activity Methods, as in mock situations, where students assumed particular roles which in turn influenced group interaction. This Shears believed encouraged 'full development of individuals and increased practice in co-operation with their fellows in handling the material used in their education'. Interaction was vital as 'different pupils bring to a joint problem different gifts and experiences' thus 'a partnership is required for a successful solution'. In class situations the teacher must 'ensure that challenging situations arise or are provided, that the pupils are given the opportunity of bringing to bear on stimulating problems their capacity for independent analysis, judgment and decision and seeing that these function in group situations where techniques for effective group action can be learned'. While Shears anticipated pupils being 'thrown constantly into situations in which they would be required to organize in order to attain their goal', activity would 'of necessity, increase the knowledge of members of one for the other and of the ways in which it is possible for a group to proceed towards its goal'. Ideally, what was achieved would be carried into adulthood and students would be equipped with the tools and experience to organise community groups cooperatively.[259]

The younger group lacked the skill attained by the older group. Shears deduced that leadership skills:

> ... related to the increasing maturity of children during adolescence, as expressed in their ability to relate generalizations and concepts to their immediate environment.

The study suggested that 'the ability to assess individuals on their possession of requirements for leading in various situations is developing during adolescence'. Results suggested the role of the school was important in nurturing appropriate skills. Shears argued that rather than selecting 'talented individuals and training them for leadership in society later on' school work should be organised 'to provide the means for acquiring practice in recognizing qualities in other individuals and for enabling as many individuals as possible to gain practice in learning and using the techniques involved in intra-group co-operation'. He explained:

> ... this does not follow formal teaching methods in which there is established a relatively rigid teacher-group relationship and which may be described in terms of varying degrees of authoritarian control. Control of this kind, whether it be in grammar, secondary modern or technical schools, tends to neglect the relationship established between children in the group. Teachers are generally aware of their relationship to the group, but it is doubtful if they have given much thought to the effect of relationships between the members

of the group they teach or the ability or desire of the children either to assimilate what is being taught, to comprehend the implications of the teaching or to respond to the stimulus involved in participation in the learning process.[260]

## A greater Britain

Mavis' Radley lineage (no known connection to Shears' Radley forebears) gave entrée to family in England. Spending Christmas with Gordon and Dorothy Radley in the village of Radlett, Hertfordshire, afforded a sense of belonging. Absence from home for extended periods was unsettling, and had caused two Imperial Relation Trust Fellows to return home, one to South Africa and one to New Zealand. Shears knew of Gordon Radley's involvement in the British Post Office and learned that his host was not just a postman but the organisation's First Engineer. With interests in wireless, telegraph and telephone systems, in 1934 Radley had presented a highly regarded PhD in electrical engineering that explored the 'interference between power and communication circuits'. Deemed an expert in the field, Radley frequently examined doctoral theses. Later knighted twice, he pioneered the coded sorting of mail and in 1955 was appointed Director-General of the British Post Office.

Predominantly Shears devoted his time to his thesis but also made time to travel. The easing of petrol rationing in July 1950 and purchase of a Ford Anglia car gave access to a greater Britain. He travelled north with Mavis and Christine to Carlisle, Kendall, Ambleside and Sunderland, crossed Hadrian's Wall and drove through the Lakes District. Travelling south on another occasion they visited Salisbury, Gloucester and Bath, Plymouth, Penzance and St Ives. Westward they drove into Wales to visit Cardigan, Holyhead and Haverford West. Shears recalled being almost penniless after one expedition so returned directly to London, 300 miles, unheard of in Britain at the time. During lecture tours they stayed at small pubs, and at night popped Christine to bed, and then spent an hour or so with the locals, chatting and sipping warm beer in the smoky saloons.

Organisers of the Imperial Relations Trust Fellowship invited colonials to talk to school groups. This was a ticket to travel with provision of payment for service, petrol and fares. Equipped with a series of slides Shears depicted 'a day in the life of an Australian'. His manner engaged listeners, whether eight or eighteen years old, though most baulked at the thought of a daily shower and were somewhat dismayed as he dispelled the 'Colonial–Chips Rafferty' Australian stereotype.[261] He visited 70 institutions. They comprised three teachers training colleges, four independent secondary schools, one independent primary school, sixteen grammar schools, 35 secondary modern schools and eleven primary schools. Retrospectively he stressed the need to 'be under 30 to get the Imperial Relations Trust Fellowship' and reflected 'the experience of the lecturing or giving little talks to schools kept me in touch with the relationship that's needed between teacher and child'. Of travel he claimed it was 'very, very important in developing character'.[262]

The travel experience afforded a general picture of education in England, Scotland and Wales. Interested in educational structures, Shears observed the system of decentralisation and how local education areas performed. He studied the variety of schools; ascertained how standards were set and maintained; observed how the *Education Act 1944* was functioning after raising the statutory leaving age imposed an extra year of compulsory schooling; and methods adopted for professional training of teachers. Triggered by his research into the educational needs of adults in rural Victoria he viewed means by which British authorities catered for youth. The opportunity to visit Sweden presented a comparative situation to his own Victorian scene.

## The educational landscape

Britain's Ministry of Education directed a complex network of schools. Due to the predominance of the Church of England for centuries past, private or proprietary independent schools, generally run as businesses, prepared pupils for entry by examination to endowed and voluntary schools. Exceptions like Bedales symbolised the passion and vision of a single educator. By 1950, the State governed two-thirds of the school population, and established a register of schools to bind the network and maintain standards. Unlike Australia where directives were 'strictly hierarchical', the four-level system in Britain involved Parliament, the ministry, local education authorities and schools working together. The structure involved:

> ... the Central Advisory Councils, the Regional Advisory Councils and Voluntary Bodies between the Ministry and the Local Authority; the Divisional Executives and the Governors and Managers between the Local Authority and the School; the Inspectorate between the Ministry and the School; the Parent Teacher Association between the teachers in the school and the pupils in the school.[263]

The roles of teachers, parents, administrators and the general public at each rung of the order influenced Shears' thoughts and he wrote, 'the system of administration demands intelligence and elicits intelligence, relies for progress on enlightened public opinion, participation of all concerned with education and accepted variety and diversification within the general framework'. He applauded these attributes but was aware of the impact of history on inter-school relationships and was aware that independent schools questioned the State's ability to satisfy pupils' needs and develop their emotional and social capacities. He noted variance in standards of buildings, equipment and the general condition of schools, and was concerned by the plight of those unable to meet financial commitments. Despite logic and order he cautioned against administrative quagmire: 'one shudders to think what would happen if all the bodies connected with education here decided to exert all the powers they had – the result would be chaos'.[264]

The headmaster was traditionally the 'head of the masters' and of 'his school'. The promotional method, unlike the lock-step approach at home, encouraged young aspirants to take command. Promotion per se enabled the emergence of young, vigorous applicants who 'grasped the possibility, accepted the responsibility and are doing a magnificent job'. Shears applauded the degree of freedom with which headmasters and school bodies operated, however questioned the 'amazing variety and breadth of standard in teaching, buildings and equipment'. Some schools he observed had no fixed blackboards and only glass partitions to divide class spaces. Some had loudspeakers in every room while communication networks in others resembled an electric power station. He considered teaching and conditions were generally good but pondered the benefits of the centralised system and the general level of efficiency such a system offered rather than diversity as he observed.[265] Commonplace, he noted, was the employment of unqualified teachers at independent schools. Empirical knowledge gained from five or six years' experience was considered suitable training.

The McNair Report (1944) had stirred debates regarding teacher recruitment. It recommended an improved salary scale, better school buildings and amenities, and smaller classes. Furthermore, it supported a supply of full-time trained and salaried youth leaders to support students beyond their traditional schooling. Shears saw the responsibility of authorities to provide adequate training salaries and conditions for teachers, activate school improvement programs and provide suitable post-schooling pathways. He took part in discussion, visited five youth clubs and gained insight into the 'youth club aspect of organization of further education'. In his report he stressed that 'the extent of the facilities and the fine work being done by the full time salaried workers is an example which could be followed in Australia, where reliance is still placed in voluntary organization with its financial and physical limitations'.[266]

Attuned to the pros and cons of centralised administration, Shears took notice of Britain's model. Locally administered, it addressed vastly diverse needs of individuals in distinct communities; such as those of specific groups he had taught in Korong Vale, Bairnsdale and the RTC. Local direction broke the concept that 'one size fits all', as revealed in his survey of adults' needs in the Upper Goulburn region. Many of the problems he witnessed in Britain paralleled those faced by authorities at home, and solutions seeded later took shape. In each situation he considered the application at home. Above all he believed in a democratic system and sought means to augment the contributions of the broader community. 'The day is passing when education and its provision can be merely the concern of governments, administrative agencies and the teaching profession. These must supply the leadership and guidance, but they must have an enlightened public behind them.'[267]

## Swedish horizons

The visit to Sweden arose when a delegation from the Institute of Education and King's College visited there. The opportunity enabled Shears to make comparisons with his local educational scene. Both Sweden and Victoria were sparsely populated and were centrally administered. He visited small two-teacher primary schools, teacher-training and adult education institutes and universities. Co-education was the norm and methods of teaching comparable, though Swedish authorities took a formal approach to art, singing and language. Unlike the emerging trend in Victoria towards consolidation, small schools were important in Sweden where travel during the winter months was problematic. The experience afforded Shears the chance to develop friendships and networks with teachers, members of professional organisations, the Swedish Institute and local people. It had lasting impact as he recognised the personal and professional benefits, and the ongoing nature of interaction.

## European sojourn

With much of Britain travelled, Europe beckoned. The summer vacation of 1951 gave time for a hotel-cum-camping tour. With their gear, including a primus stove, crammed into the Anglia's boot and tied to the roof rack, the family set off. During their 7,000-mile seven-week sojourn they visited Paris and southern France. They revitalised with a bath and meal at a Marseilles hotel. They drove along the Riviera to Italy where they stopped at Florence and Rome, lunched with a friend, then drove south past Naples to the Blue Grotto. In Germany they met Ernie Shears' timber agent Bernie Weisenberg and stopped at Gratz, renowned for fine perfumes. They found the Black Forest in Austria enchanting, in contrast to post-war devastation.

Midst rubble and rebuilding, the war cast a shadow in Britain too and raised suspicion of those who were different. There was dislike of the Germans, scepticism towards Jews, uncertainty of Asians and fear of the Russians as that nation's power increased.[268] To dispel the shadow and reclaim supremacy, British leaders promoted a new beginning in 1951 and celebrated the Festival of Britain. The Shears were there when King George, Queen Elizabeth (later the Queen Mother), their daughters Princesses Elizabeth and Margaret, and the royal entourage passed by. They were amongst crowds that waved their Union Jacks, cheered loudly and heard the 41-gun salute. On the city's south bank they saw the rocket-shaped pinnacle that transformed the skyline to symbolise the transition from severity to affluence. They were there when a pall fell over the nation on 6 February 1952 when the BBC announced:

> His Majesty, King George VI, has died peacefully in his sleep at Sandringham House. He was 56, and was known to have been suffering from a worsening lung condition.[269]

In reverence, buildings and monuments were swathed in black. Sir Winston Churchill expressed the nation's sentiment, 'We cannot at this moment more than record the spontaneous expression of grief.' Princess Elizabeth became Queen, aged 25.

Dora Gibbs' decision to sell the flat caused the Shears to seek new accommodation. Mavis and Christine stayed with the Radleys while Shears scoured the scene. In Glenhead Close, Eltham Park, half an hour from the London Institute, he found a single room for £1 a week.

Most of the time Shears was busy completing his studies or on site at schools. Mavis had long days to fill. Though a devoted mother and wife, she needed time on her own. She found care for Christine and commenced secretarial work in a solicitor's office. She had a personal income and a sense of independence. The nights were not her own. She helped with the thesis by typing questionnaires and later results that came to hand. Though she fell pregnant she worked as long as possible and typed the completed thesis to the last page. It was the eve of the baby's arrival. Shears drove Mavis to hospital and then waited at home with Christine. Next morning he welcomed his first son, Mark. While awaiting results of the thesis, as a family of four they visited parts of the country not yet seen.

The dissertation was formal, before a gathering of senior staff. Immediately after, Shears walked back to his study beside Professor James. 'Congratulations, Dr Shears,' James remarked.

# University of London

*Laurence William Shears*

of

*Institute of Education*

having completed the Course of Study approved by the University and passed the prescribed Examinations, has this day been admitted by the Senate as an Internal Student to the Degree of

## Doctor of Philosophy

in the Faculty of

*Arts*

the Field of Study being

*Education*

*3 July 1952*

*James Henderson*
Academic Registrar

Doctoral Certificate

The occasion marked the end of the doctoral journey. It was time to go home. Two adjoining cabins accommodated the family of four on SS *Otranto* in July. In January 1952 the Egyptian government revoked the Anglo-British Treaty of 1936. Britain refused to withdraw its troops after an attack that caused the death of several British officers. Negotiation failed and subsequently 50 Egyptian police officers were killed. In Cairo, anti-British sentiment targeted British interests and bombed Shepheard's Hotel. King Farouk abdicated in favour of his son. Despite restrictions on the passage of commercial vessels in the Suez Canal, *Otranto* sailed through. During the night of 26 July, as Farouk was escaping to Italy, his ship, under Egyptian guard, crossed *Otranto's* path. *Otranto* sailed on. She stopped at Colombo, Perth and Adelaide before berthing in Melbourne.

Imbued with the travel experience Shears reflected:

> You become enamoured of looking at what happens in other countries and you understand how important it is so that's where I was imbued with the idea that if I ever had anything to do with teachers they should get overseas as much as they can … the first year it took me ages to come to grips with the way in which Britain, England in particular, organised their education system. It wasn't until the second year that I really came to get to know it.[270]

When the ship berthed there was excitement at Station Pier. Passengers lined the deck rail to search the crowds thronging the wharf, eager to spy a familiar face. The Redmans and Poppa Shears greeted the travellers, and midst a buzz of conversation, hugs and kisses, they 'oohed' and 'aahed' over the new baby. The family stayed with the Redmans, who had moved to North Brighton. Christine settled into kindergarten and Shears reported back to the Education Department. He remembered how people fussed about the little doctor with all these degrees 'from some reputable university in England'. They expected his experience and knowledge of education abroad marked 'a pretty high level of intelligence'.[271] He was placed at Melbourne Teachers College but after just a week was sent to Toorak Teachers College.

CHAPTER 9

# TRAINER OF TEACHERS (1952–54)

*He who has a why to live for can bear almost any how.*

Friedrich Nietzsche

The war had played havoc with Victoria's teacher supply. As an interim measure, Melbourne TC trainees did their practical component in country regions rather than in simulated rural schools nearby. A desperate remedy for a desperate disease, claimed A J Law. In 1946, W H Ellwood, Chief Inspector of Primary Schools, argued the need to boost recruitment of trainees to 800. This would relieve pressures so apparent in the foreseeable 1950s and allow expansion of special services. The raising of the school leaving age to fifteen in 1943, the post-war population surge and the extension of teacher training to two years in 1951 exacerbated pressure on a system already depleted.[272]

Historian Don Garden described education in the 1950s and 1960s as a 'thorny political issue'. The strain of offering a good education outstripped the Department's ability to train and supply teachers. The demand had burgeoned beyond capacity despite vigorous recruitment campaigns and enticements of bursaries offered to Forms 4, 5 and 6 pupils.[273] In line with Ellwood's campaign, Len Pryor was a mover and shaker in the teacher-training domain. Taking an aggressive stance, he projected huge leaps in the school population from 115,000 in 1950 to 460,000 by 1960. He said:

> Victoria urgently needs more schools, and MORE teachers – and better teachers! … By 1955 the output must be at least 1,350, and it is probable that the demand for trained

teachers will exceed 1,750 each year as we approach 1960. And the present annual 'intake' of recruits to the Victorian Education Department is below 800!²⁷⁴

Pryor presented his views on educational reform and development in Victoria to the Council of Public Education. He recommended at least one new college to accommodate up to 1500 primary trainees and an extended timeframe to 'make teacher training a less superficial, a less hurried process … a more efficient and more pleasurable experience than the present system'. He did not favour pre-college apprenticeships for would-be teachers; he argued for direct entry to colleges for secondary-school leavers.²⁷⁵

In Victoria, funding cuts through the Great Depression and war years continued to affect the system. It was time to catch up, balance supply and demand, and thrust ahead. Until 1949, Melbourne TC was the metropolitan hub for training teachers for government schools. The reopening of regional colleges in Ballarat (1945), Bendigo (1946) and Geelong (1950) had relieved pressure on Melbourne. Founding principals were W F (Frank) Lord at Ballarat, L J (Len) Pryor at Bendigo and L G (Len) Whiteoak at Geelong. When Toorak TC opened in 1951, Lord became its founding principal.

## Toorak Teachers College (1952–53)

The opening of Toorak TC in suburban Melbourne further eased the burden on Melbourne TC. In 1951 the Education Department purchased Glenbervie, a mansion home, to accommodate a teachers college. Built in 1924, it was the home of Charles Ernest Ruwolt, an immigrant German industrialist and engineer, proprietor of Vickers Ruwolt in Victoria Street, Richmond. The company was deployed during WWII to forge heavy arms. Conversion of the home to a teachers college heralded a new era in leafy Toorak. Prefabricated buildings in its gardens provided additional teaching space but upset the neighbours who thought it disturbed the area's ambience. To provide further accommodation the Department purchased Claymore, a former factory development in Burke Road, Camberwell, but this created logistical problems. A mile from Glenbervie made timetabling complex as staff and students commuted between campuses by tram or foot along Toorak Road, or took a lift with one of the few who had cars.

Frank Lord's 'forceful personality' made him a 'legend among staff and trainees'. He is recalled as 'a real autocrat' and a man to be 'feared' who ran the college with military precision. This is understandable in view of his service in World Wars I and II. Lord took part in the Gallipoli landing, was wounded, and awarded the Military Cross for:

> ... conspicuous gallantry and devotion to duty. When his Battery was for a long time under heavy hostile shell and machine-gun fire and had suffered severe casualties, he moved about amongst the men, assisting to serve the guns and maintaining the morale of the Battery by his cheerfulness and splendid gallantry under the most trying conditions.[276]

Lord's actions marked his steadfast character and compassion. Loyal to the Crown and with high citizenship values, Lord came to Toorak from Ballarat TC where he had served as principal since its re-opening in 1945. His traditions became legend, synonymous with his name at Toorak TC. His dog, free to wander buildings and grounds, apparently held staff status.

Lord frequently mounted his wife's white horse Topper to address student assemblies in Glenbervie's garden. He dressed in uniform on Anzac Day to take the salute. During Education Week a trainee teacher was dressed in a body stocking to pose on Topper as Lady Godiva.

Lord ran a disciplined college and took a firm stance regarding attendance. During sports and interclub activities on Community Wednesdays 'trainees were checked out by marking the roll'. Despite his foibles, Lord was 'a sentimentalist with emotional depth'. He discovered that one of the Toorak trainees was living in Melbourne's squalid Dudley Flats and took great measures to find the trainee alternative accommodation, an action that revealed him as a caring man. Coupled with his emotional strength, his firm leadership qualities equipped him to found the new teachers college.[277]

'The Little Doctor', as Shears became known, was appointed Temporary Assistant at Toorak TC from 15 September 1952. Lord welcomed him, and the air of prestige his doctorate bestowed. 'He admired all that I had done and getting those qualifications as a full-time teacher and part-time student.'[278] Trainees were similarly 'impressed to have a Doctor on our staff ... quite a rare bird, an exotic creature: none of us would have ever met a real Doctor before'.[279] Lord's ongoing support encouraged Shears who established himself professionally and worked collegially. He alerted himself to college procedures and was poised to take leadership roles. Conscious of the timetabling dilemma caused by the two campuses, he worked hard to find a remedy. Aware of the need to balance theory with practice in schools, he arranged lectures, tutorials and teaching blocks for the 34 staff and 400 trainees across the two campuses. Rising enrolments in February 1953 and in July, when the mid-year intake commenced, increased the complexity of the task.

The two-year TPTC introduced in 1951 aimed to inspire initiative. Director of Education Alan Ramsay recognised its 'exploratory nature' and emphasised 'each teachers college should and will be free to evolve a plan of teacher-preparation which reflects the interests of the principal and the staff and the needs of the students'.[280] Lord went with the flow to encourage initiative among his staff. Education and Psychology Department staff – Joe St Ellen, Ron Burton and Shears – accepted the challenge. St Ellen, educated at Melbourne's Xavier College, graduated from Melbourne TC in 1935. Prior to war service in New Guinea and Bougainville he taught in rural and inner-suburban primary schools. In 1951 he became a foundation lecturer at the new teachers college. New Zealand-born Burton was educated at Bendigo HS, completed his TPTC at Bendigo TC in 1928 and studied at the University of Melbourne. He taught in country and inner-suburban schools before his appointment as lecturer at Toorak TC. Like St Ellen he had served during WWII.

The colleagues shared knowledge accrued in primary, secondary and adult settings, in country and city regions, at home and abroad. Concerned by the overcrowded nature of the curriculum, they created a sense of space by melding overlapping, isolated and repetitious units into one. Broad in scope yet deep in the fundamentals of education and teaching, the course integrated psychology principles, history and modern developments. Each of the colleagues taught one-third of the course to each of nine groups of 30 trainees. Structured to link the learning experience with the social world of the school the course involved lectures, discussion, guided reading, assigned tasks and fieldwork. In order to prepare the trainees for evolving technological change, the use of radio and film were encouraged in workshops and presentations for peers.

Thematically based, the course led trainees to understand their own situation through units entitled the Teacher; the Child; the Teacher and Child in the Classroom; the Appraisal of Results; and the Environment of Education. Collaborative working approaches applicable to their own teaching initiated a process of self-understanding to orient the trainees to tertiary study. Fundamental to their professional role was the teacher's ethical code which cast upon each teacher (and trainee) the 'responsibility to establish and uphold appropriate relationships between Teacher and Pupil; Parent; Colleague; Authority and Society'.[281] Trainees were led to think seriously about the relationships they needed to build – at college with peers and staff; at schools with pupils, parents and colleagues; and with authorities in the broader community.[282] To develop the craft of teaching, they examined various teaching methods and their origins. They explored sensory, oral and verbal approaches and looked at questioning and correction techniques. The learning process was considered holistically to give insight into the 'nature of the child at various age levels to adolescence' through the child's physical, social and emotional development. Educational theories were aligned to the nature of intelligence and the influence of heredity and environment, considered the atypical child, the qualities of each individual and intelligence testing. Members of the Education Department's Psychology Branch led discussion on assessment, evaluation, remediation and support, and their effect on vocational guidance and ongoing education.

The subject called 'Aims of Education' presented the system's historic roots and its influence on teachers' knowledge and skills. An examination of 'our present modern western society' drew comparisons and contrasts between Australian and Samoan cultures and thus alerted trainees to how an education system inducted a society's young.

Trainees next completed a comparative study between education systems in Victoria, interstate and abroad. Subsequently challenged to plan an education system, working in groups they were required to designed curriculum and assessment procedures from primary to secondary exiting levels and the administrative approach. A major focus was the school environment and the psychological influence of buildings and equipment on student wellbeing thereby generated. Ultimately each group presented a 'plan possible for educational development in Victoria at all levels' with emphasis on the primary schools. Unbeknown to trainees at the time, this paved the way for those who later sought senior administrative roles.[283]

Teachers college courses for primary and infant teachers freed universities from the task of conveying specialist knowledge, but the courses lacked university prestige and the rank of teachers colleges was often debated. Supporters upheld them as 'a centre of idealism, a laboratory of research, and the activating force behind educational development'.[284] Staff contributed to trainees' development as teachers and promoted the natural talent of each.[285] Staff members were open-minded and humane, tolerant and understanding, with enthusiasm to spark interest. Lecturers were required to be multi-talented, skilled in:

> … administration and organization; to lecture on and conduct discussions in at least one of the following groups of subjects: English, Education (History, Principles, and Modern Developments, Educational Psychology) Social Studies, Biological and Rural Science, Mathematics, and Art and Crafts; to assist in the supervision and organization of students' observation and teaching practice in training schools; and to carry out any other duties assigned by the principal.[286]

Shears contributed eagerly to this environment. His verve and vitality endeared him to the college community. In lectures he maintained authority and enlivened them with illustrations from abroad. Trainees mused at the little doctor almost hidden by the lectern. Beyond his day-to-day commitments he coached the women's hockey, men's football and athletics teams. In work or play he shared a laugh, was approachable and willing to support.[287] Younger colleague Laurie Bell recalled the support he received when he felt 'unprepared to work in that area. Lawrie convinced me I could do it.' Bell claimed this 'was one of his gifts' and reflected, 'He encouraged others too, assessed them well and set them in the right direction at the right time.'[288]

## Other dimensions of Shears

Following their British sojourn, the Shears lived for twelve months with Mavis' parents in North Brighton but like other young couples Shears and Mavis wanted a home of their own. As Melbourne's population grew, its suburbs extended and new housing estates were established. Black Rock, four miles from Brighton, typified post-war expansion. The sand-belt suburb on the fringe of Port Phillip Bay abutted Half Moon Bay, well-known for the bathing boxes that stood beneath the burnt-orange cliffs. The place-to-be for young 'up-and-comings' was set in a green wedge carved by heathlands, a golf links and parklands. Across Bluff Road, not far from the beach, Lawrie and Mavis bought a block of land 50 by 120 feet in Sturdee Road to build a three-bedroom, cream brick-veneer house.

Shears' father supplied scantling timber from Valley Sawmills at Myrtleford as high demand made housing materials scarce. Ernie had established the business in June 1945 on railway property opposite Ovens Valley Station. While Shears Senior had business skills, colleagues L Allen and G Frame had forest knowledge. The three reconstructed a disused building at Harrietville, bought a secondhand saw-bed for £1,000 and used a portable steam engine to generate power. From hardwood forests extending 30 miles north, south and east the business milled 3 million super feet annually. It employed five men in 1946 and by 1950 the number had increased to 10. Scantling and building construction timber was popular throughout Victoria and South Australia, and the mill boosted the local economy to equal the tobacco industry.[289]

Soon after the move to Sturdee Road, Mavis fell pregnant. She maintained her stamina, established the front garden with shrubs and an annual border. The back garden became Shears' domain where he composted the sandy loam and prepared a vegetable plot along the back fence. Notwithstanding his effort, Max Dimmack, colleague and friend at Toorak TC, recalled him as 'useless around the house ... the true academic. I remember going to paint his spouting; he didn't know how to open a tin of paint.'[290]

The position at Toorak was temporary. Shears sought permanency at either a teachers college or a school. Mavis balked at his proposed move to rural Traralgon 'on promotion' and preferred Principal Lord's request for him to remain for a second year. Shears' teaching record notes his suitability for college work. He was seen to be 'outstanding as a lecturer and a most capable member of staff' with 'fine personal qualities'. During his second year at Toorak he prepared for the next step, an appointment as Lecturer Grade III at the new Burwood Teachers College. A foundation staff member, he commenced duty 'on probation' on 1 January 1954.[291]

## Burwood Teachers College (1954)

On paper, the new teachers college was set to start. Situated on 30 acres of land (formerly a daffodil farm) on Burwood Road in the hub of a new educational precinct, the college adjoined Bennettswood State School, No. 4693, which also opened in 1954, and the proposed Burwood High School. Mount Scopus College was next door and the Presbyterian Ladies' College nearby. Also nearby were a school for the blind and a kindergarten for the deaf. Specifically designed, Burwood was to be Victoria's most modern and only newly constructed teachers college.

Bendigo and Ballarat operated in former State schools. Melbourne TC continued to operate in the red-brick building constructed in 1888 on the corner of Grattan and Swanston Streets. In 1950 the Department established the Secondary TC in university grounds, with a conglomeration of Bristol huts erected in the Botany School Garden to accommodate the trainees. In 1952 the Technical Teachers College became an adjunct of Melbourne Technical College, later the Royal Melbourne Institute of Technology. Former mansions in Geelong and Toorak were converted to teachers colleges and Glendonald in Kew, which trained teachers of the deaf, opened in 1954.

Donald Maine Waller was Burwood's first principal. Like Lord, he was a Great War veteran where, as a Field Ambulance Officer, he served in the AIF. He was twice wounded in action.[292] Before his appointment at Burwood he lectured in social studies at Melbourne TC where he was described as 'dry and boring'. In contrast, at Burwood, he 'distinguished himself as a college principal'. Colleagues recalled Waller as 'a quiet man with a very, very dry sense of humour. Without actually saying so, he expected you would do the very best you could.'[293] These qualities set him in high regard among foundation staff and trainees, who strove to achieve his unspoken expectations. Prior to commencement of the college year, the Department appointed 20 staff to train the 300 trainees it expected. The ratio was one staff member to fifteen trainees, and as colleagues observed, 'people who were superb in their jobs were given opportunities'.[294] The intake of 300 was reduced to 94 but only four staff members were transferred, which left a staff–trainee ratio of 1:6. However, the Department's building program was running late.

The house that had remained on the farm had been demolished, the site had been levelled and framing had commenced in September 1953 but the buildings were obviously not going to be ready for the commencement of the college year in February 1954. Waller was forced to seek alternative accommodation close to transport with facilities suitable for staff and trainees. The increasing demand for schooling in metropolitan and suburban Melbourne exacerbated his problem as available classrooms and community halls were already allocated to schools. Waller trekked the district and eventually found two halls behind the Methodist Church in Station Street, Box Hill. Oxford Hall was a solid red-brick building with a large open space and a kitchen. Behind was the Fellowship Hall, a less elaborate structure. The last resort, it proved satisfactory for establishing Burwood TC. In years to come foundation trainees met for reunions and continued to hold dear both Oxford Hall and Fellowship Hall.

Despite the urgency for trained teachers, prospective trainees underwent a selection procedure. Subject to a satisfactory report from the School Medical Officer, they were informed by mail whether or not 'you have been awarded a studentship to Burwood Teachers College'. The letter continued:

… you and an approved surety will enter into an agreement with the Minister of Education that … you will not relinquish your course of training and that you will serve the Department as a teacher for three years after the termination of your studentship. The period may be reduced to one year in the case of women who marry'.

In a subsequent letter prospective trainees were congratulated and advised 'you are fortunate in being allotted to a recently established College, soon to be situated in pleasant surroundings and functioning in modern attractive buildings'.[295]

On 16 February 1954 trainees and staff assembled at Oxford Hall. The men wore suits; the women wore modest calf-length frocks. From Melbourne's network of eastern and southeastern suburbs trainees travelled from Boronia, The Basin, Bonbeach, Heatherton, Croydon, Caulfield, Cheltenham and Edithvale. In his opening address, Principal Waller endorsed Director Ramsay's passion for the college to develop its own character. The trainees lay at the heart of this and he charged them with passion to:

> … inspire new loyalties, set worthy standards of service and achievement, and develop that indefinable 'College Spirit' which welds the constituent parts of a college into a vital and happy community … May 'Our College' grow, not only in numbers, but in strength of character and nobility of purpose. May its graduates go out with true vision of the task before them and may they retain the strength of mind and body to carry it out to the benefit of those being served and to the inner satisfaction of those giving such service to our community.[296]

Conditions at Oxford Hall were adequate but crude. The hand-picked staff met before the college year began. Max Dimmack recalled, 'I was hijacked to Burwood' to lead the Art Department beyond traditional paradigms. Chris Limb remembered leading the music course beyond the constraints of 'tafa tefas, taa taa taaas' and tonic solfa scales. Staff of the English Department indulged trainees in creative activities as well as grammatical conventions. Appointed lecturer-in-charge of 'Education and Psychology', Shears, with Bill

Watson's support, introduced the program developed at Toorak TC. Miss Alice Downward supervised social studies.

The kitchen and meeting rooms became staff offices. Watson and Shears shared a room with Miss Downward who did things in particular ways. She often pinned notes to the door asking 'Why did you …?' or 'Why haven't you …?' Oxford Hall accommodated trainees en masse for their main lectures and was partitioned for tutorials and specialist classes. Waller's desire for a 'close-knit community'[297] at the new college was satisfied in its temporary home at Oxford Hall. It was a place of bonding where staff and trainees supported each other, a place where professional and personal friendships were laid. Though he appeared 'rather dry and pedantic' Mr Waller 'encouraged us to strike out', Miss Limb recalled. His approach was good for Burwood and teaching as a whole when 'teacher education was beginning to flourish'.

Trainees as young as sixteen and just out of school faced problems adjusting. College for some was a glorified high school; others felt bored or unsuitably placed. Despite initial concerns, most settled into weekly routines of lectures, tutorials, teaching rounds and Community Wednesdays. To ease overcrowding, tutorial groups were allocated to schools in rotation, the platoon system as occurred at Melbourne and Toorak TCs. At such times they spent four days in allocated schools and joined the entire college community on Wednesdays for assembly, tutorial meetings and sport. At assemblies Waller addressed the group before a guest lecturer spoke about a specialist educational field. In small tutorial groups trainees got to know each other and gained supportive guidance regarding their teaching experience. Tutors were accessible to meet individually to discuss personal issues.[298] Club and sports activities offered leadership skills. Dimmack recalled the 'marvellous leaders' elected to head the student representative council and to establish and publish *Parabo*, the annual magazine. Through a process of consultation, he designed the college badge: a skewed hexagon portrayed Australia's earthy colours, a stylised tree represented growth and the sun symbolised enlightenment. Proud trainees wore tan blazers with yellow trim that reflected the college ethos. Guided by English lecturer Mr Fitcher the motto 'Animum, Cultum, Parabo' expressed the spirit of Burwood: 'I shall lay the foundations of a well-trained mind'. Dimmack's thoughts reflect the zeal:

> Burwood in those days was really exciting. I had this terrible urgency after five years at war, a long time, so I just pitched into anything and everything. I couldn't belong to a group if I wasn't contributing. I couldn't be a seat warmer.[299]

1954 was a vibrant year. Trainees had entered the teaching profession, received their first cheque and sealed an engagement with the Education Department to teach for three years after graduation. At the Melbourne Cricket Ground they took part in the schools' display during Queen Elizabeth's first visit to Australia. They attended balls at Toorak and Geelong TCs, and held their first college dance. They shared inter-college visits with Ballarat and Bendigo TCs, established friendships and pranked. Foundation trainees remember one of their group leapt towards Mr Waller during an assembly and cut off his tie. There was silence as they stood dumbfounded and then laughter broke out. 'It wouldn't have happened in any other college in Australia; it was one great big happy innovative family.'[300]

On one occasion when Shears was late for his lecture, trainees locked doors at both ends of the hall. He knocked unsuccessfully at one end and ran past the windows to the other end to rattle the door. Back and forth he ran until the trainees let him in. They joined in the mirth.[301]

## Other activities

The bustle of college life matched the activity in the Shears household. Aged five, Christine started at Black Rock State School, No. 3631, a 10-minute walk along Bluff Road. Mavis pushed Mark in his stroller. Growth in the suburb increased school enrolments so two prefabricated Bristol huts eased overcrowding. The Mothers Club funded a movie projector and screen for the school. Mavis was expecting another child. Shears was often home late and his use of the car isolated Mavis. She spent time with her parents and shared reciprocal visits with Peg Dimmack who lived in nearby Bentleigh.

Sometimes Max car-pooled with Shears and they ended the day with a game of squash. On Saturdays Shears was in charge of the children. Routinely they went to the park and had fish and chips for lunch. On Sundays they all went to church.

Research remained a keen interest and Shears joined the Victorian Institute for Educational Research (VIER). He thus renewed links with Professor Browne, Dr Tom Coates (awarded his doctorate a year prior to Shears), Mr Alex McDonell and Miss Alice Hoy. The VIER was foundering, with only 24 financial members among 63 who attended the Annual Meeting in 1952. Established in February 1929 under the presidency of L J Wrigley, it was one of the institutes of educational research established in various States at the time, and in August 1929 representatives from each body met in Melbourne to formulate a constitution for a national research body, known as the Australian Council for Educational Research or ACER. Even though the VIER comprised notable educators keen to circulate research, it had fallen into the doldrums during the war years and failed to gain strength.

A group of young researchers, known as the 'young Turks', who attended the Annual Meeting in 1953, was elected to form a 'new-look' VIER executive. Professor Browne was appointed president, supported by vice presidents Tom Coates and Bill Watson; Shears was secretary and Joe St Ellen treasurer. The group's verve led a 'great leap forward'.[302] The VIER encouraged inquiry and disseminated knowledge, and members undertook research. To advance these aims the executive proposed national distribution of an accredited journal. Midst debate regarding its format, Volume 1, Number 1 of the *Journal of Education* was published in July 1954. Subscription for the thrice-yearly publication was 4/- a copy, or 10/6 per annum including postage. All articles, research abstracts and books for review were sent to Dr L W Shears in Black Rock at least six weeks before the date of publication.[303] In less than twelve months the 'young Turks' established a national forum to distribute current local research. Professor Browne commended the efforts:

> ... it is easier for those interested in Australian education to obtain up-to-date information about educational happenings in USA and Britain than to secure details of devel-

opments in the different Australian States ... The Victorian Institute of Educational Research has decided to launch the journal of which this is the first issue, as an interim measure, in the hope that eventually it will be merged in a more ambitious publication, organized by and representing Australian education as a whole.[304]

As editor Shears spent considerable time at home preparing each issue. On winter nights he sat by the fire with copy strewn on the floor. The 24-page issue with red cover designed by Max Dimmack contained the inaugural Frank Tate Memorial Lecture presented by HS (later Sir Harold Stanley) Wyndham, Director of Education in New South Wales, who presented his views on 'Decentralisation of education'. Some 220 people attended the lecture held at the Masson Lecture Theatre, University of Melbourne. Browne stressed the lecture's significance and thanked book retailer Robertson and Mullens for its annual endowment. The Journal contained a feature article on research and the teacher, reports on papers presented to the Victorian Institute, abstracts of recent research and book reviews.

On 10 July Shears heard of his successful application for the position of Survey and Planning Officer to begin at the end of the month. He knew this led to administration but was sad to leave his role at Burwood and not see the year through. Staff and students felt they 'knew him long enough to appreciate all that he had done to establish our college – and long enough too, to form a great liking and respect for him'. They believed he would be 'carrying the torch for Burwood in his new position'.[305]

# Section 4:

# LAYING FOUNDATIONS

# CHAPTER 10

# SURVEYING AND PLANNING THE PROFESSIONAL REALM (1954–59)

*The desire to reach for the stars is ambitious.*
*The desire to reach hearts is wise.*

Maya Angelou

Australia was changing rapidly in the post-war years, its population growing and becoming increasingly diverse. In the intensity of nation building and reconstruction, education was the key to continued economic growth and full employment. Paralleling demand for education in primary, secondary and tertiary spheres was the upsurge in knowledge and technological advance. It was an evolution stirring 'the irresistible forces of change that promise[d] to transform beyond recognition not only a vast continent but its people'.[306]

The forces of change held promise yet also the capacity to create 'educational turmoil'. A decline in the industrial workforce and rise of salaried middle classes underlay social shifts, in turn altering traditional patterns of schooling. Young people stayed longer at school, their right, according to visiting educator R Freeman Butts, a graduate of the University of Wisconsin who was awarded a Fulbright Grant in 1954 to study education in Australia. Though viewing the system 'with an outlook conditioned by his own culture', he advocated government schooling for all. Supporting this view, James Darling, British-born principal of the elite Geelong Grammar School, disturbed the nongovernment schooling fraternity who maintained the monopoly on secondary schooling at the time. Butts censured the apathy among leaders and urged 'a great educational revival and awakening of interest in education'.[307] Seemingly harsh in the light of post-war reconstruction,

Butts' criticism alerted all to the enormity of the task ahead and the intensifying pace of change.

Throughout the 1950s developments propelled nationwide industrial 'take-off'. People held hope and desire and shared the benefits of high employment with minimal inflation. In Victoria, home building and ownership sustained momentum, with urbanisation extending along growth corridors into orchard areas in the east and the southern sand belt region abutting Port Phillip Bay. Annual population growth due to migration, rising birth rates, and the increasing tendency to stay at school beyond the leaving age of fifteen placed pressure on the education system and its administrators. The mounting prestige of education reflected a 'revolution in rising expectations' as Australian society realised the benefits of educational investment and employment opportunities.[308] Although the relationship between schooling and social mobility and the value of technical knowledge was clear, Victoria's swelling population and demand for schooling outweighed the Education Department's ability to cope. Administrators faced unparalleled challenge to purchase land in growth corridors, plan and erect new schools and add classrooms to alleviate overcrowding in existing schools.

Appointed Director of Education in Victoria in January 1948, Major General Alan Hollick Ramsay's WWI record revealed an exceptional man, a respected leader who carried things through. He had been through the ranks of the teaching profession, beginning a three-year apprenticeship as a junior teacher at St Kilda in 1912 and, on graduation, serving as head teacher at Cowley's Creek near Timboon in southwestern Victoria. Ramsay enlisted as an AIF gunner and resumed teaching after the war at inner-suburban schools and University High School (1925–27). On moving into teacher education, he taught at the Melbourne University School of Education and Melbourne TC (1928–39). He enlisted again in WWII and served in North Africa, New Guinea and New Britain. He achieved the rank of Major General and was awarded the CBE. He served as Principal-elect and Principal of Melbourne High School (1943–47) and was appointed Director of Education in 1948. His proven ability to lead troops and his knowledge of education positioned him to direct education in Victoria through more than a decade of extraordinary growth.[309]

Ramsay guided educational planning into the mid-1950s during a period of instability. Political change had activated a series of ministerial shifts. Brigadier Raymond Walter Tovell, who served as Minister of Public Instruction from 1948 to 1950 and Minister of Education in October 1952 for the Liberal Party, was alert to the shortage of teachers and accommodation in schools. Succeeding him, the Country Party's Percival Pennell Inchbold (1950–52) warned of problems associated with excessive growth. Alfred Ernest Shepherd, appointed Minister of Education in the Cain (Senior) Labor government (1952–55), endeavoured to revitalise the building program. He travelled statewide to open new classrooms and schools and assess local needs until another political change and the appointment of Sir William Watt Leggatt, who held dual portfolios of Education and Immigration in Henry Bolte's Liberal government (1955–56). The 11-year term of his successor, Sir John Stroughton Bloomfield (1956–67), brought a sense of stability.

## Surveying and planning

There was urgency to predict future needs: accommodate increasing enrolments; develop a building program to keep pace with suburban expansion and population growth; and recruit and train more teachers. Despite frequent ministerial change, Ramsay forged ahead with educational reform. To alleviate the administrative nightmare he increased the number of senior positions. He expanded the role and number of district inspectors and provided specialist supervisors to support education for the physically disabled (1951). He installed prevocational guidance officers to offer counselling services in secondary schools (1954, 1955) and developed services offered by Psychology and Guidance Branch, established in 1947. In an early move towards decentralisation, officers of 'Psych and Guidance' were located in three suburban and two country centres.

Under the new paradigm, a Survey and Planning Officer reviewed Departmental developments to predict future growth and identify particular needs. Len Pryor, appointed to the position in 1949, had knowledge of education statewide and abroad. A graduate of

Melbourne High School, the University of Melbourne and Melbourne TC (1930–33), he showed promise. He won the R G Wilson Scholarship and the Dwight Prize for top ranking in final year history at the university and shared, with Ken Cunningham, the Gladman Prize, which was awarded yearly to the best student (or in this case students!) at Melbourne TC. Pryor had lectured at Melbourne TC and tutored in history at the university. A Carnegie Fellowship and Departmental Scholarship supported his travel to Europe and the UK in 1947–48 where he was a member of the UNESCO Teacher Training Seminar at Ashridge House, in Berkhamsted, Hertfordshire. During the visit he met Ramsay, and debated local educational issues in the light of developments abroad. In the wake of England's McNair Report they considered proposals for teacher education.[310]

Aware of the difficulties faced by teachers to keep pace with evolving debates, Pryor initiated a program of residential seminars for secondary and technical teachers. These not only enhanced their professional knowledge but built camaraderie amongst those in each group. On Pryor's appointment as Principal of Bendigo TC in 1951, reopened after the war, David Satchell was appointed Survey and Planning Officer in the Education Department. A graduate of Melbourne TC with university subjects in hand, Satchell had taught at high and higher elementary schools in country and metropolitan regions. Like Pryor, he was a 'meticulous organiser who made a great success' of the position.[311] During his term as Survey and Planning Officer Satchell developed the seminar series, oversaw the establishment of Burwood TC and set in motion the purchase of hostels to accommodate country teacher trainees. Promoted to the Board of Inspectors of Secondary Schools Satchell moved on in July 1954. The position of Survey and Planning Officer advertised in the *Education Gazette and Teachers' Aid* in May 1954 sought a person to:

> ... act as personal assistant to the Director in the functions of planning and coordinating educational policy; to act as liaison officer between the various divisions and branches of the Department and between the Department and outside educational organizations; to act as executive officer of committees set up to investigate and report on particular

phases of education; and to conduct such surveys as may be required by the Director.³¹²

## Steering the administrative trail

The survey and planning officer's role required a person with initiative to see likely problems, confer with government agencies and other Departmental officers, and make recommendations to the Director who in turn presented them to the Minister. Working mainly alone to assess Departmental needs required a person with stamina, confidence and good communication skills. Shears believed the position steered the right way to administration, and once more Mavis typed his application. It was supported by references from Mr G Woodgate, Superintendent, the Department of Agriculture; Professor G Browne, Chair of Education, the University of Melbourne; and Professor HEO James of the London Institute of Education. The 37-year-old Shears had prior links with Ramsay who, with Miss Alice Hoy had lectured at Melbourne TC. Ramsay, Hoy and Shears were similarly bonded through University High School and the VIER. Shears' experience at the RTC held him in good stead administratively and his BEd and doctoral theses demonstrated his ability to conduct an educational survey of needs and identify issues of concern. Equipped with experience and knowledge of education at home and abroad, Shears felt confident to apply for the position that he believed would lead to senior administration. Though enticed by this opportunity and the annual salary package ranging from £900 to £1,025, he was aware it would distance him from direct contact with teachers and children in schools. He was cautious too of professional officers' work conditions, and realised that four weeks' annual leave would restrict holiday and family time.³¹³ His application for the job was successful.

From Flinders Street Station Shears walked briskly to No. 2 Treasury Place with his new leather satchel. His office adjoined the Director's and he became 'Alan Ramsay's white-haired boy … sitting right beside him'. Ramsay made him responsible for 'handling difficult problems and the research required for the Directors of Secondary, Technical and Primary, to make decisions'.³¹⁴ A colleague reflected:

> Alan Ramsay was a soldier and used the Survey and Planning section very much the same as a General uses intelligence in the military; to gather information for making decisions.[315]

The opportunity to work closely with Director Ramsay, and occasionally act on his behalf, imbued Shears with the politics of a large organisation. He saw how social and political forces caused it to undergo massive adjustments. From the inner circle of policy development and planning, he appraised the system, sought solutions to problems and determined future directions. He oversaw the scheduling of new schools, teachers colleges and hostels, made efforts to improve conditions, and became 'one of the important people ... obviously behind the planning'.[316] Shears became a public figure at a critical time. He was alert to educational needs. He developed his analytic skills and capacity to think and act quickly. He was involved in teacher education from go to woe. The school population was continually rising. There was a paramount need to develop and extend facilities to train teachers in the Primary, Secondary and Technical Divisions and in specialist areas. In the footsteps of Satchell and Pryor, both 'brilliant departmental officers', Shears was involved in the selection of trainees and college staff and was responsible for developing the in-service seminar series.[317]

## Inchbold's predictions

Aware of the impetus of post-war expansion and mounting demands on education, Minister Inchbold (1950–52) had warned of the 'snowballing' population and the consequent long-term problem. The development of new housing estates was changing Melbourne's suburban landscape and as the city extended, demands for schooling changed. During the period 1949–50 then Education Minister Tovel ordered 782 prefabricated two-unit classrooms. Still unable to accommodate the swelling school population Tovel's successor, Inchbold, reported the Department was 'scratching' for accommodation. The anticipated increase of about 3,000 pupils per year statewide overtaxed existing facilities. Demographic changes and

*Laying Foundations*

the explosion in demand for secondary schooling led the Department to purchase land in developing outer regions. To accommodate the new modular classroom model and provide sporting fields, 10-acre blocks were selected for primary schools and 16-acre blocks for secondary schools.[318] The Education budget of £13,000,000 for 1952 fell short and the proposal to build 500 rooms was a serious underestimate.[319] By 1954 the dilemma had reached a critical stage.

The unprecedented growth was evident in the Preston district where the school population had increased by 8,000 since 1939 but only one two-roomed unit had been provided. In addition to challenges to accommodate pupils were escalating building and maintenance costs, and the need to replace unsanitary toilet systems with septic tanks. Minister Bloomfield identified 1000 schools that remained unsewered in 1956.

Planning for the years ahead required consultation with the Public Works Department (PWD). Established in 1855 initially to construct roads, bridges and wharves, build and maintain hospitals, public buildings and housing, PWD took charge of all education buildings operations from February 1882.[320] By 1954, the primary school population had reached 235,439. Numbers in classes tapered off in the higher grades. 66,652 in Grade 1 decreased to 27,519 by Grade 6 and only 750 remained to complete Grade 8. Some 67,554 pupils attended high and junior technical schools or were enrolled in central classes, or central and higher elementary schools.[321] Shears stepped into his new job in the thick of the Department's efforts to cope. In 1954, in addition to extending the capacity of existing schools, it established nine new high schools, 27 new primary schools, and a girls' secondary school.[322] Development gained momentum in 1955 with the founding of eight high schools, then thirteen new high schools and two girls' secondary schools in 1956, when high school status was also issued to four higher elementary schools. A retrospective glance shows that the anticipated increase of 6,000 pupils in 1958 became 7,500 and growth in 1959 exceeded 10,000.[323]

With rising enrolments and accommodation overtaxed through the 1950s into the 1960s, building demands were acute. Schools designed for 500 pupils accommodated considerably more. To ease the demand corrugated iron army huts and prefabricated classrooms became commonplace. In a strange turn of events, when local materials were in short supply, prefabricated units were imported from England. Light timber construction (LTC), as Ramsay had observed in the UK in 1948, provided a low-cost alternative to 'more orthodox construction' methods. Standardised units naturally lit, efficiently warmed and speedily constructed, were an immediate solution to put pupils in classrooms. In ensuing years new schools were assembled in modular stages of 4, 6, 8 or 12 rooms to accommodate up to 250 pupils. Additional modules of the appropriate size were added in response to growth. Ideally maximum high school enrolment was 700.[324]

It was common to establish new schools before building commenced, as with Ringwood High School in Melbourne's outer east. In 1954 the year began in a scout hall, as then Headmaster Bennett recalled:

> My thoughts go back to our opening day when we held our first assembly in the Scout Hall at Croydon and the inconvenience and hardships that faced us during the first weeks of the school development. You will remember I addressed you at the assembly as the Ringwood High School, even though our building was not ready for us to occupy.[325]

As student Terrence Decini remembered, 'there were no desks, no chairs! Only the floor to sit on' but Mr Bennett 'impressed upon us that we were the new Ringwood High School and not the building that was not then ready for us'.[326] Fellow student Barry Ring concurred:

> The school year in 1954 for us started on Tuesday 2nd February in the scout hall. Mr Bennett treated it as the real school and said as the opening to his first assembly talk, 'Welcome to Ringwood High School'. He had us all believing we were there. The first day at the REAL RHS was 18 February 1954.[327]

But 'work on site and buildings continued for several years'.[328] Pupils of the time remember ear-splitting noises made by builders still at work; the day the library opened with 200 books; the blaze caused by burning the lunch papers; and the science room full of equipment not seen by the pupils before.[329]

Shortfalls in estimates indicate the importance of long-range planning. From 1954 to 1960 enrolments in Victorian schools almost doubled according to the age–grade table published in the *Education Gazette and Teachers' Aid*. The additional 60,000 secondary pupils, and 120,000 pupils overall, highlights the Department's dilemma to accommodate classes and its capacity to train teachers. Sustained growth placed enormous demands on the organisation and the survey and planning team.

Table 2. The changing face of education, classification of schools and enrolments 1954–60

| School type | 1954 | 1955 | 1956 | 1957 | 1958 | 1959 | 1960 | Increase/decrease |
|---|---|---|---|---|---|---|---|---|
| Total primary | 235,439 | 246,719 | 258,346 | 269,356 | 284,431 | 290,027 | 295,006 | +59,567 |
| Central classes | 689 | 560 | 426 | 425 | 293 | 288 | 372 | -317 |
| Central schools (Secondary) | 5,376 | 4,675 | 4,597 | 4,136 | 4,071 | 4,072 | 4,087 | -1,289 |
| Higher elementary | 3,546 | 2,823 | 2,627 | 2,386 | 2,726 | 2,658 | 2,258 | -1,288 |
| Girls' secondary | 5,837 | 6,405 | 6,610 | 7,115 | 7,292 | 5,787 | 6,410 | +573 |
| High | 31,395 | 36,499 | 42,027 | 49,258 | 56,136 | 69,617 | 78,076 | +46,681 |
| Junior technical | 18,229 | 20,105 | 22,134 | 24,590 | 27,048 | 30,573 | 34,130 | +15,901 |
| Consolidated | 1,035 | 1,114 | 1,213 | 1,266 | 1,473 | 1,548 | 1,373 | +338 |
| Central schools (Postprimary) | 1,447 | 970 | 673 | 633 | 447 | 392 | 383 | -1,064 |
| Total secondary | 67,554 | 73,151 | 80,307 | 89,809 | 99,486 | 114,935 | 127,089 | +59,535 |
| TOTAL | 302,993 | 319,870 | 338,653 | 359,165 | 383,917 | 404,962 | 422,095 | +119,102 |

Source: *Education Gazette and Teachers' Aid*, 1954–61[330]

## The case at Ferntree Gully

Growth in the hills community of Ferntree Gully stirred urgent action. A consortium of specialists from the Education Department, the University of Melbourne and the Australian Council for Educational Research met with parents and teachers to study the educational needs of the outer-eastern shire, covering 117 square miles. Dr L W Shears and District Inspectors D C Streader and R P McLellan represented the Education Department, and Dr E R Wyeth represented the University of Melbourne's School of Education.

Though new to the role of survey and planning, Shears was in his element. Radford's survey of educational needs of rural communities in the Bairnsdale district, his own research in the Upper Goulburn region, and his recent survey of schooling in Britain enriched his knowledge. Working with Streader, McLellan and Wyeth placed Shears among an elite team. Supplementing Departmental predictions, questionnaire data from teachers, parents and community representatives triggered discussion. A series of meetings followed with and among members of professional and community groups.

The report that resulted from the group's work predicted the shire's population of 25,446 would double by 1965, thus placing an additional 10,000 pupils in primary, high, technical and Catholic schools. Major needs lay in the secondary sector.[331] The report identified accommodation needs until 1960 and set new standards for new schools: 30 pupils per teacher; better staff facilities; special-purpose rooms for interviews, libraries, assemblies and gymnasiums; and allocated spaces for storage, reception and first aid. More equipment and improved amenities for washing, drinking and toileting were also required. A proposed multi-purpose co-educational secondary school would cater for school-leavers seeking jobs in and beyond the shire and for those seeking jobs in agriculture and primary production, manufacture, textiles, home-making, commerce and the professions.

Despite the consultative process not all recommendations were met. Counter to calls for a technical school, the Department advanced technical training for girls at Upwey and Boronia High Schools, the latter due to open in 1957.[332] Existing facilities exposed:

> ... marked disparity between the retention rate of girls and boys reflecting tendencies statewide. Throughout the shire in 1955, 1904 boys and 1796 girls attended state primary schools while state secondary schools accommodated 748 boys and 365 girls.[333]

To retain girls and cater for likely commercial expansion in the shire, high schools would offer core courses plus training for employment in local businesses and the Public Service.[334] Beyond education per se was the need to improve library facilities, and to provide social and cultural activities and further educational opportunities for 15- to 19-year olds:[335]

Acknowledging 'a small but important proportion of persons from non-British origin living in the Shire' the report took a strong national stance. It stressed the need for newcomers to conform to the Australian ethos, which was the 'proper basis for informed citizenship'. Undoubtedly this stirred ire among the group, many of whom worked in the manufacturing sector or on farms. Similarly greeted was the recommendation to deny them their traditional lifestyle and culture.[336] As immigrant populations grew in number and strength, such attitudes towards citizenship softened, and in forthcoming years the Education Department embarked on programs to teach English to non-English-speaking newcomers. Commonwealth finances in the 1970s supported the expansion of such programs, and corresponded with national trends and delegation by Shears of senior officers to oversee the development of these programs. Ferntree Gully's immigrant population had obviously flourished and attitudes changed as primary schoolteacher M Kocher demonstrated. In 1980 she was awarded the G S Browne Prize 'for her contribution to multicultural education and the integral role she played in establishing a multicultural centre at her school', indicating the changing social mood.

## Finding a balance: Teacher shortage and training

Although the Ferntree Gully survey focused on a discrete community, its implications for education were broad as Melbourne's suburban profile continued to spread. Survey and Planning Officer Shears was in the midst of the action to balance growth and provision. He explained that the school building program, burgeoning enrolments and the supply of enough suitably trained teachers increasingly challenged the Education Department.[337] Underlying factors were rapid population growth, the trend to keep children in school and demand for higher qualifications. Unlike education departments in New South Wales and South Australia, Victoria had ceased recruitment of teachers from the United Kingdom to fill the void.[338] Low birth rate in Victoria during the Great Depression and war years and competition from more lucrative professions affected teacher supply, making it difficult to recruit increased numbers for training.

For two decades from the 1950s the Education Department experienced extraordinary growth in the size of its pupil population, and the number of schools and teachers, as Table 3 shows.

In the decade from 1951 to 1961 the number of pupils enrolled in primary schools rose by one-third. In secondary and technical schools

Table 3. Demographics of Victorian schools and their populations

|  | 1951 | 1961 | 1971 |
| --- | --- | --- | --- |
| Primary school pupils | 205,888 | 301,514 | 367,385 |
| Primary schools | 1,949 | 1,931 | 1,733* |
| Primary teachers | 6,454 | 10,306 | 17,369 |
| Secondary (including high, central, higher elementary) pupils | 32,209 | 101,062 | 180,960 |
| Secondary schools | 135 | 257 | 303 |
| Secondary teachers | 1,469 | 3,144 | 7,223 |
| Junior technical pupils | 13,524 | 36,719 | 59,187 |
| Junior technical schools | 30 | 70 | 95 |
| Technical teachers | 703 | 1,633 | 3,754 |

Source: Garden p. 181
* The number of primary schools fell due to closing of rural schools and the swing towards consolidation.

the numbers rose by about two-thirds. The number of primary schools decreased due to consolidation of small rural schools while the number of high and junior technical schools approximately doubled. There was a rise in the number of primary teachers, a steep rise in secondary teachers and an approximate doubling of teachers in junior technical schools. The task of the three members of the survey and planning team was to forecast growth and recommend appropriate steps to ensure sufficient schools and teachers to cater for the growth in school populations and changing social demographics. For Shears this included predictions and plans for the latter years of the 1950s and continuing through the 1960s.

To alleviate the problem of teacher supply the Education Department increased the number of training institutions. It reopened Bendigo and Ballarat TCs in the mid-1940s and during the 1950s established five new colleges for primary and infant training. In 1953 the Secondary Teachers' Training Centre was converted to the Secondary Teachers College (STC). Employment of temporary teachers filled the immediate void; among them were married women no longer employable in a permanent capacity according to regulation. The *Teaching Service (Married Women) Act* 1956 (No. 6030) granted permanency to 120 women but the employment of married women raised a further difficulty. Unlike recent graduates who were assigned to remote corners of the State, the married women preferred to teach close to home.[339]

Employment of under-qualified teachers was another concern. Although the *Education Act* 1958 (No. 6240) stated 'No person shall be registered as a teacher unless he produces evidence which satisfies the Council of his fitness to teach' the crisis called for desperate measures.[340] Teachers reflected on the pressures of work. Rex Murfett, senior science teacher at Rosebud High School in 1963 recalled 'taking half an afternoon off in sports period on a Friday afternoon to teach a couple of needlework teachers some basic experiments in order that they could teach the children in Forms 1 and 2. Unbelievable!' Previously, at Leongatha High School, he ran two science prac. classes at lunchtime 'because I couldn't cope any other way. These were classes of 45.'[341] STC graduate Dick Gunstone recounted, 'you really must understand that teaching at secondary schools in the '50s was a serious job. As a first-year teacher my Lake Bolac High School Form 1 had 50 students, and I taught a Form 4 Science class with 45.' He continued:

> I was the only qualified teacher of mathematics or science in the school. Most of the rest was done by a person who had literally walked of the street and said, 'I think I'd like to teach.' He looked physically very odd and had three university subjects from 18 attempts. He was incompetent beyond belief. I had to try and hold him up.[342]

Continued growth caused problems throughout the decade. In 1956–57 Minister Bloomfield reported 'a shortage of teachers in almost all subjects of the curriculum' and warned, 'the position is likely to remain difficult for some years.'[343] To alleviate serious shortfalls in maths and science recruitment of trained teachers from Scotland and England was mooted but no action occurred.[344]

Abreast of recruitment and training problems, Shears was positioned to offer advice. Representing Director Ramsay, he was appointed Secretary, Advisory Committee on Teacher Training. While the Trained Secondary Teachers' Certificate (TSTC) helped solve the dilemma in secondary schools, changes to primary courses had ruffled feathers. The extension of the TPTC to two years in 1952 had agitated those involved in the specialist Trained Infant Teachers Certificate (TITC). Originally a 12-month extension to TPTC, the lobbying of a group led by Ruby Angus of Melbourne TC had the TITC extended to three years. Both courses continued to share a common year; however, infant teacher training of three years required revision of the curriculum. In a similar way to revamping the TPTC as a two-year course, Shears worked with infant teacher specialists to develop the curriculum yet retain the common core.[345]

Despite the extensions, training for teachers of infant and primary levels remained inadequate. Primary teachers college principals and John Cannon, Chief Inspector of Primary Schools (1956–58), promoted a three-year TPTC. Len Pryor, Principal of Bendigo TC (1951–58), lamented the lack of staff to make the required progress. He identified serious shortages among secondary teacher graduates and urged a thorough overhaul of teacher education.

## Teachers colleges

Shortage of teachers also affected the staffing of teachers colleges where temporary appointments were rife. Teachers were poached from their classrooms for lecturing positions, which left serious gaps in schools. The survey and planning team was responsible for staffing the colleges. Shears, who served as Secretary of the Special Committee for Appointments to Professional Positions in Teachers Colleges, arranged position advertisements and presented a short list to the committee. While staffing the new colleges provided jobs for 'so many good people', it created a 'problem, for without higher status and recognition, the colleges found it very difficult to attract and retain people with good qualifications and highly developed talents.'[346] Despite extensive advertising, poaching from classrooms continued.

Establishing teachers colleges in suitable premises was another major task. In 1954 five primary teachers colleges operated in temporary locations. Among them was the new college at Burwood scheduled to open in specifically designed masonry veneer or LTC buildings. By today's standards such buildings are denigrated but in the 1950s their construction was fast and efficient. Shears stressed, 'we planned teachers colleges so that they were quite different from the ordinary secondary classrooms; facilities were different.' He explained, 'I managed to persuade the Public Works Department that buildings for the teachers colleges should contain certain facilities for staff to meet together and specific groups of rooms for different faculties – practice rooms for music education, studios for art education and lecture rooms for education studies.'[347]

Administrators from the Education Department of New South Wales scoffed at Victoria's use of LTC because of its limited life span and the associated directive that school population should not exceed 700 pupils. In contrast the NSW Department constructed fewer solid brick schools each accommodating more than 1000 pupils. Victoria's philosophy impressed Dr Harry Penny, Principal of Adelaide Teachers College, who saw the attributes of design flexibility offering specialist facilities and spaces for tutorials and interviews.[348] Following a tour of the Victorian colleges with a cohort of educators and architects a second teachers college at Wattle Park in South Australia built in 1957 used LTC.[349]

## Primary teacher education

As occurred with new high schools, the Department used temporary premises to establish primary teachers colleges. Numbers of trainees entering the profession burgeoned as studentships enticed school leavers. Bendigo (1945) opened in Bendigo State School, No. 1976, known as Camp Hill, and Ballarat (1946) was established in Ballarat State School, No. 33, known as Dana Street. At Geelong and Toorak former private residences Lunan House and Glenbervie housed the initial intakes (1950 and 1951 respectively). Church halls sufficed at Burwood (1954) and Coburg (1959) and Struan, the home and practice of a local doctor, was used at Frankston (1959).[350] Staff and trainees at Ballarat TC moved into permanent buildings in 1958 and those at Bendigo did likewise the following year.

From 1957, after careful negotiation, Toorak TC was located at Stonington. John Wagner, founder partner of Cobb and Co, built the mansion and associated coach house and stables in 1890. At Federation, Stonington became Australia's Government House and home of the Governor General. St Margaret's School occupied it from 1931 and the Red Cross used it as a convalescent hospital during WWII. From 1953 the Health Department used it to rehabilitate polio victims.[351] Toorak TC outgrew the Glenbervie and Claymore sites and Stonington appeared to be an alternative. In discussion with Shears, Senior Health Officer Bertram McCloskey said, 'Get us an alternative and you can have Stonington.' Shears recalled:

> I found a suitable place in Park Street, South Yarra, providing the Health Department with facilities to meet their needs. In 1957 Toorak Teachers College moved into Stonington leaving Glenbervie available for the Technical Teachers College under Principal Blackman.[352]

Correspondingly the location of a new outer suburban college at Frankston or Dandenong was stirring debate. Shears recalled:

> ... investigating where students would come from and how they would get to Dandenong or Frankston. I spent a long time preparing the cases for each. The Chief Inspector of Primary Schools investigated the material and after talking with his Assistant Chief Inspectors went ahead with Frankston.[353]

In Melbourne's outer southeast, Frankston was close to public transport and fourteen possible training schools. Existing facilities on Struan, a property belonging to Dr Vincent, would accommodate an intake of ten staff and 109 trainees in 1959. Dr Vincent's property of just over 17 acres including an eleven-room residence and four-room cottage was purchased on 8 October 1957 for £37,500. While Shears was negotiating the purchase Minister Bloomfield advised him to accept Dr Vincent's figure. The purchase of an additional seven properties cost £18,316 which brought the total cost to £55,816. Under foundation principal Warwick Eunson (1959–62) the college grew as the new buildings and facilities were established.[354]

Coburg TC was also established in 1959 in Melbourne's northern growth corridor that attracted Italian and Greek immigrants. Proximity to transport and training schools determined the site some six miles north of the city. Four adjacent acres previously used by Pentridge prisoners as a training farm provided additional land. Guided by foundation principal Miss Ida Lowndes, the college began in a rented church hall as had happened with Burwood. The Coburg area became an educational hub with new technical and high schools nearby. Brian Carroll who wrote a history of the Phillip Institute, a later development of Coburg TC, gives colour to the early years:

> Pentridge was widely known as 'Coburg College', so the 117 students and ten staff who launched Coburg Teachers' College in February 1959, in the Methodist Church Hall on the corner of Sydney Road and Bell Street, soon found themselves the butt of many a joke. In time a number of single storey buildings on the site behind Pentridge replaced the church hall. [355]

## Secondary teacher education

From the time that the Education Department withdrew secondary studentships in 1933 the shortage of secondary teachers intensified. Soon after Ramsay's appointment as Director, the Education Department embarked on a recruitment drive and from 1950 offered four-year studentships. Awardees received a living allowance and free tuition towards a university degree and Diploma of Education. In return they were bonded to the Department for three years. Increasing the numbers of graduate secondary teachers still failed to keep pace with educational growth. To fill the void, two-year trained primary graduates taught to Grade 8 or Form 2, the equivalent of higher elementary completion or Merit Certificate. The practice caused dissent between trained secondary teachers and their 'lesser' qualified primary colleagues.

The need for more trained secondary teachers and concern regarding failure in university subjects initiated the need for alternative training measures. The Secondary Teachers' Training Centre (STTC) was established in 1950. Principal Alice Hoy led staff comprising Gwen Wainwright, in charge of English and history; Manuel Gelman, responsible for modern languages; and Harold Sargeant, who led maths and science. Wilma Hannah replaced Wainwright after Wainwright was transferred to Toorak in 1951. Staff worked under trying conditions in two Bristol huts located in the university's Botany Garden. The huts were hot in summer and cold in winter; the roofs leaked when it rained; the windows jammed; the toilet blocks were remote; and there was no phone. Gelman recalled changing a pound note into pennies and using a public phone box at the Parkville Post Office to arrange school placements and supervision.[356]

STTC staff administered allowances, supervised hostels and course content, and offered supplementary tutorials in university subjects. A safety net, according to Shears, the STTC minimised failures and provided teachers. 'Many who failed university completed secondary teacher training and performed better; others went on to do primary training. STTC graduates were among the Department's best teachers.'[357] 'Alice Hoy's Secondary Teachers' Centre', as it was known, became a college in 1953, a move applauded as a crucial advance. In 1957 the college severed connections with Melbourne TC, attuned its program to support secondary teacher training and introduced the Trained Secondary Teachers Certificate (TSTC).[358]

Doug McDonell succeeded Miss Hoy as principal in 1958. A recent Carnegie Scholar he infused the course with knowledge attained in the USA and the UK. To overcome the teacher shortage he established a developmental program to train minimally qualified temporary teachers and offered them permanency on the Secondary Classified Roll.[359] McDonell and Vice-Principal Bill Watson advocated for better facilities to prepare and train new teachers and established a timeline to introduce four-year training.

By the late 1950s plans for a new building were underway. Specifically designed for a secondary teachers college the budget was tight and space limited. Though not complete until 1962, the four-storey cream brick-veneer, named the Alice Hoy building, accepted its first intake in 1959. Survey and Planning Officer Shears, who oversaw the building's construction, reflected:

> We put it on the sanctuary of sanctuaries, namely the back paddock of the old Melbourne Teachers College, where the teachers college hockey team used to play. We knew there would only be one building, so one of the problems with its planning was that we put everything into it including the kitchen sink – everything that you needed in a secondary teachers college was shoved in. It was pretty cramped with lecture spaces, an assembly hall and office facilities for staff.[360]

By the early 1960s four institutions trained Victoria's secondary teachers. The Secondary TC and Monash TC offered TSTC whereas Melbourne and Monash universities provided courses that offered a Diploma of Education on completion of a first degree. The Education faculty at Monash University, established in 1961, was 'a matter of priority' according to the Ramsay Committee. Its initial intake of 81 Diploma of Education students was ranked second in status behind those from the University of Melbourne.

## Technical and special education teachers

Following years of stagnation in the 1930s and 40s, technical education similarly faced pressures of growth. In the Education Department's Technical Division, programs offered by the Commonwealth Reconstruction Training Scheme rehabilitated war veterans returning to civilian life. This put pressure on the Division, which was also pushed to extend certificate courses from three to four years, to educate pupils to year 12 from 1946, and to increase apprenticeships.

Within the decade from 1945 the number of technical schools rose from 32 to 45 and plans were in place to provide over 80 in the next ten years. To boost teacher numbers and train specialist teachers, in 1951 the Department established a Technical Teachers' Centre attached to Melbourne Technical College. AR Blackman was appointed principal. With an initial intake of 120 the facility was deemed too small for annual increases of 40 to 50. Negotiations with the Health Department led to the move of Toorak TC to Stonington, which left Glenbervie as an ideal location to train technical teachers and principals of technical schools.

Technical education covered a diverse field that required teachers for the core subjects of maths, science and English as well as for specific skills. Technical teacher training required specialist flair in diverse and particular fields. Such were TSTC Art and Crafts and Domestic Arts. Under the guidance of Charles Mellow, art and craft trainees completed two years at a teachers college or technical college and a further year at the Melbourne TC. Traditionally, domestic arts was conducted at 'Emily Mac', a term of endearment for the Emily McPherson College of Domestic Economy established in Victoria Street, Melbourne, in 1923. Named after the wife of patron Sir William McPherson it had offered the Diploma of Domestic Arts since 1943. The course was renamed the Diploma of Domestic Science in 1950. Neighbouring buildings in Victoria Street provided hostel accommodation for country girls and a venue for professional training.[361] 'Emily Mac' and Larnook Teachers College, established in 1950, worked in harmony to offer the TSTC (Domestic Arts) and the Diploma of Domestic Arts. From 1957 a one-year extension could be awarded to TPTC graduates to qualify them for the Trained Homecrafts Teachers Certificate. As for other specialist colleges it was difficult for Larnook and Emily Mac to recruit qualified staff and find venues for practical training until the Victorian Railways, the Myer Emporium and nearby hospitals offered to satisfy this need.[362]

Typical of the era were cramped conditions and the need for portable classrooms, as faced in the training of specialist teachers for the deaf. A sub-committee of the Special Committee on Training Teachers of the Handicapped, formed in 1953, recommended specialist training for teachers of the deaf and residential accommodation in Kew. Dr Leo Murphy established the Training Centre for Teachers of the Deaf and a certificate course at Glendonald School for the Deaf. It was recognised as a teachers college in 1954 with Murphy as its foundation principal. From the initial intake of twelve trainees from Victoria and interstate many became specialist teachers and advisers. Enrolments grew rapidly and soon exceeded the capacity of 110. A portable unit was installed in the grounds but by 1957–58 classes were held in the

*Laying Foundations*

corridor, the common room, the kitchenette and at Kew State School, No. 1075, in nearby Peel Street.[363]

Table 4 outlines the development of teacher education institutions in Victoria.

Table 4. Development of teacher education institutions in Victoria 1872–1972

|  | Teachers College | Location | Principal |
|---|---|---|---|
| 1870–93 | Central Teacher Training Institution | Spring Street, East Melbourne 1870–89<br>1888 building Grattan Street, Carlton | SC Dixon 1870–77<br>FJ Gladman 1877–84<br>CA Topp 1885–89<br>R Craig 1890–93 |
| 1893 | Training Institute closed |  |  |
| 1900 | Teachers Training College | 1888 building Grattan Street, Carlton | F Tate 1900–02<br>J Smyth 1902–13 |
| 1913 | Melbourne Teachers College | 1888 building Grattan Street, Carlton | J Smyth 1913–27<br>LJ Wrigley 1928–33<br>GS Browne 1934–38<br>AJ Law 1939–50<br>GR Mills 1951–62<br>W Eunson 1962–72 |
| 1926–31 | Bendigo Teachers College | Long Gully State School 1926–28<br>Old Court House 1928–31 | TH Scott 1926–31 |
| 1945 | Bendigo re-opened | Camp Hill State School 1945–59 | GR Mills 1945–50<br>LJ Pryor 1951–58 |
| 1959 |  | Osborne Street 1959 | SH Walters 1959–64<br>JM Hill 1964–69<br>KG Scarrott 1969– |
| 1926–31 | Ballarat Teachers College | Dana Street State School 1926–27<br>Ballarat East Town Hall 1927–31 | WH Ellwood 1926–31 |
| 1946 | Ballarat re-opened | Dana Street State School 1946–58<br>Gillies Street 1958– | WF Lord 1946-51<br>TW Turner 1951–70<br>D Watson 1971– |
| 1950 | Geelong Teachers College | Lunan House 1950–<br>Vines Road 1961– | LG Whiteoak 1950–70<br>GW Boyd 1970 |
| 1951 | Toorak Teachers College | Glenbervie, Toorak 1951–56<br>Stonington 1957– | WF Lord 1951–58<br>LJ Pryor 1959–61<br>JJ St Ellen 1962– |
| 1950 | Secondary Teachers Training Centre | Botany School garden, University of Melbourne 1950–58 | A Hoy 1950–57 |
| 1953 | Secondary Teachers College | Melbourne Teachers College grounds 1953–72; Alice Hoy Building 1962 | DM McDonell 1958–72 |
| 1950 | Larnook Teachers College | Victoria Street, Carlton 1950–52<br>Orrong Road, Armadale 1952 | AJ Pollock 1950–56<br>I Horne 1957 |
| 1952 | Technical Teachers College | Melbourne Technical College 1952–57<br>Glenbervie, Toorak 1957–70<br>Auburn Road, Hawthorn 1970– | AR Blackman 1952–72 |

161

| 1954 | Burwood Teachers College | Methodist Church Hall Box Hill 1954<br>Burwood Road/Highway 1954 | DM Waller 1954–61<br>LW Shears 1961–69<br>JM Hill 1970– |
|---|---|---|---|
| 1954 | Glendonald Training Centre for Teachers of the Deaf | Belmont Avenue, Kew 1954–57<br>Glendonald, 1957– | LJ Murphy 1954– |
| 1959 | Coburg Teachers College | Methodist Hall, Sydney Road 1959<br>Urquhart Street 1960– | I Lowndes 1959– |
| 1959 | Frankston Teachers College | Struan, residence on site 1959<br>New building on site 1960– | W Eunson 1959–62<br>GA Jenkins 1962– |
| 1961 | Monash Teachers College | Monash University 1961–65<br>Clayton Technical School 1965<br>Blackburn Road, North Clayton 1966– | HB Sargeant 1961–<br>WC Watson 1972– |
| 1970 | La Trobe Teachers College | La Trobe University 1970– | WC Watson 1970–7<br>PJ Pledger 1972– |

Source: Blake 1973[364]

## Hostels

To accommodate studentship holders from rural areas to undertake teacher training the Education Department provided hostel accommodation close to teachers colleges in regional cities and in suburban Melbourne. Approximately one-third of studentship holders resided in hostels. In 1951 thirteen hostels accommodated 38 men and 444 women but by 1954, 22 hostels accommodated 195 men and 558 women:

> Cowabee, Warwillah and 470 and 481 St Kilda Road … we put girls there but didn't know until afterwards that it had been a brothel … there was Frank Tate House in Dandenong Road near Wattletree Road; Punt Road; Patterson Street, Hawthorn; Moule Avenue, Brighton; Victoria, Walsh, Marne and Drummond Streets … they were all over the place.[365]

The purchase of hostels set in motion by Satchell became a major role for Shears. He recalled working with an agent 'who was ducking around finding them'. Frequently selected were former mansions. Three hostels integrated into the design of Burwood Teachers College were named Animum, Cultum and Parabo. Two accommodated women and the other housed men. Rather than name them hostels Shears preferred to call them 'halls of residence' as with university accommodation. Regardless of name the hostels provided secure living at minimal cost. A vital part of educational provision they catered for trainees who may have missed out on further education. Living with others of similar ilk, country students made a transition to rural towns or city life, made friends and benefited from subsidised board.

Dick Gunstone, later Professor of Science at Monash University, recalled, Kuranda, the Punt Road hostel, where there were 'only about 70 of us in 1958; 35 to 40 were first-year students'. He said others lived in Orrong and St Kilda Roads. He explained:

> I had come to the city from a very conservative rural context. From the time I was very young my mother had said I was going to go to university, otherwise we had to leave school at 12, go home and work on the farm. I had four uncles, all of them were very clear, by the time I turned 15, I should leave school and stop bludging. There was very good money to be made from splitting fence posts. They placed enormous pressure on me to leave school and certainly not do what I did. I probably would have succumbed but for one wonderful English teacher at school.[366]

Providing hostel accommodation was a recruitment tactic for the Department, but the costs – purchase/lease, upkeep – weighed against the minimal rates of accommodation charged were an ongoing cause of concern. Each year the Department's accountant requested a rise but aware of Premier Bolte's philosophy to recruit and accommodate country students at teachers colleges, Director Ramsay rejected the plea. According to Shears:

> Regular as clockwork, come the end of the financial year the accountant would send a note to Alan Ramsay. He believed we should increase the cost of accommodation because it was costing the government too much money. Alan Ramsay would dutifully hand it over to me and I would immediately write on the bottom. 'The use of hostels is a recruitment device particularly for country trainees. I recommend that no increase be made as it would cut across the policy of recruiting extra teachers who were badly needed.' Alan Ramsay said, 'No increase', so we went on hiring buildings.[367]

## Residential seminars and regional discussion groups

Beyond the scope of staffing teachers colleges and providing accommodation for country students, the survey and planning officer oversaw and developed in-service programs for teachers in schools. To upgrade teachers' skills, equip them with specialist knowledge and enhance their qualifications the Department established a series of external studies. Len Pryor, on his return from the United Kingdom and Europe as a Carnegie Fellow in 1947–48, initiated a series for secondary and technical teachers; the concept was new in Australia at the time. Offering intensive short-term study, partly during vacations, the programs satisfied teachers' and Departmental needs. Offering 10-day residential programs, Pryor aimed to help teachers solve specific problems. As a group those in attendance examined major developments in their field, then discussed methods and techniques to help them cope. Upon Pryor's appointment to Principal of Bendigo TC in 1950, David Satchell continued the work.

Participants attending the 1949–51 seminar series were accommodated in a Queenscliff guesthouse. Daytime activities took place at the Department's Health and Recreation Camp nearby, which provided midday and evening meals. The camp had space for study, discussion, recreational and social activities. Military authorities repossessed the camp in 1952 causing cancellation of the program that year. Thereafter seminar series were held at Melbourne TC and participants were housed in various Education Department hostels. Satchell competently took command until his appointment to the Board of Inspectors of Secondary Schools and in 1954 handed the task to Shears. Shears reflected on the experience of:

> … bringing together about 80 secondary and technical teachers at Melbourne Teachers College. I got experience handling them. They were very, very successful. The Director opened the seminar. It was quite an important annual activity. I developed them so that we had the same thing replicated in Ballarat, Geelong and Bendigo for teachers in country areas. We also had them at Burwood Teachers College where there was accommodation available.[368]

The seminar series were advertised in the *Education Gazette and Teachers' Aid* where Shears identified the specialist staff responsible for the program. The Boards of Inspectors of Secondary and Technical Schools recommended group leaders whom Shears contacted in turn to establish expectations. He emphasised the value of small-group discussion, time for informal study and subject-specific discussion. This approach encouraged participants to foster philosophies, develop practical skills and produce materials to enhance their teaching. By application reports were available to schools.[369]

Subject by subject, the seminars covered the secondary school curriculum. Initially two subjects were presented at a single venue but by 1956 the number expanded to eight subjects and by 1960 the seminars were held at four venues. With the system securely established, Shears introduced regional discussion groups, which offered professional training closer to home for country teachers.

The Curriculum and Research Branch, established in 1947, supported the survey and planning team by providing statistical data on pupils, teachers and schools.[370] A departmental restructure in 1959 put Shears in charge of a team of three: Bert Osmond, a statistician; Roy McLean, a Survey Officer who undertook research to guide Directors of Secondary, Technical and Primary Divisions; and Bill McKinty, who was in charge of teacher recruitment, training and in-service education.[371] When Shears embarked on a Harkness Fellowship in September 1959 McKinty acted in the senior position.

Table 5, listing seminars held between 1951 and 1961, shows development of the program and its annual focus, and identifies group leaders.

The seminar program continued throughout 1960 and in education's evolving climate change occurred. Pryor's appointment as Superintendent of Teacher Education in 1961 put him in charge of in-service training once more. He maintained the regional seminars and by 1962 they were held at five centres and training extended to leadership groups.[372] In 1961 primary head teachers met at Somers Camp and primary teachers of homecrafts met at Burwood TC. Infant mistresses held their first seminar in 1963. The purpose of the leadership seminars was apparently misunderstood and the principals

Table 5. Residential seminar series 1951-61

| Year | Subjects, Levels | Groups | Group Leaders | Date |
|---|---|---|---|---|
| 1951 | Teaching of modern languages, music, geography | | Not listed | |
| 1952 | CANCELLED due to repossession of venue by the Army | | | |
| 1953 | Geography<br>Science Forms 1 to 4<br>Commercial subjects Forms 1 to 4 | 2<br>2<br>1 | Miss R Coulsell; Mr A Moy<br>Mr J Greenwell; Mr J Stone<br>Mr R Hosie | 3–11 Sep |
| 1954 | English Forms 1 to 5<br>Social studies Forms 1 to 5 | 3 or 4<br>1 or 2 | Not listed | 1–9 Sep |
| 1955 | Mathematics Forms 1 to 5<br>Art Forms 1 to 5<br>Latin Form 5 | 2<br>2<br>1 | Mr EA Baker; Mr R Fincher; Mr E Jackson<br>Mr A. Markham<br>Miss J. Mason | 31 Aug–9 Sep |
| 1956 | History Forms 1 to 5<br>Modern languages Forms 1 to 5<br>Music Forms 1 to 5 | 1<br>1<br>1 | Mr N Curry; Mr A Jones<br>Mr R Moss<br>Miss AE Cameron | 5–18 Sep |
| 1957 | Science Forms 1 to 5<br>Geography Forms 1 to 5<br>Commercial subjects Forms 1 to 5 | 2<br>3<br>1 | Mr C Lugg; Mr I Muir<br>Mr J Bishop; Mr H Butler; Mr R. Silcock<br>Mr F de Pinna | 4–13 Sep |
| 1958 | General science Forms 1 to 4<br><br>School counselling | 5<br><br>1 | Mr H Cracknell; Mr H Ely; Mr D Lugg;<br>Mr W Muir; Mr J Theobold<br>Mr J Hall; Mr R Gregg; Mr K McLeod | 3–12 Sep |
| 1959 | Domestic science<br>Physics, chemistry, biology Forms 5 and 6 | 3<br>3 | Not listed | 2–11 Sep |
| 1960 | Dramatic work; written expression; library techniques; differential teaching of English (including remedial) | | Not listed | 31 Aug–9 Sep |
| 1961 | Coordination of plane and solid geometry; extra syllabus maths; differential teaching of English (including gifted) | | Not listed | |

Source: Education Gazette and Teachers' Aid 1951-61

questioned the virtue of specialist training. They showed little enthusiasm until Jack Howard of the Victorian Teachers Union spurred them on. He asked, 'Are senior primary teachers so lacking in professional pride that they are content to stagnate?' Those who attended saw the benefits of stimulating discussion on ways to improve their professional status. He advised, 'Here is an opportunity, grasp it.'[373]

Table 6. Regional seminar program 1956–60

| Year | Subjects | Venue | Date |
|---|---|---|---|
| 1956 | English, mathematics | | 28 May–1 Jun |
| 1957 | English, mathematics, history, science, geography, modern languages | Sandhurst Hostel Bendigo TC | 27–31 May |
| 1958 | English, mathematics, geography, modern languages, art and crafts, domestic arts, commercial subjects | 470 St Kilda Road, Bendigo, Ballarat, Geelong | |
| 1959 | English, mathematics, geography, modern languages, art and crafts, domestic arts, commercial subjects | 410 St Kilda Road, Bendigo, Ballarat, Burwood | 25–29 May |
| 1960 | English, mathematics, domestic science, commercial subjects, art, boys craft | | 23–27 May |

Source: Education Gazette and Teachers' Aid *1956–60*

## Other aspects of Shears

Shears stood at the threshold of an exciting educational era. He was becoming a powerful force. Groomed for leadership he continually strengthened professional links. He shared the platform with Ramsay, Professor Browne, Alice Hoy, Bill Radford and Alex McDonell in the rejuvenation of the VIER. The organisation shifted from 'flounder to flourish' under the new, young executive team appointed in November 1953. Invigorated by their enthusiasm, membership of the VIER grew from 30 in 1954 to exceed 400 by 1960. The major forum for educational research at the time, guest speakers from home and abroad, encouraged members to look beyond their parochial boundaries to address current issues that alerted them to forthcoming trends.[374] Browne applauded Shears on his part in the endeavour to promote and publish research, and noted his professional growth. He wrote:

> On his return from the Institute of Education in London with his doctorate he found the Victorian Institute of Educational Research moving quietly with a conventional program and a small membership. He undertook the Secretaryship and within 12 months had changed the Institute into a dynamic force in the community, attracting large audiences to its evening meetings at the University and publishing an interesting quarterly record of its proceedings, and helping to bring before the public the results of some very significant research.[375]

Shears did not rest. Eager to develop a national research agenda he encouraged the VIER to produce a *Journal of Education*. He was 33 when Volume 1, Number 1 was issued in July 1954. In the introduction Professor Browne noted:

> The Victorian Institute of Educational Research has decided to launch the journal … as an interim measure, in the hope that eventually it will be merged in a more ambitious publication, organized and representing Australian education as a whole.

The issue presented the inaugural Frank Tate Memorial Lecture[376] given by HS Wyndham, Director of Education in New South Wales. 'Decentralisation of education,' Wyndham argued, offered 'expeditious, economical and efficient administration'. He saw the Department as 'an impersonal governmental agency, with its headquarters far over the local horizon'. Local people in a decentralised system had a 'real sense of proprietorship and direct interest in the schools established for the education of the children in that community'.[377] In the same issue Director Ramsay reflected on 'Frank Tate: His life and work', Tom Coates contemplated 'Research and the teacher' and Professor Browne questioned television as a tool for learning in his article 'Television: Friend or enemy?'.

After two editions in 1954 the *Journal of Education* was published thrice yearly. Edited by Shears, it increased from 24 to 48 pages. In the light of their local success, the VIER executive persuaded the Australian Council for Educational Research to publish an *Australian Journal of Education*, as a broader research forum. Professor Browne believed Dr Shears' work contributed markedly to the appearance of this Journal. Shears claimed it would provoke thought, convey ideas, encourage questions and provide answers relevant to the present state of knowledge. He had hoped to be foundation editor but his hopes were dashed with the appointment of senior educationist Professor W F Connell of the University of Sydney and Professor C R McRae as Assistant. State Editor Shears was somewhat mollified when early editions of the *Australian Journal of Education* stated inside its front cover 'incorporating the *Journal of Education* of the Victorian Institute of Educational Research'.[378] Whether compensation or commendation, on page 27 of Volume 1 an article by Shears summarised 'Recent research on Australian secondary education.' His views on trends in primary education were published in Volume 2.

The establishment of the Australian College of Education (ACE) in 1959 was another landmark in education that offered opportunities for Shears. James Darling (later Sir), Head Master of Geelong Grammar School, and Brian Hone, Head Master of Melbourne Grammar School, had in the previous year mooted the concept of forming a national body. A provincial council was established and a draft constitution proposed. Invitations were sent to 110 highly regarded educationists who attended the residential founders' convention at Geelong Grammar School in May. The list was a veritable 'who's who' of the nation's educational leaders. Members were recognised leaders who had made significant contributions to education in private, church and government systems at all levels of provision. There were deans, professors and directors of education; rectors, sisters and brothers of Catholic colleges; high school principals; members of advisory boards; university and teachers college staff; and teachers in schools. Criteria for membership was a 'basic qualification of a first degree', 'evidence of some equivalent and appropriate academic or professional training', 'at least five years' experience in the field of education' or 'some special contribution in the field'. This prohibited entry for lesser qualified and new teachers. While ACE aimed for professional status, it was seen as elitist.

Among the founders were Dr Wyndham, Director of Education in New South Wales; Alice Hoy, founder and past principal of the Secondary Teachers College; Emeritus Professor George Browne; Dr Bill Radford, Director of ACER; and Rev Tom Timpson, Head Master of Camberwell Grammar School. At 38 years old Shears was there too, in the right place at the right time.

Victorians fared well among office bearers. Darling was elected president. Joint vice president with Wyndham was Professor Charles Moorhouse, Dean of Electrical Engineering, the University of Melbourne. The secretary was Timpson and the treasurer was Radford (ACER was headquartered in Victoria). In succeeding years leadership roles spread nationwide. State chapters of ACE ensured local focus and interest in interstate activity. Ramsay and Mr J G Baker became vice-chairmen of the Victorian chapter and Dr Coates was secretary. Ramsay advised Shears not to take a leadership role in view of his forthcoming Harkness Fellowship.

The position of Survey and Planning Officer gave Shears opportunity to grow professionally. Responsibilities he undertook reveal Ramsay's trust in his junior colleague and his leadership potential. Shears was exposed to the gamut of administrative and educational knowledge, took action on school expansion, teacher training and professional development, and among the educational fraternity was considered a stalwart of research. In a reference for Shears Radford noted his 'unsparing capacity for hard work' and wrote:

> In the field of training teachers I have found his views realistic and forward-looking, and his knowledge of practices wide and deep. His experience in research work, and his desire to create policies resting on fact and on proved practices, have enabled him already to make useful and important contributions to both practice and planning in teacher-training.[379]

Within the spectrum of this and other activity family played a central part. Ritually, Saturday mornings belonged to Mavis and he was in charge of the kids. A second daughter, Meredith, was born in 1957. On school days Mark joined Christine at primary school and Paul (born in 1954) attended kindergarten. Mavis addressed the family's needs as well as maintaining her friendships and extended family links. As often as possible they visited Poppa Shears at the Myrtleford mill. Once divorced and once widowed, Ernie Shears had met Millicent Richardson in Myrtleford and she became his third wife. In 1956 there was a family surprise with the arrival of Anne, a much younger sister for Shears.

Time did not stand still; neither did Shears. Not yet 40, he fitted the criteria for a Harkness Fellowship, and with Mavis and their family of four, set off for the United States.

CHAPTER 11

# A HARKNESS FELLOW (1959–61)

*Life is like riding a bicycle. To keep your balance, you must keep moving.*

Albert Einstein

The appointment as Survey and Planning Officer was a valuable step in Shears' career. Not yet 40, he could view the spectrum of educational needs in areas where continued growth was forecast until at least the mid-'60s. Alert to major trends, he was able to conceive strategies to ease them but was concerned by the demands of the accelerating school population and its effect on the expanding building program, and by staff shortages in schools and teachers colleges. Coupled with the need to accelerate recruitment and train new teachers were concerns about the professional status and qualifications of those teachers. Aware of shortcomings in Victoria's system where the Education Department was both training authority and employer, Shears was involved in numerous debates. Departmental certification of teachers neither equated to nor held the prestige of university degrees. Shifting control of training for primary teachers to universities was a viable alternative; however critics argued that those selected as trainees lacked academic potential. The conversion of existing teachers colleges to degree-granting State colleges was an alternative but despite the gradual introduction of technical, science and arts departments and increased course duration, teachers college courses still lacked prestige. Shears believed departmental control should continue until three- or four-year training courses were established, leading to degrees.[380]

## Commonwealth Relations Trust

These thoughts stirred Shears as he planned his next steps. Enriched by experiences with the Institute of Education at the University of London he was keen to travel and pursue further studies abroad. The Commonwealth Fund offered that chance. Established in 1918 by an endowment from Anna Harkness, an American philanthropist who wanted to 'do something for the welfare of mankind', the Commonwealth Fund, from 1925 began an international program that offered graduates from British universities the chance to study in the United States of America. Called originally 'the Commonwealth Fund Fellowships', they later became the Harkness Fellowships.[381] The creation of Dominion Fellowships in 1927 and the Dominion Civil Service Fellowships in 1929 expanded the scheme to Australia, New Zealand, Canada and South Africa. The Dominion Fellowships were open to graduates under the age of 40 to study for 9 to 15 months in the USA. The London office of the Commonwealth Fund had handled applications for all awards until it formed the Australian Nomination Committee in 1953 when it appointed local correspondents in each State and the ACT. Sir Owen Dixon was the first Chairman of the Committee and among Executive Officers was H C Forster, Professor of Agriculture at the University of Melbourne. Forster was a former Fellowship recipient during 1935–36.[382] In 1958 he chaired the panel of three to select Fellows to study abroad the following year.

Shears' 12-page application detailed his employment history, listed his publications, explained the purpose of his proposed study and outlined a tentative program. Director Ramsay believed him 'very well qualified to undertake the study he has outlined'. Ramsay wrote in a reference:

> We have in the last ten years, increased our teacher training facilities four-fold and have increased the length of the courses of training. Future developments we are now considering would be helped by an intensive study of the organisation of teacher training in the United States of America. No such study has been undertaken by an officer of the Education Department since 1932, although we are familiar with practices in the other Australian States and the United Kingdom.

The exchange of knowledge between Australia and overseas was a vital aspect of educational development. Frank Tate as Director (1902–28) travelled extensively throughout the UK, Europe and the USA to study emerging trends. In successive years Directors and senior officers similarly experienced the benefits of travel and knowledge exchange. Ramsay supported Shears 'very strongly indeed. The Minister of Education, in view of the value of the proposed study, has agreed to grant leave on full pay to Dr Shears if his application was successful.'[383]

From a field of 64 applicants the panel would select just one. Aware of tough competition Shears sought the support of Miss Alice Hoy, Professor George Browne and Dr Bill Radford. Hoy had known Shears at University High School and Melbourne TC; Browne had supported his doctoral studies a decade prior and since observed his career development; and Radford, a mentor in many respects, shared common links with Shears through service at Bairnsdale High School and BEd theses that explored educational needs.[384] All were affiliated with the VIER and among the select group to found the Australian College of Education (ACE). Each identified Shears as a protégé whose success would reward their groundwork. While they believed the Harkness Fellowship would support his professional growth, more importantly it would enrich Victoria's broader educational community.

Miss Hoy noted Shears' 'unusually varied experience in education – as a primary teacher, secondary teacher, a teacher of adults (ex-servicemen's rural training scheme), a teachers college lecturer and as Survey and Planning Officer in the State Education Department.' She continued:

> … his personal knowledge of conditions and problems of Australian education at different levels and his experience as a student of education in England have been of considerable advantage to him.

Hoy identified Shears' leadership qualities, his scholarship and sporting achievements at University High School and described his 'considerable enterprise … clear mind and enormous diligence; qualities which have enabled him to get maximum benefit from his educational experiences'. She considered his 'cheerful and friendly manner' advantageous to his work and believed the opportunity to study abroad would lead to:

> ... an executive position such as vice principal or principal of a Teachers' College or a district inspector of schools, where he would be even better placed to influence thought and policy on primary teacher training and primary education..[385]

Browne, Emeritus Professor of Education at the University of Melbourne, acknowledged Shears' 'first class mind', noted him as 'one of the best organizers we have come across' with 'distinct possibilities of securing a very important educational post in Australia in the near future'. He stressed how Shears' enthusiasm had converted the VIER from a 'conventional program with a small membership ... into a dynamic force in the community' during his first term as Secretary. Browne highlighted Shears' contribution to research and steps to persuade the 'Australian Council for Research in Education to undertake the publication of an Australian Journal of Education, which was one of the best forward moves we have had in education recently'.[386]

## Forward planning

Shears had big ideas. He proposed to leave Melbourne on 26 August 1959, arrive in San Francisco on 16 September and criss-cross the United States from north to south and east to west. He believed taking the family would 'break down barriers and enable a closer examination of the schools, living habits, interests and ideals' of the people. He stressed 'at no time will my family be a liability on the Commonwealth Fund'. Based in San Francisco he would spend the bulk of time at Californian State colleges and campuses of the State university. Leaving the family 'domiciled in California' he would complete 'the six to eight weeks of first visits to teacher education and curriculum centres in the East'. This was 'sufficient duration to allow a careful collection of data', gain insight into institutional philosophies and people across the nation and observe their attitudes to education. His travels tallied with teachers' in-service summer training and in the final 8–10 weeks he planned to attend in-service education and curriculum workshops. A visit to the UK before returning home in January 1961 would enable him to review educational developments there.[387]

Prior to leaving Melbourne Shears wrote to E K Wickman, Director, Division of International Fellowships within the Commonwealth Fund, to arrange accommodation, seek advice regarding a car and finalise details. Shears suggested the 'survey nature of my investigation' would enhance the 'international aspect of the Fellowship', and asked if the travel allowance of $175 per month could be extended from three to six or eight months. He sought additional funds to cover photographic costs as he intended to 'lecture extensively of my experiences when I return to Australia'.[388]

Conscious of the USA's east–west divide Shears knew that his itinerary irked the Commonwealth Fund organisers. In their eyes, while there were benefits of the Californian location and contact with teacher educators there, immersion in Harvard University's Graduate School of Education had greater value. Rather than evaluate teacher education and California's State college system, Harvard in the east gave access to the nation's premier teacher-training institute.[389] Wickman identified Drs Clarence Faust and Alvin Eurich, President and Vice President of the Fund, and Dean Keppel of Harvard, as renowned leaders in teacher education. He said that contact with the National Education Association, the National Association for Supervision and Curriculum Development and the US Office of Education in New York would enhance the Harvard experience.[390] Adamant that Shears start in the east, Wickman stressed the 'concentration of national leaders' and advised a flexible program to 'visit people and consult with your particular interests'.

According to Wickman, recent developments 'bear importantly on your interests and will affect your planning'. Furthermore they 'will have national impact on teacher training'. He stressed 'the Ford Foundation has just made large grants to nine institutions for the advancement of teacher training'.[391] By 1957, the 'Fund for the Advancement of Education', a philanthropic organisation established by the Ford Foundation, had provided $57,000,000 to support experimental programs, and promised to advance education in schools and colleges. Believing teacher education was the core concern the Fund had contributed $4 million over each of the previous five years – half the Fund's total expenditure for that period. The 'recruitment of able people for teaching' was crucial, and cooperation among and between teacher training institutions and school systems was considered essential. Quantity and quality lay in the balance; as new sources of teachers were required to cope with rising birth rates and the extension of schooling, the meaning and purpose of formal education required close attention.[392]

In conclusion, Wickman warned, the family 'should not take precedence over or interfere with the plan for your Fellowship program'. He had arranged a station wagon costing $120 per month, and advised that a book and equipment allowance of $300 would be available on arrival.

Despite Wickman's views, Shears stuck to his guns and made California his base.

## The American scene

Planning an overseas study tour in 1959 was a lot more difficult than it is these days with access to the Internet. Shears drew upon his network of friends with travel experience and spent considerable time researching an itinerary. In the late 1950s many Australians recognised the USA primarily for its role in WWII, its major cities and its natural phenomena. The space race, civil rights protests, unrest in southeast Asia and the rise of John F Kennedy became prominent when television brought images into Australian lounge rooms. Little was known of the more remote locations Shears chose to visit. To understand life in the USA he called on Lou Barberis, friend since teachers college, to provide information. In 1957, as a Fulbright Scholar on an educational and cultural exchange, Barberis had taken his wife and two daughters to the USA. In his own circumstance, with Mavis and four children, Shears was 'a little concerned about the conditions the family and I would face'. He was thankful that:

> ... as always, Lou came to my aid. I prepared and sent quite a detailed questionnaire and in true Lou style he responded to

each of my questions in depth. Having an idea about the situation made it easier for Mavis and me to prepare for more than a year away. Lou, Mona and their family came back in 1958 and in 1959 we set off.[393]

The Shears set off in August. They flew from Melbourne's Essendon Airport to Sydney where they boarded *SS Mariposa* bound for San Francisco via the new State of Hawaii.[394] In Honolulu celebrations of Statehood and admission to the union were underway. During the 18-day voyage to San Francisco Shears discussed education in the USA with American travellers on board. On arrival in San Francisco, the family was greeted by Stewart Morton, a Harkness Fellow of 1959, and a small group of friends. Morton had organised accommodation at 2265 Vine Street, Berkeley, an easy walk to the University of California, Berkeley. Schools for Christine and Mark within the Berkeley Unified School District offered insight into California's State regional structure. The three elder children were granted permission to enrol in school. Mark attended Whittier Elementary School where he was among 28 in Grade 3 with advanced reading skills. Paul attended the afternoon kindergarten session. Christine joined over 400 seventh-grade pupils at Garfield Junior High. Named after President James A Garfield, later renamed to honour Martin Luther King, the school had a total enrolment of 1,400.[395]

The educational scene in the USA was in a state of flux. National and international events of the 1950s had triggered curriculum reform. Russia's launch of Sputnik had created alarm and the Vietnam War was causing concern. The turn of the decade was a troubling time. In 1954 public schools were racially desegregated, and though the American Teachers' Association endorsed a 'spirit of good will and fair play', civil unrest remained. President Dwight Eisenhower maintained power for the Republican Party but in preparation for the 1960 elections John F Kennedy was gaining Democrat ground. Across the nation, educational reforms required teacher trainees to spend more time in classrooms to observe good practice and develop their skills. New professional standards were mooted across elementary, secondary and junior college levels as well as in the ranks of administration.

Counter to advice Shears located himself in the west. At the

University of California's Berkeley campus he had post-doctoral research fellow status and a small office. This was the hub from where he visited other educational institutions and met educators of national renown. Among them were William Brownell, Dean of the School of Education at Berkeley, who had a passion for research and educational leadership; Dr Simpson, Director of the State Department of Education in Sacramento, who outlined the administrative structure of California's State colleges; and Superintendent Wennerberg of the local Berkeley District. Wennerberg administered eleven schools and employed 500 teachers and an executive staff of 100. He encouraged racial integration and equal rights and offered Shears valuable insights into educational organisation. Each school had its own set of governing powers, and significant lay influence on control of the school boosted public interest in governance. As in Australia, teacher recruitment failed to meet demand. Californian superintendents made an annual trek east to entice graduates from Midwest and Southern states. They were 'armed with higher salary schedules and the lure of the climate'.[396] State funding was another critical issue but a Bill before Congress promised to finance 'the staggering increases needed' in school buildings and teachers' salaries, which lay beyond the capacity of the State and local districts.[397]

In mid-October Shears flew east 'to New York by Boeing 707, 3000 miles in five hours with barely a ripple in the plane or noise from the engines and stretched below in quick succession the Sierras; the Rocky Mountains; the Great Plains of Kansas, Nebraska and Iowa; Chicago and Lake Michigan; the Alleghenies; and New York'. The proposed eight-week tour took a strange turn when he met Wickman at the Commonwealth Fund headquarters in New York and was introduced to Dr Alvin Eurich of the Ford Foundation. Throughout the USA philanthropic investment in education was big business, with Ford as a major contributor, together with the Carnegie Corporation and the Rockefeller and Kellogg Foundations. In 1960 Ford made grants of $9,161,010 to nine centres to fund teacher preparation programs. Emphasis was placed on general/liberal education, mastery of subject-matter fields, internships, team teaching and other school improvements.[398] Upon Eurich's invitation, Shears joined a gathering of Deans of Education in Aspen, Colorado. In that single location he met a significant body of leading educationists whose diverse philosophies and knowledge enriched his entire Harkness experience.

In Aspen Shears renewed acquaintance with Dr Freeman Butts of Teachers College, Columbia University, who had been in Australia as a Fulbright Scholar in 1954. He met Dean Francis Keppel of the Harvard Graduate School, whose 'Master of Arts in Teaching Program' had become 'a model for teacher training'. He also met Dr Stinett of the National Education Association, an advocate for teachers' certification and accreditation, and Dr Hall of the Federal Office of Education, who sought social, economic and educational equity. Others he met were Dean Chase and Professor Giesecke of the University of Washington who proposed a six-year course of teacher preparation; Dr John Goodlad, Professor of Education and Director of the School of Education, University of California, Los Angeles (UCLA), who sought to improve school and classroom culture; and Dean Stiles from the University of Wisconsin (Madison), who encouraged collaboration among principals, teachers and college staff in developing a new teacher education curriculum.

Matters discussed resembled those in Victoria. Teacher shortages were prevalent, especially in mathematics and sciences, school populations had burgeoned as students stayed longer at school and among the teacher workforce some lacked suitable qualifications. Throughout the nation, since Sputnik's flight in 1957, interest rose in teaching Russian, and television was considered a new teaching medium.[399] Technology was changing the focus of and approach to education. Despite the need to forge ahead it was impossible to forecast the scope of change. Within these debates Shears was enthused. The opportunity to intersect with the 20 deans 'was the beginning of a unique experience in which I was able to talk freely for five days with professors away from the distractions of their office and to obtain a summary of what they considered were the fundamental issues in teacher education in the USA'.[400] It was:

> ... a magnificent experience because all the people that I wanted to see in teacher education were there. When I went around during the rest of that 12 months I had already bro-

ken the ice, so didn't have to establish a relationship ... the break came my way in the early part of my period there.[401]

Commonwealth Fund authorities noted the value of Shears' trip east and applauded his participation in Aspen, but remained disturbed that he was based in the west. They urged him to spend more time at Harvard, New York and Washington to gain a broad national outlook. Furthermore they failed to recognise his energy and capacity to gather detail while seemingly just skimming the surface. Wickman's comments were not complimentary when he wrote, 'he talks, he thinks, in the way he writes – about minutiae. Every plan of work or travel, every topic is broken into parts, the parts into particles, the particles into fragments ... and anywhere along the line he may be tempted to total recall or free association.' By November, he noted, Shears had examined 28 institutions in 28 days and intended to evaluate each. He wrote scathingly, 'Somehow he manages in the end an orderly loading of the freight, he assembles his freight cars from the network of sidetracks, and pulls his train triumphantly along the main line. Were he in the employ of a railroad, he would be a good traffic manager, overlooking the details.'[402]

Unaware of criticism Shears immersed himself in California's educational culture and kept abreast of developments there. In Sacramento he met with representatives of the State colleges, the California Teachers' Association, the University of California and the California Association of School Administrators, who were considering five-year training for teachers.[403] Among other issues debated were parallels with problems at home. He sought to understand the *Master Plan for Higher Education in California: 1960–75*, the culmination of a decade-long process to address future needs. Shears reflected, 'I was right in the thick of it. I visited every State college in California and the University of California. I watched while cohorts from the University of California completed their contribution to the survey of needs that was the basis for the Master Plan.' Despite the lengthy process, 'I was impressed by the momentum; in December the Governor banged his gavel; it was in the House in February and implemented in June'.[404] The Master Plan identified a 'general mission and governance structure for each of the three public higher education segments (what we know in

2014 as the University of California, the California State University system, and the California Community Colleges), and the governance and purpose of a new Coordinating Council for Higher Education.'[405] The layered system was graded by rank, each with its own set of accountabilities:

> The University of California was the premier place for research, graduate and professional education. The State colleges, administered by the State Director and his divisional chiefs embraced teachers' colleges in 1935 and from 1949 had granted masters' degrees. Junior colleges, *controlled by the local school district should admit 'any high school graduate plus any person over 18 years of age who is capable of profiting by the instruction offered', offering courses for 13th and 14th year of schooling leading to an associateship in arts or science.* They poured millions into the junior colleges and interestingly enough it was sustained. They had given all to the analysis of the needs and statistics in respect to populations and came up with this decision.[406]

Junior colleges offered general studies as well as school-to-work transition courses and vocational and technical education. Third- or fourth-year levels gave access to university or State college. The University of California admitted the top 12.5 per cent of high school graduates into bachelor, master or doctoral degrees for study and research in traditional and non-traditional fields. The top third admitted to the State colleges pursued civic and vocational competence. State college degrees held lesser rank than universities as Shears explained:

> ... they did not offer advanced graduate degrees, undertake major research activities, or train in the older professions. Their 4- to 6-year courses led to a bachelor's or master's degree in teacher training or liberal arts, occupational training, pre-professional study, adult education and community service.[407]

The Master Plan influenced Shears and became influential in his aspirations to establish the State College of Victoria, to enhance teacher education and to introduce youth policies.

A trip to the Midwest in February and March had a double agenda.

The sights were spectacular and the university visits profitable. The notion of group dynamics intrigued Dr W Wattenberg, Professor of Psychology at Wayne State University in Michigan, who obtained a microfilm copy of Shears' thesis from the Institute of Education in London.[408] At Ball State Teachers College in Indiana, Dean Richard Burkhardt was a leader in cross-cultural learning and modern languages. The University of Michigan was the philosophical home of John Dewey, the educational reformer, who advocated experiential education, problem solving, critical thinking and cooperative learning. Led by Dean Stiles, the School of Education at the University of Wisconsin (Madison) was renowned for its education, teacher preparation and internship program wherein trainees experienced a year of guided teaching before they graduated. Dr Moon, Dean of Iowa State Teachers' College, held similar ideals and placed trainee groups in schools for consecutive weeks to observe, to teach and to gain responsibility gradually.

Time did not stand still; neither did Shears. On his return to California he attended conferences held by the Council on Teacher Education (31 March–2 April) and the California Teachers' Association in Alisomar (8–10 April). Then via the Southern states he travelled east to attend the 75th Annual Convention, Association for Health, Physical Education and Recreation at Miami Beach (19 April–3 May). Records of his comings and goings show him returning to the University of California in May and in June he went to San Diego to attend back-to-back conferences of State Directors of Teacher Education and the National Commission on Teacher Education and Professional Standards (24–27 June).

An obligation of Harkness Fellows was to travel for three months. For Shears the Harkness directive provided the opportunity to mix with America's educational elite and observe the education system nationwide. It offered the chance to meet American people and see the expansive country. Late in June he and the family left California. En route to New York they travelled across the northern states and southern Canadian provinces. The tour integrated popular and out-of-the-way places with centres of educational interest. They experienced the beauty of Crater Lake, Yellowstone and Great Smoky Mountains

National Parks; Rushmore National Monument; and Niagara Falls. Shears made calls at Humboldt State College in northern California; Portland State College in Oregon; the University of British Columbia in Canada; the University of Wisconsin (Madison); and the University of Chicago in Illinois.[409] A cable from Max Dimmack, received in Detroit, Michigan, congratulated Shears on his appointment as principal-elect of Burwood Teachers College.[410]

## The Fellowship reviewed

In New York Wickman met Shears to discuss the experience and receive his report. Though Shears' verve to complete a seemingly irrational tour had baffled administrators they noted, 'he seems to have managed his cross-country drive with his large family in grand style. I can only admire such organisational skills'.[411] Administrators considered him 'competent and articulate within his field of interest – teacher training', and in contrast to earlier comments they suggested 'he will make quite an impact in that field after his return to Australia'.[412]

Shears recorded his accomplishments in his report. He stressed that his intention had been to observe the 'methods and organization of teacher education in the USA', and examine public, private and Catholic sectors. His analysis of teacher education in the USA presented a comparative and critical review. He acknowledged its attributes, noted shortfalls and identified possible corrective measures. He conceded the value of additional academic study but cautioned against any extension beyond four years with just six months' professional training. He warned against plunging graduates into a classroom with little professional knowledge. Understanding the quandary regarding end-on or parallel approaches he suggested end-on courses are dislocated from practical teaching. Parallel studies synthesised theory with practical aspects of teaching. Principal-elect of Burwood Teachers College, Shears understood effective 'intern' programs required 'professional courses, further academic study and practical teaching [to be] closely linked'. [413]

The family's presence had been contentious but Shears claimed they brought additional insight into the people, their culture and politics. His horizons broadened beyond the professional as he observed schooling 'through the children'. He observed education at tertiary levels 'through the teacher education programs and the organizational structure' and noted, 'American teacher educators are active, experimental and original'. The use of television as a teaching tool shaped his thoughts on technology while team teaching and administrative support in schools influenced his thinking. The involvement of faculty members, relationships between the university and training institutions, and the increasing complexity of courses would influence initiatives at Burwood.

The Fellowship experience compounded Shears' philosophies but in concluding the report he considered 'perhaps I am too close to the year's activity to express my feelings in true perspective'. He continued, 'At the moment I can say that for my wife, my four children and myself it has been a wonderful and exhilarating experience.' It was 'first class in terms of allowing me to find out all about administration in the various states, particularly California'. He thanked Wickman and the Commonwealth Fund organisers and before leaving New York delivered the station wagon with 30,000 miles clocked up.[414]

## Homeward bound

Under the auspices of the Education Department Shears and the family journeyed home via the United Kingdom. He explained, Director Ramsey 'was anxious that I had a look at what was going on in Britain'. They flew from New York to Glasgow on a Scandinavian Air Systems (SAS) flight on 23 August and then travelled by train to London. Lady Dorothy Radley was delighted to see Mavis, Christine and Mark once more and meet the two younger children. Sir Gordon, who had recently converted the British television system for transmission to the USA for Princess Margaret's wedding, approved of Shears' career development. The two men discussed common and specific issues facing education in the UK, the USA and Australia, and pondered the future use of technology. In the Radley family home, Meredith, Mark and Paul shared a room. Jennifer Radley moved into the study, leaving her room for Christine. Jennifer and Christine attended school together, Mark was placed in a Grade 3–4 and Paul went to Miss Bishop's kindergarten.

From the Agent-General's Office where he was based, Shears visited local education authorities (LEAs) across Britain. He travelled as far north as Scotland and returned to many places he had visited a decade before. The face of British education was changing with expansion of the tertiary sector. Prior to the Robbins Report of 1963 was the push to equate institutes of technology with universities and extend tertiary education to a broader public. This impinged on philosophies behind the 11-plus examination wherein schooling was divided into primary, secondary and tertiary sectors. The secondary sector comprised grammar, technical and secondary modern schools. Students were graded according to their 11-plus results, which determined their educational pathway. Shears contemplated these developments and throughout his career attempted to provide broad educational opportunities.

Like their travels across the USA, homeward the journey was complex. 'Aeroplanes, buses and trains,' Christine recalls, and the aeroplanes were 'very noisy and bumpy'. She associates the visit to Denmark with Anderson's Little Mermaid and remembers Poland as poverty-stricken and grey. In Greece the Parthenon impressed her as did the warmth and golden beaches of Athens. The family travelled through Africa where, staying on a farm in Rhodesia with family friends, Christine saved a little yellow bird. She remembers 'large parks with hartebeests running away … so comical with their tails up'. Mark's memories were of travelling 'down to Kenya, and then to South Africa and at Capetown we took *Dominion Monarch* back to Perth. We got picked up in a Rolls Royce and then flew back to Melbourne.'[415]

They arrived on Mavis' birthday, 5 January, and after the excitement of their welcome settled down in their Black Rock home. Mark and Paul attended the local primary school, Meredith began kindergarten and Christine started her secondary schooling at Korowa Church of England Girls' Grammar School (CEGGS). The school's musical tradition enhanced her talent as a flautist. Shears was often asked why he did not choose government schools for his children's secondary education. Retrospectively he suggested they may have been singled out, or bullied, being the son or daughter of a senior educationist. Even then he had his mind on the future and saw an escalating career.

Shears returned to the survey and planning team until he took up his appointment as Principal of Burwood TC in April 1961. In the hands of Bill McKinty the team had worked well. In April McKinty took over as Survey and Planning Officer and Shears took over at Burwood TC.

Table 7. People and institutions in the USA that influenced Shears' thinking

| Institution | Dates | Contact | Influence/Qualities |
|---|---|---|---|
| **Stage 1: California** | 10 Sep–11 Oct | | |
| University of California–Berkeley | 21–22 Sep | Dean W Brownell | Educational research–arithmetic; human/cognitive learning; national leadership; humanity |
| Berkeley City Unified School District | 23–25 Sep | Supt W Wennerberg (Supt of Schools 1958–64) | Racial integration; equal rights |
| **Stage 2: East and Midwest** | 12 Oct–1 Nov | | |
| Brown University, Providence, Rhode Island | 14 Oct | Professor Elmer Smith | Summer institutes; 1959: The Brown Plan for Teacher Education (Ford Foundation)–teacher recruitment and preparation; professional services to schools; help public resolve educational issues; interns in schools enabled teachers to complete further study |
| Harvard | 14–16 Oct | Francis Keppel, appointed Dean, Harvard Graduate School, 1948, youngest dean ever, only 32 | Teacher preparation; advanced study–Master of Arts (Elementary education); research; period of expansion; introduced TV into education; US Commissioner of Education (1962–65)–Elementary and Secondary Education Act 1965; oversaw Civil Rights in schools (1964); keen to bring in scholars from outside education |
| Ford Foundation | 19 Oct | Alvin Eurich, Executive Director (1958–64) | First president of the State University of New York (1949), assigned to bring 32 State-supported colleges under a single State university system; President Ford Fund for the Advancement of Education; President Aspen Institute for Humanistic Studies (1963–72) |
| Columbia Teachers College | 19 Oct | R Freeman Butts | |

*Laying Foundations*

| | | | |
|---|---|---|---|
| University of Chicago, Illinois | 22 Oct | Dr Kenneth Rehage | Developed undergraduate teacher training; concern for influence of teachers on students; Director Pakistan Education Program–established 43 secondary schools and educational centres at Dacca and Punjab universities |
| University of Chicago, Illinois | 22 Oct | Dr John Goodlad (1960–Prof of Ed and Director, School of Ed, UCLA) | Advocated progressive education; school and classroom culture and climate; curriculum; attitudes; 'school renewal'; identified 12 goals of American schools |
| University of Colorado, Boulder | 30 Oct | Dean Stephen Romine | '… leave it better than you found it'; concerns: accountability; instructional loads in secondary schools; subject combinations, teacher shortages |
| **Stage 3: California** | 1 Nov–7 Feb | | |
| San Francisco State College | 25 Nov | Dr Robert Smith | |
| **Stage 4: Midwest** | 8 Feb–6 Mar | | |
| University of Michigan, Ann Arbor | 16 Feb | | John Dewey, Professor of Philosophy here 1884–94, left imprint–'spirit of inquiry'; 'difference brought about by individuals, not institutions; 4-site campus divided by Huron River–swamp to Lake Erie |
| Wayne State University, Michigan | 17 Feb | Dr W Wattenberg (Professor of Psychology) | 'All men are created equal'; middle-school classroom management; discipline by influences on group; sharp variance and change in intellectual growth and emotional adjustment; knowledge of 'forces of change' only fragmentary |
| Ball State Teachers College, Indiana | 24–25 Feb | Dean Richard Burkhardt | Modern languages; cross-cultural learning; history |
| University of Wisconsin (Madison) | 28 Feb–1 Mar | Dean Lindley Joseph Stiles | Educating and preparing teachers to suitable standard; accreditation–teachers, institutions; first Research School of Ed in world; developed 'internship'–'real learners'; Wisconsin–'one of the finest places in the country for the preparation of teachers–Acting Dean, Harvard, Judson Shaplin; 'The best should teach'–Stiles' motto |
| Iowa State Teachers College, Cedar Falls | 4–5 Mar | Dr A Moon | Professional laboratory experiences of teacher trainees–period of guided teaching with increasing responsibility while working with a group for consecutive weeks; observation, participation, teaching. |

| | | | |
|---|---|---|---|
| **Stage 5: California** | 7 Mar–18 Apr | | |
| Fresno State College | 14–15 Mar | Dean D Albright | Mentoring–article |
| San Fernando Valley State College | 17 Mar | Dr Ewing Konold | Passion for education, dedicated life to help teachers with needs and problems. |
| University of Southern California | 22 Mar | Dean Irving Melbo | Authority on organisation and structure of school districts; wrote *Social Psychology of Education* (1937) |
| Long Beach State College | 29–30 Mar | President C McIntosh | Challenged by increasing enrolments, dramatic growth–keep up with faculty, staff and facilities to serve students; help those with greatest needs; cultural integration–race, religion, nationality; built up college in 'boom' time; defended tuition-free education 'voice in dark'; dealt with activism–mid 1960s–negotiate, not panic |
| Conference: California Council on Teacher Education | 31 Mar–2 April | | |
| Conference: California Teachers' Association–Alisomar | 8–10 Apr | Dr F Hile | |
| **Stage 6: Deep South** | 19 Apr –3 May | | |
| 75 Annual Convention: Assoc for Health, Physical Ed and Recreation, Miami Beach, Florida | | | Importance of health education in the curriculum |
| **Stage 7: California** | 4May–27 Jun | | |
| University of California–Berkeley School of Education | 4 May –17 Jun | | Philosophies of teacher education; structure of state college system |

# CHAPTER 12

# THE GOLDEN YEARS AT BURWOOD TEACHERS COLLEGE (1961–69)

*Hide not your talents, they for use were made,*
*What's a sundial in the shade?*

Benjamin Franklin

Remember the weeks of preparation that went into the Burwood Statement? Remember the call for, and the preparation of new courses which would bring us out of the years of complacency? They were the years of provocation – remember the startled reaction to the Statement that our methods of examination themselves required examination, that (heaven preserve us!) our examination papers were too stereotyped and were in need of an overhaul? They were the years of good fellowship, of sparkling conversation; knowing that one was a member of a closely knit and purposeful group; years of knowing that one's loyalty was well placed, and that Lawrie was as loyal to the members of his team as they were to him.

Yes! Lawrie could be relied on for the freshness and variety of his ideas, for the leadership and friendship given both to staff and students; and, in the long term, it was his warmth and friendship which remained as something to be treasured.[416]

The dawn of the new decade challenged educators globally. In Australia W F Connell, Professor of Education at the University of New South Wales, described a time of mounting economic, social and political interests as moving 'underneath the surface "down under" … one can feel the first stirrings of the irresistible forces of change that promise to transform beyond recognition not only a vast continent but its people.'[417] Expressing agreement in the inaugural Buntine Oration in 1962, Peter Karmel, Professor of Economics at the University of Adelaide, allied education to economic productivity. Vital components of a skilled workforce were 'ingenuity and inventiveness of technologists and scientists'. Education, a major factor of economic growth, was a valuable tool for 'accelerating the flow of ideas – ranging from minor brain waves to scientific discoveries, from managerial tricks to philosophies of social organization'. Increasing opportunity from primary to tertiary levels underpinned the flow of ideas. In turn, technological and administrative innovation would enhance the education system and proffer the nation a skilled workforce.[418] Karmel stressed:

> ... there must be a considerable increase over a number of years in the share of our resources devoted to education. On this there are no restraints other than those we ourselves impose.[419]

Karmel urged additional funding and long-term planning but warned 'a large increase in educational output cannot be achieved overnight'. Two years prior, delegates at the National Education Conference similarly called for additional funding. Premier Heffron of New South Wales claimed, 'If we are going to survive as a nation we must educate our people.' He argued, 'We spent a million pounds a day to carry the war to a successful conclusion. If we could do that then, in these piping times of peace we can do a better job than we are doing by way of providing finance for education.' He continued, 'This is a problem that belongs not only to the States but to the Commonwealth as well.'[420] In further debate Dr Robert Madgwick, Vice Chancellor of the University of New England, warned of a snowball effect throughout the entire education system if sufficient money were not available. He advised:

> ... without sufficient primary teachers of sufficient calibre, our secondary schools receive inadequately prepared pupils; without rapidly increased expenditure in the secondary schools, the universities will receive insufficient students – and these inadequately trained and educated; without suf-

ficient students there will come from universities too few science teachers – and these inadequately trained by universities inadequately staffed and equipped – and too few research workers and recruits for industry and government service.[421]

Madgwick stressed, 'our age is unique – never before in history have technical changes, and the social and moral issues they raise, been communicated so universally over such wide areas of the work'. While they have 'revolutionized our thinking about industrial, economic and social development' education remained 'tragically starved of funds – and of the buildings and equipment money could buy'. He feared 'loss of standards' and warned, 'competition for manpower from a dynamic expanding economy means that we cannot attract enough teachers to keep pace with the growing pupil and student population'.[422]

In Victoria the tides of leadership turned as Alex McDonell replaced Alan Ramsay, the Director who had led the education system through a decade of rapid growth. In tribute, Education Minister John Bloomfield acknowledged Ramsay's 'single mindedness', 'conscientiousness and absorption in what he was doing'. Ramsay's response expressed his ongoing faith in the schools and the teachers' commitment and reflected on his privilege to serve:

> … at a time of rapid development, to help gear up the machine to meet demands made on service since the war. In ten years the number of schools has trebled … There has been development in the training of our teachers … we have facilities for the establishment of a three years' course when the present colleges are developed to their fullest potential.[423]

The Ramsay Report of 1960 was a blueprint for Victoria's educational future. It identified that more money was vital for ongoing expansion and called for action to boost building programs for new and existing teachers colleges. However, entry standards remained a dilemma, particularly for secondary recruits. Post-matriculation three-year courses would raise academic standards but the serious shortage and demands on the present infrastructure made this unfeasible; hence a secondary teachers college at Monash University was a priority. The report claimed that courses of study should 'prepare children for a changing world' with teachers and schools increasingly involved 'in determining their content and methods of teaching'. Acknowledging that education should offer the 'fullest opportunity for every child' the report identified regional differences among the children in Corryong, Footscray, Montrose or Mansfield. Regardless of ability, aptitude, mental or physical ability, distance from school or location, equal opportunity was the ideal premise.[424]

Throughout his term Ramsay had endeavoured to increase recruitment, accelerate building programs and improve conditions in schools yet despite foresight and effort the Education Department was admonished for lethargy in planning ahead. Members of the Victorian Teachers' Union (VTU) and the Victorian Secondary Teachers' Association (VSTA) continued to agitate to boost recruitment and train better-qualified teachers, advance buildings programs and provide better work conditions.[425] Ron Reed, Director of Secondary Education (DSE), noted the impact of policy trickling through to the welfare of the child. He firmly believed the government held responsibility to organise policy and finances to satisfy the community's wishes in respect to education, arguing:

> It is the responsibility of the Education Department, to give leadership in education to the schools and to provide the teachers, buildings and equipment needed for their proper functioning, within these limits of policy and finance; it is the responsibility of the principal to establish in his school the conditions under which teachers may do their best work; and it is the responsibility of the teacher to so organise his classroom and his work that his pupils are enabled to make the best progress of which they are capable.[426]

From this environment Ramsay moved on, McDonell stepped in and Shears took his next career step. The Education Department continued to grow and, despite forward planning, found it hard to satisfy demands. Increasing intakes of new teachers and re-employment of those not currently serving barely met replacement needs caused by resignation, retirement or death let alone catering for ongoing growth in student numbers. Shears advocated the need to boost primary teacher graduates to 1,200 annually although admitting three-year training and class-size reduction would reduce the effectiveness of the increased number.[427]

Ripe for his next leadership role Shears remained enthused by the Harkness experience and enriched with knowledge of education in the USA and the UK. As he stood on the threshold of his new position, education systems across the globe prepared for the challenge ahead. American educators Spaulding and Meindl spoke of professional standards of teachers, an endemic problem requiring review. They claimed, 'we hope to make progress for our profession. Progress is not achieved by inaction'.[428] The thoughts of Shears similarly aspired to these ideals. Equipped with knowledge from abroad he stepped readily into his principalship at Burwood TC. Situated in Melbourne's outer east it was one of the State's eleven government teachers colleges. His tendrils were extending across the education spectrum. The appointment to Burwood fulfilled both Alice Hoy's prediction of his leadership potential and his next career step.[429]

Teacher training was Shears' focus. Believing the colleges were 'centres of ideas' he sought depth and consistency in course content and exposure of student teachers to the classroom. As with doctors and nurses, careful guidance was the key. He drew on his own teaching experience and recent observations in the USA and the UK. He was alert to Freeman Butts' challenge to 'permit' and 'encourage every child to climb up the educational ladder as far as his talents would take him. The dull, the normal, and the brilliant all need special attention.' Moves were afoot that 'trainee teachers master a professional body of knowledge and actual professional skill in practice'.[430] Butts believed would-be teachers [and administrators] deserved more than accumulated hints on subject matter and methods with short classroom stints. They deserved general and professional training that presented 'the foundations of education, a major field of competence, and a period of induction to teaching experience'.[431]

Agitation was rising regarding qualifications and standards. Within Victoria's growing secondary sector the system failed to differentiate between two- and three-year certificate courses for primary, infant and secondary training and university graduates who completed a fourth year DipEd. The skewed professional stakes between primary and secondary bothered Shears. He agreed with Butts that 'primary school teachers should have as much and as high-quality preparation as secondary school teachers',[432] and detested proposals to compartmentalise teachers according to their expertise with particular age levels. Believing it folly that one group should hold greater importance he refuted beliefs that primary teachers knew about children whereas secondary teachers knew about subject matter. He contended, 'in all teaching and therefore in all education, the teacher, the child and the relationship between them is as fundamental as the subject matter concerned'.[433]

## Burwood Teachers College

At Burwood TC, Don Waller, the first principal, had established firm foundations. Waller's leadership had been admirable. Staff valued the opportunities he afforded. He was 'a quiet man' with a 'very, very dry sense of humour' and 'tremendous capacity to let people go' if they had something to offer. Publications on art, English and music education had put Burwood 'on the map, not only in Victoria, but Australia and worldwide'. He had encouraged students, to 'set your course for the stars … see them clearly and follow a purposeful course'.[434] Burwood had become 'an exciting place with a sound reputation in its seven-year history'.[435] On the brink of the new era, the Burwood community reflected on Waller's 'fair-mindedness, wisdom and devotion to duty [that] inspired all who knew him'.[436] They saw the dichotomy between old and new: the staid, fatherly and encouraging Waller with the small, lithe and lively, energetic and effervescent replacement.

Shears' arrival roused 'anticipation and pleasure. He was well known amongst the educationists and teacher trainers'.[437] He was seen as 'intelligent, only a small man, he was physically active and skilful at sport and had the most persuasive manner … he got the best out of people'.[438] He acknowledged Waller's fine leadership and was encouraged by the bright, enthusiastic staff. As the new principal-cum-family man he had notable credentials but his skills were not yet tested. Aged 39, he had bypassed many on the promotional ladder, which led to jealousy by some members of the Education Department. On paper Shears had impressive credentials with three degrees and a doctorate.

Though direct teaching experience in Korong Vale, Bairnsdale and the RTC, and in England, were more than a decade past he had knowledge of teaching, and had lectured at Toorak and Burwood TCs and throughout the UK. To his credit he was abreast of developments in teacher training in the USA and the UK and aware of what schools in Victoria required. As Burwood's principal he became a member of the Primary Teachers College Principals' Association. Among colleagues were Len Pryor at Toorak, Len Whiteoak at Geelong, Ida Lowndes at Coburg and Warwick Eunson at Frankston The association promoted the status of teachers colleges in general but particularly those preparing primary teachers, and argued strongly for improved course length and depth.

On 27 April 1961 Lawrence William Shears became Burwood TC's second principal. It was a juggling act keeping pace with ongoing educational growth, settling in to college life and taking charge of 400 students and 57 staff while maintaining his family role and broader interests. Students attending the welcome assembly observed a sprightly young man. With formalities complete he perched on a chair to flap his arms and cluck as they sang 'chick chick, chick, chick chicken, lay an egg for me … chick, chick, chick, chick, chicken lay one for my tea …' While he became at one with the group he had to prove himself.

Living in residence the Shears children became popular with staff and trainees. They had space to play and the younger three walked to nearby Bennettswood State School, No. 4693. With the family all at school, Mavis enrolled in Matriculation English and prepared for tertiary studies. Each morning as he walked to his office Shears chatted with groups of students who lounged on the lawns. Between daily appointments he walked along the wide linoleum corridors to view the college in action and at day's end took the dog for a walk to check all was secure. Despite apprehension among some older colleagues, the young principal gained their respect and the Burwood community welcomed his accessibility. Though 'a prodigious worker' he had time to listen and over the years offered personal and professional support to staff and students alike. He welcomed all, whether to seek advice, share their vision or express concern. Shears became a good friend to many and was often considered one of the lads who shared a joke or had a kick. Music lecturer Chris Limb stomping into his office to state a grievance, banged on the desk with both fists. 'Lawrie took it', didn't flinch, 'a lot of principals wouldn't. He certainly didn't hold it against me or reprimand me.' The trait of knowing 'who was who' in a group or at a function held Shears in good stead. He paid attention to detail and made a point of knowing his colleagues and their professional backgrounds. New staff member Graham Corr was delighted when his rural teaching experience was acknowledged.[439]

Staff selection in the 1960s posed problems. As Pryor had claimed, the number and quality of secondary graduates was a determining factor. Burwood staff members in 1954 were a select group, several recalled that they were 'plucked from the system' and others were there by chance. Due to a fire in his school, art teacher Leon Jackman sought another position. He heard of the vacancy at Burwood and applied immediately.[440] Like others he was young, little older than college students, but he accepted the role in the post-secondary setting, and was required to support his young charges. Aware of this, Shears supported Jackman and other young staff in finding their professional feet.

Shears maintained routines established by Waller, which reflected those of Principal Law at Melbourne TC. Students were divided into clusters of 30 and with two lecturers appointed as tutors, they established friendships and received support and guidance. Lectures, assignments, tests and teaching rounds punctuated college life. Teaching methods, child development, philosophies of learning, approaches to assessment, remediation and classroom practice were part of the structured tuition program and supervised experience in schools. Easing into their roles as teachers, students moved gradually from an observational role to conducting lessons and assessing students' learning.

Fundamental to good teacher training was the relationship between the training schools and the institution. In California Shears had noted disconnection between the teacher training institute and the practising schools, a weakness that he described as 'ridiculous!'. From his own experience and now as a teacher educator he sought to establish a firm link (or consolidate the link) between the college and training schools. To ensure successful training and a smooth transition to a teaching career, college and school staffs collaborated. Lecturers liaised between individuals in their group and the schools. The Burwood Model, as it became known, was pivotal and building the link was vital. Hence, three times a year school principals and infant mistresses met with college staff. Following social interaction Chris Limb recalled 'reporting what was going on in the college and what we would like them to do. The practice schools were an integral part of the teacher education program; the institution and training schools felt as though they were one.'[441]

Tutor group interaction assisted students' social and personal adjustment and their transition to adulthood.[442] It also encouraged positive experiences, and supported the development of leadership skills and roles in student governance. Secondary teacher trainers doubted the Burwood Model applied to their specialist fields. Not afraid to speak out, Shears claimed contact between staff and schools was fundamental to all teacher training. The reality of the model's success was the relationship between specialist teachers, college staff and the school; hence the secondary training institution should:

> ... get the teachers of English, the teachers of geography, and other subjects in contact with the people who conducted the schools. Physical contact with the buildings of the training institution and the people working in them would benefit both. They would work together. I do not think it is beyond the wit of human beings to handle such an arrangement.[443]

The tension between primary- and secondary-qualified teachers remained contentious. Not only was primary training considered less prestigious, but teachers graduating from primary teachers colleges were ranked lower on the Classified Roll. Shears objected. He argued that trainee primary teachers were among the most intelligent of their age groups with average ability equal to university entrants. Though in the 1960s the number of matriculants was increasing, in 1958 only one-third of all teachers college entrants had attempted matriculation.

Eager to boost the status of courses and unite staff Shears introduced the Burwood Statement. Staff worked in faculty groups to specify course aims and objectives. Enthusiasm was amazing, he recalled, and vigour was sustained throughout. While planning ahead was the ultimate goal, the activity united staff, and boosted morale as clear goals enhanced college courses and staff confidence in what they were teaching. Retrospectively, Shears lamented that the Statement was not officially published; however he achieved his goal to generate energy, and attain valuable input from the united faculty groups.

The college timetable operated on the platoon system that Shears experienced as a trainee teacher at Melbourne TC. On Community Wednesdays when all students were present they divided into their tutor groups to share experiences. They later joined club activities and took part in their selected sport.

At morning assembly they sang the Burwood College Anthem *Animum, Cultum, Parabo* with passion; *Bush Night Song* with serenity; the *Stein Song* with vigour; and *Goodbye* with a tinge of sadness, especially when there were exiting students. In weekly addresses Shears stressed the importance of personal wellbeing in the teacher's complex task. The college program 'takes account of your needs as developing persons who will become successful teachers, citizens and scholars', he said. He promoted philosophies of Martin Buber and Arthur Jersild, which lay at the heart of teaching. 'In any teaching situation there is the teacher and the child, the subject matter and the relationship between them. The greatest joy comes in *I – Thou* relationships in which you answer for the need of others.'[444]

Academic and social events in the college program gave students room to grow and promoted personal confidence that in turn enhanced their teaching. Ultimately they would share the moment of ecstasy, as Buber described, when 'the Holy Spark' leapt across the gap. Fundamental to meaningful teacher–child relationships such 'moments' were shared from a personal perspective and from that of the child.[445] At assemblies, and in later years, Shears recited:

> A dog has looked at you, you answer for its glance
> A child has held your hand, you answer for its touch
> A host of men move about you, you answer for their need.[446]

Likewise Jersild's notion of self-understanding was essential to serving others:

While a clear picture of what you should be doing as a member of the teaching profession is of great value to you, of greater importance is your image of yourself as a teacher. This involves the establishment for yourself of behaviour patterns which are consistent with your knowledge of yourself and the demands of the career you have chosen to follow.[447]

Prominent educators who addressed the student group broadened their horizons, enhanced Burwood's profile and placed Shears among Victoria's educational elite. Invited guests included parliamentarians Minister Thompson[448] and local member for Bennettswood Mr Ian McLaren; educational leaders, Director Alex McDonell, Assistant Director Fred Brooks; and people of renown – musician Ade Monsborough, arts administrator Eric Westbrook and journalist/broadcaster Myra Roper. Save the Children Fund representatives, the Assistant Chief Commissioner of the Country Fire Authority and senior Victoria Police personnel provoked social awareness.

Burwood TC was located close to training schools but removed from major public transport. The city tram terminated a mile and a half west at Warrigal Road and a bus ran the three-mile route to and from Box Hill station. Few students had cars and parking facilities were poor. Student accounts in *Yabba* describe the 'noise of tractors, the muddy pathways … [and after] many years of deliberation, the College road is at last taking shape.'[449] Hitchhiking was common practice to and from the tram or train. This bothered Shears who held concern for students' safety. To overcome transport difficulties for the women who lived in the Patterson Street hostel in Hawthorn, he chartered a bus, as a safety factor. He invited the police to address the 'dangers of hitchhiking and gave examples about what happened to young women' at Wednesday assembly.[450]

Student life was abuzz with lectures and assignments and teaching rounds, sporting events, clubs activities and inter-college visits, dances and balls, musicals and plays, camps and tours. Welcome, mid-year and graduation dances, Christmas parties, orientations and graduations revolved through the year. Under the guidance of Ken Sargent, Head of Social Science, students performed in 'Patience', 'Brigadoon',

'White Horse Inn', 'Finian's Rainbow', 'Calamity Jane' and 'Free as Air'. Director Alex McDonell commended the team on their professional status, and considered 'White Horse Inn' to be as good as the Broadway production. During Education Week students assembled grand displays and encouraged community–college interchange. Visitors came to the college and staff dispersed to schools. Throughout the 1960s, as enrolments increased, correspondingly staff numbers increased from 54 in 1961 to 90 in 1969. The college community looked forward to a hall to seat 1000 with an orchestra pit and dressing rooms, a gym with showers and toilet, and a cafeteria to replace the tuckshop or the need to walk to Bennettswood shops.

Camps and tours were an important aspect of college life. They enriched relationships, expanded horizons and gave students the chance to explore the countryside. First-year students camped in huts at Bright, Porepunkah and Wandilagong, where they learnt about education in country areas. Chris Limb recalled:

> We stayed at an old forestry camp. It rained, the rain came through the roof, it came through onto our beds. We had a bus and we went around and saw schools. We put on a dance at the one-teacher school. Of course we had a lot of girls and very few boys. Quite a few young men from the logging came. We raised a nice amount of money for the school.

On the Alice Springs tours:

> We had tents in the bulldust. We went around in a blitz buggy which had no windows. We were covered in red dust. We got past the stage of worrying about it. Your clothes were red. Your hair was red. Everything was red.

Second- and third-year students selected low-cost destinations in Victoria or more expensive interstate options. The trips were an integral part of the course and studentship payments helped students to afford them. In the 1960s, before secondary schools established the pattern of interstate travel, Shears considered the closed lives of the Burwood cohort – 'six years primary, six years secondary, three years college [and then] back into schools'. 'What did they know about their own country?' he asked.[451]

In 1959 college students could choose between Alice Springs, Magnetic Island, Perth and Tasmania. By 1964 the expanded selection included Sydney, Perth, Flinders Ranges, Cooktown and Cairns and the Red Centre. Burwood TC was one of Australia's biggest travel customers. Proud of this feat Shears claimed, 'I used to sign the cheques – one was the largest single cheque paid to the Queensland Government Tourist Bureau. When I went to Queensland I was just about given the keys to the State.' On the Five-State Tour he experienced the 'colossal hospitality' provided at a sheep station. The host affirmed, 'If you come all the way from Melbourne to have a look at our station we ought to look after you in terms of hospitality.' Wherever the students chose to go Burwood went with them.[452] Ken Sergeant organised the tours and staff members, sometimes with their husbands or wives, accompanied the students to watch their welfare, join the fun and give advice when needed. On Rockhampton platform Mr Sargeant counselled one young lady to take care that the shy part of herself did not overpower the happy, outgoing self. Beyond the confines of college he saw her personality blossom and she remembered his counsel, 'be careful that the shy girl does not overpower the real you'.[453]

Upon graduation, exiting students, mainly female aged between just 19 and 21, were dispersed to schools across the State: small hamlets in the Victorian Alps; remote locations in the Upper Murray or the Mallee; new schools in new suburbs; or densely populated suburban locations where enclaves of migrants had settled. Raising college entry level to matriculation would have the dual role of ensuring greater maturity upon college entry and exit, and acting as a step towards raising the status of teachers college courses. This in turn would enhance primary teachers' professional status. At the core of these motives were 'the interests of pupils and teachers, [as] an essential step forward in teacher training'.[454]

Living on campus, as Shears did, blurred the boundaries between institutional and family commitment. He gave each his best effort to offer stability and optimal opportunity to grow and develop a sense of self-worth. Proximity enabled him to spend time with the growing family and capitalise on his professional activities. He and Mavis enjoyed college life – the dances and balls, musicals and dramas – and hosted social get-togethers for staff and hostel students. College facilities were available for professional development programs and research activities of the VIER and ACE. In 1962 students and staff helped members of the Victorian Chapter of ACE to collate data from the first National Survey of Teachers in Australia in readiness for the 3rd ACE annual conference in Melbourne. There was no air conditioning or computerisation in Burwood's masonry-clad buildings. 'It was hot!' so Shears provided 'jugs of iced orange and lemon juice while they all sorted the results'.[455]

## Other aspects of Shears

In his inimitable style, Shears' interests extended beyond those of husband, father and principal. Still in his 40s, he proposed his professional pathway would lead to the top. Conscious of a forewarning by Dr T L Robertson, Director-General of Education in WA (1951–66), he was aware of the likely difficulties of repositioning a career in administration. Regardless, he remained in teacher education. The position as Alan Ramsay's 'backroom boy' in Survey and Planning, his travels abroad and ongoing research activities kept him abreast of educational trends and who-was-who in terms of importance. The Burwood experience made him discernible; he was seen, mixed readily, and with the ability to work the floor at educational functions he became recognised as 'one of Australia's best-qualified educators'.[456]

Keen to advance he saw himself holding a university's Chair in Education. Previously the University of Sydney overlooked him with the appointment of Professor Bill Connell in 1955. He was unsuccessful at Monash University a decade later but shortlisted at Flinders University. Despite proven leadership skills and teacher education expertise his research activity was not current. The administrative slant on his CV and career shift to administration caused doubt in the minds of selecting committees who sought maturity, employment stability and a proven track record.[457] Undaunted, Shears developed his research profile through activity in the VIER and ACE.

Encouraged by its enthusiastic executive, the VIER continued to grow. Strength lay in membership of 'established' and 'younger members of the profession with outstanding potential'. International visitors regularly informed members of their research interests and current thinking abroad. To encourage membership in country areas the VIER established regional groups in Colac (1965), the Wimmera and Glenelg (1965), the Goulburn Valley (1968) and East Gippsland (1969). To address the needs of teachers in primary and secondary fields it introduced Primary Education Today (PET) and Secondary Education Today (SET) groups plus a research cohort. PET sustained enthusiasm throughout the 1960s but recently formed subject associations encroached on SET activities. Max Dimmack, who helped form PET, recalled, 'Nothing much happened in VIER without Lawrie Shears being involved; he was IT. Nothing happened in PET without Max Dimmack being involved because he was IT.'

As Victorian Editor of the *Australian Journal of Education* (AJE) Shears was abreast of research nationwide. When Dr Rayner from Queensland stepped aside from his column, 'Review of Education', Shears offered Burwood staff the chance to express their views to a broader circle. Those involved acknowledged how this boosted career prospects and their emergence as administrators in ensuing years.

Maintaining interest in the VIER, Shears took on its presidency in 1963. He continued to edit the *VIER Bulletin*, which disseminated research and provided summaries of the annual John Smyth lecture from 1954 and the Frank Tate Memorial Lecture from its inauguration in 1956. In the 15th Frank Tate Memorial Lecture in 1968, Dr Robertson, President of ACER, reviewed changes in education since WWII. He referred to the 'new look' in buildings and grounds; greater provision for tertiary studies; and the importance of research and planning branches. These were the 'brains trusts' of all Education Departments. Looking ahead he warned of political advisers, cautioned against the intrusion of economics over the knowledge of educators, and stressed that reform was more quickly activated by research. Robertson questioned Australia's poor support for educational research funding. 'The immensity of education in Australia is … reason for a considerable increase in investigation by research.' Among Australia's 12 million people, 3 million attended educational institutions; the sector employed 120,000; and the cost was $1,200 million each year of which only $1–1.5 million, or 0.1 per cent, was spent on educational research. In contrast S40 million was being spent in Japan and $70 million in the USA. In Australia much larger sums were being made available for scientific, industrial and medical research than for educational research.[458] Robertson's call to support research corresponded with moves to form a national research organisation. He valued State institutes' role and advocated more funding to expand research activity.

## Australian College of Education

The Australian College of Education continued to grow. Although Shears missed the first Annual General Meeting (AGM) in Sydney, due to the Harkness Fellowship, his attendance at the College's second AGM in Adelaide in 1961 established a pattern of long-term commitment to annual conference attendance. It was there that he met another feisty young educator keen to make an impression. Both were inspired by their recent appointments: Paul McKeown as third Headmaster of Canberra Grammar School in 1959[459] and Shears as second Principal of Burwood TC in April 1961, just three weeks prior to the Adelaide AGM.

The 1961 AGM was organised and formal. Beginning on Friday, delegates attended the Lord Mayor's Reception, then the President's Reception in the Cloisters of the University Refectory and finally the presentation of Fellows in Bonython Hall. Among distinguished guests were His Excellency the Governor of South Australia and Lady Bastyan and the Prime Minister, the Rt Hon. Robert Menzies, who spoke on 'The challenge to education in Australia today'. It was a fine occasion with gentlemen wearing dress suits with tails. Presenting the keynote address on Saturday, Professor W H Frederick of the University of Melbourne presented thoughts on 'The qualities and training of teachers'. On Sunday delegates attended church services and visited local places of interest.

Shears and McKeown feared that physical distance and State parochialism would cause State chapters of ACE to act independently.

They presented a motion aiming to make certain that 'College activities' would be 'at the national level' and proposed the College select at least one national issue for discussion to present in draft form to State chapters. Delegates considered ways to improve the quality of existing and future teachers and how to raise numbers, as well as issues of continued tertiary education. They settled on the first National Survey of Teachers in Australia, aiming to present at the 3rd AGM a 'picture of Australia's teachers and the facilities available to prepare them for their chosen vocation' and identify members' views on the 'qualities that should be sought in teachers, the kind of preparation that teachers should receive, and the aims that should be set and the developments fostered, to lift teaching nearer a professional level.'[460]

In conversation with Australian College of Educators archivist Tony Ryan in 2007, Shears reflected on his meeting with McKeown in 1961 and their successful effort to set in motion the first study of teachers in Australia. Shears was 'very, very taken up, seeing that chappie who was the Headmaster of Canberra Grammar School, a young fellow like me, and we moved and seconded the motion'. 'We were a bit cheeky,' he added 'because we were fairly young members of the teaching profession.' The proposal was for State chapters to collate questionnaire data (Shears collated the Victorian returns with the help of Burwood students) for the progress report to present at the 3rd AGM in Melbourne in 1962. Optimistically the College aimed to complete the report by 1963 but the draft was not complete until the Sydney AGM in 1966. The committee presented Part A at the Hobart AGM in 1967, and Part B at the Melbourne AGM in 1968, when Shears officiated because he was chair of the Victorian Chapter. He recalled that 'some States got a bit up tight' since the nature of the material was critical of their teacher education programs, namely those that didn't have full two-year or full three-year courses.[461]

On the sudden death in 1966 of Victorian ACE chapter chairman Mr A Tylee, Principal of Swinburne College of Advanced Education, vice-chairman Shears stepped in and served an extended term (1966–69). Like the 'young Turks' of the VIER, ACE members were fired with enthusiasm notwithstanding their demanding professional roles, which marked their devotion to education and the cause of the child. Members proposed that quarterly meetings embrace social gatherings and invited guests to bring local and international insights. Ideally these would be held at or near the University of Melbourne where members dined at University House. To mark the end of the first decade of the College in April 1969, the Executive held a weekend seminar at Sorrento to review the College's aims and objectives. The residential format united the group, generated ideas and gave ongoing direction.

## Australian Association for Research in Education

Stirred by the successful New Education Fellowship visit in 1937, educationists, researchers and members of State institutes of educational research saw hope for a national research body, but the war, funding cuts and shortage of manpower put paid to this. Freeman Butts, during his visit to Australia in 1953, challenged educators not to fall into post-war complacency but to seek a spirit of revival. He called for wider discussion on educational matters to involve community, and for educators to publicly express their views on the radio, in the press and in professional journals. 'Organise committees, hold meetings, conduct research, establish pilot studies, and encourage experimentation at every level of the education system,' he urged. Encouraged by his insight a flame kindled among those who sought to establish a national research body. He acknowledged:

> Preliminary discussion is already taking place on the question of establishing an Australia-wide organisation open to all those professionally engaged in education. Plans are also being made for an Australia-wide journal of education to be devoted to matters of policy and theory as well as to publication of research reports.[462]

While Butts' seeds flourished with the national journal in 1957 and a national body in 1959, it was a decade later that a national organisation with research focus was born. Recalling events Shears explained, 'We wanted to establish an Australian Association of Research, in contrast to the broader activities of the Australian College of Education.' Acknowledging the role of the State institutes of educational research he explained, 'All the institutes had delegates to ACER and they formed the ACER council. George Bradshaw was our VIER delegate from 1968 to 1975 and he was very enthusiastic about an Australian association.' Shears continued, 'Our executive passed a motion saying that we strongly supported the establishment of an Australian Council of Educational Research.' The drive of Victoria's executive had varying degrees of support from institutes in New South Wales, Queensland and South Australia. Victorians Bradshaw and Radford were a major force in the formation of the Australian association.[463]

In 1964 Radford had identified a body of 150 educational researchers nationwide whose research centred mainly in departments of education, psychology and ACER. The Commonwealth Office of Education also had a research arm, the main focus of which was fact-finding. Concerned by the hodge-podge state of affairs Radford urged rationalisation of research groups and expansion of resources. Following proceedings at a conference held at Melbourne TC in 1967 where he addressed and consulted with delegates, he emphasised the need for Commonwealth support. As Director of ACER, Radford was positioned to lead the way, his thrust strengthened by the States' research institutes The result was the establishment of two research bodies in 1970: the Australian Advisory Committee on Research and Development in Education and the Australian Association for Research in Education.[464]

Working with Radford, Shears perused statutes of the Canadian Education Research Association and the American Educational Research Association. A recommendation to the ACER general meeting in October 1969 led to discussion amongst significant people from universities and education departments. Establishing the new research organisation resembled efforts of those who established the ACE a decade before: to encourage dialogue with educational leaders abroad; establish a forum to hear, discuss recent research and publish learned papers.[465] The Australian Association for Research in Education founded in Melbourne in 1969 satisfied the yearnings of many leading educationists including Shears who was once more ideally placed to be listed among the founders.

## College of Nursing Australia (CNA)

The Burwood years provided the chance for Shears to spread his wings. Nursing, like teaching, offered female school leavers entrée into a worthwhile career. Both required theoretical knowledge and hands-on practical training. Internal conflict had caused the chair of the College of Nursing Australia to resign. An interim chairman replaced him while administrators sought an educator to fill the role. Prompted by former Director of Education Ramsay, CNA administrators identified Shears as the ideal man, and sent a 'deputation asking would I be prepared to take the position of chairman of the College of Nursing Australia?' The deputation countered his immediate reaction – 'I'm not too sure I can fit it in' – with 'it's only a finance meeting once a month and a conference once a year'. Shears was tempted, and recalled, 'largely due to the drive of people like Pat Slater I became chairman of the College of Nursing in 1963'. At the annual meeting in Brisbane the appointment became official. During Shears' term as chairman 'the training of nurses went from hospital-based to college-based. There was a lot of argument ... but that didn't stop them nursing'.[466] Shears reflected that while teaching and nursing offered comparable pathways 'the qualifications of people coming into teaching gradually increased, their secondary education gradually got higher before they became eligible; nursing followed suit but a decade or so behind'. He claimed, 'there was more objection to nursing being college-based than teaching'. He held firm views regarding training, claiming:

> If the nurses were being trained in college it was fundamental that they integrated thoroughly the theoretical work with nursing practice. It required a huge effort. Pat Slater who was the Director of the College of Nursing Australia worked very hard with Pat Osborne and her staff to bring about proper practical training which meshed in with the theoretical knowledge.[467]

Despite frustrations the profile of nurse education increased. CNA, somewhat the equivalent of the Australian College of Education but with a distinct training role, experienced a tripling in its membership. The majority of members came from Victoria where 385 Fellows and associates comprised almost half the national tally of 864. Under the leadership of Founding Director Pat Chomley (1950–64), her successor Pat Slater, honorary treasurer Jack Kennedy and honorary chairman Shears, various disparate Victorian nursing groups united into CNA and branches were established in other States. The College outgrew its premises in Slater Street, Toorak, and in 1968, after a series of moves, settled into The Mews, at 452 St Kilda Road, Melbourne. The teaching staff increased from two full-time lecturers in 1961 to ten by the end of the decade, with approximately 80 sessional staff. Acknowledged as a tertiary training institute and supported by federal funding, CNA conducted three 40-week diploma courses – Diploma of Nursing Administration, Diploma of Nurse Education and Diploma of Nursing Education (Midwifery) – and an increasing number of shorter courses.

Shears was modest about his contribution to these important developments. He considered Pat Slater and her team were the driving force; he was merely the chair. In his favour Miss Slater acknowledged that his:

> … deep commitment to education, his great capacity for work, and his lively interest and unfailing optimism were a constant inspiration to members of the nursing profession who were struggling to bring nurse education into the mainstream of higher education. His phenomenal ability to rapidly grasp unfamiliar, complex issues, to clarify and confirm differences, to direct discussion without stifling it, and to bring a topic to a satisfactory conclusion, together with the broad multidisciplinary perspectives he brought, enabled the College to develop and pioneer a new era of nursing education.[468]

## Moving on

Of change, Tennyson wrote, 'The old order changeth, yielding place to new'. In 1963 Bob Dylan wrote, '… the times they are a'changing … the present now will later be past'. Of change Shears informed Burwood students, 'Change is inevitable, desirable change is not – we must ensure inevitable change is desirable.'

Colleague and friend Ron Ginger identified the 1960s as 'The Golden Years' of education and Burwood TC lay at the heart. They were heady times when much took place in teacher education and education per se. Aligning with Shears' appointment in 1961, Monash University and Monash TC introduced teacher education courses. Richard Selby-Smith, Dean of the Faculty of Education at Monash University, appointed from headmastership of Scotch College in 1965, sought discussion with Shears. Despite advocating concurrent theoretical and practical training Selby-Smith was bound by university politics to opt for the end-on model, wherein graduate students undertook a 12-month Diploma of Education beyond their undergraduate degree. Shears reflected:

> I was on the executive board when Selby-Smith was establishing his Faculty of Education at Monash. I was very interested in the concurrent method of training as against the end-on. Selby-Smith nearly got there, but pressures were too great from the rest of the faculties. I believe that was why the end-on course was established.[469]

Burwood TC remained at the forefront of teacher education with its proud heritage of quality students who developed into quality teachers. Course standards were rising with the three-year Diploma of Teaching introduced for matriculation entrants in 1968. It gave greater depth of knowledge and placed responsibility on students to undertake research and discuss concepts of teaching. It also made three years' training available to male students. In each 11-week semester students completed four or five weeks of practical teaching and one week of exams.[470] Aligning with this, Shears' era at Burwood drew to an end. In May 1969 he stepped into more senior administrative roles. Taking his place as Acting Principal at Burwood, Ron Burton wrote:

> The sudden departure of our principal, Dr Shears, at a vital time in the year's activities, was a tragedy – and a challenge. We lost his driving energy and guidance, but found that we could accept the responsibility for our continued development. Both students and staff have been loyal to their College in the tasks that confronted them and no greater tribute than this can be paid to any leader when he lays aside his

authority. Dr Shears should be a proud man, his ideals live on in the College he loved dearly, his influence on those who worked with him is a living force and I pay my tribute to a great man and friend.[471]

Before moving on Shears alerted students of the 'change [they would face] from college to classroom, from student to professional practising teacher', counselling them to 'face this change with confidence'. Believing the program addressed student 'needs as developing persons who will become successful teachers, citizens and scholars' he claimed:

> ... the college has endeavoured to provide an environment which has given you 'room to grow'. You should have been assisted to a better knowledge of yourself and your profession by contact with colleagues who have the same vocational goals, by teaching experiences in the schools, and through the multiplicity of opportunities both academic and social which were available to you.[472]
>
> *'Animum, Cultum, Parabo'*

*1.2 Annie and Robert Shears*

*1.3 Ernest William Shears*

*1.4 Dorothy Irene Brand*

*1.5 Victoria Madeline and Josiah Brand*

*2.1 Lawrie as a baby*   *2.2 Outside Governor's Quarters, Beechworth Gaol*

*3.1 The Duke of Gloucester's visit*

*3.2 Soccer team, University High School*

*3.3 Athletics team, University High School*

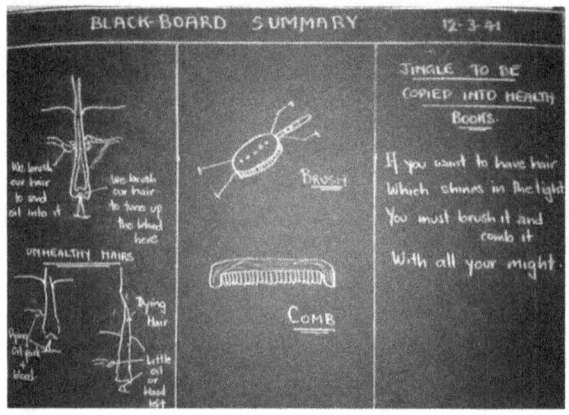

*4.1 Blackboard preparation*

*4.2 Fitzroy (Miller Street) State School*

*4.3 Shears on stage*

*4.4 College hockey team*

*4.5 Bairnsdale HS 1946, Shears with Form 3 girls*

*4.6 Staff at Bairnsdale High School 1946*

*4.7 Holiday work at the Myrtleford Mill*

*5.1 Shears' wedding to Mavis Redman*

*5.2 Huffam Hut with family members*

*5.3 RTC Football Team 1948 Premiers*

*5.4 Pete's Carrying Service*

*6.1 Graduation Lawrence Shears*

*6.2 Senate House, London*

*6.3 Lady Godiva on Topper*

*6.4 Shears with students at Oxford Hall*

*6.5 Shears with same students in recent times*

*6.6 Shears with Toorak TC Staff*

*6.7 Development of Burwood TC 1954*

*6.8 Founders of ACE 25th anniversary, Geelong Grammar School 1974*

*7.1 Harkness Fellow and family*

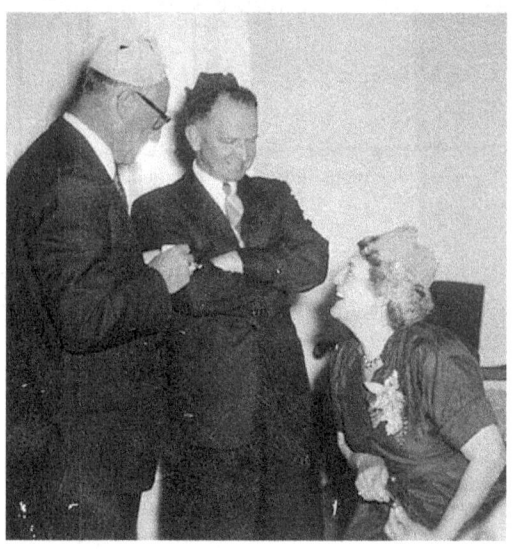

*7.2 Wallers welcome Shears*

*7.3 Fun and games on Sports Day*

*7.4 SRC Representatives 1963*

*7.5 Papua New Guinea Tour, aboard the DC 3*

*7.6 House in Hopetoun Road*

*8.1 Directors General at Standing Committee meeting*

*8.2 Opening of Regional Office with RD Ron Ginge*

*8.3 Japanese School*

*8.4a Tweedledum*

*8.4b Tweedledee*

*8.5 Drama Resource Centre 'wedding'*

*9.1 Shears and Colin Moyle*

*8.6 Thompson and Shears*

*9.2 Lawrie Shears CGE*

*9.3 Cricket field at Miller Stree*

*9.4 Miller Street classroom*

*10.1 Celebrating 50 years of marriage*

*10.2 With Ted Liefman and Geoff Stevens*

*10.3 With Field Rickards*

*10.4 At retired officers function*

*10.5 Lawrie Shears beside a portrait of Frank Tate*

*10.6 With Joan and Lindsay Thompson*

*10.7 With Doreen Falk*

*10.8 Sir James Darling Medal*

*10.9 International Teaching Fellowship Farewell 2013*

*10.10 Family at Inaugural Lawrie Shears Lecture 2013*

Section 5:

LEADING THE FLOCK

CHAPTER 13

# IN THE WINGS (1969–72)

*You are the bows from which your children as living arrows are sent forth*

Kahlil Gibran, 'On Children'

As the 1960s flowed into the 1970s, cultural shifts emerged in Australian society. Public commentary, persuasive advertising and technological advances were commonplace while people developed greater appreciation of fine arts and cuisine. Women became more professionally active and the community gained greater awareness of conserving human and natural resources. Links with Britain became subdued and bonds of tradition frayed as the Asian tiger reared its head. Authoritarianism gave way to permissiveness and time-honoured educational ideals suffered unforseen pressures.

Post-secondary pathways became a major concern. Victoria's new universities – Monash, La Trobe and Deakin – offered entry to the cream of matriculants, while the Victoria Institute of Colleges (VIC), the coordinating body for technical colleges, offered alternative educational routes. Before passing the Education portfolio to Lindsay Thompson in 1967, Minister John Bloomfield forewarned administrators 'our predecessors and contemporaries have revealed and are revealing so much that is known' yet 'so much remains mysterious. The amount to be learned and taught would be almost too terrifying if it did not hold such promise.'[473] He charged them to act with vigilance as the future unfolded. Teaching, he said, was the 'most worthy and compelling human endeavour', which required 'the fullest commitment', and 'teacher education lay at its crux'.[474]

In post-war Victoria, Directors Ramsay and McDonell laid foundations. Succeeding them, Director/Director-General Brooks guided the education system through the parsimonious 1960s during which unprecedented expansion was occurring. Robertson, from Western Australia, advised educationists to strengthen research to justify change. He cautioned them to be aware of research overseas but identify the uniqueness of local problems.[475] Influenced by Britain's Plowden Report (1967), teaching in Australia took a child-centred slant, encouraging discovery, experience and creativity. 'We have a choice in our classroom,' stated Phillip Hughes, whether to 'have a set of blank walls with no outlook or whether to take our task to be one of opening up windows on the world, of revealing insights which would otherwise be clouded'. Serving the masses, not a select few, education took on a new significance and required the dead wood of outmoded curriculum to be discarded to 'meet the needs of a world in the throes of intellectual and material development'.[476]

Funding was always a tussle and calls for Commonwealth support increased. Nationally teachers colleges needed $41m (£20.5m) during the latter half of the 1960s to upgrade buildings and replace obsolete equipment. Simultaneously attempts continued to increase teacher supply and training while reducing class size, revising curriculum and providing alternate pathways for diverse student needs. Alarmed by the scale of development and State budgetary shortfalls, the Australian Education Council (AEC), a committee of State Ministers of Education advised by their Directors-General, called for Commonwealth aid. Teacher training was an 'investment in human capital' and 'without such training the education system cannot function efficiently'.[477] Provision of science laboratories, libraries and technical training in government and nongovernment secondary schools showed signs of growing Commonwealth support, as did the funding of vocational courses through colleges of advanced education, but no aid was given to teachers colleges.[478]

To address the momentum and scale of educational development Victoria's leadership team had been expanded. John Rossiter was appointed Assistant Minister in 1964 and in 1965 W (Bill) Russell became the first Assistant Director-General of Education (ADGE). Prior to his war service Rossiter had taught in schools and later became senior lecturer in English at the Royal Melbourne Institute of Technology (RMIT). Russell had taught in country and suburban secondary settings, joined the inspectorate in 1950 and rose to Assistant Chief Inspector of Secondary Schools in 1960. Three years into his appointment as ADGE the Commonwealth of Nations Secretariat in London seconded him as Director of Education for a two-year term. He subsequently attended the Colombo Plan Conference on Training of Technicians and the SE Asia and Pacific Inspectors' Conference in Singapore and advised on education matters in India and Ceylon.[479]

Russell's long-term absence placed Victoria's administrative team under pressure. As a result, two positions for ADGE were created; one focused on planning, research and development and the other on building and equipment. Applicants required proven administrative and organising ability in education, and experience in the planning and practice of education and its organisation in Australia and overseas. Suitable personal qualities were essential. In his application Shears highlighted his qualifications and listed his administrative experience, educational knowledge and vision for ongoing growth. A forceful leverage were seven years' service as Survey and Planning Officer, as 'personal assistant to the Director of Education in the functions of planning and coordinating educational policy'. Shears' application stressed the 'need for continuity of personnel which formulate and implement our educational policies' and identified his 'full understanding of educational trends in other states and overseas, particularly in the areas of educational administration and school curriculum'. He had expert knowledge of professional and clerical divisions of both the Education Department and other government agencies. Addressing links with 'accepted educational authorities' Shears listed long-term commitment to the Victorian Institute for Educational Research and his current presidential status, the Australian Council for Educational Research where he served as VIER delegate (1957–58) and the Australian College of Education in which he was among its Founders and recent chair of the Victorian Chapter (1966–69). Chairmanship of the College of Nursing Australia since 1963 identified commitment beyond direct educational spheres, while invitations to speak at and contribute to discussion on radio and television indicated his high profile at local, state and national levels. Shears' principalship at Burwood provided extensive 'contact with local and state educational and community organizations, and renewed close association with schools and teachers'.[480]

On 24 September 1969 *The Age* announced 'Two get top posts in education'. The article described Shears as 'one of Australia's best-qualified educators', and highlighted Stewart Morton's 'reputation as an innovator in school design' in Tasmania and 'outstanding service to La Trobe University as its building officer'. Both aged 48, they were 'the youngest men given executive level jobs in the department in more than half a century'. Morton's appointment from an external source was unusual. Born and educated in Victoria, he previously served as Assistant Chief Architect, Public Works Department in Tasmania (1952–65). He was a Harkness Fellow in the USA (1958–59) the year before Shears. Morton's service as Buildings Officer (1965–69)[481] at La Trobe University proved his specialist skills. While these were vital to the Department's ongoing growth, his architectural background informed him of planning and school building operations. With these appointments the Education Department had a team of nine senior executives to administer particular functions.[482] These included the Minister and Assistant Minister, Director-General, three Assistant Directors-General and the Directors of Primary, Secondary and Technical Education.

Following Shears' appointment came widespread support. Students, teachers and colleagues, politicians and principals, members of the Burwood cohort, family, friends and various others were 'overjoyed to hear the news'. Among responses from Burwood graduates were thanks for his 'ability to make each of the hundreds of students feel they are the only one'. Staff responded, 'Hoo-bloody-ray! Congratulations and the best of luck!' They admitted 'it won't be the same without you in the chair at our meetings' but acknowledged he would now 'influence the entire system'. Correspondents 'forecast your rise right to the top' yet alerted to frustrations with 'finance or the lack of it'. Typically they admitted, 'you seem to have a way of getting what you want'.

Alice Downward from Toorak Teachers College hinted at collegial intimacy:

> Mrs Socrates hopes you enjoy your new position and wishes

you every success in it. She wishes to register her thanks to you for: getting her VW out of the trees at Blackburn School; advising her on the purchase of her house, which she still likes very much after almost four years; many discussions – even those rare occasions when she was wrong.

Shears responded:

I hope I can play out my Plato to my Mrs Socrates ... I have always enjoyed our discussions peaceful or otherwise and hope there will be many future occasions for these to take place.[483]

Norman Gill of the Board of Inspectors of Secondary Schools commended Shears for elevating the status of teachers colleges; Miss Elizabeth Butt, Principal of Fintona Girls' School acknowledged the loss to Burwood Teachers College and hoped the new 'sphere of influence will be greater'; and Rev Dudley Barrington Clarke, Principal of Peninsula Church of England School, believed having 'an ideas man with energy and ability in such a position is a major gain to the Education Department'. Professor Dellbridge from Armidale Teachers College, whom Shears had met in 1952 on the return trip from England, considered the good sense 'in making an appointment like this, instead of from the ranks of head-office administrators'. He hoped Shears would continue his 'delightful Burwood habit of sending people off to King's Cross and Macquarie and other outlandish places to see how the other half lives'.

ADGE Bill Russell wrote from the Commonwealth Secretariat in London. He acknowledged Shears' 'record of high-level service to education' and believed 'the new position will give proper scope for the use of all your skills and knowledge, professional and personal, which you have gained since I first met you 32 years ago'. From Curtin Primary School in Western Australia he was wished fulfilment 'without getting stuck in the red tape'; from the College of Nursing Australia Pat Slater identified Shears' tenacity and leadership ability; and Principal Psychologist and Guidance Officer Mr John Hall was delighted with the Minister's choice. The Hon. Jim Cairns conveyed best wishes in a telegram:

> SINCERE CONGRATULATIONS DELIGHTED TO HEAR
> OF APPOINTMENT BEST WISHES FOR FUTURE

Rev Dr Norman Curry, Sub-Dean of the University of Melbourne's Faculty of Education, believed the 'position had gone to such a worthy person … heartiest congratulations'. He warned 'it will not be an easy position to fill and I imagine there will be many worrying and sleepless hours … your background in Survey and Planning and at Burwood should give you an insight into these problems which few, if any, others have'.

Shears' appointment as ADGE began on 29 September 1969.[484] Thenceforth professionally he was in close contact with Minister Thompson. Their experience, knowledge of population growth and demographic trends equipped them with foresight to identify current educational needs and future developments. In later years Shears reflected on his role which was 'largely planning and all those things that nobody else did', and 'to be quite honest … take a bit of the burden off the Director'.[485]

## Profile: Minister Lindsay Thompson

Lindsay Thompson was born in Warburton in October 1923. His father died when he was two years old so his mother began to teach at Mentone Girls Grammar School, a small private school co-founded by his aunts. Thompson was educated at Caulfield Grammar School where he was Captain and Dux in 1941. In 1942 he joined the AIF and served in New Guinea. Under the Commonwealth Reconstruction Training Program Thompson completed an arts degree at the University of Melbourne with majors in political science and history. In 1950 he gained the exhibition in the history of education and first-class honours in practical teaching at the Secondary Teachers College. Beginning in 1951 he taught for two years at Malvern Central School, No. 1604, known as Spring Road, and correspondingly completed his BEd and thesis on 'Personality traits of leaders and rejected children at Malvern Central School'.[486] In 1953 Thompson was appointed to Melbourne High School. He taught history and supported sport in and out of school hours.

Suave, clear minded and determined, Thompson was not afraid to push boundaries. In later years he often recalled a union representative's challenge, asking what he was doing at school at 'quarter to six last night … we knock off at 4'. Thompson, who was coaching the cricket team, calmly replied, 'You decide what time you knock off … I'll decide when I knock off'. This was typical of Thompson, Shears recalled; 'if he wanted something you did not stand in his way'. By the end of the year the union representative supported after-school sport.[487]

Thompson was elected to the Legislative Council in 1955 and to the Legislative Assembly in 1970. He was appointed State representative on the Melbourne University Council (1955–59), Secretary to Cabinet (1956–58) and member of the Statute Laws Revision Committee (1955–58). He served as Minister of Housing and Forests (1961–67) and Minister-in-charge of Aboriginal Welfare (1965–67), which alerted him to Victoria's social structure, demographic change and suburban expansion, and stood him in good stead to understand educational growth. His passion for education shone through bonds cemented during his schooling and teaching and invitations to address education groups, such as teacher trainees at Burwood Teachers College where he and Shears first met in June 1966. Thompson's ultimate interest in establishing educational regions across Victoria from 1972 stemmed from his positive experience as Minister for Housing and Forests.

In his maiden speech Thompson linked education with the nation's prosperity:

> In the 167 years of this country's history, we have tilled the fields, obtained valuable minerals from the ground, and built factories and cities, but where in fact does the true wealth of the nation lie? Undoubtedly it is in the character of its people, and the education system of the State must surely be the most important factor moulding the national character. A high standard of education is particularly necessary in a democratic country because an effective government in a democracy pre-supposes an enlightened and politically conscious people.[488]

Assigned the Education portfolio thirteen years later Thompson lamented its 'Cinderella' status in State departments and determined to seek the 'first slice of the financial cake'.[489] He claimed, 'in the light of the inactivity of the 1930s and 1940s the educational developments of the last decade have been nothing short of remarkable', and stressed, 'no nations, no industry, no educational system can afford to be static in this rapidly changing world. Complacency is more likely to produce retrogression than inspire progress'.[490] Resolute in his stance, the slice of the pie increased to $105 (£52) per child, a huge leap from $4 (£2) in 1940 and $24 (£12) in 1955.[491] Yet, with the need for more schools and more trained teachers, the teacher shortage remained a major concern. Reaching a critical state by the late 1960s, it increasingly affected the secondary sector, exacerbated by study leave, employment on special staffs and teachers colleges and reducing class size and teacher work load.

Table 8. Secondary and technical enrolments in Education Department schools 1960–70

|  | Estimated growth | Actual growth | |
|---|---|---|---|
|  | August | February | August |
| 1960 | 123,834 | 128,274 | 125,633 |
| 1965 | 167,104 | 169,766 | 167,782 |
| 1970 | 205,850 | (est.) 223,000 | (est.) 219,800 |
| 1975 |  |  | (est.) 261,700 |

Source: Survey and Statistics Branch, Education Department, Victoria, cited in Thompson, 1969, p. 21.

Despite efforts to keep pace with growth, predictions fell short. The actual enrolment of secondary and technical students leapt from 128,274 in 1960 to an estimated 223,000 by 1970. The need to provide facilities and staff for the additional 94,726 students was acute. Aggravating the problem, 650 primary trained teachers who taught in secondary and technical schools were considered 'unqualified'. A further 700 teachers worked in the Special Services Division and 400 were employed in teachers colleges. Others supported education programs at the ABC, the zoo, the museum and regional art galleries, while others taught in New Guinea, and south-east Asian and Pacific regions.[492]

## Solutions from abroad

Addressing the dilemma, Shears stressed, 'while the distribution of increases will change as between primary and secondary schools, there will still be an "increasing increase" in the annual totals'.[493] Aware of teacher surpluses in the USA and UK, he believed that selecting teachers from abroad would reduce the local deficit. He proposed the Victorian Teacher Selection Program (VTSP) to provide trained secondary teachers and the International Teaching Fellowship (ITF) program. While this primarily marked distinguished service, incoming Fellows boosted the teacher pool.

Traditionally, senior administrators travelled abroad to develop professional knowledge, inspect other systems and identify trends to adapt locally. Faster, larger planes condensed the duration of travel, and in turn increased opportunities for intercultural contact. Enriched by his experience in the UK (1950–52) and the USA (1959–60), Shears believed 'the teacher of the future must have travelled or he sees things through a parochial view. If he's going to teach about a society he must know about international society.'[494] Ideally, travel embraced two years; during the first year teachers experienced an alternative education system and in the second year they understood the relationship between its philosophies and function. Hence, he envisaged the VTSP and ITF program as two-year programs.

## Victorian Teacher Selection Program

To fill shortfalls in science, mathematics, geography, English, selected languages, technical and general fields, the VTSP targeted mid-20-year-old graduate teachers from North America and the UK. Employed on two-year contracts, the Education Department funded air passages and paid incoming teachers according to the temporary scale.[495] Education departments in New South Wales, South Australia and Western Australia engaged in similar programs to fill deficits in teacher supply. The NSW Department opened 'embassies' in New York and London while the Victorian Department established centres at the State University in California, Heywood (where it appointed

Professor Clare Pederson as its representative), and at the Office of the Agent-General in London.[496]

Norman Gill of the Board of Inspectors of Secondary Schools (BISS) was seconded to Shears and Morton to help establish both programs. An apt selection, Gill's secondary teaching experience embraced regional and suburban high schools (including Melbourne HS) and he had lectured at the University of Melbourne's School of Education (1956–63) and the Secondary Teachers College (1961–64). He was appointed to the BISS in 1964, and after study abroad graduated with an MEd in educational administration from the University of Alberta (1967). While overseas he observed the Inner London Education Authority's comprehensive schools and at home had co-directed educational administrative courses. After secondment to Shears and Morton, Gill travelled abroad with senior officers to select teacher recruits in the UK, the USA and Canada. The recruitment team comprised, on occasion, Gill, Shears and Morton and Director of Secondary Education (DSE) Bert Schruhm, who took brochures to promote both the personal and professional benefits that the programs offered.[497]

---

**Teach in Victoria, Australia**
**Fly free**
**Ensure yourself a teaching appointment and travel**
**Living costs in UK equated to Common Market currency.**
**Per pound: Lamb 28 np, Beef 32 np, Butter 32 np;**
**Ladies' dresses average £9; men's suits £40;**
**20 cigarettes 20 np; petrol 24 np per gallon;**
**one bedroom flat £40 per week;**
**three bedroom home £90.**

---

*Recruitment brochure for Victorian Teacher Selection Program* [498]

In Canada Morton observed recession had halted tertiary growth. Static Year 12 enrolments reduced the trainee pool and the future for teachers looked bleak. Due to the 'grave shortage of teaching positions' he was inundated with inquiries. In the UK Schruhm noted teachers' dissatisfaction regarding non-traditional tertiary pathways. They considered Victoria the 'vanguard regarding curriculum' with opportunities to 'experiment in curriculum and method'. From 500 applicants he selected teachers with expertise in mathematics, science, English, physical education and general subjects. The tri-nation campaign harvested 680 recruits for the VTSP who arrived in August 1972 on 'a chartered Jumbo 747 and two 707s'.[499] Successively 500 arrived in September 1972, 50 in January 1973, 75 and 100 in September 1973.[500] Placed according to the needs of schools and teachers' preference, the scheme helped the Department overcome a serious dilemma and ensured an ongoing supply of qualified teachers. Aware that of recent years staffing was the biggest challenge, Shears warned, 'we must maintain vigilance to see that progress we are making continues'.[501]

## International Teaching Fellowship program

Lindsay Thompson wrote in his memoirs:

> One day the Assistant Director-General, Dr Lawrie Shears, came to me with an enterprising proposal to award what were termed International Teaching Fellowships to an outstanding teacher in each of the 50 American States and to two such teachers in each of the Canadian Provinces. A similar invitation was sent to 12 local education authorities in Britain ... The teachers were to come for a two-year period and the Department intended to ask that preference might be given to science and mathematics teachers.[502]

Thompson recalled the proposal as 'enterprising'. He saw its 'immediate appeal' and 'long-range impact'. Importantly its introduction corresponded with celebrations for the Education Department's centenary. Prior to the election of 1970 the ITF scheme gained Cabinet approval, thenceforth Treasury funding tendered prestige to 'highly selected' 'experienced teachers in their mid thirties, preferably with a Master's degree'. A letter signed by Premier Bolte and bundles of red, green and blue pamphlets were sent to the governors of every state in the USA, education ministers in every Canadian province and administrators of Britain's twelve largest education authorities. The program offered '$4800 annual living allowance plus return travel'. Shears departed in March 1970 to establish himself in London at the

Agent-General office and then went to Washington and San Francisco in the USA to establish the recruitment drive.[503]

An entourage of top brass greeted the first 81 Fellows in February 1971. The Minister hosted a reception. In attendance were Joseph Rafferty,[504] Assistant Minister of Education, the Director-General and the Assistant Directors-General. Divisional Directors and their assistants, school principals, representatives of teacher organisations and members of the press were also present. Shears introduced arrivals from 'England, Scotland, Ireland, Wales, the Provinces of Canada and the States of the USA'. He affirmed the program would ease teacher demand, establish international goodwill and 'heighten the celebration of the centenary of State education next year'.[505] Incoming Fellows were accommodated at halls of residence attached to teachers colleges for an orientation program by divisional directors and their staff who explained Victoria's culture of schooling; the city of Melbourne; and the State's political, social and environmental scene, and alluded to 'unbelievably parochial' attitudes that the Fellows might encounter.[506]

The IFT program was prominent among Shears' activities. He thrived on the hectic pace and the fanfare of greetings and goodbyes and enjoyed opportunities to travel abroad. Those involved in the program recalled often 'leaving the office on Friday afternoon and starting work in London at 9 o'clock on Monday morning'. The program flourished and became well-known in the broader educational community. At a Christmas function at Monash University in 1972, Ivan Barko, Professor of French, enquired, 'Would you and your wife like to go to France at the invitation of the French Government?' Within days Professor of German, Leslie Bodi, posed an invitation for the Shears to visit the Federal Republic of Germany in the forthcoming January recruitment drive.

In France, 50th anniversary celebrations of the Association of Pre-School Teachers stirred Shears' interest in early childhood learning. Similarly 'stimulating and challenging' were discussions concerning the nation's Five-year Economic Plan and affirmed conviction to establish long-term goals. Concepts of administration, tuition and syllabus coordination influenced his thoughts on policy development as he conceptualised the school in the wider social community. An

'Eco Model' of organisation presenting the school and community in close liaison sharpened his intent to bridge the divide. While in Paris, Shears and Mavis attended official functions and visited 'places of historic and artistic value in Paris and its environs'.[507]

Bonn and Cologne in the Federal Republic of Germany hosted discussion regarding the Report on Educational Organization and Development. Pains to boost teacher numbers and raise teachers' professional status paralleled Victoria's plight. The Republic's model of decentralisation and community involvement with parental and pupil input shaped Shears' vision 'that all levels of the school system should be considered to have equal quality and importance'.[508] Enriched by the European extension of the recruitment drive, Shears invited French and West German governments to participate in the ITF program. On his return to the office in March he promoted an 'International Teaching Fellowship Exchange Program'. He perceived 'senior outstanding teachers in Victoria will exchange on a calendar year basis with overseas teachers (possibly house, car and salary exchange as the basis of the program)'. In later years when the program was called an 'exchange' he claimed it was 'a matching procedure'.[509]

## Looking ahead: A tough row to hoe

Nationwide, Australia's education departments were challenged to keep pace, provide teachers, classrooms and schools, and look ahead in order to make viable plans. The Australian Education Council met annually to formulate policy that it hoped would alleviate problems. To address administration, teacher preparation and education, and funding for buildings, equipment and resources for the next five years, in 1969 the AEC conducted a Survey of Needs. Based on this, the State Ministers presented policy to the Standing Committee of their Directors-General to ensure desirable standards for all to complete secondary schooling.[510] Education departments faced not only financial shortfalls, but intrusion of the Commonwealth on their domain. In 1969 arguments presented at a UNESCO Conference in Canberra supported a national approach to educational policy-making. Although Directors-General rejected national control, they called for Commonwealth support. The Commonwealth department, however, was unprepared to suitably fund special grants, teacher training and capital expenditure on new buildings; and its intention to conduct its own inquiry countered the prerogative of the States. Meanwhile, pressure groups were demanding Commonwealth assistance. Maintaining their stance the AEC presented survey results in February 1970 that revealed deficiencies were common to all States.

In 1971, Vice Chancellor of Flinders University Peter Karmel took an economic stance to guarantee education met the needs of the teacher and child and satisfied the nation's citizenship ideals. Curriculum reform was a fundamental step towards unifying secondary education and securing equity regardless of background.[511] In Victoria, Minister Thompson envisaged all children should achieve 'full development of their spiritual, mental, physical and creative powers ... regardless of colour, class, race or creed' to warrant 'true equality of educational purpose'.[512]

**Table 9. Schools and expenditure**

|  | 1960–61 | 1970–71 | % increase or decrease |
|---|---|---|---|
| **Numbers of schools** | | | |
| Primary | 1,920 | 1,853 | - 3.5% |
| Secondary | 182 | 250 | + 37% |
| Technical | 70 | 95 | + 36% |
| **Expenditure on:** | | | |
| Teachers' salaries | $50,703,486 | $145,758,412 | + 190% |
| Buildings | 19,286,760 | 29,248,532 | +52% |
| Teachers colleges | 8,931,738 | 24,560,406 | + 177% |

Source: Schools and expenditure; Survey and Statistics Branch[513]

Despite these ideals the rift between promise and provision deepened. Growth was a major factor. In Victoria, costs to develop and service the system made incredible leaps. By 1971, Victoria had 30 per cent more schools than a decade before. In the same period expenditure on teachers' salaries had risen by 190 per cent, buildings by 52 per cent and money devoted to teachers colleges by 177 per cent. Vision to move ahead, plan appropriately and implement these ideals relied on ministerial sway to grasp an increasing share of Treasury funds.

Although decision-makers attempted to satisfy educational needs, teachers, union members and community groups became increasingly agitated. They were alarmed by the lack of qualified secondary teachers, understaffing, conditions in schools and non-representation of secondary teachers on the Teachers Tribunal. Frustration provoked strike action. The VSTA conducted a series of rolling strikes at Melbourne, Glenroy and Maribyrnong High Schools, and held a statewide strike and mass meeting at the Myer Music Bowl. Government proposed legislation to stop such action and in 1971 commissioned Judge Alec Southwell to conduct an Inquiry into the Tribunal's composition. VSTA executive boycotted the Inquiry, whereas the VTU and the Technical Teachers' Association of Victoria (TTAV) attended conditional upon a review of Departmental administration.

Midst this confusion the Southwell Committee wrote its review. It questioned the Department's ability to cope, criticised the supply and training of teachers, the provision of buildings and amenities and its administrative capacity. A projected restructure of the Teachers Tribunal involved a complete overhaul, with designated units allied to the teaching divisions. Each would determine qualifications and identify clear distinctions between primary and postprimary matters. Noting likely developments and ongoing growth, the report proposed a personnel branch to manage administrative matters, in turn alleviating the Tribunal's involvement in 'appeals, discipline, disputes over terms and conditions of employment and salary and allowance claims'. The report admonished VSTA tactics as a scare campaign and questioned assertions that Departmental officers underestimated the substance of VSTA concerns.[514]

Moves were already afoot in the Education Department to review administration and in June 1970 management consultants WD Scott & Co began the task. Rapid expansion made the Department unwieldy. As it grew in size and complexity traditional lines of command and divisional structures became blurred. Responsibilities of the regional directors proposed by Thompson would cut across the organisation of 'five separate divisions organised vertically'. Regional directors would take a horizontal stance to 'administrative tasks across the board and nearer to those who were to be affected'. At one extreme was the Director-General or designated Assistants. At the other extreme was the school and its community.[515]

The Scott Report (1973) accentuated 'liaison and/or communication between individuals throughout the three personnel branches and the accounts branch with particular emphasis on liaison and/or communication between the administrative branches and teachers/schools/tribunal and teacher division staff'. An examination of 'the whole structure of administration and relationships between various personnel' led to 132 recommendations, 90 of which were implemented by July 1972.[516] In response, Shears claimed 'extreme difficulty of obtaining an efficient administration when many of its decisions are in fact made by external statutory authorities such as the Teachers Tribunal and the Committee of Classifiers'. Although he acknowledged their important role, he alleged they did not have responsibility to administer the total educational program.[517]

Exacerbating communication was the matter of working conditions of senior staff. Increasing in number, they had outgrown the confines of Treasury Place. Senior officers from the Secondary and Technical Divisions shifted to 480 Collins Street and while they had better working conditions they were distanced from the administrative hub.[518] Further aggravating communication was restructure of Special Services and Teacher Education Divisions, each of which had 'particular educational demesnes of engagement and influence'.[519] Special Services, established in 1968 under Director Thomas (Les) Emerson, encompassed fourteen branches: Audiovisual Education, Curriculum and Research, Education of Backward Children (including prison education), Education of Physically Handicapped Children, Homecrafts, Music, Publications, Physical Education, Psychology and Guidance, School Camps, School Forestry, School Libraries, Speech Therapy and Welfare. The Division of Teacher Education, established in 1962 under Director Len Pryor, recruited teachers, administered studentships, staffed teachers colleges and planned in-service studies. Staffed by four in 1962, by 1971 it employed seventeen staff.

## Promoting teacher training

Throughout his career Shears honed his views on training teachers and sought to promote the profession. Au fait with the local system, he also had insight into systems abroad. Visiting Britain in 1950, in the wake of the McNair Report (1944), he had witnessed debates on training teachers and leaders of youth. He experienced the spectrum of educational provision and noted the prestige of courses presented at institutes affiliated with universities. A decade later in California, he observed the evolution of state colleges through recommendations of the Strayer Report (1947), California's Survey of Needs (1948) and the Master Plan (1960), which sanctioned the colleges as a non-university option. Under the aegis of a parent body, individual colleges pervaded traditional tertiary domains, responded to the 'professional, economic, social, cultural and vocational activities' of their communities and were certified to satisfy postgraduate needs.

Impressed by the prestige of California's institutes and state colleges and the high ranking afforded their courses, Shears continued the thrust to raise the status of Victoria's teachers colleges. He scorned financial imbalance in the funding of tertiary studies, derided 'educational elitism' held by universities and questioned the nation's failure to consider the nature and needs of the economy when determining the statutes of tertiary institutions.[520] Concerned by the bond between teacher training institutions and the employer, namely teachers colleges and the Department, he advocated 'the splitting away of the teachers' colleges from the Education Department as essential if they are going to be degree-granting institutions'.[521]

Victoria boasted three universities and a host of alternative tertiary institutes in the 1970s. Teachers colleges, senior technical schools, colleges of advanced education and specialist institutes offered courses dedicated to specific fields. Personally validating their rank as non-university options, Shears argued, 'because it is different is insufficient reason to consider it unworthy of degree status'.[522] He forecast a surge in demand for degree qualifications and derided educational planners who, despite 'the unprecedented increase in the holding power of schools' and the resulting 'wave assuming tidal proportions ... ignored the facts which were available upwards of a decade ago'. He claimed lethargy had triggered university quotas. This affected the shortage of teachers and other professionals and damaged the aspirations of young men and women.[523]

## The national outlook

Attempts to promote a more liberal approach to tertiary education were prolonged. Nationally, the Murray Report (1957) approved the establishment of new universities, among them Monash (1958) and La Trobe (1964) in Victoria, and an Australian Universities Commission (AUC).[524] In Victoria, while the Report of the Fourth University Committee – chaired by Thomas Meek Ramsay, hence Ramsay Report (1972) – sought distinction between the roles of universities, teachers colleges and colleges of advanced education, it questioned how the new university would embrace teacher education and utilise current facilities. Subsequently, the Martin Report (1964), authorised by Prime Minister Menzies, sought submissions regarding the future of tertiary education. Responses from Australia's educational elite came from James Darling (Head Master, Geelong Grammar School and President, Australian College of Education); Professors Charles Moorhouse (Dean of Engineering, University of Melbourne) and Richard Selby-Smith (Dean of Education, Monash University); Dr Bill Radford (Director ACER); and Dr Lawrie Shears (Principal, Burwood Teachers College).

Teacher education, according to Shears, lay at the source of economic development; in the hands of the country's teachers lay the futures of its youth. Likewise the Martin Report claimed the crux of development lay in training teachers whose impact flowed through all levels of schooling. To satisfy rising enrolments the report confirmed the need for more teachers to teach more classes with fewer students. It identified the trend to decrease class size and claimed the need for an additional 10,000 primary teachers by 1975. It called for more training places in secondary and tertiary sectors and a 'pressing need to improve the quality of that preparation'.[525] Advocating additional State and Commonwealth funds to promote standards[526] and questioning the nature and content of courses, the report advised 'continuous expansion of knowledge' of trainees and teachers already in the field.[527] Warning of 'dangers latent in the relationship between state departments of education and teachers' colleges', it suggested a Board of Teacher Education as a statutory body to 'ensure a continuing recruitment of high quality staff'. Open advertising was 'a prime requisite for teachers colleges appointments'.[528]

## Competing forces

The thrust to convert teachers colleges into diploma and degree institutions was echoed in technical fields. The expansion of colleges of advanced education in Victoria and their clout as a unified body, the Victoria Institute of Colleges (VIC), under Vice President Phillip Garth Law was a force for Shears to contest. Law was resolute in leadership as his reflections on his Antarctic exploration reveal:

> I didn't give orders from the top and didn't act aggressively. I used to collaborate with the men and try to enthuse them. I had very close contact working with them, leading from the front and taking part in all the difficult things, rather than sitting in an office giving instructions.[529]

Both Shears and Law held firm views regarding the development of further education. Both sought recognition of technical and teachers colleges as viable tertiary institutions of degree-granting status. Colleges of advanced education presented a united front under the aegis of the VIC instituted in 1967. Law described the VIC as 'an umbrella' organisation that coordinated the activities of up to sixteen colleges of advanced education. It took into its fold selected technical institutes that each managed their own finance, staff and particular expertise. The inclusion of Bendigo, Caulfield, Preston, Prahran and Warrnambool Technical Colleges, the Gordon and Royal Melbourne Institutes of Technology and the Ballarat School of Mines, promoted the VIC's public image.[530] Administratively, Law was responsible 'both to the Commonwealth, who were funding it, and to the State Minister of Education, who was in control of the College system'.[531] Though proud of the VIC's 'non U' status and the quality of its courses, Law was bothered by the socially constructed tertiary divide. Through ardent campaigning he believed that 'we at the VIC were responsible for the drive to upgrade the colleges to degree status'. He believed, 'the Commonwealth was violently against it'. Aware of threatened funding cuts, 'we used the Pharmacy College as the first degree institution because it had a strong parliamentary lobby in Canberra'.[532]

Law's determination expanded the scope of VIC courses to embrace social and behavioural sciences, physical education and humanities.[533] By 1972 legislation enabled the VIC and colleges of advanced education across the nation to grant higher degrees and make inroads into the universities' domain. Law's 'vision splendid' kept the VIC abreast of 'developing educational demands of our technical age'. However, preserving the VIC's unique characteristics required community pride in colleges of advanced education, which maintained strong links with industry and offered solid vocational bias.[534]

The same rang true for teachers colleges under a proposed State College mantle. As specialist institutions they were unique and maintained vocational bias with strong links to schools. Unlike the VIC colleges the teachers colleges did not receive Commonwealth funding. VIC activity and financial support niggled Shears who sought similar support for teachers colleges. The Education Department steadfastly aimed to provide specialist teacher training, and opposed the financial lure of the Commonwealth to bring them into the domain of the VIC. Shears affirmed their specialist role and signalled the VIC's technical bias. He argued, 'It was all the thing to support technology, and as a result of this we failed to consider the role that teachers colleges had been playing for many decades, the advances they had made in their courses and in their staffs, and in their student numbers, and in qualifications.'[535]

## Victoria's State College system

Debate regarding Commonwealth funds for teacher training was prolonged. The Martin Report had stressed its importance, yet despite the massive expansion of education and the need to boost teacher training (an estimated 10,000 places for primary teachers nationwide by 1975), the Commonwealth did not budge. Directors-General Robertson (WA) and Wyndham (NSW) deplored the decision not to fund teacher education knowing that Commonwealth funds were channelled towards tertiary technical colleges. They claimed 'teacher training expenditure is equally an investment in human capital [and] without such training the education system cannot function efficiently, and the financial assistance to other branches of tertiary education envisaged by the Martin Report is thereby rendered less effective.'[536]

Debate continued to no avail, and although the AEC's campaign emphasised the plight of teachers colleges, it was the CAEs that profited with Commonwealth funds. Malcolm Fraser, Minister for Education and Science (1968–69), like his predecessor Senator the Hon. John Gorton, Minister for Education (1966–68), argued that funding for teachers colleges was a State responsibility. AEC executive bewailed its 'ineffective voice in attracting Commonwealth assistance to what was widely regarded as the most pressing area of need, the schools'. In an address to the State Advisory Council on Tertiary Education in January 1969, Shears as teachers college principal had confirmed the Commonwealth's duty to finance all tertiary education. Rather than a loosely bonded specialist group of colleges he proposed multi-purpose institutes. United under a State College mantle, teachers colleges would offer liberal and theatre arts, social sciences and administration in addition to teacher education. To sustain his claim, he identified the source of trainees, staff selection criteria and projected staffing and building requirements.[537]

Shears pledged a unified front to raise the professional status of teachers and their training courses and promote an autonomous State College system. In supporting this he identified Doug McDonell, Principal of the Secondary Teachers College, as 'a driving force' who supported 'the move for independence'.[538] Shears and McDonell grieved to see colleges of advanced education functioning like the universities while teachers colleges struggled to train more teachers within the confines of State funding. They lamented classification of teachers college courses as 'Mickey Mouse' and affirmed the Commonwealth's duty 'to assist each State in the program which the State selects for the development of teacher education as part of an overall tertiary education program'. Aware of guidelines for distribution of Commonwealth money they resolved to unite teachers colleges under a State College mantle and promote teacher education and the standard of courses to university status.[539]

The quest to attain these ideals alienated Shears from teachers college staff concerned about the impact of change. They felt secure knowing 'the Education Department had always been there, the pay cheques always arrived, and the conditions were sure. If they [teachers colleges] were to be governed by a council, who knows what might happen?'[540] James (Mac) Hill, Principal of Burwood Teachers College, wanted teacher education retained as a separate sector. He feared loss of identity, of which each teachers college was proud. In response, Shears depicted 'a gradual evolution during this decade of a binary system involving the incorporation of teachers colleges within a university structure'.[541]

The pros and cons of a State College system were widely debated as the push continued. The concept of autonomy – colleges acting independently from the Education Department, the employer of teachers – complied with Fraser's guidelines. Eventually, in August 1972, the Commonwealth agreed to extend tertiary funding to teachers colleges providing they 'are being developed as self-governing tertiary institutions under the supervision of appropriate bodies in the State'.[542] Debate thence turned to the State College structure; whether to reflect the VIC model or comprise constituent parts of a fourth university.

Compliant with Commonwealth guidelines, the thrust of these endeavours led to the *State College of Victoria Act* 1972 (No. 8736). The newly established State College fostered 'the development and improvement of institutions offering tertiary education ... other than the universities of Victoria and the affiliated colleges of the Victoria Institute of Colleges'; proposed to 'co-ordinate the development of the constituent colleges for the purpose of teacher education' and offered courses to students 'other than those intending to become teachers'.[543] In a tribute to Shears, in May 1973 *The Age* referred to the 'The State College Bill' as 'his baby'. This was a tribute to a dream coming true.[544] Under Vice President Doug McDonell the State College of Victoria (SCV) began operation on 17 July, with 11,000 students and 1,000 staff. Colleague and friend Laurie Bell also recognised the passion and power of Shears to bring this to fruition. He referred to Shears as 'the architect of autonomy for the colleges and cutting them free from the Education Department'. He affirmed, 'Without Lawrie Shears that would not have happened.'[545] The SCV was a 'big step towards an ultimate objective of having a graduate teaching profession'.[546] Improving the standards and status of teacher education lay at the heart of Shears' reform agenda.

## Moves afoot

With Director Brooks' forthcoming retirement, the Assistant Directors-General each vied for his place. Coordinating centenary celebrations, sustaining smooth transition of the regional structure and promoting leadership programs, Moore was prominently positioned. Though Morton's expertise focused on infrastructure and facilities, his knowledge of growth patterns, changing demographics and emerging needs set him in good stead. During a study tour of the UK with Chief Superintendent Auman of the Public Works Department, Morton observed varying models of decentralisation, and he was alert to the necessity for central administration to remain aware of the actual need in the field. Like Moore and Morton, Shears played a significant role as an ADGE. Establishment of the Victorian Teacher Selection Program and International Teaching Fellowship showed initiative. Developments in teacher education, passing of legislation to establish the SCV, involvement in planning the fourth university showed breadth of knowledge, capacity to guide and passion to serve. Within the Department he was positioned well, having supported the launch of *Interchange*, a medium of communication for senior staff, and introduced *News Exchange*, the fortnightly broadsheet to augment dialogue between administrators and schools. Prominent in educational and public domains, Shears frequently spoke at speech nights, graduations and conferences, made media comment and published extensively on policy, teacher supply and education in general. Au fait with all aspects of the Department, though lacking inspectorial experience, he had acted as Deputy Director-General during Brooks' leave-of-absence in July 1972. During this timely appointment he reviewed the total structure of the Education Department from the Director-General down, appraised Southwell's recommendations and revised regulations as stipulated in the Scott Report.[547]

On 28 Saturday October 1972 an advertisement in local, national and international newspapers called for applications for the new Director-General of Education in Victoria. Applications closed on 27 November. 'Going – a $22,500 job', subsequently wrote Iola Mathews of *The Age*. ADGE Moore announced in *Interchange* 'the Minister will make a recommendation to Cabinet in February … the appointment will actually date from 5 May 1973.'[548]

Thenceforth each ADGE promoted his profile. Moore's appointment as Victorian Director of the Australian Education Council's Survey of Educational Needs (1969–70) and Chairman of the Department's Decentralisation Committee (1970–71) demonstrated leadership and administrative abilities. Of a similar age to Shears, Moore completed TPTC at Melbourne TC in 1941. Unlike Shears, who received an extension to university, and was duly considered secondary teaching material, Moore enlisted and served in the AIF. After the war he completed his BA under the Commonwealth Reconstruction Training Program, and for ten years taught in country high schools. Moore followed the traditional promotional path from teaching into the inspectorate, and then, granted study leave in 1963–64, he completed an MEd in educational administration at the University of Alberta. Like Shears, he rose swiftly through the promotional ranks and was appointed Assistant Chief Inspector of Secondary Schools in 1966 (later became Assistant Director of Secondary Education – ADSE). Moore's high profile in educational administration in Victoria and overseas, equipped him to direct Departmental courses from 1966 until his appointment as an ADGE in 1971. In this capacity Moore steered expansion of the regional system statewide. In November 1972 he reported, 'we are awaiting decisions on regional boundaries which are being discussed by a decentralisation committee set up by the Premier's Department'.[549] In March 1973 he visited the USA to discuss health, education, welfare and educational administration with officials in Washington DC, Sacramento and San Francisco. His knowledge of schooling and Departmental operations, his senior position and demonstrated leadership skills, presented him as a fine professional and public figure. He had an authoritative style and was a keen contender for the top job.

Similarly Shears was viewed as having potential to reach the top. His knowledge of schooling was vast, his experience broad though his professional pathway distanced him from the inspectorial fraternity. Some factions within the Department doubted his ability to lead the system, while others applauded his experience across the spectrum of schooling and his administrative skills. Some recognised attributes in his suave and profound presence while others construed his educational goings-on as egotistical, interpreted his knowledge as 'know-all', and his outgoing nature as self-centred. Despite shadows of doubt Iola Matthews surmised, on account of seniority, experience and qualifications, he might well become the next Director-General. She reported sources within the Education Department tipped him above Moore and accredited his role in the 'massive recruitment programmes of overseas teachers ... which have done a great deal to ease the teacher shortage in secondary schools'. She noted his active role in planning for a fourth university and gaining autonomy for teachers colleges.[550]

Shears had seen a glint of hope appear at Premier Bolte's farewell dinner in August 1972. He excused himself from the table where he was seated with dignitaries Louis Matheson (later Sir), Vice Chancellor Monash University, and Roger Darvall (later Sir), General Manager of the ANZ Bank, to convey his best wishes to the retiring premier. From the podium Bolte stooped and asked, 'So you want to be Director-General?' 'Yes, sir,' Shears replied.[551]

In that political climate, Thompson later admitted, Ministers ran their own departments, and as Minister of Education his authority was paramount. Aware of contenders for the top job he considered Shears as 'alert, enthusiastic and enterprising' with the capacity to lead education in Victoria. He reflected:

> He, to me, was the outstanding candidate. I had no difficulty in deciding who should be the next Director-General to replace Fred Brooks. I appointed him as the Director-

General because I thought he was the best applicant for the job on account of those qualities, being enthusiastic, alert and enterprising. I thought we needed someone of that quality, someone who could lead with vision, efficiency and enterprise.[552]

On 21 March 1973 *The Age* announced Dr Lawrie Shears to be Victoria's new education chief. Taking command of 41,000 teachers from 5 May, he maintained the virtues of travel to rid teachers of their parochial views. Impressed by his recent visit to the UK, France and Germany, he was keen to implement five-year planning and get teachers out of the classroom to broaden their minds.[553] *The Sun* reported the 51 year-old 'new man for schools' hot spot' would have fewer problems than his predecessor, while *The Australian* considered him 'relaxed about the hot seat'.[554]

## Other dimensions of Shears

Before leaving Burwood TC, Shears purchased a house in Hopetoun Road, Toorak. At home he entertained friends, colleagues and overseas guests at dinner parties, barbecues and tennis parties. Poppa Shears was open-mouthed when he first saw the big home, but was a regular visitor. He died there aged 73. Grandma Redman stayed there too following Fred's death. Mavis managed the home and family and continued her studies in arts and education at Monash University. Living in Toorak, St John's became the family church, Archdeacon Phillip Newman a family friend and Shears was appointed to vestry. He maintained stringent routines (a 'coping mechanism', he confided) and a small pocket diary listed daily appointments.

Shear's new routine resembled the busy Harkness Fellowship schedule. Shears continued to lecture in the Faculty of Education at Monash University until 1970, and he strengthened his links with Korowa CEGGS when Meredith joined Christine at the school. Anglican Bishop John Arnott had invited Shears to join the Korowa Council (1968–72), an 'interesting experience relating to the functioning of an independent school'.[555] In other domains he had served as President, Victorian Coordinating Council of the Australian Student

Christian Movement (1969–72); Chairman of the College of Nursing Australia; and adviser to Jacaranda Press apropos a research centre.

Research was important on Shears' agenda and links with research organisations remained strong. Professor Bill Connell, University of Sydney, wrote to acknowledge his 'careful editing' of the *Australian Journal of Education*. He continued, 'My faith in your judgement has been justified … and I would like to congratulate you on its production.' Shears attended annual conferences of the Australian College of Education, continued presidency of the Victorian Institute for Educational Research and was among the group of leading educators who supported the budding Australian Association for Research in Education. Overlapping his time at Burwood TC and appointment as an ADGE, Shears chaired the Victorian Chapter of ACE (1966–69) and led a review of its future direction. Due to lack of funds and encroaching lethargy the College needed a boost. National office bearers who attended a residential conference at Whitehall Guesthouse, Sorrento, were challenged by keynote speaker, Dr R D Goodman of the Queensland Chapter, who asked, 'Whither the College or where do we go from here?' Goodman identified the 'tremendous upsurge in secondary enrolments' during the span of a decade; the 'remarkable growth in numbers of teachers in training'; and the 'proliferation of tertiary institutions'. He noted Commonwealth involvement 'aiding the States with grants for science laboratories, secondary scholarships and the like'. With such changes in train he alerted delegates to an ever-evolving future and charged them to ensure the College was sufficiently 'flexible in its constitution and organisation to adapt itself to the social and educational changes of the next ten years'. Membership must expand beyond the privileged elite and 'dip into a larger group of young, qualified teachers'. He claimed there were too many drones among the current 2,500 members; only 500 were 'dedicated, hard-working, busy educationists who have a spiritual conviction that the Australian College of Education can make a substantial contribution to the improvement of education'.[556] It was time to establish a solid foundation. State chapters were detached from the central body. Council representation was askew, 'too Victorian dominated', Goodman stressed. 'If it is to be an Australian College, then we must find a formula to make the

Council representative of the whole ... whatever weakens the Chapter weakens the College.'[557] He continued, 'We are living in an educational revolution and the opportunity is there for the College to demonstrate its leadership in educational thought.'

Regardless of his position, Shears was accessible to those in need or with gripes. Professor Selby-Smith from Monash University thanked him for the copy of the Presidential Address he had been invited to deliver to the ANZAAS Conference in Perth and Professor Austin, University of Melbourne, invited him to examine an MEd thesis on teacher training. Past students, teachers, parents and acquaintances similarly requested copies of speeches, sought advice, asked for intervention on relocation, expressed thanks or simply kept in touch. A handwritten note to Dr Shears by a grandmother asked, 'Would you, could you please help me?' In later years she acknowledged 'your unfailing friendship, help and leadership in spite of so many other calls on your time'.

A public figure, Shears was open to criticism. Writing in *The Australian* Mrs Joan Kirner, President, Victorian Federation of State Schools Mothers' Clubs, alluded to the independent–government school divide. She scorned the idea of superiority of the independent schools and supported parents who 'determined to keep their child in a state school'. She believed they chose 'breadth of experience and freedom essential to the development of the child as a human through contact with other humans of every class and creed'.[558] Shears acknowledged it was wrong to 'perpetuate the myth that commitment to children's needs is a virtue reserved for staffs of independent schools, and perhaps unwittingly to cast a slur on state school teachers.' He affirmed his belief in the education system where 'state schools by the score are "living communities"' staffed by teachers with 'commitment, intelligence, creativity and empathetic understanding of other persons'.[559] His decision to place his own children in nongovernment secondary schools for their secondary education was criticised. It was a mistake on his part, some said.[560] In personal correspondence one critic wrote, 'Shame on you mate, it's obvious your ilk don't like competition for their kids ... completely dishonest like most Liberal politicians [you] send your kids to private schools where the great message is Dollars are Best.' The letter was signed, 'Yours in Disgust'.[561] Despite such criticism Shears maintained the choice of school protected the children from slurs on account of his public office. While he protected the family this cast a shadow on his own integrity.

Promotion to Director-General signalled the time to rationalise present activities to devote energy to the task ahead. Shears broke his links with Monash University, relinquished his reign as State Editor of the *Australian Journal of Education* (1956–72) and resigned as Chairman of the College of Nursing Australia (1963–72). Positions as President of the Victorian Coordinating Council, Australian Student Christian Movement in Schools (1967–72), adviser to the Educational Research and Development Centre (1969–72) and Council member at Korowa CEGGS (1968–72) became history.

A new era had dawned with new challenges ahead.

CHAPTER 14

# IN THE CHAIR (1973–75)

*A leader is a dealer in hope.*

Napoleon Bonaparte

## Becoming Director-General

On 5 May 1973, Dr Lawrence Shears stepped into shoes first worn by Frank Tate, to become Victoria's eighth educational leader. Tate, a fine administrator of considerable community status, drove development in secondary education 'for the people' and established the teaching divisions 'each with their own set of powers'. A man of 'initiative', he was 'willing to serve, but not stand still and wait … [and] retained his effectiveness because to the end he retained his enthusiasm'. Shears aspired to similar ideals. Now the permanent head, like Tate he had risen through the ranks, a 'Little God Almighty' atop Victoria's education empire. Like predecessors he held 'the responsibility of administering all Acts in any way relating to Education'.[562]

Cards, letters and telegrams offered approval, support and advice. Frank Watts, the ABC's Federal Director of Education, cautioned, 'I cannot think of anyone better equipped personally and professionally to cope with the difficulties you have ahead.'[563] Bill Radford predicted 'the present confrontation tactics are a passing phase, but they must be very galling!' Gwen Wainwright, ADSE, wished 'enduring patience and an ability to withstand the slings and arrows and such-like … we can hope that the worst days have passed and the Department can soon regain some of its former public lustre.' Historian Les Blake wrote that it 'must be one of the toughest jobs in Australia'.

Prominent educationists nationwide endorsed the appointment. Ronald Goldman, Foundation Dean of Education at La Trobe

University, stated that 'the Department will find the leadership it needs at this time'; Richard Selby-Smith, former Dean of Education at Monash University, felt 'Victoria is very lucky to have you', and Wilfred Frederick, Dean of Education at the University of Melbourne, saluted:

> ... your elevation to the top post in Victorian education ... you have a battery of qualifications, not the least open-mindedness and freshness of vision ... It pleases me, in particular, to remember that a good part of your professional life has been concerned, directly or indirectly, with what we now call teacher education ... you join hands with Frank Tate and his successors.

Norman Curry, from the University of Melbourne, acknowledged the 'well-deserved honour' with certainty that 'you will grace the position as you have in earlier appointments'. He warned of ill-informed criticism, and affirmed the support of friends 'thankful that the position is held by someone with your experience, skill and compassion'.

Alby Jones, Director-General of Education in South Australia, welcomed Shears to the Standing Committee of the Australian Education Council and his forthcoming chairmanship in June.

Phillip Law of the VIC warned of intensified challenge, acknowledged 'our odd philosophical differences in the past will doubtless continue', and assured Shears that, 'it has been possible to enjoy a warm personal relationship – long may it continue'. Ken McKinnon, Director of Education in New Guinea, felt confident 'you will accomplish a great deal ... despite "legislative and administrative" restraints'. Graham Allen, from Caulfield Institute of Technology, warned of revolutionary advances expected by some although, he said, 'I'm not!' Cabinet had made a 'first rate appointment' and he looked for 'many advances – both small and big, some even unnoticed – in your fourteen years as DGE'. Mac Hill, Principal of Burwood TC, likewise 'endorsed Cabinet's decision'; Ida Lowndes, Principal of Coburg TC expressed pleasure, and Hilma Cranley, former President of the VTU, wrote, 'I'm glad to have you for my chief'. Bert Schruhm, DSE, conveyed congratulations; Jeff Dunstan, district inspector, hoped 'you will derive much satisfaction', and Lorna Williams of the College of Nursing Australia was 'pleased to hear of your appointment'. Mick

Kent of Rural Training Centre days recalled 'the assistance you gave to our son last year', Syd Dyson from Bairnsdale HS expressed 'fond memories', and Wanda Grace (formerly Osborne) from Korong Vale asked, 'Could you be the same Lorry Shears who once taught me?' Joan Kirner, who represented the Victorian Federation of State Schools Mothers Clubs, looked forward to discussions on mutual aims.

Friends Ted and Irene Liefman from CSR's 'Roseneath' in Woodend, Lou and Mona Barberis from Latrobe High School and Ron and Melva Burton of the Burwood years acclaimed the news, and Ken and Joy Sargeant 'knew that there could be no other appointment'. The Radleys in England sent 'love and congratulations to Director General and his lady', Christine wrote, 'Congratulations to my Father ... with love from your daughter and first achievement' and Meredith claimed, 'Boy do you ever deserve it! ... from an un-biased daughter.' Shears replied 'I'm glad that you believe I deserve it, particularly as you are completely non-biased, Love Dad.'

On a small crisp card in her neat bold hand Dr Alice Hoy wrote, 'Congratulations Lawrie and good wishes for a peaceful time in Office.' Miss Pauline Knight from his Miller Street days expressed 'sincere congratulations and a little prayer that you will find the years ahead rewarding, successful and happy ... I know that you will bring dignity to this position'. In reply Shears wrote:

> ... of all the letters ... the one I appreciated most was yours. I cannot forget my first contact with teaching and my enthusiasm for it which came from those first weeks in 1939 when I was attached to your Grade 3 at Miller Street, North Fitzroy.

## The new man

Midst commands to Jezebel the dog to get off his bed, Shears presented his first interview at Hopetoun Road flat on his back. Lifting groceries from the car, he had slipped a disk. From his bed he read his address for the Drugs and Society Conference at Monash University. A press release introduced the 'youngest Director-General of Education since the legendary Frank Tate' and identified his 'contributions to educational theory and practice [that] established him in the academic world as an internationally respected authority'. To Shears it attributed the International Teaching Fellowship Program, recruitment of overseas teachers and advocacy for the State College of Victoria. It continued, 'Under the administration of Dr Shears, one would expect an emphasis on transferring decision-making to the school level' and noted the proposal to make regular visits to the 'regional directors and to regional organizations representing educationists both within and outside the State system'. He sought to be 'readily accessible to all interested parties', and 'to establish and maintain a smooth working relationship with teachers, parents, civic, and other organizations interested in education'.[564]

Shears upheld that 'change is inevitable, desirable change is not' and aimed to make the inevitable change desirable. The future lay in a modified past 'given magnetism by our hopes and aspirations'; however, 'futures for all things suffer from the pressures of tradition, habit and a general resistance to change'.[565] He acknowledged the inevitability of change and recognised the turbulent path ahead; nevertheless he was cautious of political, social and economic forces that had power to constrain. In his crystal ball he saw the challenge of a major restructure involving liberalisation of power but at the crux of educational development were the teachers and children. In his mind they were 'milling around at the crossroads': downhill lay confusion, frustration and chaos stirred by politically vigorous minority groups; uphill lay 'restored public confidence, professional unity and status ... personal satisfaction and effective teaching'. A better qualified and higher salaried workforce would ease procedural change, sustain curriculum revision and ultimately support each student's performance. While he questioned, 'Which way for the teacher?' he understood the future lay in his hands.[566]

Undoubtedly, being Director-General of Education had benefits allied to the position but numerous senior roles and membership of committees were considered par for the course. He was appointed President of the Council of Public Education and a council member of Monash University, the VIC, the SCV Senate, the State Planning Council and the Duke of Edinburgh's Award Committee. He became Trustee of the Dafydd Lewis Scholarship Trust and the State Savings Bank Bursaries Trust, Chairman of the ABC's State Advisory Committee (School Broadcasts) and a member of the Federal School Broadcasts Advisory Committee of the ABC. Holding a position of status he joined the Rotary Club of Melbourne and the Melbourne Club. Though these appointments were important to Shears and he devoted loyal service to each, his career as the educational chief was paramount. He had an agenda for reform but correspondingly the Commonwealth was increasing investment in education, taking a more pro-active stance and infiltrating the States' traditional role.

## The Commonwealth and education

The tides turned politically in December 1972 when the Whitlam Labor government ended the Liberal Government's 23-year rule in Australia. The new government challenged controversial issues, abolished the death penalty, ended conscription and established Legal Aid. Whitlam took the inaugural Prime Ministerial tour of China, purchased Jackson Pollock's painting 'Blue Poles' for the Australian National Gallery ($1.3 million), proposed 'Advance Australia Fair' to replace 'God Save the Queen' as Australia's national anthem, and projected the Albury–Wodonga precinct. A government on the move, it answered the people's call. Following Cyclone Tracy hitting Darwin on Christmas Eve 1974, the Whitlam government relocated 33,000 people and coped with the damage debt of $837 million. Not long into office Whitlam's aspirations were dashed by global forces in the form of the oil crisis and the economic downturn.

Despite ill clouds looming the new government pushed on. Presenting Minister Kim Beazley Snr with the Education portfolio, it abolished university fees and established the Tertiary Education Assistance Scheme (TEAS), later Austudy. Under the chairmanship of Professor Peter Karmel an Interim Committee was formed to survey educational needs nationwide. In response the Karmel Committee recommended to the government a 'suite of educational programs', the formation of the Australian Schools Commission and maintaining the status quo of 'free, secular and compulsory' education. The

Karmel Committee recommended the establishment of 'national goals in schools, including equality, devolution of authority, community participation and responsiveness to change'; it challenged social issues, questioned administrative structures and optimised freedom for schools to ensure that 'the educational needs of children in relation to desired outcomes are more effectively served'.[567]

These ideals were compatible with emerging trends and in line with Shears' leadership vision; however they overlay his own aspirations and restricted his ability to act. As the boundaries between State and Commonwealth involvement in education blurred, he and his team found themselves juggling parallel agendas. Upon Commonwealth directive, State education departments established a series of task forces to evaluate administration, and survey schools to assess particular needs. 'Operation Upgrade', as it was known, 'defied any existing organisational pattern or logic, and therefore its success is wholly dependent upon the goodwill and purpose of the individual member, rather than being dependent upon, and supported by, firm lines of authority'.[568] In Victoria, Operation Upgrade comprised a steering committee of seven, which guided seven smaller task forces of three members each. Throughout June 1973 task forces met senior departmental administrators and representatives of parent and teacher organisations as they surveyed the entire education system – its operations, facilities, standards, documentation, predictions, communications and costs.

Midst these goings-on, *The Age* published Shears' views in 'Educational Wisdom; Admin Muddle'. He applauded the statement of needs but criticised Commonwealth inroads and resultant to-ing and fro-ing that was affecting progress. The proposal for State committees to supervise proceedings 'was an administration muddle in the sense that you couldn't have two groups determining what would happen with the allocation of Federal money through the Schools Commission or any other Federally oriented source'.[569] Foreseeing 'an administrative machine which may be either inoperable or ineffective' prompted discussion at the forthcoming meeting of the Australian Education Council.[570]

Meeting counterpart Directors-General in Sydney in September

1973 Shears reiterated concern over the Commonwealth's infringement, the binding restrictions on spending and overlap between existing and proposed programs.[571] Victoria, like other States, was 'desperate for money for schools, libraries and science blocks' and while Commonwealth funds buoyed education coffers its intrusion created 'mini-departments' and a new layer of complexity.

Subsequent to the Interim Committee's report, the Australian Schools Commission was established in 1974. Chaired by Ken McKinnon it comprised a forum of notable educators and organisational representatives.[572] The objectives were to inform the Federal Government on the state of affairs of all schools, identify potential funding needs and administer financial support. Schooling must not assign social strata, should acknowledge the attributes of diversity, readily accept change, support emerging trends, and have greater community alignment. The Commission allocated funds for State treasuries to disperse to government, nongovernment and Catholic schools to facilitate planning, upgrade facilities, replace schools if need be, and fund in-service programs. Meetings with State representatives and two-day discussions with the Directors-General heralded an annual sequence.

In the midst of establishing himself as leader, Shears was immersed in this revolutionary education upheaval. $53 million offered by Karmel funding, while 'stirring excitement amongst administrators' required the Department to manage increased funding of 50 per cent. Addressing a conference at White Hills Technical School, Shears warned teachers not to lose sight of the teacher–child relationship; the bread and butter of their profession and the crux of learning. This, he believed, was 'one of the reasons why most magnificent teaching and magnificent education has gone on when facilities, buildings, equipment have not necessarily been at the level of which we would like them to be'. He reminded those in attendance of time restraints and though the outlook until 1979 held promise, commitment at this stage was for just two years – 1974–75.[573]

The to-ing and fro-ing to disperse funding arose before legislation was passed. In November 1973 Federal Minister for Casey, Race Mathews, questioned Minister Thompson's 'abandon' to disburse

Karmel funds 'dependent in part upon legislation currently undergoing mutilation at the hands of his party colleagues in the Senate'. In his defence, Shears cited prior approval to spend $180,000 for capital works planning. He added, 'if the Federal money doesn't come through, we will simply have to reduce the State grant ... next time by a corresponding amount.' 'We know what we want, give us the money and let us do it,' he claimed.[574] Like other Directors-General, Shears appreciated Commonwealth funds but was critical of the limitations placed on their utilisation. He affirmed his stance on States' rights during debate amongst Standing Committee members:

> The Schools Commission was established to advise the Government, not determine priorities which States should determine. The difficulties follow the restrictions laid down ... they should be determined by the State.[575]

Thompson informed Mr David Bornstein (MLA for Brunswick East) of Victoria's funds distribution. He claimed $18,130,000 delegated to recurrent grants, special education, disadvantaged schools, building programs and libraries were but a drop in the ocean. The Department had committed a larger sum to staffing and child migrant education programs, science laboratories, secondary school libraries and technical training for 1974–75. He stressed reliance on the Public Works Department and in turn the PWD's dependence on the building trade.[576]

In-service training, part of the Commonwealth deal, had become big business. $1.3m from the Schools Commission plus $65,000 allocated by the State 1975 budget serviced in-service education in Victoria. Aware that many teachers in schools remained products of two-year training Shears believed in-service training would reach out to teachers statewide, 'providing refreshment, stimulation, and knowledge of new techniques that I hope will improve the education in our schools'. He was concerned that part-time and full-time specialist training took teachers out of their classrooms. This put an additional strain on administrators and principals who knew that 'every day you still have to provide education directly to the kids in the classroom'.[577]

## The scene in Victoria

Corresponding with Whitlam's acquisition of power, Rupert Hamer succeeded Henry Bolte to become Premier of Victoria in August 1972. Previously Minister for Local Government (1964–71), Chief Secretary and Deputy Premier (1971–72), Hamer was branded a 'small l Liberal'.[578] Thompson was appointed his Deputy but maintained the Education portfolio. By 1973 Education was big business. Victoria's population had reached 3,628,000 and the Education Department was among the nation's top employers. The largest business enterprise in the State, it managed 45 per cent of Victoria's budget.[579]

Within this structure Shears, as the Department's permanent head, was subject to Minister Thompson and responsible to administer the Education Act. Legislation made him responsible for 'all professional officers, teachers and other such officers as are necessary' and gave him authority to exercise powers and duties assigned in writing and to assign duties to others whose authority carried equal force. His realm embraced all aspects of primary, secondary and technical education, teacher training, administration, buildings and lands and other responsibilities as the Minister saw fit.[580] A tier beneath the Minister, the Director-General virtually ruled Victoria's educational empire. The permanent head, he was subject to the Minister, responsible to administer the Act and obliged to offer advice on issues at stake.

Professional educators worked in unison with members of the Public Service – the Executive Secretary, the Chief Administrative and Chief Finance Officers held roles paralleling those of Shears and his Assistant Directors-General,[581] although echoes of the past remained. Historically, as implemented under the Act of 1872, the Education Department's head was the Secretary, later renamed the Director and subsequently Director-General. Members of the Public Service endorsed the authority of the Executive Secretary but the Director-General, or permanent head, was drawn from the ranks of professional officers. The matter flared in response to the Bland Board of Inquiry into the Victorian Public Service (1974), which saw fit 'to place all senior officers administering the Department and its various Divisions under the jurisdiction of the Public Service Board'. Although Shears supported 'a single homogenous integrated administration' system unifying Head Office activities he saw 'distinct danger that this would create a division within the Teaching Service of dimensions possibly greater than the Teaching Service/Public Service one it was designed to remove'. Thompson similarly opposed the Bland recommendations but saw strength in streamlining administration. Shears endorsed these ideals providing the Teachers Tribunal and the Public Service Board responded to the Education Department's urgent personnel needs.[582]

Atop the educational hierarchy Shears was betwixt the continuity of tradition and the needs of a changing world. Continuity lay in the Department's linear structure with decision-making remote from the action in schools, and partitions existing between primary, secondary and tertiary sectors; infant, middle and upper levels; and science and humanities streams. These kingdoms divided rather than united the system.[583] Looking ahead Shears aimed to soften the boundaries by dispersing powers laterally through regions to schools and their broader communities. Bridging a link between policy makers, teacher trainers, teachers, schools and school communities would enhance opportunities to maximise each child's potential. To boost teachers' professional status four-year training was fundamental. To implement this and other ideals five-year planning was crucial, line management was no longer appropriate and annual budgets were 'nearly out the door'. Proposing a system-wide restructure with a bigger administrative team and acknowledging the scope of administration at all levels, he emphasised the value of training.[584]

By the 1970s the student bulge had reached the tertiary ranks. Within a milieu of debates, plans for the Fourth University developed and the VIC and SCV vied to survive. Moves to advance professional standards continued and efforts to train new teachers fell short. To boost the teacher supply in the short-term, Minister Thompson extended the Victorian Teacher Selection Program beyond its expected 'use-by' date of 1975.

## A visionary leader: five directive papers

Shears came to the position filled with ambition to guide the system's inevitable change. He established his vision and steps to its implementation by writing five directional papers, which he methodically presented for scrutiny to the educational community and the public. Concerned by the gap between Treasury Place policy-makers and the action in schools, he supported the regional shift and encouraged school–community partnerships. Spreading the power base buoyed autonomy and leadership potential.[585] Alert to the political implications of his actions he challenged the forces of tradition with innovation. He saw:

> ... the power of the legislature to enforce its will; his power, and the power of many officers and teachers in the system rests on the power of the legislature. The source of his authority is the will of the people expressed through the legislation and the process of law.[586]

Aware of legislative constraints, a more vocal education community and increasingly interested public, Shears appointed ADGE Moore as his 'right hand man' both as an act of consolation for Moore's not getting the job of DGE and because of Moore's promise: 'of course you have my unqualified support and assistance in doing the job'.[587] This established the pattern for flamboyant Shears to follow Frank Tate's footsteps; he proposed to visit schools and their communities statewide, scour the entire educational scene, address groups and attend state, national and international conferences. Often absenting himself from the office, he authorised Moore to lead the team. Whether in the field or his office, alone in the back of the chauffeured car or in bed at night, Shears methodically fine-tuned his vision. Ambitious as always, he designed a new-look structure to streamline administration, initiated steps to broaden the regional structure, made plans to strengthen school–community links and conceived means to raise teachers' professional status.

**Paper 1:** *Structure at the State level: departmental guidelines for the future* **and Paper 2:** *Planning Services Division*

In the wake of recent political shifts Shears saw the education administrator as 'the manipulator of circumstance'. Perpetual expansion, regional development, public awareness and injections of Commonwealth money pressured the Department's day-to-day demands and endeavours to move ahead. To keep pace with decisions, deputations and daily routines he affirmed, 'not sufficient time [is] available for one person to deal effectively with these representations and their ramifications'. Aligning with counsel from external reviews he proposed 'somebody to deal with administration, somebody to deal with personnel'. He established the Office of the Director-General believing 'the more brains we have the more chance we have of reaching successful conclusions'.[588]

Two months into his term he announced a total restructure of the Education Department and by October 1973 presented Paper 1. This magnum opus of intricacy conceived by one familiar with every aspect of departmental operations detailed every particle, fragment and micro aspect. It outlined a new staffing schedule, responsibilities and salary scale, and rationale for creating the Office. National and international sourcing would afford four 'Governor-in-Council senior position appointments' for four Assistant Directors-General, one of whom would act as Deputy, responsible for finance and administration. Beneath the top leadership tier, a director, a deputy and an assistant would head the Primary, Secondary, Technical, Special Services, Teacher Education and Planning Services Divisions. Twenty-four senior personnel currently serving were unable to 'administer an organization spending $465m, employing 62,000 persons, owning 2289 separate buildings and educating 678,000 students'.[589]

Cumulative rises in school populations continued as more students enrolled and those progressing to Form 6 (Year 12) continued to rise. The 'increasing increase' demanded 'a revolution in secondary school curriculum' to meet the needs of 'the new kind of pupil who would be staying on at school'. By the 1970s schools in Victoria catered for the rank and file and academically bright as well as many for whom traditional curriculum held minimal satisfaction. The challenge to cope with the ongoing rises in school populations, teacher supply, provision of classrooms, staffrooms and schools was a major concern, and the changed composition of schools called for reform. A Planning Services Division with designated operative wings would improve administrative coordination. Subdivisions responsible for curriculum, buildings and finance would provide data for the Planning Services Division as established in Paper 2. A Curriculum Branch would enhance course development. Recruitment, re-employment, and control of entry to the teaching profession similarly underlay the need for consolidated planning.[590] In contrast to his own years in Survey and Planning, where 'there were four of us', Shears affirmed 'we needed to establish a group to concentrate on present and future planning initiatives'.[591]

Like a manual, Papers 1 and 2 identified responsibilities of each ADGE; classified the function of each Division and their research, industrial and legal arms; and defined lines of communication within and between the Divisions and with government and independent agencies. The labyrinth of detail listed duties of directors, deputies, assistants and their entourage; identified layers of seniority; itemised responsibilities; and listed appropriate salaries. Research officers would prepare ministerial letters and answers to parliamentary questions and liaise with statutory authorities on personnel matters; industrial officers representing the Divisions would handle disputes and complaints and communicate with teacher organisations; and legal officers would liaise with Police and Crown Law Departments, deal with insurance issues and tender advice.

The blueprint for the Planning Services Division was in place by February 1975. Curriculum, Educational Facilities, Educational Finance, Statistics and Operation, Post-Secondary, and Technical and Further Education branches each required a team of 50 professional officers, research and clerical staff. The appointment of research officers to support administrators (rather than secondment of teachers) reflects the complexity of the new structure and the demands placed on staff. Within the Department's divisional structure, staff aligned to particular branches ascertained needs and liaised with numerous instrumentalities including the PWD, architects, engineers, government departments and consultants, then allocated funds and resources accordingly.

As each divisional director was assigned a deputy and assistant director, layer upon layer the administrative web grew in complexity. Tiers linked horizontally and vertically to facilitate information flowing upward, downward, diagonally and crossways. A new kingdom replaced the old. Familiar ways were changing, positions were filled by selection rather than seniority, and new players in new positions confused closeknit groups accustomed to divisional demarcation and traditional lines of exchange. A sense of confusion struck some senior officers whose career aspirations paled, and their lines of communication became blurred.

Once appointments were established Shears gathered his top 50 administrators in a residential seminar at Mannix College in February 1975. He explained the administrative structure and regional development strategies, and presented a three-year plan.[592]

However, the formulation of Papers 1 and 2 by Shears and his team of educational officers raised the ire of Scully, Secretary of the Department. He claimed, 'I was not consulted, nor referred to in formulating the proposals.' He was critical of the ad hoc approach, and the lack of 'properly planned communications and coordination and soundly based appraisal of performance'. He concluded it 'will not be successful'.[593]

Shears refined his directional papers through discussion with school principals, teachers and interested persons. Eighteen months after its introduction into the educational community, the *Education Amendment Act* 1975 (No. 8768) passed on 25 November 1975, giving facility to appoint 'not more than five to be Assistant Directors-General'.[594] After advertising for the best qualified applicants, from an international field, time-honoured lines of advancement were eroded and soured many currently serving officers. Neville Barwick was appointed ADGE (Buildings) in place of Stewart Morton who had moved on. Allan Hird became ADGE (Personnel) and Ray Maddocks became ADGE (Curriculum and Planning). Tom Moore, responsible for finance and management, became Deputy Director-General. Each

ADGE dealt with senior divisional officers scattered across sixteen city locations extending from Treasury Place and the CBD to west, north and east Melbourne, Collingwood and Carlton North.[595]

**Paper 3:** *Structure at the regional level*

The formation of executive regions statewide was not new. Since 1960 the Technical Schools Division had recognised local groups with representation from schools, councils and regional industry. Each group held regular meetings and kept others informed. In 1972, Minister Thompson phased in the Education Department's regional network of administration. The success of the three pilot regions in Bendigo, Ballarat and Gippsland gave credence to expanding the system statewide. Moore was directly associated with its implementation, while Shears developed principles for administrators, guidelines for staffing and salary structure.

The Schools Commission supported regional development and by 1974 Victoria was well on the way. Paper 3 detailed the functions of regional officers and their responsibility to the schools and their populations when implementing policy. Response to public verdicts at local level was fundamental.[596] Regional directors of education (RDE), a rung below senior administrators but above the inspectors, linked administration at central office with district inspectors and school communities. Upper echelon jacks of all trades the regional directors exhibited multiple skills to do multiple tasks and were public relations officers with Departmental know-how of who's who and what's what. Charged to act on professional and managerial fronts the regional directors worked across levels of schooling and divisions to determine regional priorities, and performed other duties assigned by the Director-General. While they yielded to a new layer of authority and recognised the need to confer with regional directors, Directors of Primary, Secondary and Technical Education retained the right to implement divisional policy. Although final responsibility for what went on in schools lay with the divisional directors, matters were channelled through the appropriate RDE.[597]

Aware of the tensions these concepts imposed, Shears addressed the rationale and matters of concern at an assembly of inspectors.

He advised, 'the whole business of regions was serious'. The interdivisional approach was a means 'to mix up the people'.[598] As was his habit, after the address, Shears 'worked the room' to allay discomfort and boost morale, to 'develop common understanding [that] he knew everyone's name and something about them', and to gain support because he knew that 'working the top group massaged their egos'.[599]

The new layer of authority cut across traditional lines. As the administrative grid grew in complexity it formed links via vertical and horizontal axes. Horizontal alignment, as opposed to vertically ordered divisions, cast a net of confusion. Disarray replaced structure. Longtime inspectors squirmed at proposals to replace their Secondary and Technical Boards. This would affect their renown in the educational hierarchy and evaporate their career aspirations. They were annoyed that Shears was bumping up the regional directors while the Boards of Inspectors were downsized. If the regional structure took precedence they questioned their future.

Pilot regional directors held counter views. Colin Moyle (Bendigo) recalled 'the Secondary Division, in turmoil due to VSTA activities, saw us as intrusive; the Technical Division believed we would alleviate their administrative responsibilities; and the Primary Division, where inspectorates were responsible to central administration, saw us as a threat'. Regional directors 'interposed that line of command'. Moyle countered resistance by working in tandem with the district inspector who 'set up his office in the regional headquarters'. In contrast, another inspector warned, 'because it's you Col, we'll get on, but you stay out of my schools – they are still my administrative responsibility.' 'It was a very touchy time,' Moyle admitted.[600] Likewise Len Falk (Gippsland) worked in accord with Departmental and community groups to create the 'best possible climate for children in the region'. He acknowledged feeling isolated and believed his decisions often lacked clout.[601]

Despite these tensions, the regional directors acted as catalysts in the 'school and community movement'; a vital link between senior administrators, members of school communities and others beyond the immediate educational sphere. The regional offices softened boundaries between central office and those in the field, thus spreading the administrative burden. They similarly bridged education and community boundaries and built understanding. This, according to Shears, was 'a most important end-product of regionalization'.[602] Regional directors became involved locally and, like teachers in small rural schools, became active community members. As the regional system extended, the experience of the foundation group – Moyle, Falk and Bob Dobell (Ballarat) – influenced policy and informed the incoming group. New appointments announced in June 1974 identified eight new regional directors, six from inspectorial ranks and two school principals, to complete a network of eleven regions spread Victoria wide.

Table 10. Regional Directors: new appointments

| Region | Incoming Regional Director | Prior Position |
|---|---|---|
| Benalla | Mr Jeffrey F Dunstan | District Inspector |
| Geelong | Mr Reginald H Fisher | Principal, Ballarat North Technical School |
| Horsham | Mr John J Bishop | Principal, Moe High School |
| Frankston | Mr David C Streader | Staff Inspector |
| Knox | Mr Arthur L Harris | Staff Inspector |
| Prahran | Mr Daniel F Dee | Member BISS |
| Preston | Mr John N Roscholler | District Inspector |
| Sunshine | Mr Ronald H Ginger | District Inspector |

Source: *Interchange*, no. 32, June 1974, p.4; *News Exchange*, no. 9, 12th June 1974

## Paper 4: *The school and the community*

The school as integral to its community was not new. Devolution through local education authorities, as observed by Tate in Britain, was considered unsuitable for the Victorian scene where distance would fragment the Department. However, Winnetka and Dalton approaches, ideals of the New Education Fellowship, and Dewey's concept of 'community within the school', influenced teaching style and relationships in school populations. The concept of shared responsibility for educating children, as espoused by William Wirt, promoted self-sufficiency and productivity in the school and its community. The school was 'an oasis to instill the values of family, work, and productivity among urban students and produce an efficient, orderly society of solid, productive citizens' and 'playground, garden, workshop, social centre, library, and traditional school combined in one plant under the same management'.[603]

While community had typified living and teaching in Victoria's rural areas, formal steps for shared use of classrooms, libraries, halls and sports grounds were laid post WWI. In 1945 liaison between the Victorian Teachers' Union and the National Fitness Council led to a second such surge. The following year the Heidelberg model equipped each of three new housing developments with a school and hall in a garden setting, pre-natal and infant welfare facilities, a crèche and library.[604]

During his schooling and early teaching career Shears experienced many of these influences. Now, placed atop Victoria's education system, the void between administrators and those at the chalkface was a concern for him. Intent upon devolving central authority, albeit by evolutionary steps, Shears knew that the provision of efficient, self-governing schools in which teachers, parents and interested others made contributions, required building a link. In August 1973, just three months into office in his address to principals in the Bendigo region, Shears emphasised the importance of school community bonds.[605] From Karmel funds, a sum of $63 million was allocated, some of which was channelled to school councils and schools; this supported his thrust to 'put some power where the action is, back in the schools. Despite his driving ambition and the allocation of Karmel funds, legislation was a fundamental step.

In a Memorandum addressed to school principals in November 1973 Shears presented his case. He outlined the status quo and forthcoming changes 'during the next decade'. He proposed the Victorian Education Council to replace the Council of Public Education; it would chart procedures and update legislation to reflect a broader social conscience.[606] The Department's proposal to enlarge school councils and confer them with identified powers offered parents and community members greater say in the running of schools, *The Age* reported.[607] Shears cast the school as the major educational unit and school councils the functional management unit, supported by education committees.

He proposed the powers and composition of school councils – between five and seventeen representatives from parent, municipal and community groups plus the school principal, who could opt for full voting or observational rights. Education committee members would advise on matters that reflected the educational aspirations of the particular school and its community. Though not intended to interfere with what teachers were doing or how, the possibility of broader community members, many of whom had no educational training, permeating the teachers' domain raised concerns. School staff feared community/parental 'know-how' might undermine their professional expertise and worried that members of the school council may be too busy with their own agendas to give beneficial input, or may obscure the school's educational role.[608]

Heeding these concerns, Shears defined the school's administrative and educational functions. He spurned interference with educational activity and the basic professional and personal relationship between teacher and child. He accepted that greater flexibility and increased local participation imposed additional external pressures on decision-makers and stressed the centrality of the principal's role. It lay at the crux of implementing policy in individual schools. The three-tier system under discussion involved the Education Department, regional directors and school principals. Autonomy as proposed gave them 'freedom to make decisions without need for referral to, or ratification by, the central authority' at this stage of the decentralisation process.[609]

The school and the community movement transferred 'more power over administrative action' to the school unit. A 'desirable and inevitable' attribute, throughout the next decade the local community had 'bigger influence and involvement in its schools'.[610] Shears and the senior administrative team visited schools statewide and addressed education and other interested groups and heard concerns regarding the composition of councils, staff selection procedures, and lay persons' rights to determine education policy.

Parent advocate, Mrs Joan Kirner, related Shears' proposal to Commonwealth action when 'a lot of the stuff that we parents had fought for was happening'. She herself was breaking new ground being 'part of decision-making, not just making lamingtons' as was supposed of mothers. She claimed two hats; 'one the activist parent demanding a better delivery for our kids in Victoria', the other to dispense

Commonwealth funds to develop parental input. In reference to the Plowden Report (1967) Kirner argued, 'the major educational components of the school are the children, the teachers and the parents'. Citing Karmel, she stressed 'growing support for the involvement of all participants in the learning process'. This aimed 'for a cooperative share in what matters most to parents – the intellectual and social growth of their child out of school'. Parental voice was fundamental in principal selection, a concept principals argued against. Kirner recalled, 'You would have thought we were suggesting multi murder.'

Embroiled in 'very lively intellectual and political discussion' she noted considerable common ground between parental and Departmental views. However, Shears, who was 'very respectful of the teaching profession', represented the Department, whereas she stood for parent and community groups. We 'thought they (the Department) should have a say but not *the* say ... he (Shears) thought the parents should have a say but not *the* say'. Retrospectively Kirner conceded, 'the Department had the say'. She described Shears as 'a benevolent autocrat' who played the political game. He pleased the Minister, who 'didn't have a problem with parent participation'. His concerns 'lay with teacher participation'.[611]

Likewise Geoff Reid of the VSTA considered the right of school councils to be 'representative of the groups within the school community, viz parents, teachers and students. No one group should have an absolute majority on either the school council or the school education committee.' He claimed inadequate consultation throughout the discussion period. Counter to this Shears maintained discussion was open to schools, teachers, parents and other interested persons, and during this time he held individual and group consultations with Reid, and representatives of each teachers' union. [612]

The *Education (School Councils) Act* 1975 (No. 8799) presented in November empowered school councils to contract maintenance and improvements, supervise buildings and grounds and make recommendations to regional directors. Thenceforth they administered accountable grants, contracted to spend specific-purposes moneys and supplement funds by fundraising. They authorised shared facilities use and employment of clerical assistants, teacher aides and cleaners.

The school and the community movement corresponded with Karmel's counsel to rationalise the use of facilities, avoid duplication of plant and equipment and develop collaboration policies for schools and their communities. Beyond this bipartisan approach Shears established the Liaison Committee to develop links with the Catholic Education Office (CEO). The committee comprised six senior Departmental representatives and five CEO officers. Establishing such committees ensured efficient use of government moneys, according to Shears. Father Martin, Director of the CEO, saw that 'any moves to facilitate the sharing of facilities, both between schools of different systems and with the community at large, will have positive benefits for all the children concerned'.[613] The link was played out during a visit to Alexandra Primary School in July 1973, which celebrated the school's centenary. Asked to provide a library to mark the occasion Shears proposed a shared facility with the Catholic primary school nearby. He returned to Alexandra in November 1977 to officially open the complex.

In October 1973, the Education Department and Father Martin investigated the feasibility of sharing facilities in this and other instances. The economic impact of 'using school assets as a community resource ... not a school resource that closes at 4 o'clock, not touched until the principal walks back in the gate' reached legislation in December.[614] The *Youth, Sport and Recreation (State Schools Premises) Act* 1973 (No. 8499) permitted local councils to share management, improvements, renovations and repairs on school land. This move was beneficial to the Department and socially advantageous to the community. Such actions led to the formulation of 'Policies and Guidelines for Community Use of School Facilities'. Released at Princes Hill High School by Shears and Acting Minister of Education Brian Dixon this document guided principals and councils apropos community education activities and formed the basis for further discussion. However, Shears warned of grey areas, such as insurance, damages restitution, welfare and compensation fundamental to the concept's success and the safety of school populations.[615]

The concept of the Victorian Education Council was short-lived. Replacing the Council of Public Education its formation was an attempt to amend the council, 'little modified since 1911', to 'perform a more valuable function with a wider representation', reflecting the current scene. The proposed 35-member Council would represent the Education Department and nongovernment schools, the spectrum of tertiary institutions, teacher and parent groups and school principals. It would also involve delegates from industrial and commercial organisations, and the Australian College of Education. Led by a Chief Executive Officer, it would advise the Minister on matters of education in Victoria, other States, Territories and the Commonwealth, and of developments overseas. It would keep the Minister abreast of developments and present-day concerns. Though the proposal lost momentum, aspects of it paralleled the Director-General's Liaison Committee established in 1974 through which collaboration between government and nongovernment education systems contributed to curriculum planning and discussion regarding shared use of resources, facility and grounds.

**Paper 5:** *The teacher and the school administrator*

Rationalisation was a sign of the time. It aligned to Commonwealth activity in education, regional expansion in Victoria and the school and the community movement. Accountability to the Commonwealth, the State, the regions and the education community grew in significance and the role of the principal grew in complexity. To cope with changing and increasing demands Shears acknowledged the need for administrative training to support principals and those aspiring to hold leadership roles and was aware that some teachers preferred to remain in the classroom. Paper 5 addressed the needs of both groups. It indicated developments abroad regarding inspection and growing resistance to the time-honoured inspectorial system, and proposed an alternative promotion model.

Core concerns were the means of defining accountability and professionalism. The need to devise alternative performance appraisals was clear but required legislation. Shears proposed to 'channel discussions towards an analysis of the problem and a consequent positive solution' and from a synopsis of 'our present thinking ... policy will emerge'.[616] It was time to revise the salary structure for teachers to remain in their classrooms, establish an Institute of Educational Administration (IEA) for aspiring principals and senior teachers, and evaluate assessment modes.[617]

Accountability was a vital aspect of the reform: the government to the public, and the teaching profession to itself, its members, performance and rights. Inspection, the traditional approach to promotion, caused tension, particularly in secondary ranks. With the system of inspection falling from grace, Shears walked a fine line to find an alternative. Reflectively, he claimed:

> I tried to get a system which allowed inspectors back in schools instead of having muck thrown at them and dirt in their lockers – terrible things that went on in the late '60s and the early '70s … I used School Aptitude Assessment Panels … the unions called it SAAPs and PAAPs for senior teacher and principal appointments.

Assessment and Aptitude became the big 'A' words. SAAPs and PAAPs rated school and teacher performance and aptitude for promotion. The size and composition of the panel was reliant upon the school size and the focus of the review. Generally SAAPs comprised the principal, other teachers plus divisional and school council representatives. Senior Teacher Class panels comprised the principal, the divisional director's nominee and the applicant's choice of school staff. Would-be principals with three years' experience in the school presented their case in an interview to a similar panel in addition to other teachers and an outsider. A second interview was possible with a member of the Committee of Classifiers in attendance. The presence of a union member satisfied VSTA demands. Five-yearly reviews gave the Minister insight into the performance of each school, its teachers and allied staff. Reports were destroyed annually to maintain confidentiality.

Assessment by School Review Panels met broad opposition. Teachers were angered that panels would evaluate school policies, programs and their own potential. They considered themselves professionals who 'should not have inspectors looking over their shoulders'.[618] Panel members were concerned by the time imposed by the task and inspectors assumed authority to guide and evaluate school and teacher performance. This approach clouded traditions. They were 'committed to the notion of the inspectorate, [that] what you aspired to be part of was a wonderful thing'. The 'Little Doctor' and his policies posed a threat.[619]

Traditionally teachers had transferred between schools in pursuit of promotion. To define a good teacher and identify 'comparative assessments of teaching quality' was a problem. Shears acknowledged that not all sought administrative heights hence there was a need to 'examine present career structure and assessment procedures [and] provide incentives for teachers to remain in the classroom'.[620] While this provided stability of staffing, prolonged service in a school had propensity to create career lethargy. Such teachers required 'a fresh view of their task and its relationship to the community'; they must learn from experience, expand their horizons and travel. For promotion purposes, those with interstate or overseas experience, or the equivalent of three summer sessions of in-service education, must provide evidence.[621]

## *The selection and training of school administrators*

Leadership training gained prominence. At Queenscliff the Army established the Australian Administrative Staff College in 1946. Officers selected for senior appointments were trained 'to establish the highest standards in the entire spectrum of personal and military ethics and to reinforce the development of the total military professional'. They learnt to monitor developments in leadership theory and doctrine and ensure that a coordinated and progressive approach exists to leadership development within the Army. The University of Melbourne established the Summer School in Business Administration on the Mornington Peninsula in 1954. Founding Principal, Sir Douglas Copland, initiated six-week residential executive education programs. They extended to ten weeks in 1957, and in 1970 the university began graduate courses in leadership training. Elsewhere, the University of Queensland introduced a master's degree in 1959 and at the University of New England Professor Bill Walker introduced the first Graduate Diploma in Leadership. In 1963 he established the *Educational Administration Quarterly* (EAQ), 'the first of its kind in the world', and in 1970 partook in discussions to establish the Commonwealth Council of Educational Administration (CCEA).

## In the chair

Upon coming to office, Shears assembled a team of administrative elite. Among them were the 'Alberta Mafia', graduates in educational administration from the University of Alberta – ADGE Moore, ADGE Maddocks and senior officers Norman Gill and Robin Chapman. Moore completed an MEd (1963–64) followed by Gill (1967), while Maddocks and Chapman attained PhDs. The University of Alberta took pride in its graduates and Shears took pride in his team.[622]

Selected from local and overseas applicants, ADGE Hird had taught in primary schools and lectured at Melbourne and Coburg TCs and RMIT (1955–60). He was appointed a district inspector in 1960. Awarded a Travelling Scholarship, Hird studied at the University of Oregon (1966–67) and completed further studies in the UK (1967) where he was attached to Her Majesty's Inspectors (1968–70). Loyal to the Primary Division he became Assistant Director of Primary Education (ADPE) and aspired to become Director. His promotion to ADGE lightened the workload of Moore who delegated personnel matters to Hird. Moore maintained responsibilities with the Council of Public Education, regional directors and the finance office, and during Shears' absence served as Deputy Director-General.[623]

Barwick stepped in when Morton moved on. He flourished five successive architectural awards, the Institute Gold Medal and a couple of honours degrees. Responsible for infrastructure projects in the New Guinea highlands in the early '60s, including the Goroka Teachers College, he was affectionately called 'Xanana of the Highlands'. He had managed Melbourne Airport's construction in the mid '60s, and later, as Assistant Secretary to the Department of Housing and Construction in Canberra, supervised Darwin's reconstruction following Cyclone Tracy. He was 'travelling up and down in Hercules bombers and arranging semi-trailer loads of materials coming in from Adelaide and Brisbane and evacuating large numbers of people' when the position of ADGE (Building) became vacant. His rigorous selection process – involving the Public Service Board, a Cabinet sub-committee and the Teachers Tribunal 'each wanting a pound of flesh' – was a 'backlash' after Thompson's unilateral endorsement of Shears. Barwick presented himself in 'Territory rig – long creamy white socks, shorts and an open-necked shirt'. He remembered 'the look on Bill Sampson's face'.[624] His responses to questions about 'forward commitment patterns … and technical stuff in the field' held him in good stead as neither the educationists, the Cabinet sub-committee nor the Teachers Tribunal could clarify the 'delegated arrangements and understanding between Works and Education'. Sampson suggested he 'find that out from someone else'. According to Barwick his 'attitude of enquiring about fundamentals was part and parcel of getting the job'.[625]

Barwick showed his prowess in securing the appointment of a senior PWD officer position in each of the first three regions. He delegated Moyle to chair a meeting with senior PWD personnel in which 'hard-nosed bargaining' resulted in the positions being established and an officer appointed, responsible to each RDE. This broke the formerly inviolable responsibility of the PWD for all Education Department construction and maintenance. Both Shears and the Minister were pushing the boundaries, and the qualities of Barwick and Moyle, long serving officers and new recruits, were essential to a strong administrative team.

## Other dimensions of Shears

Shears' busy-ness persisted. He maintained connection with the VIER, ACE and CNA, and developed links with a growing number of organisations. Visits to schools and various other groups, letters to the press and media appearances in the press, on radio and on television enhanced his public profile. In October 1974 *The Age* announced that State Cabinet agreed to the Federal Government's request for him to attend the UNESCO Conference in Paris. Federal Minister for Education (Kim Beazley Snr) would lead the delegation.[626]

## Mission in Paris: UNESCO

Chaired by Magda Joboru of Hungary, the 18th General Conference debated 'Education for International Understanding and Peace'. Delegates from 134 countries included representatives from a divided Germany (German Democratic Republic, Federal Republic of Germany), the Republic of Viet-Nam, Soviet Socialist Republics of Ukraine, Byelorusssia and the Union, and the Democratic People's Republic of Korea. Presented with six questions, delegates formulated recommendations sympathetic to intercultural, international and global needs.[627]

Away from the flurry of activity at home, Shears met and mixed with an elite group from diverse social, political, economic and educational traditions. Pondering the focus on equity, access, training and opportunity, he reflected on past experiences that shaped his present conceptions: Dewey's footprint at Ann Arbor promoting the individual's capacity to make change, and the philosophy of human equality held by Wattenberg of Wayne State University. Transpiring from the Institute of Education in London were Fleming's thoughts on social psychology, Eysenck's concern with genetics and intelligence, and attitudes to race in post-war Britain addressed by HEO James and Cora Tenen.[628] His own foundation lay in Tate's legacy of secondary schooling.

The quest for 'equity of opportunity and treatment' supported his mission to 'see in each child a vision of what he can become and direct his efforts to making this vision a reality' and Minister Thompson's pursuit of 'equality in educational purpose'.[629] Shears believed that these ideals were in place in Victoria and aspired to make them universally possible. The *Education Act* 1872 had established a 'free, compulsory and secular' system, while Tate drove 'access to secondary education' for all. In contrast to countries that struggled to educate children through their primary years Victoria's tertiary sector gave 'access to higher education'. The push to implement degree-granting status at the SCV, the VIC and colleges of advanced education ensured 'standards of quality of education in public educational institutions of the same level'. Among the debates the most potent aspect for Shears was 'training for the teaching profession'.[630]

Education, it was argued, involved the entire process of social life. It was a means to reach international understanding, cooperation and peace. The Universal Declaration of Human Rights, as stated in the Charter of the United Nations, states that 'Education shall be directed to the full development of the human personality and to the strengthening of respect for human rights and fundamental freedoms'.[631] Recommendations of the Paris Conference encouraged 'an international dimension and global perspective' at all levels and in all forms, and the need to understand and respect all peoples and their social milieu. They highlighted 'increasing global interdependence', and the ability to communicate and understand the rights and duties incumbent on individuals. The call to boost teacher preparation and certification, encourage 'commitment to the ethics of human rights in a changing society', and embrace programs and materials supporting an international focus aligned with the need to 'provide those concerned, to the fullest extent, with opportunities for making direct contact with foreign teachers' and opportunities to study abroad. The award of fellowships would help 'organize or assist bilateral exchanges of teachers at all levels of education'. While administrators were urged to plan, develop and expand technical and vocational education, extend services and diversify courses, they were advised to address 'economic and social policy, labour and employment' for the various occupational sectors. Across the education spectrum it was paramount to promote in-service instruction, address training, qualifications, standards and evaluation, class ratios, curriculum and teaching materials. In all respects the need was to ensure that collaboration between authorities, schools, teachers and parents was boosted.

Consciousness of steps to embrace these issues at home sharpened Shears' awareness of challenges ahead both for the developing cultures and the system he led. While he had time to enjoy the pleasures of Paris with Mavis and renew acquaintances made in 1972, at the back of his mind issues at home stirred his mind. He was constantly in touch with those at head office by fax and phone to keep him abreast of developments in education.

Whether at home or abroad Shears kept in touch. In addition to directives, his files contain multiple letters of congratulations. Hedley

Beare, on his appointment as Director of Education in the ACT, thanked Shears and Mavis for their 'kind note of congratulations' and expressed 'mixed feelings since there are so many promising developments underway' in the education in the Northern Territory.[632] When selecting his team Beare asked Shears to confirm an applicant's 'ability to lead a professional team, the ability to speak in public and to act as an advocate for innovatory schemes, and ability as a planner'. Shears replied, 'Yes'. Paul McKeown, Headmaster of Canberra Grammar, sought advice regarding the establishment of another independent Anglican school in the ACT. On Carl Forster's retirement from the Harkness Fellowship Council Shears congratulated him on his contribution. A jointly signed telegram from Shears and Ministers Thompson and Dixon congratulated Sir Eric Willis, Minister for Education in NSW, upon his knighthood.

Education staff abroad kept him abreast of developments. Roy Senior in the UK advised that colleges offered three-year BEd or four-year BEd (Hons) courses for primary and lower secondary teachers. Most former teachers colleges were 'obliged to merge with polytechnics'. He concluded, 'the present changes will do nothing to enhance the status of teacher education'.[633] This news heralded the likelihood of forthcoming mergers at home. While Shears took heed, his immediate concerns were the rippling effect of shortcomings in funds promised by the Schools Commission. This would cripple the Department's ability to cope with a new wave of secondary school students by 1982 and shifting school populations in Melbourne's spreading outer suburbia. Once more he alerted to the need to prepare for thousands more pupil spaces.

CHAPTER 15

# IN THE HOT SEAT (1976-79)

> *There is no future without a past, because what is to be cannot be imagined except as a form of repetition.*
>
> Siri Hustvedt, *The Summer without Men*

It was a time of hope. The next decade had a lot to offer. Shears rode on a high, advancing education remained at the fore and he was never afraid to stir feathers. Speaking on the ABC he questioned, 'Education – whose responsibility?' He continued:

> Since the Second World War, the public interest in education has risen rapidly. Never have so many winters of discontent been made glorious summers by the shortcoming and difficulties which have been encountered in education. That a stormy climate of opinion exists has been evidenced recently by public meetings, at national congress, in statements by political leaders, educationists and parent groups, and in a readiness of the press, radio and television to make headlines from educational issues.[634]

The 1970s were far from mundane. The Vietnam War came to a head in April 1975 and though conflict ended, trauma continued to haunt. A more confident Australian society stood for its rights. Strength in feminist and union movements highlighted the voice of extremists. Social freedoms came in many forms: the nation's first casino established in Hobart in 1973 and the TAB in 1975. The views of those born in the 1930s, beneficiaries of the growth in secondary education, were powerful forces which often countered tradition. Barry Humphries and Tim Burstall were making their mark, Edna Everage became a Dame and Alvin Purple stepped into Australian folklore. Barry Jones shifted from State to Federal politics and Moomba became

Melbourne's Festival of Festivals. Rolf Harris, Bert Newton, Graham Kennedy and Mickey Mouse were crowned its King.

National and State politics were Liberal. Fraser had ousted Whitlam, Senator Margaret Guilfoyle replaced Kim Beazley as Minister for Education and successively John Carrick and Wal Fife took the chair. In Victoria, Rupert Hamer remained Premier but as the decade receded Deputy Premier Lindsay Thompson replaced him. Relinquishing the Education portfolio he appointed the Hon. Alan Hunt assisted by the Hon. Norman Lacy. It was a challenging time for Shears whose recently implemented policies required nurture to reach fruition. The change required him to build new relationships with the new ministers from non-education backgrounds who required knowledge of the education system and nuances of the Department.

Society's stance was born of the post-war years. Postprimary education had become the norm and administrative systems shifted from the 'para-military Victorian era, into the modern age'.[635] Educational leadership under Major-General Alan Ramsay (1948–60) paralleled the scene in South Australia under Major-General Evan Mander-Jones (1946–67). During his term Director Ramsay served with Education Ministers Lieutenant Colonel, the Hon. (later Sir) William Leggatt (1955–56) and Lieutenant Colonel, the Hon. (later Sir) John Bloomfield (1956–67). Men of such stature who led their units with military precision brought similar qualities to the Education Department. Proven leaders, they had vision to plan and execute progress. Under their direction school design changed to accommodate students in light-filled classrooms, the focus of training teachers shifted to educating teachers. School-based curriculum guided child-centred classrooms. Lingering shades of such leaders coloured Victoria's educational scene though they gradually softened under Directors McDonell and Brooks prior to Shears.

## Shears' scene

Inspired by Tate, Shears presented vision and policy to introduce change. Forceful yet egalitarian, his leadership style embraced others' views. Decision-making was a shared activity and morale was considered important. He invited two-way communication to evaluate and reposition aspects of each pursuit, yet while he yielded latitude he maintained control. Barry Hill of *The Age* described the 'refreshing new style' of leadership as 'open' and 'newly conscious of PR'. He acknowledged the practice of 'speaking at numerous public meetings, issuing policy papers for debate and ringing education reporters of daily newspapers almost every day'. Hill noted the 'striking contrast to years of administration by semi-anonymous men who were too timid to put their policies publicly on the line.'[636] Described as 'educational malaise', leadership had lacked 'dynamic and political forcefulness'. Institutional inbreeding had not produced a gutsy leader to 'rock the boat' and make waves.[637] Hill suggested that with Shears things had changed.

By the mid 1970s Victoria's Education Department employed 63,000 teachers and staff, educated 625,000 students in 2240 schools, had an annual budget of $700 million and capital investment of billions of dollars in buildings and land. The Office of the Director-General comprised Mr Tom Moore, Deputy Director-General and in charge of all matters relating to finance and administration; Mr Allan Hird, Assistant Director-General in all matters relating to personnel throughout the teaching service and public service; Dr Ray Maddocks, Assistant Director-General in all matters relating to curriculum and for the development and establishment of the Planning Services Division; Mr Neville Barwick, Assistant Director-General in all matters relating to building and accommodation.[638]

The senior administrative squad embraced a retinue of directors, deputies, assistants and specialist staff for each of the divisions. Each coordinated teams to support their specific duties. Nonetheless settling in was not easy for all. Newcomer to the administrative hierarchy Hird (Personnel) claimed lack of explicit guidelines caused confusion. Named 'Director-General in all matters relating to personnel', he felt immersed in a 'pig's breakfast' where administrative responsibility was serviced by 'the three teaching and two service divisions and the public service arm'.[639] Regional directors interrupted traditional lines of command as their power exceeded those of divisional directors. Under the new model the ADGE coordinated regional activity and oversaw the director and assistant directors of each region. Hird believed procedures were clumsy and dysfunctional. To report on developments and pinpoint shortfalls; advise on corrective action; and conduct research and present statistical data, he formed a Committee of Future Staffing Needs that met twice monthly.[640] Fracture in Departmental loyalty between senior executives was another concern. 'At least two officers wanted his (Shears) job, and were hell bent on creating difficulties.' The Department 'operated in discrete sections' rather than a united body and gave little thought to how decisions affected other parts of the whole.[641]

At the upper echelon of the hierarchy the Thompson–Shears duo became known as 'Tweedledum and Tweedledee'. In this 'Yes Minister' relationship the Director-General appeared to hold power although Shears claimed like-minded intent and the Minister's trust. In an amicable yet constructive working relationship Thompson was 'cautious and politically strategic' whereas Shears was 'full of reformist zeal'. While they worked in tandem Thompson checked Shears' 'tendency to rush in where only fools would'.[642] It appeared there was a 'chemistry between the two' who presented as 'extremely analytical, capable and intelligent' and 'persuasive' leaders. At senior officers meetings they 'mixed with the troops' though this was 'always business, never social'.[643] At regular meetings on Mondays at 9 am they updated each other before Shears briefed his Assistant Directors-General.

Administrative restructure was timely and in tune with national trends to decentralise administration and place power near the action in schools. The Planning Services Division, notably larger than the team of three Shears led in Survey and Planning, coordinated multiple functions to manage growth geared to optimise learning conditions in schools; the regional structure offered a statewide grid of authority; and authority given to school councils lifted trivia from central and regional offices. But, with unexpected twists and turns, the Director-General role was like 'riding a wild horse'. Commonwealth intrusion, increased public interest and teacher activity, the evolution of TAFE and the advance of the Catholic Education Office increased the complexity of the task. Barry Hill noted 'slight naivety of politicking that employs garrulousness as a major tool'. He pondered the constant strain and questioned Shears' belief that his forceful statements would augur accord.⁶⁴⁴

## Looking and planning ahead

Rather than one pre-determined future, Shears saw 'a range of possible futures'. Uncertainty was a common factor; the rate of recent change created new possibilities and magnified the need to steer true. As technologies advanced, the challenge to estimate, calculate and advance the state of affairs became increasingly complex. The implications of 'fast, fluid and self-regulating' technological systems of tomorrow indicated education's 'prime objective must be to increase the individual's cope-ability – the speed and economy with which he can adapt to change'.⁶⁴⁵

Looking beyond the scope of his service to education, and indeed his lifetime, Shears' crystal ball revealed escalating Commonwealth immersion. Teachers faced new challenges as the expectations of students and parents transformed. They were alert to their 'first and ultimate aim ... to enrich the lives of the pupils and students they serve'. In the new paradigm 'the stress on individual instruction, freedom to develop curricula, new technology and increasing community involvement will break down the traditional concept of the teacher isolated in the classroom ... there seems to be little doubt that the teacher's role is becoming more difficult.' Teachers must be equipped to satisfy a range of educational needs, and provide and experience lifelong learning. 'Education is Living', he proclaimed, and in line with the thrust to empower school communities, society must 'plan its facilities around the concept that Education in its broadest concept is living and vice-versa.'⁶⁴⁶

## Objectives and progress

Shears remained vigilant and sustained his vision in his mission to implement change. He had selected a capable senior management team and established a planning department; the regions extended to a statewide grid of eleven; and the school and the community movement was underway. In line with Schools Commission directives, school councils managed their budgetary needs, with moves afoot to share library, sport and playground facilities. Proposals to keep good teachers in the classroom and train leadership aspirants were not yet achieved though plans were progressing towards a semi-autonomous, 'high-powered first-quality educational management program for Principals and aspiring Principals'. Course standards would ideally surpass those offered in business administration at the Australian Administrative Staff College at Mt Eliza, would meld local and international perspectives, and would affirm the link of theory with practice.[647]

Administrative training was not new. During the 1950s and 1960s Shears and Moore conducted several intensive residential programs. Residential conferences were commonly held for principals, inspectors and senior administrators at Mannix College in Clayton and Erskine House in Lorne. Moves were afoot to develop leadership training throughout the educational domain. Karmel funding in 1975 supported training for 30 school-based administrators of the Technical Schools Division at Whitehorse Technical College where they received instruction in 'educational philosophy and administrative theory in a practical situation'.[648] Correspondingly plans were underway to establish leadership studies at SCV Hawthorn (formerly the Technical Teachers College). Under the presidency of Keith Andrews the Victorian Council of Educational Administration aimed to foster practice and study to ensure high standards of leadership preparation.[649] In August 1975 the VCEA's parent body, the Commonwealth Council for Educational Administration, conducted its conference at the University Sains in Malaysia, where issues centred on the school principal's role.[650] Meanwhile at home, Moore, Maddocks and Chapman addressed senior administrators at Mannix College to consider 'Structures and Priorities within the Education Department', exposing them to a simulated school council meeting requiring on-the-spot decision-making skills.[651]

Inspectors endorsed training and, though most had basic skills, they agreed 'there is a need for some training for administrators, including principals, to help them in developing efficient office routines and in making full and productive use of the clerical assistance provided'.[652] Forthcoming discussions across the State involved collaboration between the Department and the Catholic Education Office; staff of both met to consider 'Administration in the late '70s'. Application to attend leadership programs would require endorsement by an appropriate inspector, the principal and a colleague or school council member, supported by a principal's statement and a reference from the Committee of Classifiers, or names of two referees. But, getting back to the roots of assessment, Shears concluded, '… after careful consideration of all procedures … the best single piece of evidence of aptitude is the inspectorial assessment'. In view of turbulence caused by inspection in the secondary ranks and stigma of colleagues calling stop work action when inspection for promotion was sought, the Department endorsed teachers' requests for assessment and stressed 'the inspector enters the school to comply with the teacher's wishes'.[653] However, Shears was also convinced that promotion only by length of service or assessment failed to identify leadership aptitude successfully while graduate studies in educational administration did not provide a suitable footing. An authentic environment in a residential facility enabled like-minded aspirants to interact, develop understanding of leadership, nurture essential skills and learn about themselves. Mindful of the principal's influences in the forthcoming decade – technological advance, demands for results, financial constraints, fear of litigation, and increased complexity – Shears was certain of the need for specialist training. He believed that the complicated structure of school organisation required a person with leadership qualities and suitable personality. The person should have knowledge of technique, the capacity to understand numerous perspectives and the ability to make sound judgements. To equip a person for an administrative role within the organisation training was necessary before selection and appointment.

In the mid-1970s Professor Bill Walker at the University of New England was recognised as the leading practitioner of educational administration training in Australia. Growing interest in senior-level policy-making and observations throughout his Harkness Fellowship experience spurred Shears to initiate training for principals and would-be principals. As Survey and Planning Officer he had endorsed the practice of in-service training, and as Chair of the Victorian Chapter of the Australian College of Education he had organised the residential conference in Sorrento in 1969. By the mid '70s the push towards leadership training had gained momentum. Advocating the benefits of working and living together Shears proposed, 'training should be undertaken at a residential administrative training institute to be established' with a director or principal appointed by 'Governor-in-Council after national and international advertisement'. The institute would draw 'heavily on trained personnel in tertiary institutions, commerce or industry and on educational administrators'. Two-month residential programs held during the summer vacation would support practising teachers seeking promotion to senior positions.[654] Institute training would become a prerequisite for those with at least five years' tenure.

As the decade unfolded Shears' vision to create an institute with a worldwide reputation gradually took shape. It gained parliamentary approval in 1976. The passing of the Bill in 1977 set the scene to appoint an interim council, establish preliminary guidelines and assign the leadership team. Dr Colin Moyle was appointed Director of the Institute of Educational Administration (IEA). A former DI and RDE, Moyle had earned his doctorate in educational administration at the University of Wisconsin (Madison) with Professor Jim Lipham. Administration was a social process according to Lipham, wherein effective practice permeated the entire education system.[655] Mr Keith Andrews, former DI and in-service education officer, was appointed Assistant Director. Miss Patricia Armstrong-Grant, from outside the Education Department, was appointed Registrar.[656] Program 1 for the IEA began in 1978.

The residential program facilitated interpersonal interaction, and through a continuum of input, observation and site visits revealed leadership fundamentals. Seven days a week from 8.30 am to 9.00 pm training comprised five 90-minute sessions, private study and exercise time. Consultants drawn from universities, other tertiary institutions, industry and commerce in Victoria, interstate and abroad introduced leadership theory that participants applied to a school principal's tasks. Syndicate grouping encouraged evaluation of participants' own leadership style, self-image and self-concept. It gave them scope to analyse their attitudes and behaviour and the chance to sharpen their skills. Activity, interaction and reflection that guided knowledge development paid tribute to Shears' philosophy born almost three decades before. The success of syndicates living and learning together resembled the interaction of groups observed during his doctoral research, and reinforced his belief that residential training programs were superior to 'day' programs.

Until the IEA interim council found a permanent site, motel facilities in Shepparton, and later Geelong, provided accommodation. 13 August 1978 marked a grand occasion when the Mayor of Shepparton and town councillors, members of the interim council and a host of notables assembled for the official opening of the Institute of Educational Administration by Governor General Sir Henry Winneke. 'It has no parallel anywhere else in the world,' he believed, its seminars would 'complement existing courses' and 'stimulate further study'. The following day the Mayor opened Program 1. 'Thirty-three principals (including one from Western Australia) and other educational administrators in primary, post-primary, and administrative institutions from State, Catholic and independent systems' attended.[657]

From March 1979, the Geelong Travelodge accommodated at least three four-week programs annually. A regional city, Geelong presented as an ideal location with the full spectrum of educational institutions, from pre-school to university, nearby. Easily accessed by teacher participants it was a major centre for industry and commerce. After a lengthy search the interim council identified four acres adjacent to the Botanic Gardens, Eastern Park and the golf club. Minister Hunt announced approval for IEA headquarters at a civic reception. He identified keen interest from civic, business and community leaders.[658] Reserved 'for other purposes', the site offered provision to develop 20 acres adjoining for community and sporting use.[659]

The IEA was operational from 1978 although the *Institute of Education Act* 1980 (No. 9456) was not passed by Parliament until 16 December 1980.[660] Supported by all parties in both Houses, parliamentarians commended the new look Education Department since the restructure of 1975, the momentum of decentralisation, the progressive transfer of power through regional offices to school councils, and the thrust for common facility use. Shadow Education Minister Robert Fordham welcomed leadership training. Modern educational thinking and sound grounding in educational practice were mandatory for the principal, or chief executive officer, to administer a complex organisation, set standards to lead fellow teachers, appoint support personnel and ensure the school's operation.[661] The project was funded by the State Government and managed by the Geelong Regional Commission. Rather than the estimated $3 million the cost exceeded $4.5 million. Site works involved demolition at the Geelong oval and trotting track. Architects' plans accommodated three distinct syndicate areas for small group interaction, plus communal spaces.[662]

Table 11. Inaugural council of the Institute of Educational Administration

| | |
|---|---|
| Dr LW Shears | Chairman of the Council of the IEA |
| Mr ADP Dyer | Principal, Camberwell Grammar School |
| Dr R Fitzgerald | Dean, Planning and Development, Burwood State College |
| Mr M Hughes | Principal, Winchelsea Higher Elementary School |
| Mrs J Kirner | Executive Officer, Victorian Federation of State Schools Parents' Clubs |
| Assoc Professor R McCulloch | School of Education, Monash University |
| Dr GR Maddocks | Assistant Director-General of Education |
| Dr TJ Moore | Deputy Director-General of Education |
| Mr G Newitt | Principal, Waverley High School |
| Mr F Rogan | Supervisor of Secondary Education, Catholic Education Office |
| Mr RL Senior | Director of Teacher Education |
| Mr JS Smith | Retired Professor of Business Administration, University of Melbourne |
| Professor KB Start | School of Education, University of Melbourne |
| Professor WG Walker | Chairman, Professorial Board, University of New England |
| Mr Q Willis | Lecturer in Educational Administration, Royal Melbourne Institute of Technology |

Source: Handbook of Educational Leadership Program 1, Sunday, August 13–Friday September 8 1978, Parklake Motor Inn, Shepparton

## Table 12. Executive staff of the Institute of Educational Administration

| | |
|---|---|
| Dr CRJ Moyle | Director |
| Mr KC Andrews | Assistant Director |
| Miss PJ Armstrong-Grant | Registrar |

Source: Handbook of Educational Leadership Program 1, Sunday, August 13–Friday September 8 1978, Parklake Motor Inn, Shepparton

## Table 13. Presenters at IEA Program 1

| PROGRAM 1 | Parklake Motel Shepparton, 13 August–8 September 1978 |
|---|---|
| Dr James Lipham | Professor of Educational Administration, University of Wisconsin–Madison |
| Dr Hedley Beare | Chief Executive Officer, Australian Capital Territory school system |
| Dr Ronald K Browne | Secretary, Australian Education Council |
| Mr Anthony B Conabere | Headmaster, Wesley College, Melbourne (Waverley); Executive Chairman, Victorian In-Service Education Committee |
| Dr Philip Creed | Acting Assistant Director of Teacher Education (In-Service Education) |
| Mr Arthur E Crook | Principal Lecturer in Psychology, Department of Applied Psychology, Caulfield Institute of Technology |
| Mr Ken E Davis | Syndicate Leader, Australian Administrative Staff College, Mt Eliza |
| Dr June M Hearn | Lecturer, Industrial Relations Program, University of Melbourne |
| Mr Albert W Jones | University Fellow, University of New England, formerly Director-General of Education, South Australia |
| Dr Warren Lett | Reader in Education; Chairman, Centre for Study of Teaching and Human Interaction, Latrobe University |
| Mr Robin J Matthews | Senior Lecturer, Curriculum and Teaching, State College of Victoria (Rusden) |
| Dr Warren Mellor | Senior Lecturer in Educational Administration, Monash University |
| Professor Ross Thomas | Associate Professor of Educational Administration; Head of the Centre of Administrative Studies, University of New England |
| Dr AW Willee | Reader, Chairman, Department of Human Movement Studies, University of Melbourne |
| Mr Antony Williams | Lecturer in Education, Latrobe University, Centre for the Study of Teaching and Human Interaction |

Source: Handbook of Educational Leadership Program 1, Sunday, August 13–Friday September 8 1978, Parklake Motor Inn, Shepparton

**Table 14. Presenters at IEA Program 2**

| PROGRAM 2 | Travelodge Motel Geelong, 4–30 March 1979 |
|---|---|
| Dr R Bryce | Professor of Educational Administration, University of Alberta, Canada |
| Mr NJ Barwick | Assistant Director-General of Education (Building) |
| Dr RK Browne | Secretary, Australian Education Council |
| Mr AB Conabere | Headmaster, Wesley College, Melbourne (Waverley); Executive Chairman, Victorian In-Service Education Committee |
| Mr AE Crook | Principal Lecturer in Psychology, Department of Applied Psychology, Caulfield Institute of Technology |
| Mr KE Davis | Syndicate Leader, Australian Staff College, Moondah, Mount Eliza |
| Dr JM Hearn | Lecturer, Industrial Relations Program, University of Melbourne |
| Dr P Hughes | Head, School of Teacher Education, Canberra College of Advanced Education |
| Dr GR Maddocks | Assistant Director-General of Education (Curriculum |
| Mr RJ Matthews | Senior Lecturer, Curriculum and Teaching, State College of Victoria (Rusden) |
| Dr W Mellor | Senior Lecturer in Educational Administration, Monash University |
| Dr TJ Moore | Deputy Director-General of Education |
| Dr W Mulford | Lecturer in Educational Administration, Canberra College of Advanced Education |
| Professor R Thomas | Associate Professor of Educational Administration; Head of the Centre of Administrative Studies, University of New England |
| Dr RE Potter | Professor of Education, University of Hawaii, presently teaching at the Centre for Administrative Studies, University of New England |
| Mr KA Smith | Principal Lecturer, Coordinator, Graduate Diploma in Educational Studies, State College of Victoria (Hawthorn) |
| Miss R White | Partner, Lindsay A White and Associates |
| Dr AW Willee | Reader, Chairman, Department of Human Movement Studies, University of Melbourne |

Source: Handbook of Educational Leadership Program 2.

Shears reflected on the IEA's development, organisation and success. Every program was opened by someone of importance at a black-tie function. He said this was an integral part of the program because it gave teachers status as they mingled with political, educational and industrial elite. Planning came to fruition in 1983 during the term of a Labor government when Premier Cain officially opened the purpose-built facility as well as the program, despite scorn from some members of his party that he was being elitist. The Institute gained status too and held national and international appeal. A Thai government observer examined the training model and building design in respect to replicating an IEA in Thailand, and the Sultan of Brunei wrote, 'I wish to send all the principals of my schools to the Institute of Educational Administration.' There were criticisms too. Reliance upon restricted numbers posed financial problems regarding 'its size in comparison with the size of its task'. While training boosted participants' confidence and modified their behaviour, post-course evaluation failed to show attitude change. Use of overseas consultants was another burning point even though the printed elements of their planning and other contributions were vetted intimately to ensure broad compliance with the underlying principles of Victorian education. While cost was a factor, international consultants brought international perspectives at a time when global communication was accelerating as the 21st century approached.

Proud of his achievement, Shears was present at every opening and closed every program. Director Moyle stressed Shears' loyalty and support and in turn 'no-one associated with the IEA would let him down. Loyalty begets loyalty.' Moyle remembered their verbal jousts that let participants see the human side of their Director-General and noted Mavis, always present, 'meant so much to his infrastructure … she backgrounded herself [but] she was always 'there' for Lawrie.'[663]

IEA training satisfied the promotional needs of selected senior staff; however School Review Boards continued to evaluate promotional potential and learning programs in schools. Since their inception in 1975, the composition of each Board embraced a larger share of the school community.[664] Keeping good teachers in the classroom remained a puzzle that Shears had not implemented during his term, and then, as now, there was no clear definition of a 'good teacher'.

## Shears' broader embrace

Whether the writer or a reader of Lawrie Shears' story one must pause to consider the mind of the man who conceived the five papers, the intricacies involved in their development and the skill required in their implementation. The evolution of change was underway and while Shears' pioneering changes took shape he was actively involved in other activities within and beyond the borders of the education spectrum.

He remained an advocate of sound teacher preparation, supported the International Teaching Fellowship program and its extension to new horizons in Europe and Asia. This corresponded with policy shifts to multiculturalism.[665] Parallel thrusts were the evolution of technical and further education (TAFE) and the continuing development of teacher education.

Shears continued to acclaim the benefits of overseas travel. Short study tours gave glimpses of the way things were done in other cultural settings while the two-year International Teaching Fellowship offered deeper insight into the beliefs and practices of other cultures. Victorian teachers returned enriched by their knowledge, which put them in good stead to understand the immigrants' plight. Matching Fellows from home and abroad came at a critical time with the push to teach English as a Second Language (ESL) and extend opportunities to learn Languages Other Than English (LOTE).

Among the incoming waves of non-English speakers were arrivals from Southeast Asia. Beyond the traditional school classroom was the need for adults to attend classes, as with limited English language ability, overseas professionals could not find appropriate work. Since 1940 3 million immigrants had arrived in Australia of whom 400,000 were not fluent in English.

The *Migration Act* 1958 (Cwlth)[666] had triggered English language support through adult migrant English programs but despite the prominence of immigrant children in inner-suburban schools little action took place to support their needs. By 1967, they totalled over one-third of the population in 68 schools within a 4-mile radius of Melbourne. Two schools recorded more than 70 per cent. Under the Commonwealth's *Immigration (Education) Act* 1971,[667] services increased and options for English language learning extended to workplace programs and home tutoring for new arrivals. From 1971 to 1975 the Commonwealth Government funded four-week intensive courses for experienced teachers and developed curriculum. Subsequently, in 1977, the Federal Curriculum Development Centre prioritised multicultural education. It stipulated:

(i) the rights of ethnic groups to maintain and foster their ethnic languages and cultures;

(ii) the need for all Australians to promote cultural interaction; and

(iii) the task of developing and sustaining core values and understanding in a pluralist society.[668]

The Galbally Report (1978) recommended orientation programs, extended English language instruction and boosted child migrant courses. It triggered a network of migrant resource centres, ethnic radio and television. In 1975 the first SBS radio broadcasts took place in Sydney and Melbourne and in 1979, through ABV2, Sunday morning transmission of SBS television began. The following year, on United Nations Day, Channel 0/28 transmitted its first program 'Who are we?' hosted by Peter Luck. Urgent action was critical to provide trained specialist ESL and LOTE teachers, and ethnic support staff.[669]

Among the cohort of alternative schools that had sprung up in the 1960s were those that taught bilingual and ethnic programs to satisfy distinct language groups. The Greek Orthodox, Italian and Jewish communities taught their own language and culture while the French opted for a 'school within a school' or 'La petite école' at a Richmond primary school. French diplomats' children studied the core curriculum in French but joined the broader school community for sport, art, craft and music activities.[670] Secondary students located at John Gardiner High School followed the French Ministry's correspondence course. In Victoria's La Trobe Valley, the children of Japanese workers followed a curriculum set by the Japanese Education Ministry, as happened in 73 other schools across the globe:

> In 1980 the Victorian and Japanese Governments agreed to develop a coal-to-oil project in Morwell. In 1981 a meeting was held with the Education Department to determine how education would be provided for children of Japanese workers. A 'school-within-a-school' was proposed. In April 1982 two Japanese students enrolled at Morwell (Commercial Road) Primary School and in September 1982 the Japanese Centre was built at that school. In 1983 the first Japanese teacher arrived to teach the seven enrolled students. The 'Japanese School' was officially opened in April 1983 and an additional classroom was built in July 1984

to house the increasing numbers of students. The highest number was 40 in 1989, but between 1983 and 1991 133 primary school students went through the Japanese School and 21 high school students took Japanese language tuition there after hours while following the normal curriculum at Morwell High School. One student completed his VCE at Morwell and was accepted into Monash University.

*Brief history of the Japanese school at Morwell*
*(Keith Brownbill, former Principal of Morwell High Schools)*

Beyond traditional school programs Saturday classes (the Saturday School of Languages had begun in 1935) found new energy to support LOTE programs and hone immigrant children's first-language skills.

Despite these moves, the ongoing influx of immigrant children sent ripples through the teaching fraternity. Pressure to conform and parental expectations affected the children; teachers felt unprepared and ill-equipped; and schools with high immigrant populations queried the best means of support and requested additional staffing.[671] The complex array of demands set the Department in turmoil and disturbed 'the normally imperturbable' Shears who was seen to become 'unexpectedly acerbic'.[672] While the Department struggled to service commitments it was publicly scorned. Teacher unions complained that insufficient teachers and poorly managed programs showed gross ignorance of migrant needs. Critical of its staffing for 1979 Albert Park High School teachers identified only four specialist teachers to provide ongoing intensive language support for 60 per cent of its 850 students:

> ... any notion of equal opportunity becomes meaningless and 'normal' classes become increasingly hampered by large numbers of students unable to cope with the required level of language skills ... to propose that four teachers represent a 'more than adequate' provision for the language needs of so many students is educational nonsense.[673]

There were difficulties, Shears admitted, and with the 'Premier breathing down my neck' he blamed lack of funds. To uphold escalating needs he stressed the Department's endeavours to satisfy shortfalls. By 1978 it employed 920 specialist teachers, a gain of 100 since 1976, plus a supply of remedial teachers. He did not specify teacher expertise or the number of language specialists.[674]

Though disturbed by the waves of discontent, Shears maintained faith that International Teaching Fellows would awaken cultural understanding. On visits abroad he supported recruitment drives and sought opportunities to expand the program. The UNESCO experience in 1974 had stirred the extension of the ITF program to Europe and prompted two-way matches, and the UNESCO Conference in Nairobi in 1976 was another opportunity. The Conference broached educational policy, planning, structures and management; content, methods and techniques of delivery; higher education and personnel training; the status of teachers; equality of opportunity and special programs. Debate apropos the 1974 Paris Conference and development of adult education supported the concept of 'Learning to Be'. Influenced by the Faure Report (1972) education was considered a lifelong transformative, liberating force that affected broader society.

Following the Nairobi conference Shears travelled to the UK via Greece where the Greek government had pre-arranged interview venues for him to recruit Greek-speaking teachers. Mavis had flown ahead and on his arrival they lunched at the residence of the Australian Ambassador to Greece. Professionally and socially Shears was on top of the world and Mavis enriched his pursuits. The recruitment drive took them over mountains and through small villages and exposed them to Greek culture. Shears explained in an interview I conducted in 2008, 'In the 1970s we had the second largest Greek community outside Athens; our Greek community welcomed the group of sixteen bilingual Greeks employed as foreign language assistants.'[675]

In England the final recruitment campaign for the Victorian Teacher Selection Program was taking place. Since its commencement 1971, the number of 3238 imported teachers included 2647 from the USA, 380 from Britain and 211 from Canada. Current shortfalls for teachers of physical education, music and maths, and horticulture specialists in technical schools, led to a final intake of 22 from Britain. On arrival in Melbourne they faced protests and a threatened boycott by unions and unemployed teachers.[676]

Discussion to expand the ITF continued. *The Age* reported 'Teacher swap with Russia' and negotiations with Russian education officials. It stated 'Japan and Greece have also been approached and Israel has become the first country to approach Victoria about the scheme.' Regarding the Russian proposal Shears explained 'It would probably take much longer to complete arrangements ... because of their total bureaucracy and [the] general isolation of Russian educators from the Western World.'[677]

Groundwork to expand the program involved first-hand contact in which Shears excelled. Whenever possible he renewed or made contacts abroad. In his persuasive manner he presented the proposition in depth to enhance its international status. By appointment, Rex Murfett was introduced to Alan Wilcox, Principal of the United Nations International School (UNIS) in New York. Wilcox explained the school's status, one of the big three international schools in the world; he had been there for thirteen years. Keen to engage Australian and New Zealand teachers he had already met successfully with Director-General Bill Renwick in New Zealand. Wilcox proposed, 'If we paid their salaries the local education departments could pay the teachers' fares'. He recalled:

> Dr Shears was sitting behind a huge desk. He was very much a 'get to the point' top man. I explained the deal: It's a wonderful school, it's an opportunity for teachers' professional development to go to the United Nations school and be on show. This is a school that's connected with the UN. It has the children of all the diplomats; George Bush's daughter, all the hoi polloi of New York, anybody who was anybody – that was just the society.
>
> I sat down and said, 'Here's the deal: I'll pay for the salaries of the teachers if you pay for the fares.' Without batting an eye, Dr Shears turned to me and said, 'You pay the fares and I'll pay the salaries.' I looked at Rex and queried, 'What he is saying is we'll pay you $50,000 a year if you pay $2000?' In shock, I responded 'No, no, we'll pay the salaries if you pay the fares.' He said, 'I'll pay the salaries!' I said, 'That's fine – for two teachers starting one year apart.' 'Yes,' he confirmed and said to Rex, 'Take care of it.'
>
> I went into the deal to ask the guy for a couple of thousand dollars for the fares, to put them on a level playing field, and

he gave me, like $300,000. I went out with Rex who said, 'If that's what he wants, do it; it's part of a program he's developing, part of the ITF program.' I got in touch with Renwick and explained what they did in Victoria and he did the same.[678]

In 1979 the ITF reached new horizons. In addition to matching 47 Victorian ITFs, Mr Ray Daniels from Blackburn South High School began a two-year appointment at the UNIS, New York. Subsequently a two-year matching appointment initiated a long association. Another advance was the matching of principals with principals and an administrator with another from the Canadian Education Department. The first Catholic ITFs appeared in 1981 when France and Germany took part, and matching with China and Yugoslavia began in 1982.

## *Lifelong learning*

Lifelong training was UNESCO's call to promote adult learning. The Victorian Education Department advanced this through increased support for the Council of Adult Education, developments in colleges of advanced education and the expansion of TAFE. As with all aspects of education the quality and preparation of teachers lay at the heart of learning.

Despite efforts to promote the status of teacher education there remained a rift between courses offered at universities and alternative institutions. In this debate the Commonwealth's role in education was increasingly evident. The Murray Report (1957) had identified the need for more highly educated people in more walks of life. It stressed the nation's need for a 'very large number of very highly educated men and women', promoted science and technology to support national growth and accentuated the critical shortage of graduate teachers. It acknowledged that universities must guard their intellectual integrity but saw an enormous gap between the nurturing school environment and the 'sink or swim' attitude of universities. High first-year failure rate was an extravagance the nation could ill-afford while increased numbers of part-time students were an essential aspect of growth.[679] The Martin Report (1964) accentuated the university–non-university divide. Though the report stipulated broad comprehensive tertiary studies it also acknowledged the value of a binary system that offered knowledge-based or vocational focus to satisfy students' ability and purpose.[680] The proposal to promote the status of teaching was common to both the Murray and the Martin Reports, which led to numerous State and national studies.

Like former investigations, the Swanson Committee on Teacher Education (1973) had endorsed the binary system wherein universities prepared graduates for the professions while colleges of advanced education and teachers colleges addressed vocational needs. Despite inconsistency of status in graduate preparation, a focal shift occurred from training to educating teachers. Education began at pre-service level and continued career long through professional development and in-service activities.

Correspondingly, the Kangan Committee (1973-74) was a major step in the advance of TAFE. A Whitlam initiative, the Kangan Committee signalled funding shortfalls that left 400,000 students beyond the Schools Commission jurisdiction. As new industries emerged and technology advanced, the Committee addressed the priorities of technical and further training, and their importance to the nation's education and economy. By the 1970s the workforce had altered; hence the need to train more women and adults as well as school leavers. The birth of TAFE as a body to offer post-secondary studies in professional, para-professional, trades, other skilled areas, preparatory and adult education aimed to elevate the status of the tertiary underdog.[681]

The Commonwealth Tertiary Education Commission, established in May 1975 by Kim Beazley (Snr), Commonwealth Minister for Education (1972-75), united the Universities Commission and the Commission of Advanced Education. Notwithstanding economic pressures, the succeeding Liberal government maintained momentum to review secondary and post-secondary education. The Committee of Enquiry into Education and Training promoted 'balanced development of the whole area of tertiary education as provided in universities and colleges of advanced education' yet for funding purposes maintained distinction between tertiary ranks. State ministers, critical of their non-representation and of the lack of secondary education expertise of committee members claimed the Enquiry measured education on a 'specialized basis rather than trying to perceive the educational scene as a unity'. As consolation they made a submission, analysed data relating to their particular State, and conferred with the Committee of Enquiry and President Professor Bruce Williams.[682] The Williams Committee (1976–79) accentuated more effective teaching to develop basic skills, identified education as more important than preparation for work and stressed the need to develop the TAFE system. Albeit a prolonged evolution, the Williams Report led to the first nationwide review of teacher education and was fundamental to the evolution of TAFE.

## Teacher education on the national front

Following consultation with Senator Carrick, Commonwealth Minister for Education (1975–79), the AEC nominated six members of a 15-person committee to participate in the National Inquiry into Teacher Education (NITE). As a member of the Inquiry committee Shears' Burwood experience, knowledge of teacher education in local and international domains and aspirations to boost professional status held him in good stead. He understood that preparation and graduation were but steps in each teacher's career. Chaired by Professor James Auchmuty,[683] the National Inquiry endeavoured to influence education in all its manifestations for the next 25 years; transform preparation 'from a narrow trade-based vocational approach to a broader more professional approach'; and continue 'the shift from certificates and diplomas to degrees in education'. As the Swanson Committee had found in 1973–75,[684] 'a continuous process of personal and professional development' was the ideal.[685]

Paralleling the NITE Inquiry was the Victorian Enquiry into Teacher Education chaired by the Hon. Mr Justice Asche. Departmental officers RL Senior and JF Wilson were appointed as Deputy Chairman and Executive Officer. Members of the 22-person committee included representatives of metropolitan and regional universities, the State College of Victoria, government and nongovernment schools, community services and industry. Five thousand copies of the 553-page Interim Asche Report distributed to school councils, regional offices, teacher-training institutions, and State and federal instrumentalities involved in education gave a thorough overview. Consultants from a spectrum of educational interests included Dr P Creed, Acting Assistant Director of Teacher Education, Victorian Education Department; Dr C Moyle, Director, IEA; and Mr J Izard, Australian Council for Educational Research. Respondents included universities, the Victorian In-service Education Committee, the Catholic Education Commission, the Free Kindergarten Union of Victoria, representatives of schools and community groups, technical colleges and colleges of the SCV.

Proposed policy changes reflected social and demographic change that affected education systems. In response to Mr Al Grasby's claim that 'Australian schools today are educating children of 140 ethnic backgrounds and cultures, 90 different home languages, and 40 different religious affiliations ...', the Asche Report stressed the complexities of Australia's pluralist society. Schooling must avoid 'cultural elitism without depriving anyone of their cultural heritage' avoid 'fostering cultural separation or assimilation without recognition of the practical importance of students learning the skills and customs of the dominant culture' and the 'inclusion of opinions and judgments of all people in actions undertaken with regard to education'. Within the social framework such ideals were difficult to bring to fruition.[686]

Toffler's philosophies, noted by Shears in 1975, stated that 'the rate at which man in the future will have to abandon the familiar to grapple with the novel will create great psychological strains, which it is suggested, will require increased human adaptability.' In alignment with these predictions, the submission from SCV Rusden indicated:

> The rate of change may outstrip our ability to deal with new realities ... in a dynamic world where skills date rapidly, a sound general education offers the best guarantee of a flexible workforce whose members are capable of turning to new tasks.[687]

To cope with these possibilities, plus many not yet identified, the complexity of the teacher's task continually increased. Across the profession teachers faced a range of needs. Beginning teachers required careful induction and the bond between them, the training institute and the school was a vital link, whereas priorities for practising teachers and the broader school community were support to cope with emerging issues. The Asche Report emphasised, 'teaching is for most a very demanding occupation in terms of nervous strain. With increasing demands upon schools this is likely to become worse rather than better.' It stressed the personal and professional benefits of further training.[688]

Common to the Asche and Auchmuty inquiries was the thrust to extend the duration of teacher-preparation courses as concurrent or end-on programs. Both sought to promote the status of the profession, ensure ongoing options for professional development and maintain close liaison between training schools and institutions. Indirectly involved in the Asche Enquiry, Shears was briefed on progress and recommendations by senior staff. Directly involved in the Auchmuty Inquiry he claimed 'quality not quantity' was the aim. Of the lengthy process of meetings and forming conclusions he reflected:

> After many weekend meetings, visits throughout Australia, public meetings, and more than 153 written submissions, we were able to sign a document for submission to the Federal and State ministers of education which I hope will have a significant influence on future teachers. Emphasis on the development and maintenance of quality teaching from the time a young person decides to enter the teaching profession until s/he leaves it should provide an excellent starting point for the implementation of the Committee's recommendations.[689]

Future focused, the NITE Report stated that the computer industry would affect teachers' traditional role and stipulated that post-secondary pathways must embrace 'special preparation for work, job retraining, and increased leisure'. Teacher education required a core set of studies, four-year training with a clear bond between theory and practice, and careful supervision.[690] Philosophies reflected in both reports resembled those progressively sought by Shears and others keen to elevate the professional status of teaching. While they marked a stage in an evolutionary process, revolutionary changes were taking place in Victoria. Newly appointed, Minister Alan Hunt and Assistant Minister Norman Lacy supported proposals to strengthen teachers' basic skills and endorsed developments in technical and further education.

## *Technical and further education (TAFE)*

Declining school enrolments, lower retention rates in senior classes and youth unemployment were a major concern. Improved quality and diversity of TAFE courses was the key to smooth the transition from school to work.[691] Prior to the Hunt–Lacy era developments were underway. The Kangan Report (1974) stressed the importance of TAFE as a vital part of the nation's education system. Its primary role was to provide vocational choice for individuals within the context of industry's needs. The report detailed Commonwealth financial requirements.

Shears acknowledged the social contribution of technical education and in Paper 1 addressed the need to expand postprimary schooling. In the concept of lifelong learning the integration of primary, secondary, technical and post-secondary domains created a complete educational unit and was a step towards merging school, education, living and leisure within the community. 'Education for Complete Living' was the logo for the New Education Conference (1937) and 'Learning to Be' was the theme at the UNESCO Conference in Paris (1972). 'Education is Living,' Shears proclaimed. Every part of the whole had a task to perform[692] and 'only an overall lifelong educational plan can produce the kind of complete man and woman needed in our society in the future.'[693] These beliefs remained firm in Shears' mind while discussion apropos vocational pathways continued. The *Post-Secondary Education Act* 1978 (No. 9145) authorised an Accreditation Board to investigate 'course content and academic standard, and facilities available in connection with courses of study occupying not less than one year's full-time study or equivalent'.[694] Emeritus Professor William Connell, University of Sydney, chaired the Accreditation Board, with Mr James (Mac) Hill, former Vice President, SCV, and

*Leading the Flock*

Dr Graham Whitehead, Assistant Director of Special Services, among board members.

The birth of TAFE in Victoria was continually fraught with frustration midst Commonwealth threats to withhold money. With $52 million spread nationwide in 1979 the Commonwealth claimed the state of technical education in Victoria did not warrant its share. Victoria was criticised for its poor forward planning. Unless the Department set a realistic target date for its building program it would not receive funds. Shadow Education Minister Robert Fordham hoped it was not too late. Shears, in response, claimed the TAFE Council had ignored details of planning and building operations and long-term plans recently presented.[695]

In March 1980 Minister Hunt announced government policy to develop TAFE. A TAFE Board led by Mr Ian Predl, consisting of not more than ten members, would determine policy subject to ministerial constraints; determine distribution of funds; authorise and accredit new TAFE courses and developments in existing courses to ensure effective use of resources; and make recommendations to relevant ministers. The TAFE Board's role was in policy rather than administration. Current services were cost effective and did not need duplication.[696]

TAFE offered a complexity of courses beyond traditional tertiary bounds. The Education Department (through its Technical Schools Division), the Council of Adult Education, the Department of Agriculture and independent colleges were TAFE's four recognised providers. As the State authority, the Education Department formulated priorities with business and industrial groups and coordinated funding for TAFE colleges under its jurisdiction, the TAFE modules presented in secondary schools, community education courses and evening classes. The Technical and Further Education Administrative Committee coordinated broader activities and the State Council for Technical Education advised the Minister.

Explaining the structure to the educational community through *News Exchange* Shears envisaged that each of the four providers would have stand-alone strength but he warned against a premature move to become autonomous, as had occurred with the SCV and VIC.[697] The

T of TAFE represented the Technical element whereas FE, or Further Education, was a vital part of the whole. By September 1981 the Education Department's technical colleges were incorporated under the *Victorian Post Secondary Education (Amendment) Act* 1981 (No. 9711) and Ian Predl was appointed Managing Director of a group of five metropolitan and nine country TAFE colleges. A Post-Secondary Education Committee was set up as a part of the Albury–Wodonga Development Corporation.[698]

Table 15. Victoria's four recognised TAFE providers

| Needs ascertainment | Education Department | Council of Adult Education | Department of Agriculture | Independent colleges |
|---|---|---|---|---|
| Policy determination | TAFE BOARD Representative of all interests with a small Statewide executive body and expert committees to allocate resources among providers | | | |
| Policy implementation | Education Department | Council of Adult Education | Department of Agriculture | Independent colleges |

The four recognised providers work with business, industry and community groups to prepare details of needs. These needs are transmitted to the TAFE Board where policy is formed and resources are allocated. The four recognised providers implement the policies to meet the needs of their clients.

Source: Adapted from *News Exchange*, no. 9, 10 June 1981

## Institutional unification

While TAFE was expanding, moves were afoot to consolidate the VIC and SCV.

The concept of mergers met disapproval. Students and staff took pride in their institution and the institutional identity they created. But economy overruled loyalty and even Shears conceded the economic benefits of post-secondary mergers. Ensuing was the merger of the SCV with the VIC. In June 1981 Dr Graham Allen, Chairman of the Victorian Post-Secondary Education Commission, announced Federal Government recommendations for the 1982–84 triennium. Immediate change presented 'academic, financial and administrative strength to maintain the quality of advanced education in Victoria ... use more efficiently the physical resources available in the Metropolitan area' and formed a foundation for the growth of advanced education through the next 20 years.[699] The identity of former teachers colleges dear to Shears' heart (Burwood and Toorak) was further diminished by uniting with SCV Rusden and Prahran CAE under the name of Victoria College, founded in 1981. 75 per cent of the Victoria College students were enrolled in teacher education but by 1988 language, business and nursing diversified options.

Table 16. Institutional mergers from 1981 and Shears' connections

| Institute | Proposal in 1981 | Development | Connection |
|---|---|---|---|
| SCV Burwood SCV Toorak SCV Rusden Prahran CAE | Multi-campus, multi-disciplined college, governed by a single council; offer advanced educational studies on three campuses | Victoria College of Advanced Education (1981); Burwood, Toorak and Rusden became part of Deakin University (1992), Prahran CAE became part of Swinburne University of Technology (1992) | Survey and Planning Officer (1954–61)–involved in site purchase of Toorak TC and development of Burwood TC Lecturer, Toorak TC (1952–53); Lecturer, Burwood TC (1954) Principal Burwood TC (1961–69) |
| Lincoln Institute of Health Sciences SCV Coburg SCV Melbourne | Consolidate on to two campuses governed by a single council, offer advanced education studies | Lincoln merged with LaTrobe University (1988); SCV Melbourne became part of the Faculty of Education University of Melbourne (1989); SCV Coburg, Preston Institute of Technology became Phillip Institute (1982) and merged with RMIT (1992) | Survey and Planning Officer (1954–61)–involved in site purchase and development of Coburg TC |

## On the industrial front

Industrial unrest was a hallmark of Shears' years in administration though much of the cause lay beyond his reach. Financial constraints imposed by the Schools Commission hindered education departments nationwide. Loss of recurrent funds impeded maintenance and developments in Catholic schools and loss of capital funds crippled the Victorian Education Department's building program. The effect rippled through the educational community, roused parental concern and teacher militancy. Unions had become powerful forces and the VSTA the most effective. However, problems of the 1970s and 1980s stemmed from the 1960s when unrest created a nightmare. Former activist Gerry Tickell explained:

> Funds for education had been parsimonious; we had a desperate shortage of teachers until well into the 70s. I had a department of 16 teachers at Glenroy Tech ... about three of us had BA or DipEd. Lawrie ran into a period when the unions had been making a fair bit of progress but were starting to encounter resistance. As the government's Chief Officer he was obliged to hold the line ... there were no grounds for thinking that he was personally hostile.[700]

In a letter to *The Age* Shears expressed concern about severe funding cuts and their effect on education:

> If the community wants to avoid the problems of the 1950s and 1960s; if we are to maintain our present level of provision in the face of increasing school populations and inflationary costs; and if the 'young marrieds' of the past 10 years are to obtain for their children who have been born during this time an education at least level to our present services – there must be no cuts.[701]

The unions demanded urgent reform. Publicly they pounded Shears' handling of their concerns and yet they built an alliance with him. His diaries record weekly meetings that show 'I gave them plenty of time'. At times, he admitted, discussion became heated whereas VSTA executives acknowledged 'he gave as good as he got – the little bugger'. Bob Jenkin of the VSTA Executive recalled, 'the guy we conflicted with on industrial issues didn't sit back and take it' but he improved dialogue between teachers, the government and the Department.[702]

Bill Hannan witnessed discussions 'off the record'. He described parley around a coffee table instead of sitting on 'opposing sides of a massive ornate desk'. Geoff Reid described this as 'sporadic intercourse on a waterbed' wherein substantial pummelling led to compromise. An observer claimed Shears had the capacity to placate the unions whereas others objected to disruptions to schools and their personal time. Witness to a deputation being bundled out of the office of an ADGE Reid contemplated the extremes: 'Shears would have handled it differently, been more conciliatory; he wanted to maintain good relations with everybody.'[703]

The unions fought for their cause. They wanted immediate action to improve physical and employment conditions and enhance teacher training. They strived for professional status. Shears acknowledged concerns and affirmed steps to recruit and train teachers, raise standards and keep pace with growth. Both parties agreed that 'conditions of work for secondary teachers are so important an issue the matter cannot be decided without proper consultation' but delays stirred continued strike action. From a common platform they argued their case from different texts.

A school-by-school survey indicated teachers' work conditions were at least equal to colleagues elsewhere and better in many respects.[704] Class size, Shears argued, gave a 'rough measure' and was not the sole criteria; however he saw the need to differentiate between inner-suburban schools with high migrant enrolments and those in high socio-economic locations.[705] As a new wave of students reached secondary levels there was a need for more money, more schools, more teachers and more specialist staff.

Table 17. Secondary teachers' working conditions: Analysis of State, national and international practices

| Source of information | | | |
|---|---|---|---|
| Australia | USA | Canada | UK |
| 6 replies | 20 replies from 14 States | 13 replies from 6 provinces | 7 replies from 7 local education authorities |

| Hours of instruction and teacher attendance per day | | | | | | | |
|---|---|---|---|---|---|---|---|
| Australia | | USA | | Canada | | UK | |
| Instruction | Attendance | Instruction | Attendance | Instruction | Attendance | Instruction | Attendance |
| $5^{1/3}$–$6^{1/3}$ | $6$–$6^{2/3}$ | $5^{1/2}$–$7$ | $6^{1/2}$–$7$ | $5^{1/2}$–$7^{1/4}$ | $6$–$7$ | $6$–$6^{1/2}$ | $6^{1/2}$–$7$ |
| Suggestion: $5^{1/2}$ hours of pupil instruction, 6–$6^{1/2}$ hours' attendance. | | | | | | | |

| Hours of face-to-face teaching per week | | | | | | | |
|---|---|---|---|---|---|---|---|
| Australia | | USA | | Canada | | UK | |
| Range | Average | Range | Average | Range | Average | Range | Average |
| 20–$21^{1/3}$ | 20.5 | 18–25 | 22 | 18–26 | 22 | 20–24 | $21^{2/3}$ |
| Suggestion: 20 hours' face-to-face teaching excluding sports supervision | | | | | | | |

| **Percentage of face-to-face teaching time allowed for preparation and correction during school instructions hours** | | | |
|---|---|---|---|
| Australia | USA | Canada | UK |
| 20%–33% | 15%–40% | 15%–33% | 15%–20% |

Suggestion: 25% of face-to-face teaching allowed for preparation and correction during school time.
Note: Responses varied due to length of instructional day e.g. one US State had a 7-hour day, so more time allocated to these duties.

| **Participation in sport and/or study supervision** | | | |
|---|---|---|---|
| Australia | USA | Canada | UK |
| 1+ hours | 1–4+ hours | 1–4+ hours | 2+ hours |

Supervision of sport or study is a universal expectation set on the basis of stated hours or voluntary. Participation 'should be voluntary in Victorian schools but where it is undertaken 2 hours or 2 forty-five minute periods should be allowed for it in addition to face-to-face teaching time and preparation and correction time. It could be a deduction from the total teacher attendance time.'

| **Participation in extracurricular activities** | | | | | | | |
|---|---|---|---|---|---|---|---|
| Australia | | USA | | Canada | | UK | |
| Hrs stated | Voluntary | Hrs stated | Voluntary | Hrs stated | Voluntary | Hrs stated | Voluntary |
| 1 | 5 | 5 | 12 | 4 | 9 | 11 | 32 |

3 responses from the USA and Canada indicated teachers did not participate in extracurricular activities.
Suggestion: Keeping in practice with other countries, extracurricular activities other than sport and study supervision should be encouraged but remain voluntary and related to teachers' personal and professional commitment.

**Emergency teaching and/or taking 'extras'**

(a) Steps should be taken immediately to develop
    (i) a larger full-time itinerant relieving staff
    (ii) a list of emergency short-term relief teachers
(b) While relieving teachers are being recruited, emergency teaching or taking extras should be restricted to a system involving not more than 2 hours per week for those whose teacher-attendance has not been absorbed in study, sport or extracurricular activities.

Source: Working Conditions of Teachers in Secondary Schools: An Analysis of National and International Practices pp. 1–5[706]

**Table 18. Analysis of class size**

| Analysis of class size | | | | | | |
|---|---|---|---|---|---|---|
| Year level | Range | Australia | USA | Canada | UK | Average |
| Forms 1 & 2 | 27–37 | 32–36 | 27–37 | 30–35 | 30–35 | 30–35 |
| Form 3 | 25–35 | 30–35 | 25–35 | 25–35 | 30–35 | 30 |
| Form 4 | 25–35 | 30–35 | 25–35 | 25–35 | 30–35 | 30 |
| Form 5 | 20–35 | 24–30 | 20–35 | 25–32 | 25–35 | 30 |
| Form 6 | 15–35 | 20–30 | 15–35 | 20–30 | 15–20 | 30 |

Replies indicate objectives to reduce class size have not met our expectations.

Suggestions: Victoria could accept the best of the range of class size but in borderline cases classes could not be split to a larger number of class groups until they were above a certain percentage above the objective:

| | |
|---|---|
| Forms 1, 2, 3 | 30 pupils (15%) |
| Form 4 | 30 pupils (10%) |
| Forms 5 & 6 | 25 pupils (10%) |

Source: Working Conditions of Teachers in Secondary Schools: An Analysis of National and International Practices[707]

To-ing and fro-ing between the unions and Shears was an ongoing saga where each side selected criteria to suit their case. Professionalism was paramount and while Shears heralded the role of professional organisations, the unions upheld their own associations. With pride, the VSTA had framed its constitution on the Australian Medical Association's model to promote a professional body. In rebuttal Shears claimed professional groups controlled their membership whereas teachers had 'lost the ability to discipline their members'. As a consequence, many secondary teachers were not members of the VSTA. [708]

Acknowledgement of their commitment was insufficient. Secondary teachers emphasised the breadth of their work – face-to-face teaching, correction, preparation, extracurricular activities, emergency teaching and ancillary duties. They disputed requirements to work beyond the regulation 38-hour week. Out-of-hours activities were part of their duty, claimed Shears. He calculated a 44-hour week in line with the public average of four weeks leave plus approximately one week of public holidays (i.e. a working year of 47 weeks at 40 hours a week or 1880 hours), which gave teachers an additional six weeks of duty-free leave (i.e. a working year of 41 weeks at 44 hours or 1804 hours). He specified:

| | |
|---|---|
| Face to face teaching | 20 hours |
| Preparation and correction during school hours | 5 hours |
| Other duties during school hours | 7½ hours |
| Out-of-school obligations | 11½ hours[709] |

The unions were not impressed. During those volatile times Shears was 'doing the government of the day's bidding … staunchly supporting its policies'.[710] Yet some of his action caused confusion. At times he seemed to be a firm yet interactive negotiator in contrast to a group of abusive, disrespectful senior officers about him. Some who were involved categorised him with the abusive group while others queried the democratic leader who tolerated their antics.[711] Newspaper headlines reflected the tension. 'School union "plays games" '[712]; 'Shears raps VSTA'; 'Promotions bring school rift'; 'School row looms'; 'Strikes threat to cash: Shears'; and 'Sack Shears say strikers'. Not afraid to face his foe, like Daniel, Shears walked into the lion's den, to uphold an engagement to address a regional VSTA dinner. In the midst of a rolling strike regarding the 'right to strike' he looked at education issues rather than union action. In a letter to *The Age* he questioned 'Who should run the schools?'

> They (the unions) are saying to the Director-General, who is accountable to the Minister for the administration of Government schools: 'You shall not give instructions or directions to any secondary teacher if these instructions contradict what we say should be happening.'

He continued, saying that, by law:

> … no Minister or permanent head can forgo the responsibility he has to account to the Government and to the Parliament. No teacher can refuse to accept his responsibility as an employee to carry out lawful instructions of the properly appointed educational ministers.[713]

Union executives opposed the Minister, Shears and the Education Department. The Minister had failed to hold promised discussions and Shears was 'skating over unrest' and making staffing decisions without consultation. Enraged by the decree to accept staff ceiling and work condition criteria 'without negotiation', the union leaders sought to 'rescind the un-negotiated decisions and start afresh … with ample negotiation or even a joint union–department working party.'[714]

Analytic and tactical, Shears preferred to 'negotiate rather than resist'.[715] He held regular meetings with union officials though they claimed he swayed debate from the root of the cause. 'Waterbed tactics', Hannan said. He emphasised Shears' sophisticated and tactical analytic ability, and his capacity to float 'novel solutions and alternatives without prejudice'.[716] However, publicly Shears blasted the VSTA over increasing industrial stoppages. He claimed inaccurate rationale augured strike action and jeopardised performance of students in schools. Teacher militancy led to anarchy. Such action 'threatened the whole structure of local involvement in schools', a principal claimed.[717] After consultation with Thompson, Shears presented a Statement of Research Needs in April 1979. It defined teacher surplus; teacher shortage; optimum allocation of staff resources; and source and supply of teachers. It identified research related to selection, preparation and induction of new staff. It identified timetabled duties and emphasised the 'Right to be Taught' as opposed to the 'Right to Strike'.[718]

Betwixt the to-ing and fro-ing, the pull and the tussle, Shears' leadership was put to the test. The size of the task for educational leaders and their line of accountability cannot be overlooked; the Department to the government, the Minister, schools, teachers, children, parents and the broader community. With authority to lead, his innovations had created waves, and he dealt with glitches and difficulties. He was seen to bear the brunt of the burden. Described as 'relaxed, but sometimes angry ... sometimes unpredictable' he appeared 'more like a diplomat than an educational supremo' who 'radiates energy and enthusiasm'. Energy, enthusiasm and passion were vital characteristics that carried him through.[719]

## Other dimensions of Shears

Professional demands had their lighter side too. Like a hound with its nose to the ground, he was always alert. Impressed by London's Cockpit Theatre he thought Victoria should have one too. With expansion of the Drama Resource Centre the Bouverie Street Theatre was born. During its 10-year existence under the Education Department those involved toured to London, Sydney, Adelaide and statewide across Victoria. On the occasion when the Centre received an official bus, a 'wedding' was performed in Carlton's Lincoln Gardens. Father of the bride/bus, Shears, handed over the keys to the 'groom', Denis Gill of the Drama Resource Centre, with DRC colleagues as witnesses.

Hopetoun Road was a haven. Away from the office it was a venue to entertain. Mavis and the family catered for tennis and swimming parties and barbecues, and presented grand dinner parties for friends, colleagues and overseas guests. Walking the dog was a pleasant pastime Shears undertook gladly and the block that had been purchased at Aireys Inlet was a pleasant retreat. But such breaks were short, as duty called.

Shears remained loyal to the VIER where he maintained presidency, attended meetings and supported primary, secondary and regional groups. He attended annual conferences of the Australian College of Education and retained interest in the AARE. Alert to developments in education he was quick to respond and share his views as guest speaker at gatherings of numerous organisations. His lecture 'Go, not woe' for VIER's Primary Education Today group was well received in 1980. While his contributions to VIER gained him Honorary Life Membership, several protégés who played active roles continued their upward professional climb – Dr Graham Allen (Treasurer 1960–66) Vice President 1969–82); foundation student at Burwood TC Dr Graham Whitehead (Treasurer 1967–70, Vice President 1983–87); Dr Leo Foster (Delegate to ACER 1985, Vice President 1989).

Activity in the College of Nursing Australia began to fade after Shears' senior appointment though he maintained connections and received an Honorary Fellowship in 1978. The IEA demanded increased attention as plans for the Geelong headquarters took shape. Expansion of the ITF continued to challenge and the link with UNIS added a new dimension in the arena of international schools. A ceremony in Melbourne in 1978 marked this significance with a plaque presented to Shears as a representative of the Education Department. The Australian Ambassador attended a corresponding ceremony at the United Nations headquarters in the USA.

Rotary lunches at the Windsor Hotel and gatherings of sub-group

'Toorak Number Two' offered community service opportunity. As a member of the Duke of Edinburgh's Award Committee Shears attended awards presentations at Government House, met the Duke of Edinburgh, and received an award for his own service. Membership at the Melbourne Club continued to grant prestige; the Club was a venue to host interstate and overseas guests, educational colleagues and up-and-comings. Among other activities Shears led the education delegation to the ABC Commonwealth Conference (1975) and chaired both the Liaison Committee he had set up between the Department and the Catholic Education Office (1974–82) and the Social Resources Committee of the State Coordination Council (1974–83). He served on the Latrobe University council and the vestry at St John's Toorak.

# Section 6:

# NEW ERA

CHAPTER 16

# TURBULENT TIMES (1980–81)

*We must accept finite disappointment, but never lose infinite hope.*
Martin Luther King, Jr.

Shears knew education. As the new decade dawned he had much to be proud of. The decade past had been marked by social ferment, increased affluence and sexual freedom. In that volatile climate Shears established policies to guide education into the 21st century. He orchestrated the restructure; steered devolution of power through regions, thus spreading the power base; forged closer relationships with the community; conveyed financial autonomy to school councils; and formalised administrative training.[720]

Victoria had made significant steps towards school and community education projects with joint planning and shared use of facilities. School councils had greater monetary discretion; the total amount of money available to school councils showed a rise from $3 million to $38 million in the last decade. In the broader scheme the Liaison Committee promoted cooperative planning between government, Catholic and independent schools; 'Books on Wheels' enhanced literacy prospects for rural children; the TV news program 'You, me and education' produced in conjunction with Channel 7 was presented in schools; and the work experience program catered for 60,000 secondary pupils.[721]

In business terms Shears described the magnitude of the educational enterprise. Allocated 36 per cent of the State budget, the Victorian Education Department was the nation's third largest government enterprise. Across eleven regions and 50 district inspectorates it comprised 2200 'branches' (schools of varying kinds), employed 60,000 staff, and serviced 700,000 customers. It injected the largest single cash input into most cities and shires and had constructed the equivalent of one 15-room branch every week, 52 weeks of the year for the last 30 years.[722] It embraced general and specialist schools whose statewide clientele had particular needs; staffed cultural attractions; embraced research and development; offered specialist training; and provided overseas opportunities. In all aspects of educational provision the Department was accountable to the government, teachers, pupils and parents, the broader community and industry.[723] A complex organisation, its tendrils were far-reaching.

Not content to rest on his laurels, Shears believed the crux of progress lay with the quality of education. At its heart, 'a school system can be regarded as successful to the degree to which it fulfils its basic aim'. It must 'prepare the younger generation adequately for the world of tomorrow … no school can perform its proper function in a vacuum isolated from the community'. Ongoing discussion determined the most appropriate means of teacher recruitment and training, and the best way to monitor standards. 'Sound mastery of reading, spelling, and elementary mathematics' was essential to 'effective progress at school and in later life' and effective transitions from school to employment or tertiary studies.[724]

Shears adhered to the philosophy that 'a future is the past modified by the present, given a special magnetism by our hopes and aspirations'. His crystal ball revealed prospects for growth in buildings and site development; improved industrial relations, staffing and professional pathways; increased opportunities for reciprocal school, parent and community activity; means to address special needs, such as migrant and disadvantaged groups; administrative review; and coordination of post-secondary education. The evolution would be ongoing but the structural niggles would smooth out. Circumstance was rife to enhance the profession, enrich educational provision, and expand the International Teaching Fellowship, thus encouraging cultural understanding. Money was vital, leadership essential and cooperation with State and Federal authorities and numerous bodies with educational interests fundamental.

Throughout his term as Director-General of Education Shears had admired his predecessors' 'commitment and vision' and aspired to similar acclaim. He assumed those engaged in education understood its nuances and shared his vision. He admitted to emulating Tate who had travelled Victoria to visit inspectorial districts and the teachers and pupils in schools. Like Tate Shears ventured across the State, and abroad, to peruse the impact of change, assess the social/economic/political climate, seek new knowledge and affirm connections. Out and about, he attended official functions and addressed various groups as his diaries and records suggest. As each year began he informed senior colleagues of his commitments. Accompanied by a year planner, a memorandum dated 19 January 1979 to his Assistant Directors-General informed them of a tight timeframe for meetings, 'a means of communicating with all who are involved in our common undertaking. I extend my best wishes for a very successful 1979'. Writing to them on 22 January he outlined meeting dates and attached copies of letters sent to directors of the divisions and organisations he intended to visit. He aligned visits to schools with formalities on his agenda, such as attending the opening of the Horsham Civic Centre, a cooperative venture between the Education Department and the Wimmera Shire; speaking at the National Final of the Plain English Speaking Award; opening the Curriculum Development Centre Conference in May and the first national conference on work experience in August. He addressed Rotary groups, named libraries, unveiled portraits, and officiated at openings of halls, libraries and swimming pools.

At the official opening in February 1979 of the recreation room at Camp Balook, belonging to outer suburban Westall High School, Shears commended the school community's enthusiasm and the concern shown for the needs of all children. Aware of the school's multicultural nature he maintained:

> There is no better illustration of this than the decision to provide relevant information in other languages for students and their parents – with various ethnic backgrounds … Living as we do, in a society growing ever more complex, and at a time when many Victorian youths are faced with possible, and indeed actual, unemployment, it is essential that we do all we can to provide our school children with those experi-

ences that will enable them to make the most satisfactory career decision and adjustment to adult life.

Opening the Basic Modern Teaching Conference (Modern Teaching Methods Association) in May 1979, his keynote address alerted those in attendance to the increased difficulty of 'forecasting future directions in education with preciseness and with confidence'. He claimed 'the community expects economic relevance in our performance as teachers ... what is *relevant* today in terms of preparing students for employment is not necessarily relevant for tomorrow.'

An invitation to be guest speaker at celebrations of Cheltenham Primary School's 125th anniversary (15 October–21 November 1979) was one he could not refuse. The principal wrote:

> Dear Lawrie ... I am aware that this school has special significance to your family as I see Mavis Redman, Dux 1940, on the Honour Board.

Year by year his busy round of meetings and events continued. Miss Alice Downward's farewell took him to Bendigo in March 1980. A stalwart of Burwood TC, she was a member of the college's foundation teaching staff and coordinator of its infant teaching program. 'There can only be One Alice,' he said, to whom 'thousands owe a debt of gratitude.'[725] A woman of keen intent she had energy, was reliable, capable, cooperative and not afraid to be forceful. Also in March he addressed the Long Gully Primary School Centenary and attended the official opening of the Myrtleford High School library. At the Victorian Primary Principals' Association Conference, 26 April 1980, he alerted attendees to 'a new accountability in terms of [your] own values and ideas, those of the staff and of the community'. He claimed:

> We who are in positions of responsibility within the Education Department are surely accountable for how effective we are in using the human resources available ... So much is talked about and written about a lack of professionalism among today's teachers yet I believe that they remain education's greatest single resource. The vast majority of people are as dedicated today as they ever have been and are, on top of this, *better* trained to help meet the changing needs of society.

In October 1980 Marie Neale, Professor (Exceptional Children) and Director of the Krongold Centre at Monash University, invited him to deliver the opening address at the Special Education Workshop sponsored by the Australian Development Assistance Bureau. In December 1980 Shears and Thompson, now Minister for Police and Emergency Services, both spoke at the launch of a new course at Moorabbin Technical College aimed at motorcycle riders, a joint venture between the Education Department and the Road Safety and Traffic Authority.

On every occasion Shears spruiked his philosophies and made his mark, but a powerful force, guided by the newly appointed Minister of Education, changed the course of educational history. The 'pressures of tradition, habits and our resistance to change' began to crumble.[726]

When Lindsay Thompson completed his 12-year term as Minister of Education in May 1979 the new team heralded a new era. Directives from Minister Alan Hunt and Assistant Minister Norman Lacy caused major disruption. The political duo was intent upon making their mark. To 'clean up the Education Department' Hunt brought in a vacuum cleaner rather than sweep with a new broom. Immediately the Ministers began to audit the system. Not of the educational fraternity, they were blind to both traditions and new directions. Abandonment of familiar ways of doing things, the way things had been done with Thompson, caused Shears to grapple with their powerful force. They began to smother his role and command his educational empire. Senior colleagues, though they came to grips with the new leadership team, queried 'Can a person from the general community have all of that knowledge; speak in parliament about its direction? Could they be as good as the Directors-General over history?' The political change cast shadows through Departmental ranks but Shears maintained his grit. 'Other people walked away. He didn't. He went on to do what he thought would be best.'[727]

Since the inception of the Director's role in 1902 the chief administrator's domain had gradually diminished and his executive powers were reduced. This was evident during Shears' era when institutions such as the VIC and the SCV became self-governing, and with the rising intervention of the Commonwealth government. Likewise, the formation of the Advisory Committee on Tertiary Education (1968) and the Victorian Post-Secondary Education Commission (1978), the inclusion of persons other than Directors-General on the AEC Standing Committee (1979), the composition of the Victorian Institute of Secondary Education (1979), the establishment of the TAFE Board (1980) and the separation of TAFE colleges from the Education Department (1981) reduced his powers. Correspondingly increased political persuasion determined educational direction.[728]

Under the Westminster system the Director-General had the 'responsibility of administering all Acts in any way relating to education' but the new political pair stifled this. Replacing Shears as the face of education, the views of the party determined the Department's management function and the Minister was in charge. Unlike Thompson, their predecessor, Hunt and Lacy had little hands-on experience in schooling and held no professional teaching credentials. Aware of the tension between knowing and not knowing the Education Department's unique culture Shears took on a mentoring role. In accordance with the Westminster System he endeavoured to guide the Ministers. Intent upon overhauling the Education Department, 'they really were ruthless. They came in from the top and imposed all sorts of things.'[729] They deduced current practices were ineffective and prior reviews mere band-aid devices.

Hunt had a reputation for a hard-line stance. A powerful force in politics he 'rated three in the Cabinet: Leader in the Upper House and lead Minister after Hamer and Thompson'. He had cleaned up the Country Roads Board (CRB) and was intent on doing likewise with the 'gargantuan department' not 'guided by any particular philosophy'. Hunt confronted in Shears the man whom Phil Law later called the 'Father of Education'. Loyal to the Department, Shears' record exhibited a man of knowledge and broad experience. Hunt admitted a close working relationship, accepted Shears' advice, but made his own decisions. Hunt saw 'an exceedingly able man ... one of the best administrators in private or public enterprise' but his leadership was inept. He was an expert at problem solving but neither he nor his team had 'confirmed views on where they were going'.[730] Suffice to say, Hunt's views overlooked Shears' strenuous effort to embrace public voice to shape the policy papers in the recent restructure. Questions were asked. Was Hunt blind to recent events in the evolving history of education; was he intent to do it his way? Did Hunt understand the nuances of the system, demands upon teachers and pressures on the Department post-war? Did his legal knowledge and restructure of the CRB equate to Shears' lifetime devotion to teaching and 'its advancement, with rolled-up sleeves and chalk dust in his throat?'[731]

Conflict appeared as two powerful forces met: Shears led the educational team and Hunt the political opponents. They viewed aims and objectives from different perspectives. Shears, who had introduced structural change and liberated administrative powers, had vision for ongoing developments while Hunt observed a tangle of structural confusion, tension between tradition and innovation, and no plausible direction. Under Hunt's regime educational history underwent a massive restructure. After just a fortnight he and Lacy launched 'an inquiry into the aims and objectives of education'. Hunt 'envisaged a pretty simple procedure. We produced a Green Paper and went to a White Paper. I appointed Norman as Chairman of various committees to increase his confidence and to increase his knowledge by close association with top people in education and industry.'[732]

Like Hunt, Lacy attacked educational administration and claimed the need for reform. Appointed to Cabinet and Assistant Minister of Education in May 1979 he thenceforth worked with Hunt. While Lacy was elated with this promotion he was also alert to Hunt's displeasure upon having the education portfolio and to his ambition for higher positions. Both Hunt and Lacy claimed to mastermind the reform and the Green and White Papers.

## What Hunt saw

Hunt acknowledged the close working relationship between Thompson and Shears. In Shears he faced 'an administrator of proven excellence' but lamented the bitter attitude and lack of trust by the unions and parents to the Department. The Department lacked direction. It required 'clear and defined aims and objectives to which the public contributed'.[733] Rather than time-honoured traditions and the expertise of educational administrators he established direction. Chaos rather than order, competing loyalties rather than trust, confusion rather than clear lines of command and tension between tradition and innovation challenged his leadership style.[734]

Upon taking office Hunt commenced a preliminary review of the Department's executive measures, aims and objectives, policy development, dissemination and the Ministry in general. Rather than clear statements Shears had provided 'a number of papers purporting to explain the organization, but nowhere was its rationale explained'. Hunt observed unclear lines of communication, duplication and even triplication. He upheld 'the fundamental maxim that an organizational structure must be simple to be effective' but as this maxim had not been applied, the Department had 'grown like Topsy' with potential for misunderstanding and conflict between its divisions.[735]

## What Lacy saw

Prior to his appointment as Assistant Minister Lacy had chosen departmental administration as a case study at the Australian Administrative Staff College. He subsequently became Chairman of the Parliamentary Liberal Party Education Committee in 1976 and completed an Advanced Management Program at the College the following year. Set the task to analyse the structure of an organisation he selected the Education Department. This led him to believe in the need for its restructure and to 'insert in place of a permanent head a board consisting of a group of managers, of which the Minister was one'. Answerable to Cabinet, the Minister shared his responsibility with members of the administrative board. Abolition of the divisions and elevation of regional directors formed part of Lacy's scheme.

Given authority over the Buildings Operations Division, the Special Services Division and later the Planning Services Division, Lacy sought to avoid duplication and believed others supported his views. He became aware of total lack of concern for administrative efficiency … no clearly defined and understood goals … no management information system, no accountability procedures, a hopelessly outdated accounting system, and no corporate plan or system of policy development.[736]

## What DDGE Moore saw

Deputy Director-General of Education Tom Moore recalled the challenges of the 1970s. The student flood of the 1960s ebbed and gave time to 'stabilize structures and procedures'. Nevertheless teacher unions continued their persistent militancy. Moore saw Hunt as a 'strong man' who aimed to 'restore order in the industrial relations arena and, in short, to put Departmental affairs in order'. However the role Hunt took as executive leader stirred friction between himself, Shears and senior officers.[737]

Moore was surprised by the appointment of the two new Ministers. Experience had shown that two Ministers 'tended to split the Education portfolio in a rather artificial and unworkable manner … creating difficulties for administrators and the school system'. Moore was equally surprised by Hunt's appointment, a shift from holding smaller portfolios to 'the biggest and most complex area of Government'.[738]

## What Norman Curry saw

Vice President of the State College of Victoria Norman Curry was concerned that continued public criticism eroded morale. Suspicion stirred in the minds of senior staff. Shears, so much in the public eye, was being viewed as responsible for increased budgetary constraints because of the cost of regional expansion. The regional structure that offered three-fold lines of responsibility caused confusion and blurred communication channels and left people in schools perplexed: Did they go to a region? Did they go to one of the divisions? Did they go to an Assistant Director-General?[739] Curry saw confusion.

## A regional director's view

Jeff Dunstan, Regional Director for Benalla since 1974, saw value in the proposed restructure as 'massive growth was moving towards massive dysfunction'. Traditionally the Primary, Secondary and Technical Schools Divisions comprised three mini-departments. Service divisions pioneered in the 1960s imposed a layer of complexity and the regional structure inflicted another. The Office of Director-General, whereby each ADGE held specialist responsibilities, added a further layer and aggravated tension among and between the competing forces.[740] Horizontal and vertical lines of communication resulted in mish-mash and confusion.

The Primary Schools Division exemplified this when Harry Nixon was appointed Acting Director while Kevin Collins was seconded to the Implementation Task Force. Supporting Nixon were:

> HVF Sloane, Acting Deputy Director (In-Service Education)
> RA McLeod, Assistant Director (Staffing)
> DC Holloway, Assistant Director (Curriculum)
> HS Hobbs, Assistant Director (Buildings)
> HM Adamson, Acting Assistant Director (Inspection)
> HE Dawson, Acting Assistant Director

Each was assigned specific duties that aligned with those of an ADGE. It was a similar scenario in the other divisions and the regional offices. Administrative overload and blurred communication channels resulted and Hunt was determined to render a change.

## A view from the outside

Joan Kirner, Executive Officer, Victorian Federation of State Schools Parents' Clubs, observed the unfolding drama. Whereas Thompson and Shears had formed a cohesive political–educational team, dynamics between the new Ministers and the Director-General showed fractures. Hunt was determined to handle industrial relations, administration and devolution while Lacy examined core curriculum, special services and Ministerial control. In line with their scrutiny, a public enquiry led to the Green and White Papers on Government policy and ultimately an enquiry by external consultants.[741]

Shears attempted to contribute but Hunt held the reins. Situated between the two, Kirner had a good working relationship with Shears and they held mutual respect. She also worked well with Hunt and was enticed by ideas of 'modernising and reorganising the department' and 'willingness to have people like myself and my organisation involved'.

Astute as she was, Kirner saw multiple agendas: the Minister's, the second Minister's and Shears', the parents' and school councils'. Lack of money invested in the State system was a further agenda. Though she grasped the chance to contribute she felt the means was not 'truly democratic'. Potential political change was creating strife.[742]

## A proliferation of committees, confusion and a wild goose chase

Minister Hunt established a Ministerial Consultative Committee, an Organisations Reference Group, and an Implementation Task Force with an Implementation Steering Committee. Appointed Chairman of the Ministerial Consultative Committee and the Implementation Steering Committee, Lacy ostensibly advised himself. The Consultative Committee comprised senior education officers and representatives from the Public Service and industry. The Implementation Steering Committee consisted of Ministers Lacy (Chairman) and Hunt, Shears, Moore, Ron Cullen of the Public Service Board, Michael Deeley of Dulux, and Emeritus Professor Bill Walker. Robin Chapman, Director of Planning Services, was Chairman of the Organisations Reference Group and the Implementation Task Force, and liaised between the Ministers, the Steering Committee and the Task Force.

The politicisation of educational decision-making was under way, working around the Director-General rather than through him. Shears could see but not do. By appointment he met the Ministerial Consultative Committee or its members if they wished to seek clarification or ask his advice. In compliance with the Ministers' directive he attended to his own duties as best he could. Being out and about, he was out of the way.

Procedures changed. Hunt replaced the Director-General's Policy Committee,[743] the advisory group directed by Shears, with a Corporate Management Group. Richard Bates referred to the 'rhetoric of efficiency, effectiveness, control and accountability', general myths, he claimed for organisational reform.[744] Areas of administrative overlap, as in the divisions, were replaced by new chains of command. The first ran through the Director-General, regional directors and principals of school while a less explicit chain of command monitored systems of accountability and evaluation through deputy regional directors and the Deputy Director-General back to the Corporate Management Group. Intended to establish a structure that ensured the communication and implementation of policy throughout the organisation, it was evident that 'despite the rhetoric of devolution' central decision-making became strengthened 'in the hands of a firmly politicised top echelon'. Despite apparent devolution of authority and decision-making, the corporate management system 'effectively excluded those very interests it was supposed to serve – the local communities to which power was (rhetorically) devolved'. Although the bodies established appeared community-based, Hunt 'was determined to brook no meddling interference'. Decision-making under the new organisational structure effectively bypassed Shears.

ADGE Allan Hird was alert to the turmoil created. Proud of his own loyal stance, he admitted they were testing times. Hunt became both the Minister and Director-General, the antithesis of Thompson's 'rather gentle and subtly self-effacing' approach. 'Prone to fume and bluster', Hunt had replaced a man of 'capacity and integrity who dedicated himself to education'. Hird saw that Thompson's hesitancy to hasten reform played into the hands of a man with 'capacity to grasp and appreciate the worth or otherwise of a submission', appraise the facts and with commendable skill dictate a response. He implied that Hunt had 'little regard for the needs and aspirations of those who worked with him or the teaching service in general'. They were 'merely the cogs in the machine'. He destroyed the credibility of senior officers, created a climate of fear and distrust, and denigrated his predecessor and the Director-General. In conference with senior officers as well as outsiders, Hird witnessed an 'unedifying experience' when Hunt provoked a slanging match with Shears.[745]

The line of authority had been the Department's safeguard and strength. Though the process of disseminating power was in train, legally the Director-General remained in control. He was the link between the Minister and the administration of schools. Hunt's defiance of tradition caused confusion right down the line. Hec Gallagher, Acting Director of Secondary Education, recalled Thompson as 'a marvellous Minister, who would support his Director-General and go through the appropriate lines'. Hunt on the other hand completely disregarded the Department's established lines of authority. Senior staff was torn between support of their Director-General or enticement by the Minister's kudos. They were in an unenviable situation. On an occasion when Gallagher questioned the legality of Hunt's instructions to 'take a team of inspectors' to Seaford–Carrum on Monday morning he sought Shears' advice. On Saturday morning he found Shears 'in his working clothes cleaning out gutters and drains' at St John's, Toorak.

While Hunt was the executive powerhouse, Lacy had his own agenda. He was often at odds with Hunt, particularly in regard to the Corporate Management Group. The 'last ditch stand of the old guard', the group lacked sway. Whereas Hunt was prepared to negotiate, Lacy determined direction. Advised by his 'hand-picked' group of senior staff, his announcements generally bypassed regular channels.[746] Two months into office Hunt formed a Ministerial Consultative Committee that consisted of some of the nation's leading educationists and business leaders. Members conferred to identify the aims of education, the means to achieve these and to consider an approach to administrative change. Sectors of the educational community welcomed the review but expressed concern by their lack of representation. Members of the Victorian Teachers' Union claimed no teachers were involved while Kirner, unaware of the new Committee, claimed, 'Mr Lacy's method of operation is 10 years out of date. If he wants participatory decision-making he must begin with those at the bottom of the pyramid.' In response, Hunt stressed the professional standing of committee members.[747]

Robin Chapman, who chaired the Implementation Task Force, directed Education Department personnel on the Implementation Steering Committee, established in December 1980 and January 1981; he reported directly to Lacy, effectively bypassing Shears. Senior staff seconded from departmental divisions staffed working parties that were aligned with the Implementation Task Force. Assembled thus were Regional Directors, Reg Fisher and Jeff Dunstan; Director of Primary Education Kevin Collins; Acting Deputy Director of Technical Education, Noel Watkins; Acting Director of Teacher Education,

Philip Creed; secondary inspectors Doris Embling and Don Sinclair; primary and technical inspectors Ian Jobling and Norm Shearer; Tony Allan (Management Services), Charles Butler (Planning Services); Graham Whitehead (Assistant Director Special Services), Ian Hind (Assistant Director Planning Services), Errol Hutcheson (Assistant Director Personnel Division), Frank Tinney (Senior Guidance Officer, Counselling, Guidance and Clinical Services).[748] In Departmental ranks some considered the resulting leadership vacuum a conspiracy to undermine the system and the Director-General.[749]

Members' 'unquestioning acceptance of Ministerial instructions' appalled Kirner, one of only three women on all the committees, midst almost 50 men. Members failed to consider, 'What will happen to the current Director-General?' She questioned, 'Is management or learning the centre of the education structure? How can structures facilitate participation and equity?' The turn of events observed by ADGE Hird was as if they held a gun at Shears' head. Kirner claimed, he was kept 'in the dark as much as anyone else'. Departmental staff:

> ... fought their own rear-guard actions over the more destructive ideas floated by either the Steering Committee or the Task Force. Mostly they lost, because the totally 'insider' nature of the Steering Committee and the Task Force left them without allies in breaking the iron-clad management direction of the PA consultants and the Ministers.[750]

## Controversial issues, pros and cons

To initiate the implementation process senior officers attended a three-day residential seminar in August 1979 entitled 'Controversial Issues'. Those assembled addressed the pros and cons of education in order to try to establish a clear set of aims and objectives. In early September Shears distributed 800 copies of 'Controversial Issues: Pros and Cons', for groups and individuals to evaluate fourteen identified issues and add others as they saw fit. The 82-page document defined accountability under the Westminster system and the 'American overlay' wherein the community held responsibility. Implementation of the five directional papers had been vital towards this end.

'Pros and Cons' addressed school and teacher accountability; the continuum of schooling from pre-school to post-secondary; school choice; curriculum; and finance. The document sought views on the divisions and regions; rationalisation of resources; teacher training, classification and registration; principal and staff selection; and the Teachers Tribunal. Responses were 'thoughtful, well-prepared and fully acceptable' with 'substantial common ground' but had little influence on the Ministers' enquiry. Shears later conceded, 'they were determined [the responses] wouldn't'.[751]

On 12 December 1979 Hunt presented his *Statement of Aims and Objectives for Education in Victoria* to Parliament. It offered education an emergent sense of direction, consistent means of decision-making and a framework to boost delegation of power to regions and schools. Despite questions of cost and the means of implementation, the sustainability of recommendations, and possible furore, confusion and loss of morale among staff, the mechanics of changes continued.[752] Further submissions received in March helped formulate the Green Paper on Strategies and Structures for Education in Victoria that Hunt presented to Parliament on 8 May 1980. Submissions responding to the Green Paper closed on 30 September 1980.

## Meeting in Warburton

### *Hunt's stance*

The forthcoming elections of 1982 played significantly in Hunt's resolve to hasten change. The Liberals had polled poorly in 1979 and education was a major concern. The teacher unions were offside and the public was critical. Prominent Departmental staff and commercial leaders helped drive the campaign that stirred ripples throughout the educational and broader communities.

With the election in sight Hunt met Lacy and Shears at Warburton on Saturday, 18 October 1980 to review final submissions to the Green Paper and formulate the White Paper, which would in turn lead to further investigation. Despite gaining a 'clear sense of direction on major educational issues and questions of school governance' further consultation was necessary. 'The fundamental questions on structure, organisation and management' were 'demonstrably urgent from every viewpoint'.[753]

Hunt spent the week prior in Warburton at the secluded Seventh Day Adventist facility. He recalled, 'with the 2000 responses in three cases I went by myself and booked in for a week, worked 12–13 hours a day, read the lot'. Each day he walked to refresh his mind and contemplate – 'wasn't interrupted, no phones, nothing' – on the emergent themes and the respondents' words. He claimed that Lacy and Shears 'agreed on all of the main principles for the White Paper'. Such a 'shake-up' required determination, careful analysis and a rigid timeline. Unless he improved efficiency in his first term his efforts were doomed to fail.[754]

### Lacy's stance

Lacy was keen to make his mark. He was proud of his rise through the ranks of trade, self-initiated university studies, service as a clergyman and his election to politics in 1973. Even before the 1979 election he had been keen for a major review of education policy and saw himself as having a lot to offer.

Lacy believed it was he who orchestrated and steered the change with the support of back-room and front-of-house relationships formed with key personnel. Despite criticism that he had breached Departmental order and the Director-General's decision-making line, he claimed support for his 'well-developed preconception that a review was necessary'.[755] At the Warburton meeting with Hunt and Shears he reviewed the Green Paper submissions. Shears helped formulate recommendations; a necessary move as the current was too strong for sustained opposition. Like other senior staff he swam with the tide. To execute recommendations Lacy seconded senior staff to the Implementation Task Force: Robin Chapman, Director of Planning Services, and Kevin Collins, Director of Primary Education.

## Shears' stance

Shears accepted that change was in train, as with previous reviews, most notably Scott. The current review would pursue his vision, commenced during Brooks' governance, and detailed in his five policy papers. Satisfied with the introduction of 'functional coordination across the teaching divisions, regionalisation, putting 'power where the action is ...' – into schools and the community – parent involvement, training of administrators and community review of schools' this review would fine-tune issues that niggled. The seeds sown germinated in the fruits of the Green and White Papers. Aware of pressures imposed by the Liberal Party, the speed of change caused concern; 'evolution became revolution, community and teacher analysis became business management analysis and time for adjustment became action to a timetable dominated by the next election.'[756]

## Harman's observation

Grant Harman, Reader in the Centre for the Study of Higher Education at the University of Melbourne, was approached on Shears' advice. Subsequently Hunt appointed Harman, whom he described as 'an expert educational bloke ... a real thinker', to evaluate responses within the tight timeline.[757] Harman questioned the practicality of three major issues. The tradition of central control, so well entrenched, hindered decentralisation and devolution, which had been initiated in recent years but the lingering forces of the centralised body hindered momentum, cut across departmental divisions and governmental policy domains. Legislation to support equal opportunity and anti-discrimination impinged on it too, and the 'power of the purse' influenced progress at State and Federal level.

Harman questioned the necessity of structural reorganisation to 'achieve change in management policies'. He signalled the personal trauma on those affected and warned that 'organisational change may become an end in itself and the real reasons for change may be forgotten.' His swift but efficient review led him to question the underlying rationale: a shake-up to demonstrate managerial decisiveness; a means to streamline the organisation, minimise overlap and reduce costs;

or focus on a unified direction. The state of school funding, particularly in secondary schools, stratification between high and technical schools; the morale and aspirations in school populations; and the sense of mediocrity displayed by the state of buildings were certainly major concerns. In line with these observations he noted many senior officials, school principals and teachers sent their children to non-government schools.[758]

## PA consultants

Hunt presented the first draft of the White Paper on Strategies and Structures for Education in Victorian Government Schools to Parliament on 10 December 1980. Throughout 1981 intense action took place. The Implementation Steering Committee was formed in January, in February the Implementation Task Force commenced duties and the Corporate Management Group met. In April PA Consulting Australia (PA) reviewed results, made further inquiry and gave counsel. Lacy, appointed Minister for Educational Services on 17 December 1980, wrote to Shears on 8 April 1981 to confirm the Ministers' resolve to pursue the White Paper's proposals in a responsible and expeditious manner. He insisted 'this endeavour [must] have the very highest priority in the Education Department and that all officers [must] cooperate fully with the effort'. He required Shears to 'earmark an adequate implementation fund and financial account number this week' and 'see that adequate clerical staff is seconded to the team as required'. He advised that DDGE Moore and DPS Chapman would form a sub-committee to review organisational changes that arose. An enlarged Implementation Task Force began its duties in May, their task paralleling timelines for PA's appraisal.

In the meantime Shears briefed senior officers of the moves in train. Subsequent to meeting the Ministers in Warburton he claimed, 'unanimous decisions were made on the problems of funding the implementation program, the time-span for the program and the allocation of resources ... the way now is an all-out attack on the implementation'. In reference to his directional papers he believed current views 'reflected the educational thinking and developments which have been canvassed over the last decade. The White Paper accelerates the inevitable moves along these paths. As educational administrators we should appreciate the democratic process which has produced these decisions, and be keen to activate the goals which have been laid down.'[759]

Briefed to develop an implementation program, PA identified three key themes. There was a need to reorganise regional functioning and consider the economics and efficiencies of assigning responsibilities; redistribute aspects of devolution, governance and consultation; and review schools and their educational processes. Like their political masters they tackled administrative structures and noted 'you cannot know who will occupy the positions that are detailed. Thus you cannot assume a particular style of management will be used in a particular position.' Restructure must be stable and function regardless of the incumbent's management style and 'regardless of changes to the incumbent'. Alert to possible breakdown in loyalties they predicted those with reduced powers to be seen as 'losers' while those with increased powers were considered 'winners'. Despite these conjectures, Shears considered his position safe.

To gain insight into operational nuances, staff selection was the key. An informed cohort of 'high fliers' established collegial credibility. Likely supporters of change, their support would trickle through the organisation. In less than half a week selected staff commenced training to develop a unified sense of purpose. The Implementation Task Force established conditions for change, expanded initiatives of the White Paper and identified a framework for implementation. Indeed Shears' initiatives formed part of PA's analysis; his five papers were listed along with 62 submissions and over 600 letters passed to the Task Force. In addition there was material sustaining the Green and White Papers; documents prepared by the Assistant Directors-General and former studies including the Ramsay, Southwell, Scott and Bland Reports (1960, 1971, 1973, 1974), the Curriculum Services Enquiry (1975), the Interim Report of the Committee of the Victorian Enquiry into Teacher Education (1980) and a draft statement of roles and responsibilities of regional directors, prepared by Dobell, Falk and Moyle (1972). PA carried out interviews across a broad range of

Departmental staff, but missing were Shears and Moore and the majority of directors or assistant directors of divisions. From an extensive list of Victorian bodies and Departments of Education in Queensland and New South Wales, the Victorian Teachers' Union, the Victorian Secondary Teachers' Association and the Technical Teachers' Union of Victoria declined to be interviewed.

In the chain of events the Ministers, Shears, Moore and the Assistant Directors-General had select agendas. Hunt wanted to streamline departmental operations and Lacy was intent on getting rid of Shears who in turn assumed loyalty. Shears maintained trust in his senior officers, unaware that some saw the chance to move up the hierarchical ladder or take his place, as they were led to believe. Under the proposed change the DDGE would have greater responsibility and eminent status. Loyalties were lacking according to ADGE Hird, who over time observed the antics of 'organisations purporting to represent teachers … [that] destroyed the credibility of the administrator'. The public and political parties thus questioned 'the viability of the structures and the capacity and honesty of the administrators'. 'Lack of loyalty' was obvious, Shears' leadership style at fault, and 'over-criticism of the Director-General, stemmed from his own office.' A witch's cauldron began to boil.[760]

## Bypassing Shears

Hunt as executive leader was the driving force, sustained by Lacy and the eloquent few. In tough political times support for the Labor Party in opposition had surged in 1979. Education offered the chance to accelerate the momentum of change and exhibit the Liberals' action. A lot was at stake as the Party looked to another term in office.

Apart from the Implementation Steering Committee and regular meetings with the Ministers, Shears had little involvement. He busied himself with executive duties and addressed numerous groups at conferences, centenaries, speech nights and special occasions. From the Ministers' viewpoint he was out of the way.

Sanctioned by the Premier's Overseas Division and the Hon. Tony Street, Minister for Foreign Affairs, Shears travelled with Hunt to China, 12–15 May 1981, to pursue cultural cooperation. With the Chinese ministerial entourage they laid plans for RMIT to support management and electronic engineering programs, and offer an exchange scheme at master's degree level. Broader discussion centred on the presentation of kangaroos to the Nanjing Zoo and re-afforestation of botanical gardens, parks and tourist attractions. They considered water conservation, animal husbandry, artificial insemination and pasture establishment on hills, and coastal revegetation. They addressed the commercial viability of cultural exchange and contributions by Dr Westbrook of the National Gallery of Victoria, David Wang and Myer to this. Extension of the ITF to China afforded possibilities of staff recruitment for teachers colleges and secondary schools and gauged interest at university level.

Like his whirlwind tour of the United States in 1959, Shears travelled on to Tokyo, Athens and then Paris where he joined the Education Committee at Chateau de la Muette at the 23rd Session of the OECD Conference. Delegates considered trends in labour supply and their educational implications; education and working life; policies for higher education in the 1980s; youth unemployment; and young foreigners in the world of work. Shears went on to London where the focus of discussion was the decline of recruitment for the ITF in the UK, because of lower salaries in Victoria than in the UK and because similar programs had been initiated in other Australian States. Another aspect of the visit was to cement arrangements to embrace the UK into the Plain English Speaking Award, instituted in Victoria in 1977 as part of the celebrations of the 25th year of the reign of Queen Elizabeth II. Shears was a committee member for the Award. Moving on to New York, at the International School he was presented with an Award which he accepted on behalf of the Education Department of Victoria. The award acknowledged the Department's contribution to 'World Peace through International Understanding in (our) support of the International Teaching Fellowship (UNIS, NY)' in 1979. The next leg of his journey took him to Canada. Funded by the Institute of Educational Administration he travelled to Banff to meet Dr R Kissinger of the Kellogg Foundation. Shears sought funding to expand multi-media resources and a resource bank to service continuing educational activities in educational administration in Australia and SE Asia.[761]

In September 1981 the Japanese government invited Shears to participate in an exchange of ideas with Japanese scholars and educationists from France, USA and West Germany. The group observed Japanese society and considered how 'Japanese education, arts, and culture will be stimulated, and a contribution will be made to international exchange in these fields'. While this augured well with the ITF and its embrace of Japan, Victoria's industrial development was of particular relevance. Discussion focused on educational facilities for children of Japanese people associated with Gippsland's brown coal and oil. In this situation 'education provision involved in the provision of social resources with sufficient time to enable the requirements to be met'.[762]

Shears was out and about across the State, the nation and the globe because he trusted his senior team to act appropriately in his absence. Lengthy telexes to Acting D-G Moore informed him of the status quo abroad and faxes informed Rex Murfett of developments in the ITF program. Unlike others on recruitment campaigns who sent information by mail, Shears sent his by fax. 'I can remember walking through the office dragging Lawrie's fax, his fax details of the teachers!'[763] Murfett explained that detail had to come back in order to assess compatibility of teachers and suitable locations of schools. Negotiations with China came to fruition in October when the first Fellows arrived to lecture in higher education institutions. Correspondingly he held discussions with Croatia, Greece, Italy, Yugoslavia and Croatia to further expand the ITF program.

## Educational soothsayers

Overlays of excitement and satisfaction concealed Shears' concerns during those turbulent times. The Ministers thwarted his recommendations and he remained sidelined. Hunt's tactics troubled senior officers but an Act of Parliament secured the position of Director-General. Maslen was alarmed in 1979 when the Ministerial committee was formed to assess the aims and structures of education.

Lacy held secretive meetings with Sir John Buchan, Professors Bill Connell and Kwong Lee Dow and Ron Fitzgerald and formed a committee to assess the Department's operation within a four-week span. Hunt stressed the expertise of the group, the VTU welcomed the review although no teachers were present, and 'Controversial Issues' was Shears' response.

Throughout Shears maintained routines, met the Ministers each Monday at 9 am and the Assistant Directors-General at 10.30 am. In 1980, when ADGE Barwick was appointed Director-General of Youth, Sport and Recreation, Stewart Morton rejoined the team.[764] As events unfolded Shears informed the wider educational community, and though control was beyond his reach, developments centred on the policies he had established. In a letter sent on 13 April 1981 to 'all members of the Director-General's Policy Committee, all regional directors, all members of the Implementation Steering Committee and the Implementation Task Force and the PA Australia consultants', he supported 'an all-out attack on the implementation'. Progress:

> ... reflected the educational thinking and developments which have been canvassed over the last decade. The White Paper accelerates the inevitable moves along these paths. As educational administrators we should appreciate the democratic process which has produced these decisions, and be keen to activate the goals which have been laid down.[765]

In contrast, correspondence from the Corporate Management Group[766] in May 1981 addressed 'problems and possible solutions'. The letter commented on Shears' busy schedule, denigrated his capacity to cope and effectively excluded him from the inner circle:

> ... the Director-General cannot become au fait in such short time with experts' papers, cannot provide across-the-board consideration of functional papers and his role is reduced to irritating cross-examination rather than consideration and leadership. Although caught up in the same situation, Ministers can exercise ministerial prerogative and position to overcome this difficulty.[767]

According to Richard Bates, Associate Professor (Educational

Administration), School of Education at Deakin University, the sequence of events and their culmination:

> ... spelled an effective end to the long-sustained tradition ... of the separation of political and administrative functions enshrined in the Westminster tradition. In particular it politicized the senior echelon of Departmental officers in a manner that overrode the independent, expert and professional role to which such officers were traditionally supposed to conform ... thus, Ministerial political control was extended over processes of implementation and over the administrative officers themselves.'[768]

The Ministers were wielding their power and squeezing the Director-General out. The political masters had taken control, diminished Shears' credibility and distanced him from the activity. In August 1981 Shears advised the Assistant Directors-General that 'any divisions of education functions between Ministers means a strong likelihood that the DG will be by-passed'. In fact this was already so. The political power mongers were in for the kill.

Throughout the drama Shears concealed his inner feelings in the face of proposals and surreptitious actions to reduce his powers and boost those of his minions. Many saw new possibilities, a career boost and hierarchical elevation. The Director-General had had his day. Shears acknowledged a spill of senior officers' positions but his own held firm despite counsel 'that the new Ministers of Education – or at least one of them – intended to remove the Director-General early'. The *Education Act* offered protection. In the unlikelihood of such an event, he maintained, the government must table in Parliament the grounds for his dismissal and allow seven days or the community to 'pray' for his reinstatement.[769]

Despite Shears' air of confidence, rumblings extended into the broader community. On 29 September 1981 Maslen queried Shears' stance when senior positions down to regional director level were tipped to spill. He wondered about Shears' ongoing ties with the Department or perhaps he would take a UNESCO post.[770] Meanwhile Minister Hunt finalised the White Paper to present to Parliament on 10 October 1981. In an exceptional move he gave a copy in confidence to Labor Party counterparts, Evan Walker, leader and educational spokesman in the Upper House, and Robert Fordham, Deputy Labor Leader and Shadow Minister of Education. Hunt believed their preview of the White Paper stirred well-informed debate rather than its adjournment.

## Execution

The axe fell. The Act was changed. Under the new administration, criteria for the role of Director-General differed vastly from the old. The position was no longer valid. Shears' era ended. Industrial unrest that constantly shadowed him had undermined his power, now political antagonism was his foe. An observer believed flack over lack of educational investment and appalling treatment of the teacher unions made him the focus. 'He was hung out to dry ... He wasn't the problem. He was made to be the problem.'[771] Premier Thompson's priority to save the government prevailed above saving the Director-General.

Hunt affirmed the need to change in order to save the government, which left no alternative. He and Lacy briefed Shears at 9.30 on 12 October; Shears in turn briefed the Assistant Directors-General. In preparation for a meeting of the Australian Education Council Shears met Bert Osmond (then Survey and Planning Officer) and at 8.00 pm he attended the monthly vestry meeting at St John's. Among commitments the following day he met Sue Green of *The Age*. Later on 13 October 1981 members of the educational hierarchy assembled at Parliament House. The atmosphere was electric. Kirner wrote:

> ... the impossible happened. Dr Shears, Director-General of Education in Victoria from 1973 was removed – publicly and arbitrarily – by the Government that appointed him. An amendment to the Act had deprived him of his protection, the Government of the responsibility to fully justify their action, and the community of the opportunity to challenge the decision.[772]

The debate continued till morning. Intent on removing the Director-General, Lacy had pinned him down. Shears was shaken and broken, publicly ridiculed by his execution. The Opposition's request that he retain his position unless the government could justify the removal under existing power was to no avail. Shears was an outstanding educator and administrator; there was no evidence of failure, according to Robert Fordham. The government had breached conditions of Shears' appointment, claimed Peter Ross-Edwards, the National Party Leader. It had acted in a 'morally wrong and devious way'. In his response Lacy admitted Shears' competence, high intelligence and foresight, but spoke of inequity unless all senior positions were spilled, as in recent restructures of the Housing and Health Commissions.[773]

The *Education (Amendment) Act* 1981 (No. 9582) established a blueprint for a new structure. The Director-General was removed. A corporate management team replaced him. Chaired by one of the Ministers, the new Director-General with reduced powers would be part of the group composed of the two Ministers, the Deputy Director-General and two Executive Directors. Advertisements were placed in the *Education Gazette*, State, national and international newspapers to seek a new senior officer and 59 middle-level administrative positions.

## In praise of Shears

People were appalled; not with the Bill, though it heralded unprecedented change, but by the treatment of people who had made major contributions to education. They considered it unacceptable and disrespectful.

Ross-Edwards' accusation of the devious manner in which the government had bypassed Shears was supported by Milton Whiting, the Party's Deputy Leader, who worried that Shears' surreptitious removal might lead to similar occurrences with other permanent heads. The Deputy Opposition Leader in the Legislative Council was appalled that appropriate legislative procedures were breached. Shears' removal was 'subterfuge of the worst kind'. It required agreement by both Houses for approval on two successive sessions in the Legislative Assembly. Parliamentarians, the education community and members of the public accused Hunt of taking these actions because personal differences prevented a good working relationship. Hunt, in response, admitted Shears was an educationist of great reputation. Rather than foul play a revised nature of the Director-General's role made the position obsolete. Its new specifications required the best person sourced from a global field. Fordham claimed 'shabby treatment' and proposed to reinstate Shears as Director-General if Labor gained power before the Bill was passed.[774] In *The Age* Maslen referred to Thompson's respect for Shears throughout their 12-year association, questioned lack of collegial and parliamentary support, and assumed Thompson's obligation was to the Party rather than Shears, in lieu of political debts incurred to retain his own position. He identified the ploy directed by Hunt and Lacy to change that Act, oust incumbent Shears and gain power over the Department's day-to-day operations and appointment of its senior staff. Whatever decision he made would be costly. Rumour suggested an appointment with responsibilities overseas would keep him out of the way. Lurking in the shadows, prospecitve suitors for the new role of Director-General were Professor Kwong Lee Dow, Dean, Education Faculty, the University of Melbourne, and Graham Allen, Chairman, Post-Secondary Education Commission. In praise of Shears, Maslen saluted his 'enormous enthusiasm' and the best developments in educational progress that he 'personally engineered'. Maslen lamented the bitter sting of the Government's cowardly treatment and long-term ramifications on senior administrators in other government departments.[775]

Coping with the loss of position, authority and an uncertain future had the propensity to leave Shears in a state of despair. With family and collegial support he overcame grief, carried on with his duties and got on with life. Moyle told of how he took it on the chin and maintained commitments. Shears' diaries show his attendance at the Rotary luncheon on 14 October, meeting the International Teaching Fellowship Committee and dining at Burke Hall. Next day he met the Ministers prior to a meeting of the Australian Education Council in Queensland.

While Shears moved on, his execution caused public furore. Its effect rippled throughout the community. In a letter to *The Age* J Clark, G Murray, G Bowles, T Barr, L Barberis, and J Eldens, principals and council presidents of University, MacRobertson and Melbourne High

Schools expressed grave concern:

> Dr Shears is held in high esteem as a person, as an educationist, and as an administrator, by colleagues and clients within the system and beyond it. Over almost a lifetime of service within the Education Department, and especially as its Director-General, he has demonstrated a thorough familiarity with and concern for all facets of the State system and has worked with a deep commitment and a unique expertise to promote it, often in the face of well-orchestrated opposition.
>
> To direct the smooth transition of changes recommended in the PA consultants' report recently adopted as Government policy, while at the same time fostering survival of many worthwhile initiatives at present in train, will require great strength of purpose, consummate administrative talent and the widest and deepest familiarity with the existing organization.[776]

The group encouraged him to offer himself for candidature to ensure at least one among the applicants possessed all the necessary attributes to facilitate ongoing progress. By reapplication he would not deny the selection committee the opportunity to consider the suitability of others 'against his undoubted qualifications for the post'. [777]

On behalf of the Burwood cohort, Ken Sargeant wrote:

> As colleagues of Dr Shears at Burwood Teachers College (now Burwood State College) we can testify to his excellence as an educationist, to his warmth in his personal relationships, and to his humanity, most especially in his approach to problems of young people. It is a matter of deep concern that we see his position of Director-General of Education being advertised in what we consider a complete breach of the original contract, and the end of a long-standing tradition in the affairs of the Education Department.
>
> In the sensitive area of education, continuity in planning and administration is all important. The fact that the position of the director-general can be declared vacant at a time when there is to be a complete reshuffle in all senior positions, or indeed what might well be complete replacement of

all senior staff, presents us with a situation which is serious in the extreme. Can the public believe that the administration of a Government department be improved by the appointment of a new director-general complete with a new set of top officials? Where is the continuity?

Has the public a right to ask for a statement on the cost of such an operation? Will the public be faced with a double bill for salaries? Will the schools suffer as a result?

Dr Shears must, in the public interest, apply for reappointment to the position of director-general. We understand how he must feel, but we also understand that there must be a person of his qualifications and abilities available for service in education. We urge him to apply.[778]

The Editor noted a letter received from members of the VIER and staff of the Faculty of Education of the University of Melbourne, and indicated that they were amongst supporters who expressed their views. Though not published, a copy of this letter in Shears' personal file endorsed his 'outstanding service in the position'. Among the signatories were George Bradshaw, Imelda Palmer, Ross Millikan, Peter Nattrass, Max Boyce, Kevin Hall, Roderick Fawns and Mary Ainley. They wrote '… we strongly urge that he apply for re-appointment.' [779]

The State Opposition also urged Shears to apply. The Liberals had treated him unfairly and denigrated the position. Shears bore this in mind but he had to move beyond the hurt. Though tempted to apply, he made other plans. The last two years had been fraught by tension wherein his role, his knowledge and his capacity to lead were marginalised. The election in May 1982 offered either more of the same, or a change in government and further uncertainty. Unsure of his actions he prepared an application few others could match: qualifications, departmental know-how, experience and knowledge of education and other fields. His global networks, track record and broad recognition set him apart. He did not know who other applicants would be and had no surety of selection. The position he undertook in 1973 was not the one advertised in 1981. His term was cut short, his policy changes were incomplete but at just 60 years old he would not be left on a limb.

Not only Shears, but at least ten other top senior administrators were tipped to lose their posts. In addition to the two-year exercise that culminated in the PA Report at a cost in excess of $300,000, the collective annual price tag of the respective officers amounted to $700,000. With this burden to bear the Ministers were keen to maintain face. The position of Director-General had become a poisoned chalice, and expected aspirants, including the most favoured, Kwong Lee Dow, did not apply. Neither did Shears. His comprehensive application dated 14 November remained in his files. The selection committee comprised Ken McKinnon, former chairman of the Schools Commission, current vice chancellor, Wollongong University; Dr Ron Cullen, chairman of the Public Service Board; and Emeritus Professor Bill Walker, Principal of the Australian Administrative Staff College at Mt Eliza. Purportedly two of the three were unlikely to favour Shears' candidature. His stance on educational concerns often countered their opinion. Always enterprising, Shears approached Minister Hunt and Cullen. An unadvertised position of Coordinator-General nominally offered him the most senior position and got Hunt out of a Liberal pickle.

CHAPTER 17

# COORDINATION (1982–84)

*... how sad and bad and mad it was – but then, how it was sweet*

Robert Browning, 'Confessions'

The onslaught crumbled tradition; order was disarranged. The Ministers had shifted the locus of power from the professional team. Their educational empire had suffered massive upheaval. And unrest. Shears pondered commitment to this environment.

Hunt faced continual censure for his treatment of Shears. The unseating created a new dilemma. Reappointment was not an option despite the absence of an application from Hunt's favoured candidate Professor Kwong Lee Dow.[780] Shears' disappointment was bitter and the Ministers were perplexed over what to do. People asked why Shears had been dumped after twelve years' leadership and a lifetime of service. Was the senior public servant to remain idle until his retirement? Rebuked in educational, public and political spheres the ministers created a new position. Unadvertised, the position of Coordinator-General, would nominally coordinate all aspects of education in Victoria. The most senior rank in the Education Department, this key role in name, though not in nature, permitted the Ministers and Shears to maintain face.

In response to a letter from Hunt, Shears indicated acceptance apropos salary, superannuation, long-service, sick and recreation leave and other entitlements that matched those of the Secretary of the Premier's Department and Chairman of the Public Service Board. He wished to retain his office, his secretary, and car and chauffeur as approved by the Teachers Tribunal, and required a staff of five. He assumed his right to remain Chairman of the State Coordination Council, Social Resources Group and Institute of Educational Administration and fill

Victoria's third position on the Standing Committee of the Australian Education Council. He wrote, 'I would appreciate your concurrence in writing and would then be willing to accept the invitation you have extended.'[781]

Newspapers publicised Shears' new job and described his future role. The position, according to Hunt, filled an 'important gap which had emerged and widened as functions, once the prerogative of the director-general, have been parcelled off to other bodies'. There was 'need for coordination at the highest level to ensure a proper balance between claims of all sectors'. The task required 'a person who possesses full knowledge and experience of the whole range of educational functions, who has a demonstrated breadth of vision, and would be acceptable to the educational community as a whole'. Shears stressed 'supreme importance' of the role as 'an effective means of coordination between the various sectors'.[782] While the solution eased pressures on Hunt, Shears' supporters, among them cohorts from Burwood TC, the University of Melbourne and the VIER, hoped the Minister would take advantage of Shears' wisdom and experience. Others expressed concern. Peter Vaughn of the VSTA alerted to cost: $250,000 per annum to service a position shaped 'out of thin air'.[783] Emotionally moved, Shears used the media to thank colleagues, groups and the public for their support, and the government for interpreting their wishes.

Meanwhile the selection committee whittled applications for Director-General to the final three. After consultation with Shears they appointed Rev Dr Norman Curry. Ordained as a priest in 1961, Curry had broad experience and knowledge. A graduate of Melbourne High School, he attained his BA and MEd at the University of Melbourne and his PhD at the University of London. A teacher educator and administrator, he had progressed through the ranks of tutor and lecturer at the Secondary Teachers College (1952–58), to lecturer, senior lecturer and sub-dean in the Faculty of Education at the University of Melbourne (1959–74). He was a visiting scholar at the Institute of Education, University of London in 1972, was appointed Vice-Principal of State College of Victoria, Melbourne in 1975 and Principal of SCV Toorak in 1977. Council membership on nongovernment schools, the SCV, the Victorian Teacher Education

Inquiry and the Institute of Early Childhood Development provided extensive knowledge of education and training across the spectrum of schooling in government and nongovernment systems, and the post-secondary sector. As he was ten years younger than Shears, the appointment offered the opportunity for a decade of service.

On 31 December 1981 *The Age* reported six senior positions were reduced to four. While Shears and Curry were secure, junior officers and outsiders displaced Assistant Directors-General Hird (Personnel), Joy (Finance), Morton (Buildings) and Maddocks (Curriculum), and Deputy Director-General Moore. Kevin Collins, DPE, ousted Moore who became visiting professor at the University of Melbourne funded by the Education Department. Ian Allen, Principal SCV Coburg, and Ron Ritchie, Acting Director, Technical Education, were appointed Executive Director (Educational Services) and Executive Director (Personnel and Resources) in place of the deposed Hird, Joy, Morton and Maddocks.[784]

Victoria's public criticised the escalating cost of the upheaval. They questioned the Department's justification to subsidise salaries until these men reached 65 and its decision not to employ 1,000 secondary teachers classified in excess. In a letter to *The Age* 'a parent interested in the future of our Government school system', wrote, 'such actions certainly don't reflect parent priorities for Government expenditure in education'. She questioned why and how Mr Hunt could find positions and subsidise salaries for the administrative group made 'in excess'.[785] '$40,000 a year for six without official positions' headlined *The Age* on 23 January 1982. A further round of appointments revealed additional job losses that left gulfs in senior ranks. Regional directors were hard hit as Robin Chapman, DPS, Bob McLeod, ADPE and Dr Noel Watkins, ADTE, replaced Noel Brain in Bendigo, John Roscholler in the Northern Metropolitan region, and Daniel Dee in the Central Metropolitan Region. Dee stressed his loyalty and constant effort to implement policies; with six years to serve he elected to remain in the Department and to work in an unknown capacity.[786]

By February 1982, the Education Department announced replacement positions for former Assistant Directors-General. Morton became Executive Director (Facilities) and Maddocks coordinated the

Policy and Planning Unit that developed policy options as requested by the Director-General or his Deputy. Joy resigned to enter private practice while Hird, disappointed to miss out on the Deputy's position that he was led to believe would be his and affronted by the offer to be a consultant, retired, using accrued leave to allow him to finish work at the earliest opportunity.[787] He later wrote of the Minister's underhandedness in concealing events from Shears. He claimed Hunt 'openly solicited applications for Director-General' at the October meeting of Ministers and Directors-General. 'The matter of a forced early retirement or a movement sideways loomed large in the mind of the Minister.' Hird knew Shears had rallied support and prepared an application to withhold until the death-knock. According to Hird, Hunt presented an alternative that got himself off the hook.[788]

On 27 January 1982 the Office of the Director-General was disbanded. Norman Curry came in as Director-General. Shears and senior staff were relegated to other duties, retired or selected another career. In an effort to maintain face Shears wrote a letter to the press in which he claimed there were two top jobs, the Director-General's and his own. He and Curry vied to be Number One, deservedly so for Curry, who had received Ministerial appointment, and understandably so for Shears, who had been dethroned. Curry believed, 'the role of the director-general is to be responsible for the education system within the State' and he upheld the importance of Shears' appointment, which was 'an attempt to provide an overall look at education within the State'. Though he admitted some overlap he stressed 'it does not impinge on the role of director-general specifically.'[789]

To allay confusion and clarify roles, Shears and Curry co-authored a letter to *The Age*, published on 10 February. They claimed 'we are working with harmony and understanding towards the achievement of our objectives. Both of us are required to represent the Minister for Education on various state and national bodies.' The letter explained:

> Dr Curry is responsible for the administration of the newly structured State Education Department in the same way that the director-general was previously. He will be Chairman of the Non-Government School Registration Board and when requested will provide personal advice to the Minister on any matter in education.

> The role of the Coordinator-General of Education, Dr Shears, is advisory, investigatory and conciliatory. He will be concerned with priorities and balance between the major segments, with cost effectiveness, and with the establishment of guidelines for future developments in the total educational provision for the State. He will be Chairman of both the Victorian Education Council and the committee of chief executives of the various segments.
>
> The work of the director-general in the newly restructured Education Department and that of the coordinator-general give an opportunity for exciting cooperative developments in providing the best possible education for all people in Victoria.

The letter smacked of Shears. He promoted the responsibilities of director-general yet elevated his own. In support of this and censure of the restructure, he stressed erosion of the Director-General's role. The *Education (Amendment) Act* 1981 (No. 9582) made way for vital coordination. He explained, 'The Government has chosen to create under the Public Service Board the "Office of the Coordinator-General of Education", the Permanent Head of which is the Coordinator-General of Education'.

In contrast to his public front, frustration and disappointment burned inside. Despite elevating the position, the educational fraternity and public saw the reality that it placed Shears in an administrative backwater. In the true spirit of Shears, rather than appear defeated, he maintained a prominent profile. 'Make something of yourself,' advised long-standing friend Ken Sargent. 'Identify specific needs; define your role; establish a position of worth with a sense of authority; set an agenda to develop a series of projects, and travel.' [790]

## Changes afoot

In the unfolding months of 1982 another change was afoot. In pre-election hype, education was a hot topic. The Liberal Party's performance, the restructure debacle and underhand tactics exacerbated concerns. Complexity imposed by the Commonwealth swelled the dilemma in education as razor gang cuts targeted amalgamation of SCV Melbourne, Hawthorn Institute of Education, the Institute of Early Childhood Development and the University of Melbourne. Education needed a greater share of Treasury coffers. $15m promised to fund building and maintenance and $7m to provide non-teaching staff was considered a trifling share of the Department's $1500m annual budget. An 11 per cent pay increase cost the government $100m yet teachers felt short-changed. As the election hype continued Premier Thompson wooed independent schools to broaden support. People contrasted Thompson's diplomatic style with Hunt's militant approach. During two years' agitation Hunt had not achieved all he intended and Lacy was considered a hindrance. Though gearing towards an election Hunt failed to attend a pre-election press conference in March. In his absence Lacy blundered about literacy rates and failed to answer questions. Those in attendance criticised lack of aims and direction in education and requested an update from Curry.[791]

The Teachers Tribunal was a stumbling block that the unions detested, especially the VSTA. Disparity between their views and the Department's bolstered the campaign to oust the Liberals. Activist Brian Henderson recalled:

> ... intense hatred of the Education Department bureaucracy, which came about through years of successive Liberal governments ... the government had in place bureaucrats that were doing what the government wanted and that generated enormous hatred of those people.
>
> We campaigned relentlessly for the Labor Party ... made a $50,000.00 donation. The Victorian Teacher's Union donated $100,000. None of the Teacher's Unions are affiliated to the ALP and never have been, so for us to make that donation was a very big political gesture. People were campaigning to get rid of Liberal Government.

Henderson explained, 'Tribunal reform, control of entry, conditions, had been running battles for years and years and years. Labor offered greater investment ... promised "we will fix these things".'[792]

Labor toppled the Liberals in the April 1982 election. Hunt held his seat but Lacy was out. Robert Fordham took on the education portfolio. Fordham had attended Footscray North State School (No. 4160) and Essendon High School, and then the University of Melbourne where he completed two degrees, a rarity for a Footscray boy. He described himself as:

> … far from one of the brightest kids and I was the only one to go on to University. That was symptomatic of the changes that had to be made if we were to cope with the enormous social and economic changes that were happening in our workforce and business life. Education became the focus; through the Commonwealth Government and changes that Whitlam brought and pressures on the State Government through the seventies.

Elected to parliament in 1970 Fordham was 'a product of the education system' who had served as Shadow Minister. Now the Minister, Fordham was 'quite assiduous … conscious that I was spokesperson on the biggest portfolio.' Throughout his parliamentary service, interactions with Shears were courteous and appropriate. Shears outlined what was happening in education and what was proposed. The Labor Party identified funding stringency, committed to boost literacy and numeracy standards and provide more and better-qualified teachers. It prioritised the thrust to service the needs of minority groups: immigrant, 'handicapped', female and rural students, but industrial relations remained contentious. Maintenance and improvement programs lagged behind the school building boom of the fifties, sixties and seventies; masonry veneer and portables constructed to ease the school population boom were obsolete. Fordham received constant complaints about faulty toilets, insufficient classrooms and inadequate buildings. It required a quantum leap in commitment to remedy these and other concerns.

## Fordham's platform

Fordham was elected to Parliament in 1970, and appointed education spokesperson for the Labor Party. Of the times he noted:

> From the sixties on education had become more and more

a political issue at elections and in public discourse ... one of the peaks was the election of the Whitlam government in '72 and the involvement of the Australian government in education issues. That wasn't just done in a vacuum; it reflected an increasing public concern about education as a public issue. Australian society had changed through the sixties as a result of post war migration, the development of technical skills was extremely important, skills that required a higher degree of education than had been the case in the past and so the capacity of our education systems, primary, secondary and post secondary were very much under scrutiny.

Throughout the 1970s, Director-General Shears and Shadow Minister Fordham had a good working relationship. Retrospectively Fordham noted Shears' loyalty to his Minister and to the government he served, and willingness 'to talk with me and to respond to issues that I'd raise'. Fordham was prepared for his own Ministerial role. The policy statement for education he prepared in 1976 addressed multiple issues that continually niggled educational development. He wrote, 'If we are to achieve the social reformation for which we stand, real educational opportunity must be readily available to all in our society.' It was the Party's intent 'to ensure that not only is every man, woman and child allowed access to the educational stream of their choice, but also that the quality of education be such as to allow full development of their capacities and talent.' Critical of elitist Liberal policies the statement lamented, 'Neglect must not go unchallenged, for surely it is fundamental to our concept of democracy to provide an equal opportunity for education to every man, woman and child irrespective of income or social status.'[793]

In the flurry of the Hunt/Lacy saga Shears' policies appeared to be swept aside. Although innovation and change as he saw it seemed forgotten, the five directive papers continued to guide reform. Under Fordham, there was yet another administrative restructure, yet the regions developed, and schools within each were grouped into clusters to service local and individual needs. The school and community movement expanded as school councils attained additional powers. With greater community interface, they gained curricula sway, attained control of maintenance and capital works, and employment of ancillary staff. Administrative training was seen as advantageous, while study leave and enrichment programs proposed to minimise teacher loss.

Unlike aggressive change imposed by Hunt, Fordham attempted to restore faith in 'our Department', and loyalties to traditions and those who served. Leadership turned from executive rule to school-based reform. Fordham's diplomatic approach silenced protagonists whom he appointed to committees, inquiries and reviews to highlight concerns. A further channel of advice was the State Board of Education, a Schools Commission look-alike. The Victorian Teaching Service Conciliation and Arbitration Commission similarly reflected its Commonwealth counterpart. Well versed in educational matters Fordham gave teachers a 4.5 per cent pay rise, repealed stand-down legislation that hindered temporary and emergency teacher employment, increased the number of teachers for migrant English programs and provided more clerical staff in schools. He reached agreement with the VSTA, abolished the Teachers Tribunal and revoked corporal punishment.[794] Of recent events and the treatment of Shears Fordham observed that Hunt and Lacy 'chose to take Lawrie from the centre stage and put him into this backwater called the Coordinator-General's role'. He continued:

> What they did, I regarded as highly improper … there was an election due, and the idea of changing the Director General, some months out from an election goes against the principals of the Westminster system. It was the responsibility of the incoming government to either make or not make and to replace Lawrie with Dr Norman Curry was, I think, inappropriate.

Fordham regarded it 'as an act of desperation on the part of those ministers, an act that did not prove to be successful as it turned out'. Sensitive to the people involved in these matters, upon taking office, he ostensibly gave equal billing to Coordinator-General and Director-General yet in truth there was a divide. He described the Coordinator-General's position as a 'cul de sac' and though Shears wrote some worthwhile reports they were not centre stage. Fordham sensed:

> Lawrie was highly conscious of that of course. The working arrangements he had in the building, knowing that Norman Curry, by definition as being Director General, was dealing with the critical issues ... he found that extremely difficult.

With the education portfolio in hand Fordham picked up on policies initiated by Shears and continued their development. He reflected:

> Lawrie had started to go down the path of issues that in the end became my ministerial papers, dealing with the regional development of education, far greater involvement of parents, development of school councils and all of those moves, were in his mind as well as my own. Although we were working separately ... we were both responding to the problems of the time. There's no doubt about it. We were heading very much in the same direction.[795]

## Fordham's policy papers

### Paper 1: *Decision making in Victorian education* (1983)

Devolution remained a priority by which school communities shaped policy and practice through 'strong representative school councils, regional boards and the State Board of Education'. Ministerial advice was thus channelled from the community to the Education Department and to the State Board, chartered to offer advice on strategies to improve schools and the curriculum. Fordham believed 'the real work is in the schools, where teachers, students, principals and parents ... make the decisions that are wisest for the school.' He challenged schools to foster a 'broad general education' through a curriculum to ensure students understood their world and the wider society. 'Cooperation and collaboration amongst schools', the focal point in the educative process aimed 'to meet the needs of the total community'. Fordham noted significant advances with the regional structure and the consultancy services that supported the development of school-based curriculum. He supported 'collective responsibility' involving departmental administrators, regional staff and entire school communities working toward common objectives.

'Together we are about to embark on fundamental reforms of the education system – a sharing of responsibility in the continuing task of improving the schools within the State system of education to serve the people of Victoria.'[796]

## Paper 2: *The School Improvement Plan* (1983)

Paper 2 presented the rationale to establish a Working Party, convened by Joan Kirner, MLC. Two basic principles were:

> The determination of educational policy for each school is a cooperative task which must be carried out principally by the school community itself.
>
> The education system is responsible for providing resources and services to schools in ways that meet their identified needs and which result in coordinated support for schools.[797]

Paper 2 identified aims, principles, processes and general criteria for inclusion and funding. It addressed Management Structure in minute details (as Shears did in his Paper 1), spelt out responsibilities of committees, the secretariat and the standing committee, and distinguished roles and relationships between them, and between the School Improvement Plan and other policy initiatives. Fundamentals underlying the development of State education were 'relationships based on mutual respect; collaboration in decisions about what is learned and how it is taught; the active redress of disadvantage and discrimination; the empowering of the school community; and processes of shared responsibility'.

The School Improvement Plan assisted schools to improve students' learning experience, and review their policies, practices and programs. An approach to appraise school and teacher performance bore semblance to strategies Shears presented in his Paper 5. Another step away from inspectorial visits, it signalled the inspectorate's demise.

## Paper 3: *The State Board of Education* (1983)

To monitor the entire educational scene Fordham established the State Board of Education. Like Shears, he believed the Council of Public Education was ineffective. Whereas Shears proposed the Victorian

Education Council within the Departmental structure, the State Board was an independent entity. The State Board of Education was a key advisory body geared to inform Fordham of educational matters in a similar vein to advice offered by the Director-General. It was an attempt to build transparency into the process of policy-making: operating in the public arena; publishing reports, papers and research findings; and presenting critical analysis. To ensure success the State Board would operate across the spectrum of schooling, report major matters to Parliament, have access to all Education Department information, and negotiate with the non-government sector.

Paper 3, a comprehensive document, listed the Board's priorities regarding policies, needs, curricula, and structure. The paper identified the need to define relationships between schools and other providers, establish long-term planning, set budgetary priorities, study the impact of new nongovernment schools and establish collaborative processes at school council and proposed regional board levels. Chaired by Ken McKinnon, the State Board drew two full-time and eleven part-time members from 'various groups with a legitimate concern for the future of primary and post-primary education in Victoria'. Members included Dr Norman Curry, DGE; Professor Peter Fensham representing tertiary education; Mr Gerry Tickell, a government schoolteacher and advocate of alternative schools; and Mrs Pat Reeve representing school organisations (full-time members); Mr Bob Dobell, Regional Director; Mr Jo Lo Bianco representing ethnic communities; Father Tom Doyle representing Catholic education; and Dr Ray Maddocks, seconded from the Education Department. Policy analysts and researchers brought broad expertise and diverse perspectives. Advice offered to the Minister by the State Board would complement that of the Director-General. On 28 June the *State Board of Education Act* 1983 (No. 9929) was enacted. The influence of the State Board was dependent 'upon the quality of its advice and the persuasiveness of its ideas'.[798]

**Paper 4: *School councils* (1983)**

School councils under the *Education (Schools Councils) Act* 1975 (No. 8799) became legal government agents and offered advice on educational matters. While Hunt had purportedly continued the thrust to devolve the power-base, his actions regarding the treatment of Shears and senior officers gave those 'sentiments a somewhat hollow sound'.[799] Fordham, whose views embraced the broader public, encouraged authentic school and community interaction. The essence of accountability, he claimed, was to the school community rather than the bureaucracy. Collaboration was critical to ensure teachers and parents shared 'common concern and a common responsibility for the education of children'.[800] Shared central and school responsibility required cooperative policy development and planning to identify roles and responsibilities of school councils and principals.

As bodies corporate, school councils were obliged to satisfy financial and auditing conditions and strengthen relationships between each school and its community. Rather than accountability to the distant Department, school councils were accountable to the entire community of students, teachers and those beyond school boundaries. Fordham identified council membership and representation, and the requirement to draft procedures in compliance with government policy and reflective of local community needs. Within the Education Department, a School Councils Services Unit maintained a central registry of membership and constitutions, supported skills development and provided training and consultancy services through regional offices. Reconstitution of school councils by the end of 1983 preceded the establishment of regional boards.

**Paper 5:** *Regional boards of education* **(1984)**

Regional boards, a 'mechanism for collective decision making by school councils in a region' were an important part in the program to develop an administration system responsive to the needs of schools. The mechanism enabled two-way dialogue between the school community and the Minister through administrative layers comprising school councils, regional boards and the State Board. Based on 'participative, collaborative decision-making' the regional board was a step beyond the school and regional expansion and the community movement initiated by Shears. The motif to establish a bureaucracy responsive to the needs of clients emulated previous aims to satisfy the teacher and child in the classroom. Regional boards were a vital link between school communities, the State Board and the Minister. Their role included staff selection, school cluster development and coordination of in-service education.

The evolution of education during the decade past affected the role of regional offices and services. Beyond bringing centrally controlled services to schools, their role was more fluid as they responded to the needs of the schools in their geographic locations and to advice given by school councils. Planning, liaising and coordinating bodies, the regional boards would select regional staff, assume responsibility for State- and Commonwealth-funded programs and funds, establish guidelines for support personnel, identify priorities and guidelines for programs and resource allocation, and cooperate with the State Board and the Director-General.

Paper 5 defined the size of regional boards, enumerated the composition of elected, nominated and co-opted members, and defined the electoral process, the operation of the boards and the review process. The regional structure expanded with clearly defined layers in an attempt to further disseminate power.

## Paper 6: *Curriculum development and planning in Victoria* (1984)

Subject to accelerating social, economic and technological change, increasingly curriculum became a political concern. Though it remained a statement of knowledge, competencies and values, schools adapted to ensure ongoing relevance to students' needs. Interchange between central authorities and the schools guaranteed progression in all learning domains from Preparatory Year to Year 12 (Years P–12) and through to post-compulsory schooling. Beyond this, Fordham referred to 'the effects on student learning of such matters as staffing policy, facilities, teaching and learning styles, school organization, and assessment and reporting procedures'. Implicit and explicit values formed the basis of curriculum policy, such as common ground, honesty and justice.

Paper 6 established guidelines for school councils to follow as young people undertook worthwhile work and participated in societal improvement. The paper stimulated discussion about ways to implement policies and practice. Fordham stressed the milieu of multicultural Victoria and the vigilance required to maintain educational standards. Guided by the former Curriculum and Research Branch experts, it addressed needs of students at all levels of schooling in the evolving social scene. Schools were charged to adjust their curricula in response to change and to ensure their relevance in preparing young people for productive life in their society. This required 'providing all young people with experiences that cannot be readily or universally gained through other life experiences and that are necessary for them to become effective adults'.[801]

It was the school's responsibility to provide access and success, building on previous knowledge, measuring ability and catering for a range of students' needs. School councils were responsible for ensuring the program was planned and challenging to enable students to understand the world and its people, participate in Australian society, achieve personal fulfillment, gain technical competence and gain enrichment through studies of science and mathematics, literature and the arts. Such development through the regions strengthened the link between head office policy makers and those responsive to the immediate needs of students in regional areas and local schools.

## Reflections

Fordham's papers, comprehensive and insightful, showed his knowledge of education, identified his aims, and revealed his commitment to providing positive and nurturing learning environments in which students could grow. Fordham, like Shears, was aware of the risk of the gap between head office bureaucracy and schools, and acknowledged recognisable foundations in the policies established by Shears. Many of the people interviewed by the author likewise saw evidence of the Shears footprint on the system as it evolved. Lindsay Thompson considered the departmental restructure important, particularly the establishment of the Office of Director-General; Kevin Collins identified greater community responsibility and increased power to school administrators; and Norman Curry noted the regional concept and accountability given to schools. Devolution to regions and school councils was a vital reform, according to Neville Barwick, while John Pascoe noted the shift in school councils' role from advisory to operating councils, and moves toward their role in principal selection. The importance of the IEA became obvious because devolved authority revealed the need to train principals. Significant for Brian Henderson was curriculum. He claimed, 'the educational philosophy and certain arguments about curriculum and assessment are still underpinned by a lot of the work Lawrie oversaw at the time.' Henderson continued:

> When you look back in history and see what he has done, you can see that he has made a significant contribution. While we weren't necessarily on the right side of that, you still have to acknowledge that ... the impression from the union was that it was Lindsay Thompson pulling the strings; Lawrie doing all his dirty work, would be how I would describe it.[802]

## Shears' new command

On 27 January 1982 Norman Curry was officially appointed Victoria's Director-General and Shears became its first and only Coordinator-General. After a scuffle to accommodate the two senior officers, Shears began the year with a round of meetings. Attendance at the Australian and New Zealand Student Services Association Conference at La Trobe University gave insight into student engagement, wellbeing and development as well as into problems confronting young people. That conference prefaced his appointment to chair a task force to identify options and cost implications of formulating a comprehensive youth policy. He attended AEC Executive meetings and the AEC conference in Alice Springs, and attended policy and finance meetings of the IEA, which became an important part of his life. Reappointed to the UNESCO Committee, a reception in Canberra gave him entrée to representatives from Japan, China, Yugoslavia and Russia, and supported developments of the ITF Program. Representing the Federal Government he visited the Asian Centre in Bangkok and attended the UNESCO General Conference in Paris. Despite the advent of mass schooling worldwide, literacy levels had decreased.

In October 1982, Executive Director of the Office of Coordinator-General Elizabeth (Lee) Dale looked after the office while Shears travelled abroad. A maths and science teacher, she moved into teacher education at Toorak TC and at the VIC served as Registrar (1977) and Deputy Vice-Principal (1980), under the leadership of Phillip Law. A feisty woman, she described Shears as amiable, charming and kindly to 'even the most junior typist'. His ego was 'high enough not to be tackled' and though he liked top billing she saw he needed support 'not be knocked out of the ranks'.[803]

Shears heeded Sargent's advice to make something of himself and the position. Major issues that challenged education were curriculum planning, youth policies and the emergent use of computers in schools. To attain a global perspective of these required overseas travel. Some critics said it was an inspirational move on the Minister's part to send Shears. Shears was delighted. Coupled with UNESCO commitments, he undertook research on four definitive papers that provided up-to-date data and a unique collection of contemporary material on basic education issues. During three months abroad he visited eleven countries to observe youth policies, computers in education and administration. In a comparative study he examined the alignment of Victorian with overseas programs, and whether orientation to British traditions disadvantaged studies of European and Asian culture and history.[804]

## Ministerial reports

Between October 1982 and June 1984 four reports were written. Shears undertook data collection overseas while staff in his office collected local data. Jenny Matthews was involved in preparing the reports on youth policies and curriculum, Lee Dale supported computers, and Shears compiled and presented the administrative study alone.

### *Youth policies* (1983)

A job for life was no longer viable nor was an open cheque policy for education. Economic and social change and international recession affected traditional transitions from youth to adulthood, school to work and a secure career. Angry, ill-equipped and estranged, young people were edging towards 'social disaffection and destructive behaviour'. In response, governments attempted to engage the 'energy and intelligence' of young people in 'socially valued and personally beneficial activities', offer them hope, training and skills.[805]

In Australia, economic regression, unemployment and fewer job opportunities affected school retention rates. Despite strong white-collar sector expansion, teenage employment declined; girls were hardest hit. Work or apprenticeships held greater attraction than Year 12 completion as the prospects for graduates reduced and tertiary studies had few financial benefits. Study deferral and mature-age entry increased enrolments in TAFE and offset the decline in full-time education. The relationship between education and work, the curriculum and the environment were fundamental to explore. The findings would for the basis of advice to governments and voluntary sector agencies that supported transition by way of accommodation, finance and disadvantage, health, recreation and specific needs.

Examination of youth issues at home and abroad revealed diverse definitions of youth. Australia, like Thailand, France, and the UK, identified youth according to younger and older age groups. Youth age extended from birth to 25 in Thailand and Japan, 27 in Yugoslavia and 30 in China. Neither Sweden nor the USA had a defining age. The diversity of groups was responsible for diverse structures, services and evaluation processes. Education, training and employment issues were common, and financial and social support were recognised in some countries. Although each country addressed youth issues, in some cases evaluation was ad hoc.

The report on youth policies made 27 recommendations, among them, that coordination and engagement of young people in decisions regarding their future were vital; and that a National Committee on Youth Policy with replicate State agencies, and Offices of Youth Affairs, be established to conduct research, disseminate information, and maintain and evaluate policies and their progress.[806]

## Computers (1983)

Scepticism towards computers in classrooms echoed doubts about radio and television as learning tools. Idle students resulted, opponents claimed; horizons broadened, advocates argued. Governments, administrators and teachers questioned the pros and cons, and agreed that the key to successful utilisation was 'effective preparation and involvement of teachers'. The Victorian Education Department conducted an inquiry into the use of computers in 1982 but as an isolated case. There was need for a collective investigation to ascertain their use in broader segments of the educational community. At a recent meeting of the Australian Education Council Victoria and New South Wales had set in train guidelines for a national enquiry. Aligning with this, Minister Fordham sent Shears to examine attitudes abroad. In the report, Shears categorised three groups of countries according to their use of computers in schools: 'under-developed and uncertain' as in China, Thailand and Yugoslavia; 'developed but reluctant' as in Japan, Germany and Sweden; and 'developed and committed' as in France, UK, USA, Canada and Norway.

In China's 'predominantly rural culture and economy' the teacher–pupil relationship was fundamental. Authorities feared that computers would have an adverse effect on the teacher's role and students' learning. Nevertheless, elective studies at universities and colleges offered familiarisation courses, and small centres gave instruction in chemistry and mathematics. Thailand's Ministry of Education had installed a computer centre for management information systems and statistics and acknowledged advantages in administration, timetables and budgets. Although familiarisation programs were introduced computers had minimal educational benefits. Yugoslavia saw benefits of familiarisation and established model centres.

Despite Japan's expertise in microelectronics and access to high-quality equipment, only 10–20 per cent of its schools had computers. They were considered a teaching gimmick, beneficial to industry not education. Though trials in secondary schools were underway and teacher-training centres had been established, educational application was primarily for payroll, personnel and building data.

Germany too had access to computer resources but authorities feared breakdown in the teacher–student relationship. Nonetheless its three regions exhibited vast attitudinal differences. Although North Rhine–Westphalia sustained limited use in schools, the region supported familiarisation programs and the use of computers in and vocational and tertiary training. Bavaria equipped 400 schools with terminals, offered community guidance and teamed up with IBM for research, administration and tertiary study. Hamburg afforded minimal options.

Though Swedish and Norwegian authorities acknowledged administrative and learning advantages of computers, commitment in Norway was greater. Sweden introduced them into upper secondary schools and teacher in-service programs whereas in Norway they supported vocational and academic courses in many senior secondary schools. Regional colleges taught computer science and the Norwegian Television and Broadcasting Commission presented visual training for teachers.

Authorities in France, the most advanced European country, believed the teacher held the key, and sound technological skills underpinned a complete education. Computers were standard classroom aids, four universities offered training for teachers and a program was underway to equip high schools. Though less developed, the Microelectronics Program in England, Wales and Northern Ireland prepared children for life and adjustment to new technologies. Despite in-service training, curriculum planning and support, sceptics remained. Scotland had its own agenda.

Most schools in the USA were equipped with computers. Despite random enthusiasm and coordination, research revealed learning gains. In Canada computers were regarded as intellectual amplifiers, however provincial variations in supply, application and acceptance were apparent. Computer science was taught at secondary and post-secondary levels in British Columbia where private enterprise support was encouraged. In Ontario learning materials were catalogued and teachers were familiarised with the curriculum. Saskatchewan authorities aimed toward computer literacy for all students by Year 8. They developed curriculum and provided consultants. Schools in Alberta used computers across the curriculum whereas progress was slow in Manitoba.

Research across Australia revealed commitment to computer education but expense was a concern. State-by-state strategies indicated lack of guidelines and coordination, minimal software development and few details of computer use in post-secondary schooling. Fundamental to initiating computer education in schools was to establish a set of aims and objectives and commercial links to ensure provision of suitable equipment, with appropriate hardware and software. Pre-service teacher training and in-service education were also essential. Educational rather than administrative use was a priority plus the use of computers in special education and distance learning. University and TAFE courses with academic, vocational and specialist orientation had potential to link schools with industry.

## *Curriculum* (1984)

A coordinated and structured curriculum underlay successful education. Previously Shears had acknowledged this with his appointment of ADGE Maddocks in charge of curriculum, and the development of the Curriculum Branch. Alternative school structures with P–12 schools and senior high schools and colleges, e.g. Bendigo Senior Secondary College, were occurring in Victoria, making curriculum a critical issue.

Unlike previous reports on curriculum in Victoria (such as the Curriculum Services Enquiry of 1976 and various smaller studies including the St Albans Curriculum Development Project conducted in 1975 to seek to overcome the underlying causes of educational disadvantage among primary schools in the area), data presented in this report were limited to overseas sources in the hope that international philosophies would ignite 'a spark of creativity'. This would in turn 'avoid the dangers of isolation and parochialism'. Interview data was geographically classified according to Asian, European and American perspectives, with consideration given to history, culture, social structure and politics. In Japan, China and Thailand national benefits ranked above personal commitment to moral, social and ethical values. Rationality and intellect, valued in France, produced a managerial and intellectual elite, whereas ability-based provision in the UK filtered students into comprehensive or vocational schools.

The Norwegian system encouraged tolerance, equity, cooperation and freedom of thought, whereas Sweden valued high standards of social welfare. Both Nordic countries, like America, promoted advancement, social mobility and bonds.

Control of curriculum reflected degrees of authority and autonomy. Ministerial management, as in Japan, China, Thailand and France, contrasted with mixed mode approaches in Norway, Sweden and Canada, and decentralised systems in the UK and the USA. Greater consensus on content was evident in primary schools where the 'common curriculum' comprised native language, science, mathematics, and physical, social and visual education while greater diversity existed in secondary systems. Tension between general and vocational learning created a rift in perceptions of equity. A transferable common core in Norwegian and Swedish systems minimised this.

Frequently achievement provided foundation for further study. Basic skills in primary classes were taught rather than acquired as students progressed towards promotion. Apart from Thailand and the City of New York, promotion hinged on successful completion, and remediation was the preferred option. Leaps from lower to upper secondary, termination of schooling and selection for post-secondary studies depended upon performance measured by combinations of internal and external assessment.

Of particular interest were the vast open spaces in Sweden that paralleled those in Victoria and influenced the location and composition of schools, and the local voice still evident in educational matters in the USA, a feature that had guided Shears' own policy papers. The drafting of students into academic, vocational and functional streams according to the 11-plus assessment continued in the UK.

Recommendations of the curriculum report were geared towards Victoria's education policy developing an international outlook. Immigration had placed increasing demands on the system and, reinforced by research, Shears adhered to his views on travel awakening international understanding. He cautioned against assessment at Years 4 and 7 levels, as in New York City, and 'the danger of defining the outcomes of primary schooling in terms of a range of basic skills'. The report stressed that education required financial and physical support and additional teaching resources. The trend towards comprehensive secondary schools observed abroad, as was occurring in Victoria, was a vital link between primary and post-compulsory schooling. Complexes of three or four year levels were optional models to consider. Post-compulsory complexes would allow students to continue their schooling and keep open their options for study or vocational pathways. Youth services integral to each, or assessment at stipulated levels, would enable teachers to evaluate, diagnose and resolve problems. The report identified a descriptive profile of achievements and certification of post-compulsory completion as a reliable resource for tertiary entrance and employment. However, policies must be framed to consider 'the educational needs of all children not those at either end of the spectrum, i.e. not the most able and privileged or the less able and disadvantaged but all children'. Equity was fundamental to personal fulfilment and had broad social benefits.[807]

## *Administration* (1984)

The fourth report was a survey structures throughout Australia and abroad. Interviewees represented government ministries, educational leaders, executive officers and expert advisers from educational, public and private enterprises. Data reflected social, philosophical and political values that characterised each system and the 'intellectual talents and personal relationship skills of those who are selected to make them work'. Strong words, yet poignant, in the light of recent events; the holy spark so important in classroom interactions played a key role in educational administration.[808]

The report reviewed Victoria's administrative history since the Department's founding in 1901. Fragmentation began in 1965 and slicing off of component parts continued until the *Education (Amendment) Act* 1981 (No. 9582) segmented the final portion, removing the Director-General's power and vesting it in the Minister's hands. The report identified the Coordinator-General as the senior adviser (albeit a myth). Backlash of the Hunt–Lacy saga created chaos, which Shears described as an 'unusual combination of administrators disaffected in their hundreds' and 'the political desperation of teacher organisations' that left the Liberal Party 'to lament the confusion and discord of its attempted revolution'. On coming to power, 'the Labor Party began the task of picking up the pieces and implementing its own educational policies'. Thenceforth the Minister of Education politically and administratively arbitrated educational decision-making subject to the policy platform of the Party.[809]

A national survey of education departments identified administrative units of one person or more. Queensland, Western Australia and Tasmania employed the one-person model of a single minister and senior administrator. A single minister governed systems in South Australia, the Northern Territory and New South Wales, where two administrative units functioned under a Director-General of Schools and a Director-General of TAFE.

Victoria's system remained unique where a proliferation of statutory authorities tendered advice. To reflect ministerial authority, the report suggested a Ministry of Education was appropriate. The report proposed a Director-General of Education to govern the Schools Division, and a Managing Director to administer TAFE. A Victorian Education Commission would streamline communication, channel recommendations of the State Board, VPSEC, the TAFE Board and other authorities to spearhead advice to the Minister.

The four reports renewed the opportunity for Shears to act as Ministerial adviser. Data provided insights to shape educational policy.

## Attitudes towards the reports

Attitudes towards the reports were muted. Youth policies received greatest acclaim. Questions were raised about the suitability of the current curriculum to prepare young people to make transitions from school to work and provide structure for their post-secondary. The environment was ripe for the study and the community was eager to receive the report. The teenage jobless rate was 30 per cent and rising, school retention rates were falling and youth homelessness was an increasing concern. Tackling this grim scene 'in a hopelessly piecemeal and ad hoc fashion', State and Federal governments had created a 'bewildering array of uncoordinated support services, training schemes, and transition to work schemes, run by a plethora of committees, departments, instrumentalities, statutory authorities and voluntary aid groups'.[810] Costly and controversial, the administrative maze was ineffective.

Proposals in the youth policies report gave a whiff of what to expect, stirred debate and highlighted the gravity of concerns facing youth and those responsible for support. In 1979 Fraser tried to sell the idea that unemployment was 'the least attractive option' but youth unemployment had since soared 200 per cent. Federal Labor's promises to present a comprehensive policy, boost school retention and numbers entering universities and colleges were too little, critics alleged. In response to the formal release of the youth policies report in June, Prime Minister Hawke suggested teenage kibbutzim, and Peter Tannock, chairman of the Schools Commission, urged enticement for early school leavers to stay on. *The Age* education reporter Geoff Maslen acknowledged the report as 'commendably coherent and its arguments cogent and persuasive' but it failed to 'acknowledge the crucial factor that there are not enough jobs for those who want them – whether they are old or young. Furthermore, ahead lay 'the prospect that Australia may have a large core of permanently unemployed young people'.[811]

Shears slammed Canberra's youth policy, its ad hoc and ineffective coordination and few common goals. Reaction highlighted a history of futile efforts, lack of action and 'appalling waste of our national human resources'. Alan Wright of Ballarat despaired to see 25 to 30 per cent of young people 'move out of school into a life without structure, without direction, without opportunities to feel socially useful and valued, without appropriate income and encouragements that offer some hope for the future.' Federal action was critical but the major thrust ought to be towards empowering local communities to share in decision making about their own social futures, and those of their young'. Wright pleaded for strong incentives to strengthen consultation processes, and develop local, social priorities and objectives. He prayed 'that those in positions of power will heed the import of Dr Shears' report.'[812]

The report jolted debate and action, though not immediately. Young people's role in decision-making was vital. The enticement of additional schooling removed them from the workforce figures but this was quickly recognised as a cover up. 'Young people want jobs' became a familiar cry. In the interests of youth Shears pleaded for action and argued the case for education and cooperation by Federal and State governments, institutions, employers and other agencies. He sought youth hubs to offer guidance and support, and to provide opportunities for cooperation with employers.

## Other aspects of Shears

Making the most of opportunities, life as Coordinator-General resembled an Indian summer. The four reports raised discussion, particularly regarding youth; however observers noted 'nothing much came from the work he'd done'. They wondered 'how much he saw himself removed and how much he saw himself promoted' to his present position. 'The general view in the system was that the job he'd been given was not a serious job'. Similar doubts stirred in his inner thoughts, but seemingly undaunted, and encouraged by Sargent's advice, he battled on. He plunged himself into affairs of the IEA, where he remained Chairman of the council. He regularly attended council meetings and opening and closing ceremonies and worked towards completion of the new complex. He immersed himself in expanding the ITF program and continued rigorous recruitment campaigns to broaden its base. On the social front he enjoyed occasional lunches with the Trios Femme, three reporters from *News Exchange*. 'It became a personal relationship when we had the lunches,' one recalled, 'it was just a very private thing between the four of us.'[813]

VIER held special appeal and meetings were clearly marked in Shears' diary. During his presidency several up-and-comings had made their mark. Peter Natrass became Principal, SCV Burwood; Dr Graham Whitehead was appointed Executive Officer of the 1976 Curriculum Services Enquiry; Max Boyce, became Senior Lecturer, SCV Toorak; and Leo Foster was appointed Principal, Phillip Institute. The Frank Tate Memorial Lecture remained an important occasion with Professor Emeritus Selby-Smith from Monash University, Professor Eileen Byrne from the University of Queensland, Professor

William Cooley from the University of Pittsburg, and Peter Tannock, Chairman of the Schools Commission among the speakers. Professors Richard Selleck and Richard White, Monash University, and Ronald Goldman, La Trobe University, presented the John Smyth Memorial Lectures (1982–84). The George Browne Prizes continued until 1983 but the Primary and Secondary Education groups had faded.

At meetings, lunches or dinners Shears kept in touch. He frequently lunched with Graham Allen at the Melbourne or the Athenaeum Club, and considered the youth dilemma and post-secondary options. Tony Delves, Grant Harman, Bill Walker, Peter Tannock and Joan Kirner were among others he met. Featured among Shears' commitments were ACE, VIER, ITF, and IEA functions, Rotary and vestry meetings, special occasions and conferences. Out and about within the State, a regular traveller interstate and abroad, he nevertheless considered himself a homebody. He exuded charm wherever he went, or entertained friends and guests at Hopetoun Road. When time allowed he secluded himself with the family in their two-bedroom shack at Aireys Inlet.

But summer's winds and heat in 1983 caused disaster. Much of Victoria burned. Lives were lost. The Surf Coast turned to a charcoal desert. Huddled on the beach locals saw the horror; the choking smoke, the blood-red sky and flames that leapt across treetops. Among houses gone was the Aireys Inlet holiday cottage. Shears, recently home from the study tour, was at a UNESCO meeting in Canberra. His concern centred with others who lost their homes. The Shears rebuilt.

1983 marked other losses. Abolition of the divisions and the inspectorate soured careers' end for many. David Holloway, ADPE and former inspector, recalled a memorandum from D-G Curry forewarning him. Subsequently Curry met each inspector by turn. Holloway observed 'grown men [and women] who had nurtured the department, in a lifetime of service' come back in tears ... 'kicked fair in the midriff'. There was 'no farewell, no thanks, no recognition that the inspectorate, ever since 1851, had built the school system ... they built it, taught it, guided it, introduced new ideas, looked after it in every way.'[814] Similar events stung divisional directors, deputies and assistants whose careers fell apart, displaced by the regional expansion.

Shears expressed empathy for those who lost out.

The trip between Hopetoun Road and Aireys Inlet became frequently travelled with rebuilding the house and supervising progress of the IEA complex at Geelong. With architectural drawings complete, the site was prepared and construction commenced. Wearing a hard hat Shears regularly frequented the site. Being chairman of the IEA council gave him kudos and 'though not as administratively powerful as before, [he] was not afraid to rattle a few cages to ensure the IEA received its due'.[815]

The diversity among those who attended IEA programs, the power of the group, the insights and understanding enriched people's lives, and in turn the lives of those in their professional realm. Participants benefited from the mixed social fabric of groups, teaching backgrounds, leadership roles and traditions of education in government and nongovernment systems in Victoria, interstate and abroad. International guests continued to feature and participants from Brunei attended.

The ITF program continued to offer enrichment. In the heyday of the 1980s it catered for up to 80 incoming and exiting teachers each year. 600 Fellows had experienced life in one of ten other countries since 1971. Rex Murfett reflected:

> Our student base was pretty diverse through immigration. With a large number of students from Greece, Yugoslavia, Croatia and Serbia, we wanted to assist their assimilation, let them see that teachers from their own countries were welcome here, and send our teachers over there. The real point of the ITF exchange program was to give our experienced teachers another view of education around the globe.[816]

In Canada, Fellows experienced darkness falling at 3.15 pm, and the cold of minus degrees. Some visited Great Bear Lake and those based at Port Radium travelled to school by bus with the miners. 'Back to basics' was common across the USA, as in Mohawke Valley where the results of regular standardised tests were published in the press. In that conservative district traditional teaching methods prevailed. Staff assembled at 7.50 am in California and the first students arrived at 8.20 am. Highly regulated days, tight curriculum and lack of concrete teaching materials required unfamiliar teaching techniques. Fellows located in Inner London faced cross-cultural and discipline problems. The reality that 'poorly qualified white boys and girls have a better chance of securing employment than better qualified blacks' was confronting. Elsewhere in Britain 'Bloody Saturday' occurred during the Brixton Riots. The 500 students involved were 50 per cent of the school population. A Fellow in a market town in France's Loire Valley felt a long way from home despite a French romance. The first Fellow to Macedonia, though 'transplanted' to Australia only fifteen years prior, was daunted by re-immersion in the culture and language. 'Communication and transport were fraught with difficulties ... I was looked on as a visitor despite my attempts to achieve worker status'. The ITF experience became comfort for some and challenge for others, coupled with a spirit of adventure for all as they thrust new frontiers. Learning about others, they learnt about self, and brought enrichment into their classrooms.[817]

The ITF and IEA programs gave great satisfaction in Shears' fulfilling career. Evolution of his vision outlined in the directional papers and address of current and emerging issues in the four reports marked his enduring dedication to education. From humble beginnings, the boy born on a kitchen table, educated in the government system and, by a twist of fate, introduced to the teaching profession, rose to top rank in education's hierarchy and brought others along in his wake. The exemplary service of this single man was dependent upon his team who jointly upheld loyalty to the Education Department and commitment to the teachers and those they taught. A fulfilling life and brilliant career, seeds sown were harvested; it was time to move on. Minister Fordham announced the retirement. The position of Coordinator-General created in 1981 would be abolished. He commended Shears' outstanding service.

## End of the road

'Education chief stepping down after pursuing his hobby for 45 years' *The Age* reported. 'End of the road for a pace-setter' it announced. Geoff Maslen reviewed Shears' career and the remarkable change he had engineered. To mark the announcement Shears visited Merri Primary School, his beloved Miller Street State School, where his teaching career began in 1939. Unlike then when rows of desks for 60 pupils cluttered Miss Pauline Knight's Grade 3 classroom, he perched on a chair midst a composite class of 21 children in Years 2 and 3.

Maslen marked Shears' key legacies as:

> ... giving local communities a greater say in the running of schools; giving school councils more powers and responsibilities; shifting power from the centre to the regions; introducing the International Teaching Fellowship ... and during the critical shortage of teachers in the early 1970s, supervising and hiring 3000 teachers from overseas.[818]

He noted Shears' working relationship with Thompson, his fall out of favor with Hunt; his removal and public reaction; and his caution not to spill the top posts. Shears served in the top three positions longer than any predecessors apart from Frank Tate. In tune with administrative trends Shears introduced change and presented new ideas that 'only now have gained wide currency and become part of the conventional wisdom of education'. Before the lingo became vogue, and before Hunt's sweeping change, Shears had established school and community discourse, initiated the devolutionary process and empowered school councils. Evolutionary not revolutionary, he sought solutions beyond the square and encouraged others to share his visions. Invariably, financial restraint or wariness of difference curtailed him. Highly visible and outspoken, he frequently ruffled feathers, most notably those of the VSTA and custodians of Commonwealth funds. Maslen reflected on events that affected Shears' undoing. Attempts by Hunt and Lacy to reshape the departmental pyramid were 'a shabby and shameful legislative device that avoided the government having to sack him'. He acknowledged Shears' preference for 'a job in the hand' rather than 'his life in the bush', his 'irrepressible optimism and good humour' with which he tackled the Coordinator-General's role, and the significance of the four reports.[819]

## Finale

The night of tributes: an affair to remember. Lee Dale and Hec Gallagher, Special Assistant to Director-General Curry, prepared the retirement function – a grand farewell at Camberwell Civic Centre, as Fred Brooks had received. The Civic Centre was full. Among 400 present were the notables of education and Parliament, plus guests from the RTC, teachers colleges and other career phases. Feeding them became a catering challenge when half the electric ovens failed. Cutting the beef into steaks turned possible disaster to triumph. Half the guests had steak the others roast beef with gravy.

In tribute to Shears Neville Barwick recalled the 'heady days' when education integrated trends from abroad; the optimism and innovation allied with expanding horizons. 'Lifelong education, community development and comprehensive services were being articulated.' He highlighted the emergence of participative processes and regionalism, and concerns regarding the transition from school to work. Management structures created dynamics, nourished by vision, opportunity and idealism. The potential 'education renaissance' aligned with technological change, but economic fluctuations, population growth and changing employment prospects had no single solution. Despite the stress that fraught others, Shears 'fairly sparkled'; despite dark days, he bounced back. It was sheer effervescence.

Recorded in a memento of L W Shears[820] presented on the night Hilma Cranley, former infant mistress (1933–75) and President of the Victorian Teachers' Union (1965–67), considered Shears was a 'true teacher, innovative, ahead of his time'. He was 'vitally concerned with practical teaching and in giving teachers opportunities to broaden their experience'. She claimed, 'we are indebted to him as an understanding practitioner in the teaching profession'.

David Mossenson, Chairman of the Secondary Education Authority in Western Australia, recalled Shears as the 'doughty protagonist resisting Federal inroads into State education … ever alert to all the implications' and 'always ready to defend the historic role of public systems'. Jack Ford, former DSE, stressed the international significance of his activities. Many enjoyed benefits arising from

'Shears-sponsored international relationships'. 'Consequences of his overseas contacts should linger in Victoria's list of credits'. Shears was skilled in the public and political arenas and Ford recalled how he negotiated between 'employer, employed, public, politicians and press'. In pursuit of this he surely knew 'loneliness as he searched for others who believed'. A 'power-house for progress', his cleverness and courage buoyed his doubters, countered his attackers and guaranteed his ability to rebound.

'LAWRIE SHEARS EDUCATION WRECKER' painted in black on a railway bridge evoked Ron Reed's memories. On becoming Director-General Shears had 'plunged immediately into a period of restlessness, angry and uncertain change that might well have taken as its symbol a perambulating guillotine looking for heads'. He not only survived but also directed the restless energy to benefit education. In football terms 'Lawrie scored many educational goals, but he also kicked a few behinds.'

Joe St Ellen and Ken Sargeant reflected on teachers college days. St Ellen recalled the contribution of Shears, Laurie Bell and Ron Burton at Toorak Teachers College, when they devised a new course and systematically investigated the teaching styles employed. In the 1950s research dissemination was not easy so Shears persuaded the VIER to establish the *Journal of Education*. First published in July 1954, it was a forerunner of the *Australian Journal of Education*. Even at that stage Principal Frank Lord predicted the 'little doctor' would become a 'future Director of Education'. Sargeant recalled the startled reaction of staff to the Burwood Statement, its examination of the courses and of itself. Preparation of new courses in response provoked staff to move beyond years of complacency. Of the 'Golden Years' at Burwood he recalled good fellowship and sparkling conversation, and the close-knit purposeful group of staff and students, supported by well-placed loyalties. Shears' fresh ideas enthused the entire community; his warmth and friendship were treasured.

On behalf of the College of Nursing Australia Pat Slater acknowledged Shears' contributions. He guided the 'small struggling institution on a shoestring budget, with a handful of students and staff' to become a 'well-funded college of advanced education, affiliated with the Victoria Institute of Colleges, and [having] two thriving branches in Perth and Brisbane'. Slater admitted arguments with Shears but with common goals she learnt to be 'flexible in dealing with current issues and problems and to alter programs and structures in the light of new information, while maintaining direction'. His 'unfailing optimism' inspired members of the profession to bring nurse training into mainstream higher education. Above all she admired his 'humanness' unequivocal sensitivity to others, and his wise leadership.

Colin Moyle, Director of the IEA, spoke of Shears' leadership, vision and personal qualities:

> [He] exemplified the fundamental human qualities of integrity, dedication, openness and creativity for one who holds wide-ranging leadership positions. Nowhere has this been more apparent than in his commitment to the development and growth of the Institute of Educational Administration.
>
> Projecting into the future, he predicted that administration would become increasingly complex and challenging. The IEA residential complex, soon to be completed in Geelong, will serve as a tangible reminder, to all who served with Lawrie for decades, of the indefatigable, feisty and visionary leadership he has given to a variety of institutions and trailblazing projects.

Lawrie as administrator, educator and man was signalled in all accolades. Doug Swan, Director-General of Education in New South Wales, recalled a particular meeting in Canberra. He observed 'a man who cared about people, his staff and the pupils in schools ... I was there when he was put to the test – and passed.' In 1983 fires had ripped through Aireys Inlet, taking the Shears' house and its treasures:

> Lawrie's thoughts were only for those less fortunate than he, those who had lost their only home ... I saw no self interest, no self pity ... I saw and witnessed his great concern for others.' It was a rare opportunity to 'know that much of the educational rhetoric which we preach and teach was real for at least one man.'

Absent that evening was Lindsay Thompson. He was overseas but he wrote that Shears had 'occupied every conceivable post with the exception of two, Infant Mistress and School Cleaner'. He committed dedication and distinction to every role, and an impact that usually brought about progress and desirable change.' Thompson concluded:

> His career, without doubt, was an outstanding one. Any impartial historian writing a history of the Education Department in the years to come will undoubtedly give a very prominent place to the name of – Lawrence William Shears, BA, BCom, BEd, PhD (London), FACE, FAIM, ABPsS, MAPsS, BWD (To the ignorant and uninitiated, BWD stands for 'bloody well done').

## In response

*In appreciation* of those present Shears acknowledged politicians, educationists, community leaders, friends and family who embodied the scope of his life from school days, teachers college, service to education and other organisations in which he was involved.

*In praise* of Mavis he described the school leaver who entered the typing pool after secretarial training. As a banker's daughter she had moved from town to town, and as the wife of a roving educationist she had journeyed with children to England and the USA by ship and across the USA by car. In her life's journey she returned to study, matriculated, and with a BA with Honours and a DipEd became a teacher and linguist. A hostess on numerous occasions she was above all his companion and friend.

*In thanks* for his own opportunity he considered the influence of school: the teachers at Windsor State School, Mr Vroland at Elsternwick State School and Stanton Sharman at University High. School was a haven for achievement and friendship for the lonely only child. As a student teacher at Miller Street, engagement with children nurtured his love of people, satisfied his yearning for companionship and sense of being worthwhile. He remained forever grateful that:

> I struck a Head teacher and staff who worked hard to make the student teacher system a success and who created an environment that when I looked inward on my heart and mind I found children and people – there was no need to

look further on my career. Since then, there have been many times in teaching when I have experienced that remarkable moment of successful relating, of successful teaching when, in Buber's words, 'the Holy spark leaps across the gap', that despite the calls of commerce and business, I knew there could be no change.

*In retrospect* he contemplated the building of bridges. Like a dream coming true he had witnessed members of educational and allied associations support 'the professionals in the advancement of parent/community/teacher/child relationships'. Though the thrust was well on the way he counselled, 'the school and its total community' movement 'must be encouraged and nurtured'. Likewise he promoted the 'valiant attempt to reduce barriers between the different facets of education provision'.

*On reflection* of 30 years administering, policy-making, leading and creating, the final fifteen were the most daunting. Decisions affected so many lives in the day-to-day organisation of pupils, teachers and schools, and programs to enrich and support. He highlighted the ITF program, the IEA, the Drama Resource Centre and the Equal Opportunity Unit, which augmented teachers' knowledge and improved educational provision.

*In recalling* the trajectory of his life he found himself remembering a series of images:

> *Bairnsdale*: a city teacher in the bush; boating on the Mitchell River; youth and sports associations; Mavis the major prize.
>
> *Dookie days*: 100+ diploma students and 1000+ completing short courses; farm practice, 'elevenses' when horses, carts, drays, tractors and men gathered Huffam Hut.
>
> *London*: doctoral studies.
>
> *Toorak and Burwood Teachers Colleges*: their struggle for course status yet the certainty of 'intellectual stimulation, argument, warmth and understanding'.
>
> *The Golden Days at Burwood*: coined by Ron Ginger at a farewell gathering the week before.
>
> *Administration*: when one removed oneself from easy access

to people but decisions made profoundly affected more

*Farewell Fred Brooks*: eleven years before and the beginning of a 'unique, out of this world experience yet one which was most fruitful and rewarding'. Diverse prior experience, such as his, was a solid grounding.

*In respect* to colleagues he contemplated, 'people who are at the heart of the movement are so numerous and so dedicated they are often overlooked'. Though most remained nameless he expressed thanks to them all, identified the leadership team of Deputy Tom, Assistants Alan, Ray, Neville, Stewart, and Barry, Directors of the teaching and administrative divisions, and the Policy Committee. At the heart of achievement lay 'integration of home, work and play as a firm basis for a satisfying life for the individual and highly productive for the team and individuals in it'.

*In recognition* of successors, he praised their worth: Fordham whose service as Shadow Minister prepared him for the Ministerial mantle; Curry a 'man of purpose and high ideals and a capacity for hard work and devotion to the cause'; Graham Allen, Chairman VPSEC, Peter Kirby, Director of TAFE and Ken McKinnon whose 'broad experience and intelligence [were] guiding the first steps of the State Board'.

*In praise* of tertiary education he acknowledged his alma mater, gave thanks for his grounding and the reference written by the late George Browne that established his doctoral candidature. He commended the pioneering efforts of Richard Selby-Smith, Ron Goldman and their staffs who established schools of education at Monash and Latrobe. He was thankful for his involvement in each and the position he held on both university councils and recalled the drama when locked in the council chamber by disgruntled students. He marvelled at the phenomenal expansion of tertiary provision through new universities, colleges of advanced education and TAFE institutions. In addition to communication between educational sectors he sought 'interface between education, the world of business, commerce, industry and the Trade Unions ... recriminations arise out of ignorance, and dialogue is essential'.

*In contemplation* of the intimate groups with which he served he recalled the 'dedicated unselfish people who have provided an incomparable and varied range of experience and added a dimension of riches of inestimable value not only to me but to the causes they serve'. Since entering teachers college he had kept in touch with the College 1941-ers, some of whom joined the VIER, which provided the 'cheapest in-service education for teachers'. The ACE had waved 'the flag of unity in education through all the states and across all barriers', the College of Nursing blazed the trail for college-based programs and the Duke of Edinburgh's Award Committee celebrated contributions of the young. Through association with St John's, Toorak, he understood that 'faith and accompanying peace which passes all understanding' have provided 'inner strength to cope with external difficulties when they have occurred.'

*In respect* to the four reports, he considered them timely. It was an 'excellent precedent' to send a senior administrator 'out to pasture to investigate an activity of importance to government without the other administrative work around his neck yet with access to top-level contacts built up over the years'.

*In retrospect*, he was thankful for family and lifelong friends 'who admit no pretence, allow no ego-trips, yet provide the continuity and normality essential to a life highly geared and connected to long and sustained public exposure'.

*In appreciation* of the grandeur of the occasion he likened it to the Opening of the 1956 Olympic Games. The gathering of people represented different groups that held different ethos and values. He recognised the 'common bond which binds us ... the advancement of our community through education, through lifelong education, through continued and integrated education'.

He recited words that had shadowed his life:

> A dog has looked at you, you answer for its glance
> A child has clutched your hand, you answer for its touch
> A host of men move about you, you answer for their need.

In conclusion he added, 'If I have answered the need of some of that host of men, women and children I am well content'. [821]

Melbourne,

23rd September, 1969.

*It is submitted for the approval of His Excellency the Governor in Council that* in pursuance of the powers conferred under the provisions of Section 4 of the Education Act 1958 he will appoint Lawrence William Shears, B.A., B.Com., B.Ed., Ph.D. to be an Assistant Director General of Education at a salary at the rate of $13,000 per annum from and including the 29th September, 1969.

Dinner Party 29 September 1984

Minister of Education.

BY THE GOVERNOR IN COUNCIL
23 SEP 1969

CLERK OF THE EXECUTIVE COUNCIL

GAZETTE
-1 OCT 1969

**Remembering the official appointment of Shears as ADGE**
[Shears personal collection]

*At a special dinner following the grand farewell, guests signed the letter officially appointing Shears as ADGE 15 years previously*

CHAPTER 18

# BEYOND (1984– )

*Now this is not the end. It is not even the beginning of the end.*
*But it is, perhaps, the end of the beginning.*

Winston Churchill, November 1942[822]

## Taking stock

Political, economic and social change had reshaped the nation. The increasing momentum within Shears' lifetime shifted the economy base from agriculture and manufacturing. Traditional technical training became obsolete and employment patterns changed. The recent reports presented to Fordham stressed the need for curriculum review, urgency to address policies for youth and post-compulsory schooling, and acceptance of new technologies in schools. These corresponded with the Blackburn Report (1985)[823] apropos post-compulsory schooling and proposals to bond general and vocational streams. The Quality of Education in Australia Review Committee (1985) argued for the expansion of senior curriculum to embrace new knowledge, and emphasised the need for better-educated, innovative and receptive teachers in response to technological advance. It stressed equity across social groups and circumstances, and the community role in the education spectrum.

Opportunity for every child in the hands of caring, qualified teachers in communities that put 'power where the action is' was central to Shears' ideal. During 40 years' service he laid foundations for this, and shaped policies that influenced the State's education system. With each turn of the page he had played a part: the war years and post-war expansion; provision and training of teachers; devolution of power through school council governance by principals, teachers, parents and pupils; and the movement to bring closer together the school and the community. He had led a diverse team that stirred the Department and carried bureaucracy to support essential change. With this in motion he remained optimistic and looked ahead.

## Looking forward

In the opening address at the 4th National Conference of the Australian Association for Community Education in December 1984 Shears considered 'The challenge to change'. He cited the certainty, posed 'What is desirable?' and mused:

> ... isolation of teachers, parents, community members and community educators from one another would be disastrous ... members are growing more and more in need of support as the fabric of their lives grows more complex. Breaking down these barriers and building a new edifice based on co-operation is one major goal for our future.[824]

Invited to present the 32nd Frank Tate Memorial Lecture he pondered 'Reflections of an optimist – a future for education', and argued:

> A future is the past modified by the present and given a special magnetism by our hopes and aspirations. Futures for all things suffer from the pressures of tradition, habit and a general resistance to change. In education these include the conservatism of parents and teachers, the reluctance of politicians, including teacher politicians, to risk the result of the next election, the restricted expectations and requirements which the private sector have of education, and the reflection of all these on administrative practices.

At last, the man who had organised the first eight Frank Tate Memorial Lectures was honoured to speak. Following those chaired by Professors Brown and Frederick and Dr Tom Coates, since 1961 Shears had chaired 22 of the next 24. On this night of nights the Tate family 'gathered to listen and honour the memory of Frank Tate – a great scholar, educator, administrator, teacher, patriot and person.'

The address tackled change that affected educational advance. *Political influences* had modified the Westminster system; Ministers added 'administrative function to their policy role'. Political heads were 'on stage' and 'backstage' and subject to party politics. This he considered unsettling for 'children who are trying to learn, teachers who are trying to teach and parents and the business community who are trying to understand and participate'. *Personal influences*, as espoused at Burwood TC, relationships shared among students, teachers, parents and community must prevail. 'Put power where the action is,' he decreed, and challenged the school and its community unit to turn outward rather than inward. He saw administrative shifts taking place, set in motion by his policies. The regions and subsidiary authorities facilitated local administrative zones wherein collaboration avoided duplication of human and fiscal resources. *Industrial, material* and *technical influences* likewise influenced education, the purpose of which exceeded that of 'cramming students [and teachers] into little boxes' as if 'all are equally endowed in various aspects of human behaviour'. He observed education 'tottering a little further along the road to the recognition of individual differences in our practices as well as in our pronouncements'. Present too were *Spiritual influences* wherein 'religious experience, morality, the application of a value system, or the expression of human emotions' fused to shape belief systems.

Shears stressed the vital role of the VIER in educational research but saw new fields of need. He assumed a continuum of learning from Prep to Year 14, academic and technical distinctions renounced, and provision at all levels combined. It was mandatory that 'skills and knowledge 'of tomorrow's workforce' were 'broadly generic rather than fitting any specific occupation category'. He enumerated the four Ministerial reports and five policy papers and challenged the audience to ponder 28 ideals.[825]

## New ventures

Shears remained loyal to his various committees and professional groups and the other people involved in them. Equally, members of these fraternities held him in high regard. Everyone knew him or knew about him. His high profile drew interest, and other organisations sourced his skill, knowledge and networks. On retirement at just 63 he was ripe for new challenge.

Soon after Shears left Treasury Place, Dr Peter Tannock, Chairman of the Schools Commission since 1980, employed him to conduct a review of over 30 Commonwealth-sponsored education centres. The sense of community was crucial in the nationwide network, particularly in remote regions. Initiated by teachers, parents and local groups to overcome social and professional isolation, the network of centres expanded rapidly after the delivery of the Karmel Report (1973). 'They served a function for teachers outside the bureaucracy' (i.e. those not working full-time in schools, perhaps working part-time, seconded to organisations outside the Department etc.), provided in-service training, curriculum support and consultancy, and became a 'catalyst for organizing and supporting teachers and parents working towards the betterment of schools'.[826]

Supported by a committee of three, Shears undertook the evaluation of the centres between August and December 1984. Accompanied by a committee member, Shears visited each centre in turn to review its relationship with the Schools Commission as well as its management, maintenance and commitment to staffing, facilities and programs. The review probed State and Commonwealth roles, identified community attitudes to the centres and circulated a questionnaire. The 'long and arduous task … produced some vigorous forthright discussion' but the tight schedule to present the report on 14 December 1984 made the process a 'hectic run'.[827] Funding cuts that eventually closed the network 'broke an important link and placed little value on the successful local partnerships'.[828] Finished by Christmas, Shears undertook a new mission. The second consultancy took him to the Solomon Islands where daughter Meredith and her husband were volunteers. Employed by the R E Ross Trust, a perpetual charitable trust established in Victoria in 1970, Shears was charged to select good secondary students for 'residential positions at Melbourne Grammar School or Geelong College'. He doubted the success of this and imagined the culture shock and awkward transition from an island community to the privileged private school system. 'What are they going to do when they get back to their village?' he asked. He proposed the program address the primary to secondary transition and subsequently the continuation of schooling. Training was the key, and selected teachers completed specialist programs at either the IEA or Hawthorn Institute of Education. Subsequently the Ross Trust Board extended the program to teachers in Vanuatu and Western Samoa and in successive years approximately five Fellows were trained annually at the IEA and up to fifteen as technical teachers at Hawthorn. The Trade Education Project begun in 1973 became the RE Ross Fellowship Program in which adults from South Pacific islands undertook short-term study to enhance their instruction techniques and trade skills. From 2005 the focus shifted to supporting health professionals undertake study at Melbourne's Royal Children's Hospital.[829]

Post-retirement activities had a low profile and were short-lived. From 1983 Shears chaired the AEC History Committee until the launch of *A History of the Australian Education Council 1936–1986* in 1987. He worked with a small committee and credited Alby Jones, former Director-General in South Australia, who scrupulously read the drafts. He noted the support of Ron Browne, Peter Tannock, and Andrew Spaull, author.[830] 'Life. Be in It'[831] posed another interesting task. A concept cultivated in collaboration between the Hon. Brian Dixon, Assistant Minister of Education, and the Education Department in 1975, the Commonwealth adopted the program in 1978 but withdrew funds in 1981. Thenceforth it became a community organisation. Ian Bennett, formerly of the Education Department, then the program's Chief Executive, invited Shears to join the board. Roused by commitment to youth development and health education, and keen to maintain his public image, he welcomed the opportunity.

Integration of education, health and community services lingered in Shears' psyche; thus he was enticed by plans to establish the Baranduda community near Wodonga. Like the Heidelberg model established in 1946, the proposal embraced community educational, recreational, cultural and health services. Though the Baranduda project failed to generate interest, later developments emulated the concept. Reliant on independent financial support, private enterprise activity such as this lay outside the system that Shears had known. Regardless of semblance, his expertise and connections in education did not always relate. Proposals for a residential conference facility near Alexandra also failed to reach fruition, the Australian Youth Olympic Program fizzled out, and the development of Agribusiness with entrepreneur Doug Shears (no relative) despite the verve of colleague Deborah Towns, came to nought. However, he maintained a public profile, wrote to the newspapers and frequently aired his views.

Meanwhile, steady advance in computer technology alerted educationists to consider computer use in schools. Postulation that computers would have greater impact than earlier technologies prompted ACER to undertake a 12-month study in 1994. Chairman of the investigative committee, Shears saw computers had potential to transform work and leisure. He argued that computer literacy was essential and 'there was no point involving computers with teachers unless the teachers were sufficiently trained'.[832] For the duration of the study ACER provided the institutional base while Toshiba (Aust.) Pty Ltd offered financial support and supplied 25 laptops to each of ten schools. After a nine-month trial, teachers and principals completed a questionnaire. The rising use of computers was initiating social change. As with all innovations, cost created a gap between schools embracing computers and schools that did not. School characteristics, student use at home and at school, and use by teachers for teaching were among the problems to be faced. Mismatch between teacher and student knowledge was apparent. The invitation to conduct the study and work with colleagues at ACER meant kudos for Shears. ACER Chairman Barry McGaw welcomed the vitality Shears brought to the study and to the others involved. McGaw noted the personal phone calls Shears made to get responses, his 'warmth to encourage and the confidence to cajole', and his insistence that 'quality is produced and deadlines [are] met'.[833]

Since his rise to senior administration, Shears had entered

appointments in small pocket diaries. He frequently jested the preference to be minus his trousers rather than his diary. In his diaries he recorded meetings and conferences, lunches with friends and members of various organisations, birthdays, celebrations, contact details, Rotary lunches, fireside chats, annual dinners and reunions. Functions at Burwood TC and, from 1996, those held at the RTC he held most dear.

Throughout the 1990s Shears regularly attended St John's and in 1994 took charge of the organ restoration appeal. Built in 1913 by Hill & Son in London, its tonal qualities were distorted by the installation of an electro-pneumatic mechanism and oak case modification in 1960. Supported by the National Trust, the appeal raised $300,000 to restore the organ to its original specifications.

Among other activities marked in the diary were functions for Korowa, the IEA, the ITFP, VIER and the Duke of Edinburgh's Award Committee. A mentoring project at Montague Special School helped young people's quest to achieve the Duke of Edinburgh's Bridge Award. Shears welcomed appointments to act as Director, Health Education Seminar, Doctors and Nurse Educators (1987); member, St John Ambulance Marketing Committee (1990–98); and Chairman, Australian Red Cross National Committee for International Humanitarian Law (1990–94). He kept dutifully busy but his public profile faded from media prominence.

Over the years he met friends and associates at celebrations, retirements and final farewells. Bill Moore, Lou Barberis, Ron Ginger, Noel Watkins and Colin Moyle retired in 1986 or 1987. Geoff Stevens and Ted Liefmann turned 70 in 1990, Lou Barberis took his turn the following year, and Ken Sargeant turned 80 in 1993. Sadness struck in 1993–94 with the deaths of Uncle Stan, Mavis' sister Betty and his granddaughter Layla, aged two.

By the early 1990s 'the children had vanished' from the family home in Hopetoun Road. After 25 years there were just 'two of us rattling around in 57 squares'. A sea change in the truest sense came about when Shears and Mavis shifted to Aireys Inlet. They became involved in community activities and St Aidan's church, rebuilt after the Ash Wednesday bushfires, although Shears attended St John's regularly for several years. Twice he and Mavis travelled abroad, reunited with family and renewed friendships. On extended visits to the city the Melbourne Club became a home away from home. When Mavis was hospitalised and diagnosed with cancer, the Melbourne Club was his refuge. Her sudden death in 1999 left him a lonely man.

## Looking back

In the cottage at Aireys Inlet, Lawrie sits on his leather chair, one of a pair. Outside cockatoos squawk in the scraggly gums. Blue wrens dart on the grass and magpies scavenge for worms. His diary and *The Age* lie on the table nearby and he reads a draft of this biography. He pauses to contemplate, then comments that the directional papers are his most significant contributions he believes.

On the dining room table are other reminders: the Annual Conference of the Australian College of Educators in June 2013 and the dinner at which Barry Jones speaks; the Len Falk Memorial Lecture in Morwell; the RTC reunion and the 33rd reunion of the liveliest program group that went through the IEA (Program 8, July 1980) both in September; a letter sent at Christmas by a foundation student at Burwood TC. After almost 60 years she dares to call him 'Lawrie'. From the US where she lives she will attend the October reunion. An ex-serviceman gives a change of address into residential care, and another is unable to make the reunion. In a photo Shears poses with Education Minister Peter Hall at the government reception for International Teaching Fellows in 2013. On the sideboard is a view from the top of Mt Major, and on the mantelpiece are family photos.

Shears reflects. The Office of the Director-General, instituted in 1973, preceded a series of changes outlined in the policy papers. The administrative structure triggered later moves towards decentralisation of power. He remembers the team and contributions of each individual. The regional structure transformed administration; power vested in regional officers was a direct link with schools and their communities. In turn, authority given to school councils gave budgetary discretion. Correspondingly, school and community borders softened.

Small-group function, embodied in his doctoral research, was fundamental to residential leadership training. The IEA's state-of-the-art centre opened in January 1985 brought a dream to fruition. Envisaged in the Liberals' heyday, the Labor government 'built it, set it up and got it going'. Advocates claimed it second-to-none while opponents asserted the 'memorial to Lawrie Shears' produced a 'cult of leadership that was potentially elitist'.[834] Although successors endorsed the IEA and its programs, residential training drew to an end. The cost of running the $3 million complex for 52 weeks exceeded the hire of a motel for its four-week programs. Victim to Premier Kennett's economic restraints, the IEA building was sold to the Salvation Army in 1996. Shears rues this unfortunate event.

Upon retirement Shears looked forward to spending time with Mavis. Although their time together was punctuated by his official interests, they travelled extensively, twice abroad and several trips throughout Australia. When at Aireys Inlet they walked together, hand in hand, along the cliff tops, across tidal plateaus of rocks and vast stretches of beach. When Mavis died the world stopped. Life had no meaning. His soulmate was gone. Family and friends supported him through dark days of mourning but loneliness lingered.

Over the years friends and colleagues passed on too – Ted Liefman (2005), Lou Barberis (2005) then Geoff Stevens, Lee Dale, Tom Moore, Phillip Law and Lindsay Thompson. He paid tribute to each of them in lengthy death notices in *The Age* that detailed their contributions to education in Victoria. The loss of Lindsay saddened him particularly. In that notice he reflected on the intertwining of their personal and professional lives:

> When you worked with a man like Lindsay Thompson you were certain of wisdom, vision, foresight and understanding, particularly of the needs of children. He was quickly in command of new ideas and sought to obtain the means to bring them to reality. I met him first in 1955 and it was a satisfying pleasure to be involved with him in the overseas recruitment program, the International Teaching Fellowship, now in its 37th year, regionalisation, school councils and their communities, training of principals, improved conditions for teachers, and a whole series of advances which

typified the 1970s. A fine gentleman in manners, always in control of himself, the STATE of Victoria and Education generally is deeply in his debt.

Of Lou Barberis he wrote, 'His Principalship of Melbourne High School was a triumph of his personal ability, compassion and understanding', and of Tom Moore, 'He valued the history, achievements and traditions of the Victorian Education system to which he made a most significant contribution'.

On the death of Phillip Law he wrote:

> A fine man of adventurous nature and determination he successfully pushed boundaries. It was a privilege to work with one whose foresight, command and true leadership led the Victorian Institute of Colleges (VIC) as Vice President and many other activities. His legacy in education stands particularly in the strength and status of institutions associated with the VIC.

And of Lee Dale he said, 'An outstanding colleague, she acted with aplomb in multiple roles across the spectrum of education ... A fine lady who contributed greatly to education in Victoria.'

## Kaleidoscope of life

He ponders. Friendships mark milestones. As though viewing a newsreel, his life screens before him: homes in Newry and Pakington Streets, family, childhood, Windsor and Elsternwick State Schools and University High. At each his teachers boosted him on. Spellbound at Miller Street State School, teaching became his career. Guided by illustrious staff at teachers college and university, in time it was his turn to inspire in classrooms and communities in Korong Vale and Bairnsdale. At the RTC he played a vital role in the rehabilitation of ex-servicemen, where his service to them allayed his remorse for not being able to serve. His contributions were noted and references that supported his doctoral studies at the Institute of Education gave entrée to renowned educational psychology researchers. The opportunity to experience other education systems and design a study of small groups shaped philosophies that he imparted to others. Back home he leapt ahead of the pack. Teachers college lectureships preceded advance to Survey and Planning. He gained insight into the entire education system, met the 'who's who' in the chain of command. Aged 38 he assembled among Foundation members of the Australian College of Education. Aged 39, as a Harkness Fellow, he scoured the education scene in the United States, met a network of deans, and witnessed major development in education and massive social reforms. In Britain he observed progress since the McNair Report (1944) and philosophies that had underpinned the Robbins Report (1944).

A proud moment it was when he took command at Burwood TC where he ignited the 'holy spark'. He fostered relationships among staff, students and teachers in training schools and the bond between theory and practice. Pivotal was the drive to promote the status of teachers colleges and boost teachers' qualifications. He encouraged research and participation in professional groups and travel to broaden teachers' minds. The Victorian Teacher Selection Program and the International Teaching Fellowship nurtured understanding, united peoples and wakened participants to the world beyond the classroom and to another educational ethos. These initiatives also provided teachers when the shortage in Victoria was dire.

From murmurings of the mind he jolts back to the present. Meredith drops by from time to time. He's just a 20-minute drive from her home so she keeps check. As her father was, she is employed in education, in fact by the Department of Education and Early Childhood Development, the Education Department under a new guise. Her focus is on youth and post-school pathways. Shears bred a family of teachers with Meredith, Mark and Christine joining the ranks. The highlight for Mark was his time at Williamstown High where he supported the down and outers. Linguist and musician Christine taught secondary English – 'very well', people recall. Working now as a private tutor she still gains respect and as a musician she earns global applaud. Paul became an engineer, metallurgical; then putting that aside became an entrepreneur in the photography field. Family photos on the mantelpiece show the family at key life stages and grandchildren now grown and building careers of their own.

On their Great Ocean Road escapades friends visit too. He recalls Alan and Mavis Wilcox dropping by and a wonderful day with Kevin and Dorothy Collins when they dined together. Annually Robyn Whiteley and John Collins pause for coffee and a chat. As the book takes shape they have so much to share. Cousin Barbara Brand makes fortnightly visits. She and Lawrie talk and talk, drive to the lighthouse, the coalmine or Lorne and have lunch. Like others, she makes frequent phone calls.

BALMORAL CASTLE

25 August, 2004

Dear Dr. Shears,

I have been told that you are retiring from membership of the State Award Committee of Victoria after 31 years' service. This is a remarkable record of commitment and I am quite sure that everyone involved in the Australian Award would like me to send you an expression of gratitude and appreciation for your exceptionally valuable contribution to the success of the Award in Australia.

I also have no doubt that there are many young people in Australia who have every reason to be grateful to you for the chance the Award has given them to make a difference to their lives.

Yours sincerely,

Philip

*Letter of apprecation from the Duke of Edinburgh [Shears personal collection]*

Reminders of his life fill the room: photographs of family, the fireplace set by son Mark who died in 2011. In the study a seascape painted along the Great Ocean Road by Burwood colleague Chris White was a gift on retirement. Books stacked on overflowing shelves run the length of the room. The history-filled library holds books from school, student teacher notes, his theses and those of others nurtured. There are Mavis' recipe books, sequential copies of the *VIER Bulletin* (rarely found elsewhere), poems by TS Eliot and Browning, anthologies, Shakespearian works and numerous books he has read. On the opposite wall his portrait depicts a contemplative pose. Beside it is a letter signed *Philip*, Duke of Edinburgh, acknowledging his contribution to the Duke of Edinburgh's Award. There's a photograph taken with Her Majesty at Royal Park in 1977 as part of her Silver Jubilee celebrations. She asked, 'Will you give the children a holiday?' On the small corner table in a velvet box is the Sir James Darling Medal. Awarded in 2009, it celebrates Shears' contributions to the ACE and, more importantly, his legacies to education. Honorary Life Membership of AARE also honours his worth.

'Has my life been worthwhile?' he asks.

'Yes,' others reply.

They see a reformer, a rationaliser rather than a revolutionary, who introduced progressive change. They acknowledge a man of vision, integrity and competence. Responsive to wider educational developments and aware of movements underway, he saw how they might be applied. A pragmatist and an able manager with a clear sense of vision as to what education should be about, he opened the black box of an internalised system. They witnessed the movement to displace centralisation and supported the belief that power shared was responsive and less likely abused. Shears endeavoured to shape a system with:

> ... teachers as educators and parents as contributors ... everybody could make a contribution whether they were parents or janitors or whoever, if they were making a contribution to State education they were part of his team.[835]

Described by Philip Law as the 'Father of Education', Shears was dedicated, committed, showed care and concern. He believed in the system and the people within, had faith, held a clear sense of vision that he ably pursued. Though seen as tenacious he was able to flex; though a good listener he didn't cave in; he remained steadfast and 'he gave us an awful lot'. Hard steps to follow, he laid the foundations and others continued the educational evolution. 'Footsteps of his leadership remain embedded … the basis for things done now, the improvements.'[836] Multiple images through the eyes of others expose a complex man, admired for what he pursued. Even former contenders hold him dear, as revealed in the grip of a handshake and intensity when eyes connect. On his lap is a book with a loose page marking the place – an announcement of the 'Lawrie Shears Lecture and Doctoral Scholarship', an honour endowed by the 'Department' and bankmecu, the bank that grew out of a teachers' credit union.

He sighs, he shuts the book, his eyelids droop. Of education, his life and worth he ponders.

> This above all: to thine own self be true,
> And it must follow, as the night the day,
> Thou canst not then be false to any man.[837]

# ENDNOTES

## Chapter 1

1. According to the *Port Phillip Gazette*, Wednesday, 12 December 1841, the barque *Alan Kerr* docked at Williams Town on 10 December.
2. Register of ships arriving in Port Phillip in 1841 details the captain, crew and passengers, http://search.slv.vic.gov.au/primo_library/libweb/action/dlDisplay.do?vid=MAIN&reset_config=true&docId=SLV_VOYAGER1635770; R Broome, *The Victorians: Arriving*, Fairfax, Syme & Weldon Associates, McMahons Point, 1984, considers the time taken for the journey pp. 52–3.
3. A Dingle, *The Victorians: Settling*, Fairfax, Syme & Weldon Associates, McMahons Point, 1984, p. 48.
4. H McCrae (ed.), *Georgiana's Journal: Melbourne a Hundred Years Ago*, Angus & Robertson, Sydney, 1934, pp. 7–23.
5. Description of Collins Street, 1841, www.melbourne.vic.gov.au/AboutMelbourne/History/Pages/Streetsandroads.aspx.
6. As described by R Annear in *Bearbrass: Imagining Early Melbourne*, Vintage, Milson's Point, 1995; Georgiana McCrae describes the tendency of indigenous people to use language to indicate flowing, such as the tidal flow at the river's mouth, McCrae, 1934, p. 31.
7. The city was founded in 1835 by John Batman and officially named in 1836. Almost a century later, in 1934, the Duke of Gloucester visited 'to commemorate the centenary of the State of Victoria and the founding of the City of Melbourne'. He launched celebrations on 18 October and they concluded with a parade through the city on 19 November. http://australianscreen.com.au/titles/centenary-celebrations/clip1/. The report in the *Port Phillip Gazette* claims that in 1841 the population doubled in two years http://home.vicnet.net.au/~pioneers/pppg5bl.htm. Broome's figures differ (p. 57) as do records of the Catholic Church that calculate the population of Port Phillip as 11,638 with 2,411 being Catholics. The great expansion is in line with Cochrane's review of the population of the colony between 1836 and 1941 when it rose from 77,000 to 130,856. During the same period the ratio of free people to convicts rose from 2:1 to 4:1 – P Cochrane, *Colonial Ambition: Foundations of Australian Democracy*, Melbourne University Press, Carlton, 2006, p. 10.
8. McCrae, 1934, p. 54.
9. http://www.ballaratgenealogy.org.au/art/loddon.htm#SQUAT.
10. Dingle, p. 48; Georgiana's recounting of Aleck Hunter's writing suggests 'men to be had for £25, women from £10 to £15', which is a slight variation (McCrae, 1934, p. 25). Her record of the sale of her cow and calf bringing £100 helps to demonstrate the conditions on board ship when the minimal space was shared with stock.

11  Broome, p. 57, describes the hardships faced by immigrant workers at the time.
12  Cochrane, pp. 44, 63, 65, looks at sufferings during the depression years.
13  http://www.germanaustralia.com/e/chron/chron3.htm.
14  L Blake (ed.) *Vision and Realisation: A Centenary History of State Education in Victoria*, 3 vols, Education Department of Victoria, Melbourne, 1973, vol. 1, pp. 154–8, gives an account of Industrial and Reformatory Schools.
15  A Hird, *Limited Tenure*, self-published, Melbourne, circa 1985, p. 7, describes his parents' journey by horse and gig with three young children. They left the goldfields in Heathcote to go to Sandy Creek in Victoria's northeast and camped beside the road.
16  E Anderson, oral history interview conducted by the author, 2008.
17  R Selleck, *Frank Tate: A Biography*, Melbourne University Press, Carlton, 1982, pp. 210–30, describes in detail the fervour as men and women rushed to enlist, describes the war as it unfolded, and the serious loss suffered by individuals and the nation. He lists the contributions of the school community, inspired by the Director, Frank Tate.
18  This description typified the patterns of selection as settlement fanned eastward from South Australia, westward from Port Phillip and northward from Portland Bay. Many selectors were Australian-born of English and German descent. Among 320 names listed in L Blake and K Lovett *Wimmera Shire Centenary: An Historical Account*, Shire of Wimmera, Horsham, 1962, p. 59, approximately half were of German origin.
19  http://www.swvic.org/byaduk/byaduk_pioneers.htm.
20  M Clyne, *Community Languages: the Australian Experience*, Cambridge University Press, Cambridge, 1991.
21  Public records have alternative spellings: Byaduk or Viaduct and Madeline or Madlean.
22  http://en.wikipedia.org/wiki/Battle_of_Grand_Port.
23  Catherine's record states departure from Cork on 5 December, a week earlier than the shipping record shows.
24  *Sydney Gazette*, 12 August 1815, states the ships' departure date from Cork as 5 December.
25  ibid.

## Chapter 2

26  *The Education Act* 1872 (No. 447), An Act to amend the Law relating to Education, 17 December 1872, to come into operation on 1 January 1873; *The Common Schools Act* (No. 149) repealed from 31 December 1872; section 5.
27  Selleck, 1982, notes the professionalism of departmental employees, p. 19.
28  *The Education Act* (1872), section 3.
29  ibid., section 12.
30  Goold was appointed Archbishop of the Melbourne Diocese in 1874, a position he held until 1886.
31  Report to the Committee on State Education in Victoria (Ramsay Report), 1960, p. 11.
32  Selleck's 1982 summation of Tate's attitude during his years as inspector (1895–99) based at Charlton in Victoria's northwest.
33  Attitude expressed by John Robertson, reported by Selleck, 1982, p. 31. Robertson was later appointed an inspector. According to D Holloway, *The Inspectors*, The Insti-

tute of Senior Officers of the Victorian Education Services Incorporated, Melbourne, 2000, p. 154, Robertson was a constant critic of authority.

34  Blake, vol. 1, p. 437.
35  B Jones, 'Our education failures', Dean's Lecture, the Faculty of Education, The University of Melbourne, 30 May 2007 www.theage.com.au/news/opinion/our-education-failures/2007/05/29/1180205246158.html; Selleck, 1982, pp. 23, 24.
36  L Burchell, *Victorian Schools: A History of Government Architecture, 1837–1900*, Melbourne University Press, Carlton, 1980, p. 130.
37  History of Gold Street, Clifton Hill, http://www.cliftonhillps.vic.edu.au/sub/about/history.html#submenu3.
38  Burchell looks at schools and their construction. He describes the Buninyong model in Chapter 8 and rural schools in Chapter 9, with the description on pp. 98–9, and of later urban schools on p. 130, where he refers to the 'fledgling Education Department'.
39  Blake, vol. 1, p. 848.
40  ibid., p. 826.
41  Selleck, 1982, p. 27.
42  M Boyce, oral history interview conducted by the author 2008; extract from Boyce's grandfather's memoirs.
43  D Garden, *The Melbourne Teacher Training Colleges: From Training Institution to Melbourne State College 1870–1982*, Heinemann Educational Australia, Richmond, 1982, describes the expansion in depth on pp. 25–6, and on pp. 45–6 describes the opening of the College.
44  Selleck, 1982, p. 125, identifies Tate's reform agenda; p. 128 lists influential reform movements.
45  ibid., p. 69.
*  New Education was a movement that developed in the 1920s in which ideas about education concentrated on the child and each child's learning rather than on 'mass' teaching. By the 1960s perhaps the term 'teaching for individual differences' was a development of New Education.
46  Blake, vol. 1, p. 437, and Garden, p. 71, and http://adbonline.anu.edu.au/biogs/A080524b.htm give details.
47  Selleck, 1982, describes the results of the *Education Act* 1901 (No. 1777), pp. 130–2; a subsequent Act specified terms and conditions for employment and promotion according to the Classified Roll – *An Act to Amend the Law Relating to State School Teachers* (No. 2006), 12 December, 1905.
48  Copy of Licence to Teach awarded to Mary Grace Cuthill on 18 May 1906, reproduced in Blake, vol. 1, p. 867.
49  Selleck, 1982, describes Tate's vision and the challenges he experienced when he introduced change, pp. 136–41; Selleck describes the feelings of Bagge and Stewart, p. 136.
50  Blake, vol. 1, pp. 297, 309, 437, 439–40, and Selleck, 1982, pp. 130–1, describe Tate's philosophies prior to the Fink Royal Commission. See also http://adbonline.anu.edu.au/biogs/A120189b.htm; references cited in Selleck, 1982, p. 147, from Tate's 'Report of the Director of Education upon some aspects of education in New Zealand', September 1904.
51  F Gladman, *School Method*, Jarrod and Sons, London, 1877.

52 Garden, pp. 99–101.
53 http://adb.anu.edu.au/biography/browne-george-stephenson-9604.
54 *Education Gazette and Teachers' Aid,* Education Department of Victoria, Melbourne, July 1920, cited in Blake, vol. 1, p. 364.
55 Broome, p. 141.
56 Details of Clapp and his contribution to Victoria's rail network, agriculture and tourism: http://adb.anu.edu.au/biography/clapp-sir-harold-winthrop-5657.
57 1881: Registration Number: 10074 (Prahran: PH); land auctioned by G W Taylor & Co at the home of E J Dixon, City of Stonington Archives.
58 Meccano sets were invented in Liverpool, England, and patented by Frank Hornby in 1908. In 1925 new models were marketed of the familiar red and green, coinciding with the 25 anniversary in 1926.
59 Each day the milkman delivered milk. From a large metal can he poured the milk into a smaller tin or enamel billy waiting on a hook. A billy is like a can with a handle.

# Chapter 3

60 'State school' was the official term for schools taking pupils in Grades 1 to 8 until 1969 when the term 'primary school' became accepted for schools taking pupils in Grades 1 to 6 and 'central school' was used when Grades 7 and 8 were included.
61 *Education Act* 1905 (No 2005), An Act to amend the *Education Act* 1901, 12 December 1905; Blake, vol. 1, pp. 371–2 details regulations governing the Qualifying and Merit Certificates. A J Law, Principal, Melbourne Teachers College (TC), opposed the examination system that involved inspectors. He believed the headmaster's certification should suffice.
62 Blake, vol. 1, pp. 368, 369, reviews arguments to accept or reject developments proposed by K Cunningham, G S Browne and C McCrae.
63 Blake, vol. 3, p. 360.
64 ibid., and Burchell, p. 134.
65 Shears, oral history interview conducted by Tony Ryan, archivist for the Australian College of Educators, 2004.
66 The hinged leather bag with rigid frame and two compartments was made of stiff leather. The late 19th century French invention was popularised by William E Gladstone (1809–98), four-time Prime Minister of Britain, who travelled extensively. Working men in Australia used to carry their lunches to work in a Gladstone bag. The bags could accommodate half a dozen bottles of beer.
67 B Bessant and A Spaull, *Politics of Schooling*, Pitman Pacific, Carlton, 1976, pp. 11–14.
68 http://adb.anu.edu.au/biography/vroland-anton-william-rutherford-11928/text21371.
69 District Inspector Saxton's report, 1924, cited in Blake, vol. 3, p. 390.
70 Blake, vol. 1, pp. 338, 367, describes Dr Leach's contribution. His philosophies and interest in geography, nature study and Australian birds infiltrated educational thinking through the Gould League of Bird Lovers, established in 1909.
71 Preface, *Victorian Readers: Eighth Book,* Education Department of Victoria, Melbourne, 1928, p.v.
72 Blake, vol. 1, p. 368, discusses the work of Rosalie Virtue and the introduction of these activities in 1922; the Ramsay Report, 1960, considered sporting facilities in the planning of new schools, pp. 13–4.
73 Garden, p. 220; Deans' Lecture, Graduate School of Education, the University of Mel-

bourne, 9 September 2008.
74 Bill Woodfull captained the Australian cricket team in 1930, 1932–33 and 1934. He was Principal of Melbourne High School from 1956 to 1962.
75 Blake, vol. 1, pp. 539–46, describes the Ramsay Report in detail.
76 Shears, oral history interview conducted by Tony Ryan, archivist for the Australian College of Educators, 2004.
77 Ramsay Report, 1960, p. 20.
78 ibid.
79 ibid.
80 A Hoy, *A city built to music: the history of University High School, Melbourne, 1910 to 1960*, University High School, Melbourne, 1961, pp. 2, 3.
81 R Selleck, *The shop: the University of Melbourne 1850–1939*, Melbourne University Press, Carlton, 2003, p. 458; Garden, p. 85.
82 Hoy, p. 3. Motion passed at a conference attended by representatives of the University, the Education Department and the Association of Secondary Teachers in Victoria, circa 1906–07.
83 Hoy, 1961, p. 69.
84 L Thompson, *Looking Ahead in Education*, Education Department of Victoria, Melbourne, 1969, p. 14.
85 Garden describes Stanton Sharman as innovative; Blake, vol. 3, p. 234, says Sharman held his position 'with great distinction'.
86 W Law Suart, *Golden Morning: An Australian Childhood*, Dingo Books, Bordon, Hampshire, 2001. Wendy Suart recalls her days at University High School, where she began her secondary studies in 1936.
87 Bruce (pale blue), Burrows (pink), Hancock (red), Duff (yellow), Langford-Brooke (purple) and Saltau (royal blue).
88 Hoy, 1961, p. 38. Sharman's philosophies, presented at Speech Night 1919, echoed throughout the years of Shears' time at the school.
89 Garden, p. 108.
90 *The Record*, University High School, Melbourne, 1935–37, philosophies espoused in editorials.
91 ibid., June and Christmas 1938.
92 Jean Muir became Jean Blackburn and contributed to the Karmel Report of 1973 and the Ministerial Review of Compulsory Schooling in 1985.
93 Shears, oral history interview conducted by the author, 2007.
94 During the war Merv Finster was a member of the 24th Flying Squadron that flew Wirraways out of Townsville. Aircraft A20–118 crashed on 30 June 1941 when one of its wings collapsed during dive-bombing practice. Merv and his flight companion Albert Glance lost their lives. http://www.adf-serials.com.au/2a20b.htm.
95 *The Record*, Christmas 1938.
96 Shears, oral history interview conducted by Tony Ryan, archivist for the Australian College of Educators, 2004.

# Chapter 4

97 Garden, p. 139. Between 1927–28 and 1933–34 funding dropped from £3.37m to £2.53m. Financial support for teacher education dropped from £27,319 to £20,375 in

the same period.
98  ibid., pp. 141–2. Numbers fell from 610 to 233 between 1929 and 1933.
99  ibid., p. 143. One of the 1931 cohort later became a Rhodes Scholar and another became a Rockefeller Research Scholar at the University of London.
100 M Boyce, *A Perspective of the VIER: A View of the First Sixty Years of the Victorian Institute of Educational Research 1929–1989,* Victorian Institute of Educational Research, Melbourne, 1992. Foreword by Shears identifies factors that underlay the establishment of ACER.
101 B Williams, *Education with Its Eyes Open: A Biography of Dr K.S. Cunningham,* Australian Council for Educational Research, Melbourne, 1994, pp. 161–8, lists the 10 candidates and their individual attributes; Garden, p. 117, and Williams, p. 161, outline Cunningham's professional interests.
102 Garden, pp. 142–5.
103 Blake, vol. 1, p. 897; Acts 4205, 4207 dated 29 December 1933, *Teachers Act* 1933, and *Education (Fees) Act* 1933; Garden, p. 147.
104 ibid., p. 1437, McDonell lectured at Melbourne TC from 1929 to 1932 and again from 1934 to 1937.
105 Seitz succeeded McRae in 1936; Garden, p. 155, details friction between Seitz and Professor Browne. Seitz, who needed teachers for the Department, wanted authority over their training, as did Browne, who stood by his professorial status. Eventually Seitz established control and had Browne removed as Principal in 1939.
106 Garden, pp. 148, 156–7, 165.
107 Shears, oral history interview conducted by Tony Ryan, archivist for the Australian College of Educators, 2004.
108 P Law, oral history interview conducted by the author, 2007.
109 Shears, oral history interview conducted by Tony Ryan, archivist for the Australian College of Educators, 2004.
110 Shears, oral history interview conducted by the author, 2009.
111 ibid.
112 ibid.
113 Seitz was appointed in 1936; Shears, oral history interview conducted by Tony Ryan, archivist for the Australian College of Educators, 2004.
114 Prime Minister's declaration broadcast to the nation. http://www.menziesvirtualmuseum.org.au/1930s/1939.html.
115 During the evacuation at Dunkirk 338,000 troops were rescued. Despite the huge loss Churchill declared that 'Britain will never surrender'. http://en.wikipedia.org/wiki/We_shall_fight_on_the_beaches.
116 Heathcote's report noted on Shears' teaching record. Inspectors always used abbreviations – v.g = very good, S.T. = student teacher. Teachers spoke of 'getting' a g, a vg or an os (= outstanding).

## Chapter 5

117 Garden, p. 167; the figure rose to £40 in 1943. Students in residence received £70 a year, which rose to £90. Allowances had been abolished in 1933–34 when funds were cut, p. 142.
118 *The Trainee*, annual magazine of Melbourne TC, editorial, December 1939, p. 8.

119 ibid., December 1939, p. 8.

120 Garden, p. 85, describes this group as former trainees in the teacher workforce who were furthering their qualifications. Their status as such was a source of jealousy within the Department. Selleck, 1982, p. 157, believes McRae's experience contributed to his attaining the high rank of Director.

121 http://adbonline.anu.edu.au/biogs/A100354b.htm

122 *The Trainee*, December 1939, p. 9.

123 ibid., Non Omnis Moriar translates from Latin to mean 'I shall not wholly die' (Merriam-Webster's Online Dictionary).

124 ibid., p. 15.

125 Garden, p. 150.

126 *The Trainee*, December 1940, p. 9.

127 P Law, oral history interview conducted by the author, 2007. Law, who established himself in the sciences and Antarctic exploration and later became an educational leader, preceded Shears' years in college.

128 http://adbonline.anu.edu.au/biogs/A100354b.htm.

129 Shears, oral history interview conducted by the author, 2009.

130 Blake, vol. 1, pp. 897, 898.

131 Garden claims the college as an avenue for new ideas and experimentation ceased in the 1930s, p. 167.

132 P Law 1967, lecture presented to the Victorian Institute of Educational Research, 10 March, and printed in *VIER Bulletin*, no. 17, cited in Garden, pp. 146–7; Shears, oral history interview conducted by the author, 2009.

133 *The Trainee*, address by the principal, December 1940, p. 7.

134 *The Trainee*, editorial, December 1941, p. 7.

135 *The Trainee*, address by the principal, December 1942, p. 9.

136 *The Trainee*, 1941, pp. 31, 32.

137 Shears, oral history interview conducted by the author, 2009.

138 *The Trainee*, College highlights, by M Kydd, December 1941, pp. 10, 11.

139 *The Trainee,* sport, December 1941, p. 51.

140 Garden, p. 167.

141 Council of Public Education Victoria, Report on Educational Reform and Development in Victoria, 1945, p. 29, cited in Blake, vol. 1, p. 906.

142 Shears, oral history interview conducted by the author, 2009.

143 A Law, *Modern Teaching,* Robertson & Mullins, Melbourne, 1940, p. 31, quotes W James, *Talks to Teachers on Psychology*, chapter 8 'The laws of habit', 1890, http://ebooks.adelaide.edu.au/j/james/william/talks/chapter8.html.

144 Blake, vol. 3, p. 140. Staff included Chief Inspector OC Phillips, Director of Primary Education RP McLellan and District Inspectors WJ Braden and HA Fleigner.

145 Shears, Notes of Lessons, Teachers' College, 1941.

146 Blake, vol. 1, pp. 519, 1070. Loader was an activist in the Victorian Teachers' Union (VTU). In 1942 he became permanent assistant to John A Cole at the Curriculum Research Office.

147 A Law, p. 93.

148 Shears, Notes of Lessons, Teachers' College, 1941.

149 'Your experiment was hard work for you. The class got restless because there was too much that was formal about it ... they appreciated your reading of it which was very well done. You had done an enormous amount of preparation, but the class hadn't, so you were disappointed that they were not so interested in the experiment as you were. You were trying very hard to get them to do something but they did not quite enter into the spirit of it. If you had taken the poem and discussed it with them and shown them what you had seen – with not so many facts – they would have grasped more of it.' Another comment: 'A strenuous period in which much work was done.'

150 Blake, vol. 1, pp. 400, 401, details rural school enrolment, maintenance costs and closures in the 1940s.

151 James, 1890, http://ebooks.adelaide.edu.au/j/james/william/talks/chapter8.html.

152 *The Trainee*, 1942, p. 33.

153 Shears, oral history interview conducted by the author, 2009.

154 *The Trainee*, 1942, p. 50.

155 Garden, p. 162, describes precautions taken at the time.

156 *Griffin* was a monthly publication. Very few copies from the era exist.

157 *The Trainee*, 1942, p. 7.

158 Shears, oral history interview conducted by Tony Ryan, archivist for the Australian College of Educators, 2005, and subsequent discussion with the author.

159 The original Wilson Hall, a Gothic Revival style building was designed by Reed and Barnes in 1879. It burned to the ground in 1952.

160 *The Record*, June 1941, p. 15.

# Chapter 6

161 Blake, vol. 1, cites the ninth annual conference report, VTU, 1935, p. 517.

162 Education Department of Victoria, Report of the Minister of Public Instruction for the year 1936–37, Government Printer, Melbourne, 1938, p. 19, cited in Blake, vol. 1, p. 518.

163 Education Department of Victoria, Report of the Minister of Public Instruction for the year 1942–43, Government Printer, Melbourne, 1944, p. 24, cited in Blake, vol. 1, p. 520.

164 D M Waddington, W C Radford, J A Keats, *Review of Education in Australia 1940–48*, Melbourne University Press, Carlton, 1950, p. 183.

165 Education Department of Victoria, Report of the Minister of Public Instruction for the year 1943–44, Government Printer, Melbourne, 1945, p. 31, cited in Blake, vol. 1, p. 520; Waddington et al., p. 183.

166 Blake, vol. 2, p. 502. Korong Vale was classified as a primary school but 'functioned as a central school until 1945'.

167 Korong Vale was ripe in the Gold Rush Era and maintained popularity because of its position on the railway line linking Bendigo to Boort, Inglewood, Robinvale, Murray Bridge in South Australia and later to Wedderburn. The *Lance and Northwestern Advertiser* was published there from 1896 to 1915, and the *Korong Times and Farmer's Advocate* was established in 1920.

168 Blake, vol. 2, p. 502.

169 Selleck, 1982, p. 238–9.

170 Blake, vol. 2, p. 451.
171 Blake, vol. 1, p. 405.
172 Blake, vol. 1, p. 405.
173 Selleck, 1982, p. 81, describes Tate's experiences.
174 Holloway, p. 291.
175 Teachers began in fifth class and gradually climbed through the ranks.
176 Shears, oral history interview conducted by the author, 2009.
177 ibid.
178 Browne, in the John Smyth Memorial Lecture, 1941. Instituted in 1928 by Smyth's former students, the John Smyth Memorial Lecture marked Smyth's contribution to teacher training and the development of education in Victoria. Recently retired Director of Education Frank Tate presented the inaugural lecture held at Melbourne High School on 22 September 1928. By 1961 organisational interest had diminished until enthusiasm was stirred among members of the VIER. The lecture was re-introduced in 1964 and conducted annually by the VIER, which faded from existence in the late 1990s.
179 The tap installed in 1943 was still there when Shears made a visit to the school as Director-General.
180 Bessant and Spaull, pp. 23.
181 ibid., pp. 21–6.
182 When Shears visited Korong Vale as Director-General 30 years later, a past student produced a copy of the book.
183 Shears, oral history interview conducted by Tony Ryan, archivist for the Australian College of Educators, 2005.
184 T S Eliot, 'Preludes', 1910–11.
185 W Radford, *The Educational Needs of a Rural Community*, Melbourne University Press in conjunction with Oxford University Press, Melbourne, 1939, p. 3, presents the situation in 1938, six years before Lawrie's appointment.
186 ibid., pp. 45–7.
187 Blake, vol. 3, pp. 1159–63, relates the history of Bairnsdale Technical School; Holloway, pp. 256, 257, outlines Clark's career and the development of technical education; R Whiteley, Donald Clark, the first chief inspector of technical schools, Master of Education thesis, University of Melbourne, 1980, details Clark's time in Bairnsdale; Selleck, 1982, pp. 202, 203, gives an account of Clark's philosophies towards technical and high school education and their suitability for specific outcomes.
188 ibid.; Thompson, 1969, p. 33; *Bairnsdale Advertiser*, 22 December 1944.
189 *Bairnsdale Advertiser*, 5 May 1943, reported their concerns, the response appeared in the paper on 23 May; The Head Master's Plan of School Work, *The Cygnet* 1946, p. 1. *The Cygnet* was not published in 1944–45 because of the war but the school followed the three-strand course of study; Selleck, 1982, p. 203, considers Tate's belief in equity in schooling and those of British Labor spokesman RH Tawney, whose review of the Hadow Reports is found in *Melbourne Studies in Education*, Faculty of Education, University of Melbourne, Melbourne University Press, Carlton, 1972, pp. 180–1. The Hadow Report(s) were six reports produced from 1923 and 1933 on education in England by various consultative committees chaired by Sir William Henry Hadow.
190 J Darling, *The Age*, 19 May 1943 – report of the Educational Reform Association meeting at the Melbourne Town Hall.

191 *Every Week*, 29 February 1944, reported on the meeting of school councils and committees and the Educational Reform Association held three days prior; *Every Week*, 1 February 1944, discusses the options, p. 1.

192 *Bairnsdale Advertiser*, 1 February, 22 August 1944; *Every Week*, 28 March 1944, p. 5, 16 May p. 1, 22 August.

193 *Every Week*, 28 March 1944, p. 5.

194 *Bairnsdale Advertiser*, 2 and 6 February 1944; *The Cygnet*, 1943–46.

195 Blake, vol. 1, p. 380, presents developing philosophies and the 1934 curriculum pp. 379–85.

196 *The Cygnet*, Bairnsdale High School magazine, published after suspension during the war years, 1946.

197 ibid.

198 ibid.

199 Radford, p. 3; *The Cygnet*, 1946.

200 Shears, oral history interview conducted by Tony Ryan, archivist for the Australian College of Educators, 2005.

201 Shears' teaching record; Shears, oral history interview conducted by Tony Ryan, archivist for the Australian College of Educators, 2006.

202 *Bairnsdale Advertiser*, 11 May 1945.

203 *Every Week*, 24 March 1944, p. 1.

204 *Bairnsdale Advertiser*, 5 June 1945.

205 Shears, oral history interview conducted by the author, 2009.

206 *Every Week*, 6 April 1944, p. 1; *Every Week*, 12 May 1944, p. 4.

207 Shears, oral history interview conducted by Tony Ryan, archivist for the Australian College of Educators, 2004; Shears, oral history interview conducted by the author, 2009.

208 Shears, oral history interview conducted by Tony Ryan, archivist for the Australian College of Educators, 2004.

209 *Every Week*, 3 March 1944.

# Chapter 7

210 *Dookie Collegian*, 1948, Rural Training Centre (RTC) editorial p. 44.

211 H Gallagher, *We Got a Fair Go: A History of the Commonwealth Reconstruction Training Scheme 1945–1952*, self-published, Melbourne, 2003, p. 35.

212 Blake, vol. 1, gives insight into the development and contributions of technical training. The Commonwealth Defence Technical Training Scheme later combined with the Commonwealth Reconstruction Training Scheme, pp. 675–702.

213 http://en.wikipedia.org/wiki/History_of_the_Royal_Melbourne_Institute_of_Technology looks at the impact of WW II and gives details of the Melbourne Technical College courses during the war years. Also see http://access.prov.vic.gov.au/public/component/daPublicBaseContainer?component=daViewAgency&breadcrumbPath=Home/Access%20the%20Collection/Browse%20The%20Collection/Agency%20Details&entityId=1046

214 Gallagher, p. 72.

215 Gallagher details the development of the Commonwealth Reconstruction Training Scheme. The Industrial Training Division conducted Repatriation training under the Commonwealth Technical Training Scheme (CTTS), which operated during war-

time, pp. 19–20. Gallagher identifies the work of the CTTS and difficulties encountered, pp. 52–67.

216 R Smallwood, *Hard to Go Bung: World War II Soldier Settlement in Victoria 1945–1962*, Hyland House, Melbourne, 1992, presents insights identified in *Mufti* that gave voice to those who served. Smallwood cites arguments contained in the Pike Report and analysis of the post WWI scheme.

217 *Dookie Collegian*, 1948, history of the RTC.

218 ibid., pp. 45, 46; memories shared by those attending the 2008 RTC reunion celebrating 60 years since graduation.

219 B Gleeson, in conversation with the author, 2008.

220 Blake, vol. 1, p. 1437. Alexander McDonell moved on to become Chief Inspector of Secondary Schools in February 1953, Assistant Director of Education from September 1958 and Director of Education from 13 March 1960 until 1965 when he retired. He understood what it took to teach adults from experience at Melbourne TC 1918–21, 1929–32.

221 L Bell, oral history interview conducted by the author, 2007, shows that this was the case at Dookie College.

222 R Aldridge, *Dookie College: The First 100 Years*, Victorian College of Agriculture and Horticulture, Melbourne, 1986, p. 122.

223 Shears, oral history interview conducted by the author, 2007.

224 G Woodgate, reference for Shears, 1950.

225 Dookie Collegian, 1947, editorial, p. 39.

226 W Wordsworth, 'Daffodils', stanza 1. 'Daffodils' appeared in *Victorian Readers: Sixth Book*, p. 172.

227 Memories shared by ex-servicemen at the 2008 RTC reunion.

228 At first vehicles were to be kept outside the college grounds. Authorities later gave permission for the men to park them under the sugar gums.

229 Shears, oral history interview conducted by the author, 2005.

230 ibid.

231 *Dookie Collegian*, 1948, RTC section, pp. 57, 58.

232 ibid., p. 47.

233 Web records suggest the Dookie Collegians won the premiership rather than the RTC team as reported in the *Dookie Collegian*, and as told in interviews by the author with Shears and some of the men; Goorambat, premiers the previous year, defeated Swanpool 8.7(55) to 7.7(49); http://www.foxsportspulse.com/assoc_page.cgi?c=0-6146-0-0-0&sID=112066. Records show that Dookie Agricultural College commenced in 1886 although it was run as an experimental farm prior to that. If the '62 years' that Shears and the men use in their stories is correct, then 1885 is the year the Dookie team began.

234 Shears, oral history interview conducted by the author, 2006.

235 *The Age*, 28 May 1946, reported on the short courses at their commencement; *Stock and Land*, 31 August 1949, Soldier Settler column reported on progress and outcomes of short courses to date.

236 L Shears, The educational needs of adults in rural areas, Bachelor of Education thesis, University of Melbourne, 1949, p. 23.

237 Shears, The educational needs of adults in rural areas, p. 24.

238 *Sun*, 22 September 1948.

239 *Dookie Collegian*, 1947, p. 45.

240 Memories shared by ex-servicemen at the 2008 RTC reunion.

241 Shears, oral history interview conducted by the author, 2006. Shears took 'first place in Bachelor of Education' because he received the highest marks for his practical and theoretical study.

# Chapter 8

242 Tate's report titled 'Some reflections on education in New Zealand'; Blake, vol. 1, p. 1514.

243 Blake, vol. 1, details overseas travels of Victoria's former Directors of Education, pp. 1491–3; History of UNESCO; http://www.unesco.org/new/en/unesco/about-us/who-we-are/history/.

244 Williams, chapter 10, gives a description of Cunningham's travels and international links; reference to Clarke cited from p. 222; Isaac Kandel, Professor of Education, International Institute, Teachers College, Columbia University. He was previously the Joseph Payne Lecturer at the University of London. In 1937 he presented the 10th John Smyth Memorial Lecture, The strife of tongues, for the VIER. In Chapter 11 Williams describes the NEF Conference in detail.

245 Garden, p. 80–2; http://adb.anu.edu.au/biography/smyth-john-8566.

246 Imperial Relations Trust established to administer £250,000 placed anonymously and at the disposal of the British Prime Minister in 1937 to provide grants to individuals who contributed to strengthening ties among the Commonwealth countries.

247 Thomas Hampton Coates later became Headmaster of Wesley College, Melbourne (1957–71). His research interests lay in moral education.

248 G Browne, Reference addressed to Dr Jeffery, Director, Institute of Education, University of London, 1950, in possession of Shears.

249 Institute of Education London, http://www.ioe.ac.uk/about/761.html.

250 R Aldrich, *The Institute of Education 1902-2002: A Centenary History,* Institute of Education, London, 2002, p. 125.

251 http://www.aim25.ac.uk/cats/5/2322.htm.

252 The McNair Report, 1944, http://www.educationengland.org.uk/documents/mcnair/mcnair19.html.

253 Aldrich, p. 148; Vernon identified *Intelligence A* as influenced by genetics and mediated by the nervous system, *Intelligence B* as reflected in behaviour, ability, efficiency and perception, and *Intelligence C* as the IQ score from a particular test; www.intelltheory.com/vernon.shtml

254 http://www.a2zpsychology.com/great_psychologists/hans_j_eysenck.htm.

255 L Shears, The dynamics of leadership in adolescent school groups, doctoral thesis, Institute of Education, University of London, 1952, p. 1.

256 ibid., p. 79.

257 ibid., p. 325.

258 ibid., p. 324, underlining by Shears when he read a draft of this chapter in January 2012.

259 ibid., pp. 327–9.

260 ibid., pp. 321, 322.

261 Shears, oral history interview conducted by Tony Ryan, archivist for the Australian College of Educators, 2004.

262 ibid.

263 Shears, The dynamics of leadership in adolescent school groups, p. 15.

264 ibid., p. 20.

265 ibid., pp. 20, 21.

266 L Shears, 'A report to the Imperial Relations Trustees: an account of activity under the Award of the Imperial Relations Trust Fellowship 1950–1951', Institute of Education, University of London, 1952, p. 29; Youth club activities embraced sport, gymnastics, art, drama, discussion and music.

267 Shears, The dynamics of leadership in adolescent school groups, pp. 23, 24.

268 S Garfield, *Our Hidden Lives,* Random House, London, 2004, reveals post-war attitudes held by civilians; HEO James & Cora Tenen, *The Teacher Was Black: an experiment in international understanding sponsored by UNESCO*, Heinemann, London, 1953, indicates attitudes to colour.

269 1952: King George VI dies in his sleep; http://news.bbc.co.uk/onthisday/hi/dates/stories/february/6/newsid_2711000/2711265.stm.

270 Shears, oral history interview conducted by Tony Ryan, archivist for the Australian College of Educators, 2006.

271 Moyle, oral history interview conducted by the author, 2006.

# Chapter 9

272 Blake, vol. 1, A J Law as Principal of Melbourne TC, p. 903; In late 1946 Ellwood was appointed to the Teachers Tribunal; Cannon travelled abroad in 1938–39 as Assistant Chief Inspector of Primary Schools, p. 1400.

273 Garden, p. 182.

274 *Letters from Abroad: Replanning Teacher Education in Victoria*, http://www.ascd.org/ASCD/pdf/journals/ed_lead/el_195002_pryor.pdf

275 Blake, vol. 1, pp. 912, 1455; L Pryor, The training of primary teachers, September 1969, typescript, cited in Blake p. 912.

276 Citation from the Military Cross awarded to William Francis Lord as quoted in C Gervasoni, William Frank Lord, www.ballarat.edu.au/centres/art-and-historical-collection/ub-honour-roll/l/william-frank-lord-1969.

277 Blake, vol. 1, p. 904; Gervasoni, 1969; Shears, oral history interview conducted by the author, 2009; M Waugh, oral history interview conducted by the author, 2007.

278 Shears, oral history interview conducted by Tony Ryan, archivist for the Australian College of Educators, 2004.

279 Personal communication: Toorak TC trainees 1952–53.

280 Blake, vol. 1, p. 913, quotes these words of Ramsay and cites 'Department Teacher Training – New Two-Year Course of Training for Primary Teachers, 21 Sept. 1950, p. 1. (Revised 1958, see General Directive from Advisory Committee, MTC archives)'.

281 J St Ellen and L Shears, 'An experimental course in education for teachers' colleges', *The Forum of Education*, vol. XII, no. 3, April 1954, pp. 89–101.

282 The teachers' ethical code to which Shears adhered was embraced by the Australian College of Education and eventually published in G Bassett, *Teachers in Australian Schools*, Australian College of Education, Melbourne, 1980, p. 14.

283 St Ellen and Shears, pp. 89–101.
284 Gallagher, p. 72, presents the debate regarding the teaching of education and agriculture.
285 Views correspond with those of H Menzies-Smith, 'Desirable training of teachers' in P Partridge, *Teachers in Australia: an appraisal, including the 1966 Buntine Oration* [Papers presented at the Seventh Annual Conference of the Australian College of Education, held at the University of Sydney, 1966], published by Cheshire for the Australian College of Education, Melbourne, 1966, p. 79.
286 *Education Gazette and Teachers' Aid,* 13 July 1953; positions vacant at Toorak TC.
287 Personal communication: Toorak TC trainees 1951–53.
288 Bell, oral history interview conducted by the author, 2007.
289 K Robertson, *Myrtleford: Gateway to the Australian Alps,* Rigby, Adelaide, 1973.
290 M Dimmack, oral history interview conducted by the author, 2008.
291 Shears' teaching record.
292 Service record of Donald Maine Waller, http://naa12.naa.gov.au/scripts/imagine.asp?B=8399914&I=1&SE=1.
293 Dimmack, oral history interview conducted by the author, 2008; C Limb, oral history interview conducted by the author, 2008.
294 Shears, oral history interview conducted by the author, 2007; Limb, oral history interview conducted by the author, 2008.
295 Letter in personal file of former Burwood student.
296 *Parabo,* 1954.
297 Limb, oral history interview conducted by the author, 2008; Dimmack, oral history interview conducted by the author, 2008.
298 Anecdotal accounts of participating staff – Dimmack, Bell, Nixon, Limb.
299 *Parabo,* 1954, p. 14, describes the meaning of the Burwood TC badge; Dimmack, oral history interview conducted by the author, 2008.
300 Dimmack, oral history interview conducted by the author, 2008.
301 ibid.; anecdotal accounts of foundation students, 2009 reunion at Oxford Hall.
302 Boyce, pp. 20, 21.
303 *Journal of Education* vol. 1, no. 1, 1954, p. 25.
304 ibid., p. 1.
305 *Parabo,* 1954, p. 14.

## Chapter 10

306 R Jackson, *Emergent Needs in Australian Education,* ACER, Melbourne, 1962, pp. 31, cited in Connell, W *Reshaping Australian Education 1960–85,* ACER, Hawthorn, 1993.
307 R Butts, *Assumptions underlying Australian Education,* ACER, Melbourne, 1955, pp. 77–9. Butts attended a meeting of the Victorian Institute for Educational Research and the New Education Fellowship on 12 November 1954.
308 Bessant and Spaull, pp. 80, 81.
309 Blake, vol. 1. pp. 1492–3.
310 ibid., p. 1455.
311 W McKinty, oral history interview conducted by the author, 2007. McKinty joined

the Survey and Planning team and was senior officer in 1959–60 during Shears' term as a Harkness Fellow.

312 *Education Gazette and Teachers' Aid*, 21st May 1954, p. 302.

313 ibid.; Shears, oral history interviews conducted by the author, 2006, 2008.

314 Shears, oral history interview conducted by Tony Ryan, archivist for the Australian College of Educators, 2004.

315 McKinty, oral history interview conducted by the author, 2007.

316 N Curry, oral history interview conducted by the author, 2007.

317 Shears, oral history interview conducted by the author, 2008.

318 *The Age*, 16 August 1948; Ramsay Report, 1960, p. 134, cited in Blake, vol. 1, pp. 539–46.

319 R McDonnell, W Radford and P Staurenghi, *Review of Education in Australia 1948–1954*, ACER, Melbourne, 1956, p. 97; Blake, vol. 1, p. 387.

320 Blake, vol. 1, p. 261; Burchell, pp. 162, 163; Blake describes how William Collard Smith who served as Minister of Education from 1878 to 1881 dictated building policy. Commissioner of Public Works Charles Young, in discussion with Collard Smith and Chief Secretary James McPherson Grant, subsequently agreed that from 1881 the PWD would undertake work pertaining to Education Department buildings.

321 *Education Gazette and Teachers' Aid*, 1954–61.

322 McDonnell et al., p. 97.

323 Blake, vol. 1, p. 532 cites details form from Reports of the Minister of Education for the years 1954-55; 1955-56; 1957-58; 1959-60; Education Department of Victoria, Report of the Minister of Education for the year 1958–59, Government Printer, Melbourne, 1960, by Assistant Chief Inspector of Secondary Schools, Alex McDonell, p. 24.

324 McDonnell et al. describe the situation in Victoria and compares its situation with other States, p. 98.

325 J Bennett, principal's address in *Yakkity Hi*, magazine of Ringwood High School, 1954.

326 T Decini, *Yakkity Hi*.

327 B Ring, personal communication with author.

328 Blake, vol. 3, p. 586.

329 *Yakkity Hi*.

330 *Education Gazette and Teachers' Aid*, 1954–61.

331 ACER, 'The Shire of Ferntree Gully and its educational future: A report compiled in collaboration by officers of the Australian Council for Educational Research, University of Melbourne Faculty of Education, Victorian Education Department … at the request of the Combined State Schools' Committees' Conference of the Shire of Ferntree Gully', ACER, Melbourne, 1956, pp. (i), 51, 52. (hereinafter 'Ferntree Gully Survey').

332 Upwey Higher Elementary School became a high school in 1944 with WM Woodfull its first head master. Boronia High School began in 1957 in the local Progress Hall with 115 students under headmaster HA Russell.

333 Ferntree Gully survey, pp. 9, 53.

334 ibid., pp. 45, 53.

335 ibid., recommendations, p. 54.

336 ibid., p. 54; Rizvi's 1991 reflection on social attitudes cited in E Peeler, Changing culture, changing practice: Immigrant teachers in search of self, Doctor of Education thesis, Monash University, 2005, p. 10.

337 Shears, oral history interview conducted by the author, 2009.

338 McDonnell et al., p. 179.

339 Blake, vol. 1, pp. 536–8, details staffing in the 1950s and on pp. 546–7 gives an account of the 1960s and numbers of classified and temporary teachers employed.

340 R Gunstone, oral history interview conducted by the author, 2008; L Thompson, oral history interview conducted by the author, 2007; *Education Act* 1958 (No. 6240).

341 R Murfett, oral history interview conducted by the author, 2007.

342 Gunstone, oral history interview conducted by the author, 2008.

343 Murfett, oral history interview conducted by the author, 2007; Report of the Minister of Education for the year 1958–59, p. 30, cited in Blake, vol. 1, p. 537; overseas recruitment through the Agent-General's Office in London.

344 Education Department of Victoria, Report of the Minister of Education for the year 1956–57, Government Printer, Melbourne, 1958, p. 27, cited in Blake, vol. 1, p. 537.

345 Shears, in an oral history interview conducted by the author, 2009, stressed the lobbying power of the TITC clique at Melbourne TC; Shears, 1959, curriculum vitae. Garden describes the activities of Angus pp. 68, 191, 198.

346 *Education Gazette and Teachers' Aid*, 13 July 1953, pp. 176–81; Shears, oral history interview conducted by the author, 2007; Garden, p. 184.

347 Shears, oral history interview conducted by the author, 2008.

348 Shears, oral history interview conducted by Tony Ryan, archivist for the Australian College of Educators, 2004.

349 Report on Additions to Adelaide Teachers' College, 1959, p. 48; Shears, oral history interview conducted by Tony Ryan, archivist for the Australian College of Educators, 2004.

350 Blake, vol. 1, p. 912.

351 Stonington Mansion http://en.wikipedia.org/wiki/Stonington_mansion; Shears, oral history interview conducted by Tony Ryan, archivist for the Australian College of Educators, 2004; Shears, oral history interview conducted by the author, 2007; A Catrice, Foundations of Burwood and Toorak Teachers Colleges, *Glenbervian,* May 2009.

352 Shears, oral history interviews conducted by the author, 2006 and 2009.

353 Shears, oral history interview conducted by the author, 2007.

354 Shears, oral history interview conducted by the author, 2007; http://books.publishing.monash.edu/apps/bookworm/view/Still+Learning/143/xhtml/title.html

355 B Carroll, *A Decade of Achievement: Phillip Institute of Technology*, RMIT Press, Melbourne, 1995.

356 Garden gives a detailed description of secondary teachers colleges, chapter 7, p. 207-308.

357 Shears, oral history interview conducted by Tony Ryan, archivist for the Australian College of Educators, 2004.

358 Blake, vol. 1, pp. 920–2.

359 Garden, pp. 192–211; Blake, vol. 1, pp. 537, 922.

360 Shears, oral history interview conducted by Tony Ryan, archivist for the Australian College of Educators, 2004; Shears, oral history interview conducted by the author, 2006. Gelman Hall was named after Manuel Gelman, an original staff member.

361 Blake, vol. 1 pp. 703-9.

362 J Docherty, *The Emily Mac: The Story of the Emily McPherson College, 1906–1979*, Ormond Book and Educational Supplies, Melbourne, 1981; Holloway, p. 379; Blake, vol. 1, pp. 703–9; N Schiegel, *Larnook – our thoughts to thee will fly: a book of memories 1952–1983*, Berri Publishing, Glen Iris, 2005.

363 P Duerdoth and N Vlahogiannis, *More Than a School: Glendonald School for the Deaf 1951–1991*, Victoria College Press, Melbourne, 1992, pp. 76, 77, 81.

364 Blake, vol. 1, pp. 910–11.

365 Shears, oral history interview conducted by Tony Ryan, archivist for the Australian College of Educators, 2004.

366 Gunstone, oral history interview conducted by the author, 2008.

367 Shears, oral history interview conducted by Tony Ryan, archivist for the Australian College of Educators, 2004.

368 ibid.

369 Generic notice in the March and April issues of the *Education Gazette and Teachers' Aid*; Shears, oral history interview conducted by the author, 2009.

370 Blake, vol. 1, details the genesis of the Curriculum and Research Branch, noting the early work of George S Browne, the ACER, impetus of the New Education Fellowship Conference in 1937, the influence of Dr Edwin I Leach, John A Cole and Harold Loader, pp. 1068–73.

371 McKinty, oral history interview conducted by the author, 2007.

372 *Education Gazette and Teachers' Aid*, 24 August, 1962; Blake, vol. 1, p. 1168.

373 *The Teachers Journal*: journal of the Victorian Teachers' Union, May 1962, p. 116.

374 Blake, vol. 1, gives an overview of the development in the VIER, pp. 1230–3; Boyce records its history and influence; Shears supports these views.

375 Browne, reference for Shears, 1958.

376 Boyce, p. 82, identifies origins of the Frank Tate Memorial Lecture. At the Annual Meeting of the VIER Executive in 1953 ER Wyeth put forth the proposal, seconded by Shears, that an annual oration celebrate the work of Frank Tate.

377 *Journal of Education*, vol. 1, no. 1, July 1954, pp. 5–9.

378 Shears, oral history interview conducted by the author, 2006.

379 W Radford, reference written October 1958 to support Shears' application for a Harkness Fellowship.

# Chapter 11

380 L Shears, 'The training of teachers for primary schools', *Australian Journal of Education*, vol. 2, no. 3, 1958, pp. 175–7.

381 http://www.commonwealthfund.org/About-Us/Foundation-History.aspx

382 Howard C Foster, a Commonwealth Fund Fellow (1935–36), was appointed Professor of Agriculture in 1953, a position he held until 1972. After retirement from Methodist Ladies' College, his sister lived close to the Shears at Aireys Inlet and attended St Aidan's Church with them.

383 A Ramsay, 20 October 1958, in Shears' application for a Commonwealth Fund Dominion Fellowship, later renamed, and hereinafter referred to as, Harkness Fellowship. The Shears file, containing the application and all letters, memos and reports, is at the Rockefeller Foundation, USA, and the National Library of Australia, ACT, nla.gov.au/nla.ms-ms9258.

384 In 1938 Radford's thesis The Educational Needs in the Rural Community studied the

situation in Bairnsdale and in 1950 Shears' survey 'The educational needs of adults in a rural community' covered the Upper Goulburn Region nearby to Dookie Agricultural College where he was employed at the RTC 1947–50.

385 Hoy, 25 October 1958, in Shears' Harkness Fellowship file – underlining present in copies obtained from Rockefeller Foundation.

386 Browne, 20 October 1958, in Shears' Harkness Fellowship file – underlining present in copies obtained from Rockefeller Foundation; the *Australian Journal of Education* developed from the *Journal of Education* published by VIER from 1954.

387 L Shears, application for a Harkness Fellowship, 14 October 1958; Shears, Letter to Wickman, Harkness Fellowship file, 10 April 1959.

388 L Shears, letter to Wickman, 10 April 1959.

389 RHG [not traceable to full name] memorandum to EKW [Wickman], Harkness Fellowship file, 14 April 1959.

390 E Wickman, letter to Shears, Harkness Fellowship file, 16 April 1959.

391 Memorandum to EKW, 14 April 1959, from unknown source; Wickman, letter to Shears, 16 April 1959, both memo and letter are in the Harkness Fellowship file. The memo lists recipients of Ford Foundation funding: Barnard College $70,000; Brown University $1,047,000; University of Chicago $2,400,000; Claremont Graduate School $425,000; Duke University $294,210; George Peabody College for Teachers $600,000; Stanford University $900,000; University of Wisconsin $625,000; Harvard University $2,800,000.

392 Ford Foundation, *New Directions in Teacher Education: an interim report of the work of the fund for the advancement of teacher education and recruitment*, Ford Foundation, New York, 1957, pp. 4, 5.

393 Shears, oral history interview conducted by the author, 2009; L Shears, memoir of Lou Barberis, 2009, written at the request of Alan Gregory for forthcoming Melbourne High School publication.

394 Hawaii became the 50th State of the Union on 21st August 1959.

395 L Shears, 'My American diary', *Teachers' Journal*, July 1960, p. 214.

396 ibid.

397 ibid.

398 Ford Foundation 1962, http://www.fordfound.org/archives/item/1962/text/20 [see note in bibliography]; RHG memorandum to EKW, 14 April 1959.

399 W Brickman, 'Educational developments in the United States during 1956', *International Review of Education*, vol. 4, no. 1, 1958; the number of institutions teaching Russian had increased from 16 in 1957 to over 400 by 1959.

400 L Shears, 'My American diary', *Teachers' Journal*, August 1960, p 268.

401 Shears, oral history interview conducted by Tony Ryan, archivist for the Australian College of Educators, 2004.

402 Reflection by EKW (Wickman), Berkeley, November 1959.

403 Shears, 'My American diary', *Teachers' Journal*, August 1960, p. 269.

404 Shears, oral history interview conducted by Tony Ryan, archivist for the Australian College of Educators, 2004.

405 Calisphere, University of California 2011, *A Master Plan for Higher Education in California, 1960–1975*, http://content.cdlib.org/view?docId=hb9c6008sn&chunk.id=div00072&brand=calisphere&doc.view=entire_text; Document submitted to governor for legisla-

tion, February 1; Statutory Bill passed April 14; Constitutional Amendment passed in November 1960, http://sunsite.berkeley.edu/uchistory/archives_exhibits/masterplan/1960.html.

406 Shears, oral history interview conducted by Tony Ryan, archivist for the Australian College of Educators, 2004; text in italics quoted from a submission by Shears to the Committee for the Development of Tertiary Education in Victoria, 29 September 1961.

407 Shears, oral history interview conducted by Tony Ryan, archivist for the Australian College of Educators, 2004.

408 Shears' original copy was lost. When asked for a copy, the University of London did not reply but librarians at Wayne State University used microfilm held in their archive to copy the thesis.

409 L Shears, Harkness Fellowship Report, 1960.

410 Shears, oral history interview conducted by the author, 2006; McKinty, oral history interview conducted by the author, 2007.

411 Unidentified memo in Shears' Harkness Fellowship file.

412 Shears, Harkness Fellowship file, 1960.

413 L Shears, Harkness Fellowship Report, 1960.

414 ibid.

415 Christine Shears, personal reflection with author, 2010; Mark Shears, oral history interview conducted by the author, 2007.

# Chapter 12

416 K Sargeant in *A Memento to L W Shears*, 3 August 1984.

417 Connell, 1993, p. 2.

418 P Karmel, Some economic aspects of education, the Buntine Oration delivered to the Australian College of Education, 3rd Annual Conference, 18 May 1962.

419 Karmel, p. 23.

420 Karmel, p. 20; Heffron 'Educate or Perish': Premier's address, Report of the National Education Conference, Leichardt Stadium, Sydney 21 May 1960, p. 4.

421 Dr (later Sir) Robert Madgwick, Education – a challenge to Australia!, Special Address to the National Education Conference, 21 May 1960, pp. 6–7. Madgwick, first Vice Chancellor of the University of New England, was a pioneer of distance education. He was appointed Chair of the ABC in 1966 and served two terms.

422 ibid.

423 Alan Ramsay's address at the 34 Annual Conference of the Victorian Teachers' Union; *Teachers' Journal*, March 1960.

424 Ramsay Report, recommendations, pp. 34, 147–9, 157.

425 W Hannan, *The Best of Times: the story of the great secondary schooling expansion*, Lexis, Northcote, 2009, p. 72.

426 R Reed, 'The organisation of secondary education', 14th Frank Tate Memorial Lecture, 27 June 1967, printed in *VIER Bulletin*, November 1967 pp. 8, 9.

427 Shears, 1958, 'The training of teachers for primary schools'.

428 W Spaulding and G Meindl, 'The institutional recommendation for certification', *Journal of Teacher Education*, June 1960, vol. 11, pp. 243–9. Dr Spaulding was chairman of the Division of Education, Portland (Oregon) State College and Mr Meindl

was attorney for the Oregon Education Association, Portland.
429 Hoy, 1958.
430 Butts, p. 4.
431 ibid., p. 7.
432 ibid., pp. 5–9.
433 L Shears in his principal's address, *Parabo*, 1965.
434 Waller in his principal's address, *Parabo*, 1957. Dimmack wrote *Modern Art Education in the Primary School,* which was printed in Australia, England and Jamaica. Frank Higgins wrote *Music in the Primary School*, Graham Allen wrote *Social Studies in the Primary School* and George Patrick wrote *English in the Primary School.*
435 Dimmack and Limb, oral history interviews conducted by the author, 2008.
436 D Keillerup, 'Retrospect', *Parabo*, 1961. Dennis was the son of Frank Keillerup who taught with Shears at Bairnsdale 1944–46.
437 H Nixon, oral history interview conducted by the author, 2007.
438 Dimmack, oral history interview conducted by the author, 2008.
439 Limb, oral history interview conducted by the author, 2008; G Corr, oral history interview conducted by the author, 2007.
440 Reflection by Fran Jackman, wife of Leon Jackman.
441 Limb, oral history interview conducted by the author, 2008; Corr, oral history interview conducted by the author, 2007.
442 *Yabba,* vol. 6, no. 6, August 1962. *Yabba* was the twice-yearly student magazine at Burwood TC, probably parallel to *Griffin* at Melbourne TC.
443 Shears, oral history interview conducted by the author, 2007.
444 L Shears, principal's address, printed in *Parabo*, 1967.
445 L Shears, principal's address, The personal meaning of education, 25 September 1963.
446 Shears frequently quoted these thoughts of Martin Buber in public presentations in later life.
447 L Shears, principal's end-of-courses address, 'Some thoughts on self-understanding', influenced by A Jersild, '*When Teachers Face Themselves,* Teachers' College Press, New York, 1955.
448 Thompson accepted the Education portfolio in 1967 and Brooks succeeded McDonell in 1965.
449 *Yabba,* June 1962, vol. 6, no. 5, p. 1.
450 Bell, oral history interview conducted by the author, 2007.
451 Shears, oral history interview conducted by the author, 2008.
452 Shears, oral history interview conducted by Tony Ryan, archivist for the Australian College of Educators, 2004.
453 Reflections by the author on Ken Sargeant's wise words given in 1962.
454 Shears, 1958, 'The training of teachers for primary schools'.
455 Shears and Paul McKeown initiated the survey of teachers in Australia at the second annual conference of the Australian College of Education in Adelaide in 1961. Results were presented to the third annual conference in Melbourne in 1962 and published in 1963 by the Australian College of Education; Shears, oral history interview conducted by Tony Ryan, archivist for the Australian College of Educators, 2005.
456 *The Age,* 4 September 1969.

457 Richard Selby Smith, born in 1913, came to Monash from the position of Principal, Scotch College, in Melbourne (1953–64). Initially appointed Foundation Professor of Education, he became Dean in 1965 and held the position until 1971. William Ernest Connell, born in 1916, had extensive experience as a headmaster, Lecturer in Education (1945–46) at the University of Melbourne, and Senior Lecturer (1951–53) and Reader (1954–55) in Education at the University of Sydney. He had extensive overseas experience at universities in the UK and the USA. Both he and Shears were Foundation members of the Australian College of Education and were made Fellows of the College in recognition of their extensive and ongoing commitment to education.

458 T Robertson, 'Educational research in Australia', 15th Frank Tate Memorial Lecture, *VIER Bulletin*, no. 19, 1968.

459 http://austcolled.com.au/notepad/article/tribute-paul-mckeown

460 Teachers in Australian Schools, A Report by the Australian College of Education, 1968 pp. 3, 4. (Comment upon this publication by Lawrie Shears: Paul [McKeown] and I met as members of the Australian College of Education, founded at Geelong Grammar School in 1959. At the second annual conference held at Adelaide University in May 1961 Paul and I presented a motion urging that the College pursues its activities at national level. From this motion the first comprehensive study of teachers in Australian schools took place.)

461 Shears, oral history interview conducted by Tony Ryan, archivist for the Australian College of Educators, 2006.

462 Butts, p. 80.

463 Shears, oral history interview conducted by Tony Ryan, archivist for the Australian College of Educators, 2006; views reflect those expressed by B Bessant and A Holbrook, *Reflections on Educational Research in Australia: a history of the Australian Association for Research in Education*, AARE, Coldstream, 1995, pp. 36, 37.

464 Connell, 1993, pp. 254, 255.

465 At the annual Conference in 2009 members of the AARE celebrated contributions to research over the past 40 years. Several Founders were present including Shears.

466 Shears, oral history interview conducted by the author, 2008.

467 ibid.

468 P Slater in *A Memento of L W Shears*, 3 August 1984, p. 16.

469 Shears, oral history interview conducted by Tony Ryan, archivist for the Australian College of Educators, 2006.

470 L Shears, principal's address, *Parabo*, 1968.

471 R Burton, *Parabo*, 1969.

472 Principal's addresses 1962–69.

# Chapter 13

473 J Bloomfield, Address, *Teachers Journal*, March 1967.

474 ibid.

475 Robertson, *VIER Bulletin* No 19, p. 4, 1968, 15th Frank Tate Memorial Lecture.

476 P. Hughes, VIER Bulletin, No 20, 1969, p 11. Hughes was Director-General of Education, Tasmania (1965–69).

477 Case for funding presented by the Australian Education Council, cited in A Spaull,

A *History of the Australian Education Council 1936–1986*, Allen and Unwin, Sydney, 1987, p. 148.

478 Commonwealth funding began in 1964; the *Victoria Institute of Colleges Act* 1967 (No. 7644) passed on 19 December 1967 although the first student intake occurred in 1965; school leaving age extended in 1965; examinations terminated in 1967.

479 Blake, vol. 1 p. 1460; ACIS became ADSE under the *Education and Teaching Service (Amendment) Act* 1967 (No. 7533).

480 L Shears' application for the position of Assistant Director-General of Education (Position 2) advertised in the *Education Gazette and Teachers' Aid*, 26 June 1969.

481 Blake, vol. 1, p. 1446.

482 Frank Tate, Victoria's first Director of Education appointed 1902, aged 38 years; *The Age*, 24 September 1969.

483 L Shears, personal files from 1969.

484 Morton commenced duty on 6 October 1969, according to Blake, vol. 1, p. 570.

485 Shears, oral history interview conducted by Tony Ryan, archivist for the Australian College of Educators, 2004.

486 Blake, vol. 1, p. 1385.

487 Thompson, oral history interview conducted by the author, 2007.

488 L Thompson, Maiden Speech, Legislative Council, 16 June 1955.

489 Education Department of Victoria, Report of the Minister of Education for 1967–68, Government Printer, Melbourne, 1970; *Teachers Journal*, March 1968, p. 13; further reference to the Cinderella portfolio in the *Education Gazette and Teachers' Aid*, April 1973, p. 34, where he highlighted comparative educational expenditure.

490 Thompson, *Looking Ahead in Education*, 1969, pp. 3, 4.

491 Education Department of Victoria, Report of the Minister of Education, 1967–68; *Teachers Journal*, March 1968, p. 13; Victorian State treasury papers cited in Thompson, 1969, p. 3.

492 *Interchange*, no. 2, November 1971, p. 4; 400 primary teachers were placed in secondary schools and 250 in technical schools; *News Exchange*, no. 5, 1973.

493 L Shears, Secondary education for the seventies, Lecture 3: The supply of teachers – with some digressions, presented in the Secondary Education Lecture Series of the Victorian Institute for Educational Research, 20 September 1971.

494 *The Age*, 21 March 1973.

495 *Interchange*, no. 6, March 1972, p. 6.

496 *Interchange*, no. 3, December 1971, p. 2.

497 *Teachers Journal*, May 1969 p. 13; *Interchange*, no. 5, February 1972, p. 3; *Interchange*, no. 9, June 1972, p. 3; *Interchange*, no. 10, July 1972, p. 1.

498 Copy of original document from Shears' personal files; the United Kingdom became a member of the European Economic Community on 1 January 1973.

499 *Interchange*, no. 10, July 1972, p. 3; *Interchange*, no. 11, August 1972, p. 5.

500 *Interchange*, no. 11, August 1972, p. 5; *Interchange*, no. 14, November 1972, p. 4, 5; *Interchange*, no. 12, September 1972, p. 4.

501 *Interchange*, no. 18 March 1973, p. 1.

502 L Thompson, *I Remember: an autobiography*, Hyland House, South Yarra, 1989, p. 97.

503 Thompson 1989, p. 97; Thompson, oral history interview conducted by the author,

2007; *Interchange*, no. 6, March 1972 gives an overview of the program from its inception, p. 6; Shears, oral history interview conducted by Tony Ryan, archivist for the Australian College of Educators, 2006; *The Age* 12 August 1970.

504 Rafferty had an educational background with experience in special education. He served as Assistant Minister of Education (August 1972–May 1973), Minister of Health (May 1973–March 1976), Minister of Special Education (March 1976–May 1979) and Assistant Minister of Education (August 1970–72).

505 *The Age*, 15 February 1971.

506 Murfett, oral history interview conducted by the author, 2007.

507 Correspondence, Shears' personal file.

508 Report on Educational Organization and Development in the Federal Republic of Germany in 1970–71, pp. 8, 9.

509 Undated statement from Shears' chronologically collated personal files.

510 Spaull, 1987, see pp. 169–86 for details; AEC recommendations followed the Survey of Needs

511 AW Jones, 'P Karmel: The Greatest Educational Statesman of the Century: The unification of South Australian secondary education, 1970–1977', http://www.lythrumpress.com.au/vision/261.html;

512 Thompson, 1969, pp. 4–5.

513 Survey and Statistics Branch; *Interchange*, no. 7, April 1972, p. 3.

514 Blake, vol. 1, pp. 1149–51 outlines the Southwell Report; Hannan, 2009, presents a union view of the Report pp. 298, 302-303; Brian Conway, Secretary, VSTA, letter to *The Age,* 23 March 1972.

515 Moyle, oral history interview conducted by the author, 2007.

516 *Interchange*, no. 23, August 1973, p. 3.

517 ibid.

518 ibid.

519 Blake, vol. 1, pp. 1354–55.

520 L Shears, opening remarks at a meeting of the Council of Teachers' College Staff Association Victoria (CTCSAV) entitled 'The origins, progress and future of the State College of Victoria', 6 April 1973, Melbourne TC; ideas reflect those presented in The McNair Report (1944) 'The supply, recruitment and training of teachers and youth leaders', as presented by D Gillard, *Education in England: a brief history,* 2007, www.educationengland.org.uk/history.

521 L Shears, 1973 'The origins, progress and future of the State College of Victoria', pp. 4, 5. Although he presented this view in the mid 1970s, it was affirmation of his aspiration to develop teachers colleges as autonomous tertiary institutions.

522 L Shears, 1961, submission by Shears to the Committee for the development of tertiary education in Victoria, pp. 7, 8.

523 L Shears, 'Tertiary Education – Can we provide it more economically?', unpublished article submitted to *The Australian*, 19 March 1965, filed with letter of apology from the Editor, Shears' personal files.

524 Monash University, founded in 1958, had its first student intake of 347 students in 1961; La Trobe University was founded in 1964 and its first intake of 500 students was in 1967; under the *Australian Universities Commission Act* 1959 the AUC was a statutory body established to advise the Commonwealth Government on university

matters nationwide.

525 *Tertiary Education in Australia*, report of the Committee on the Future of Tertiary Education in Australia to the Australian Universities Commission (Martin Report), Emeritus Professor Sir Lesley Martin, chairman, Government Printer, Canberra, vol. 1, August 1964, chapter 4 (v, vi, vii), p. 103.

526 Martin Report, chapter 4 (v).

527 ibid. (xi, xii, xiiv).

528 ibid. (vi, vii, x).

529 VIC statutes, approved by Governor in Council, 7 May 1974; *Victoria Institute of Colleges Act* 1965, (No. 7291); P Law, oral history interview conducted by the author, 2007.

530 J Polesel and R Teese, *The 'Colleges': growth and diversity in the non-university tertiary studies sector (1965–75)*, Department of Education, Training and Youth Affairs (Evaluations and Investigations Programme), Canberra, 1998.

531 P Law, oral history interview conducted by the author, 2007.

532 ibid.; The Pharmacy College, affiliated with the VIC, was granted permission to award the Bachelor of Pharmacy degree in 1967. The college thus became the first non-university institution in Australia to offer a bachelor's degree. A Master of Pharmacy degree followed in 1970.

533 *Interchange*, no. 6, March 1972, p. 5.

534 P Law, lecture presented to the Victorian Institute of Educational Research, 10 March 1967, printed in *VIER Bulletin*, no. 17, p. 45.

535 Shears, 1973, The origins, progress and future of the State College of Victoria', pp. 5.

536 AEC, Commonwealth financial assistance for capital expenditure to teacher training, 1966, pp. 8–9; AEC Council Meeting 1966, pp. 6–7, cited in Spaull, 1987.

537 L Shears, paper presented to the Australian Association of Teachers' College Principals in Brisbane on Saturday, 18 January 1969; projections for 1975 included a trainee source of over 11,000 nationwide.

538 Shears, oral history interview conducted by Tony Ryan, archivist for the Australian College of Educators, 2004.

539 Shears, 1969; Shears, oral history interview conducted by the author, 2008.

540 Shears, oral history interview conducted by Tony Ryan, archivist for the Australian College of Educators, 2004; oral history interview conducted by the author, 2007.a

541 Senate Standing Committee p. 478, cited in T Batrouney, Tertiary education in Victoria from the Murray Report and the State College of Victoria Act manuscript: an analysis of the changing definitions of tertiary education in Victoria and the educational ideologies which underline them, Master of Education thesis, Monash University, 1973.

542 Parliamentary Debates, Senate, vol. 12, 27th Parl. 2nd Session, 17 August 1972. pp. 202–3, cited in Batrouney; the AEC Standing Committee on Education, Science and the Arts and the Australian Pre-School Association were among those that offered support.

543 *State College of Victoria Act* (No. 8736), 19 December 1972, http://www.austlii.edu.au/au/legis/vic/hist_act/scova1972241/; the Act advanced the 'Provision of Tertiary Education in Branches of Learning of Importance in the Preparation of Teachers and especially in the Arts, Humanities and Sciences'.

544 *The Age*, 8 May 1973.

545 Bell, oral history interview conducted by the author, 2007.
546 Director-General's column, *News Exchange*, 7 July 1973.
547 L Shears' CV (1972, 1981) identifies his involvement in the Senate Standing Committee on Education, Science and the Arts (Teacher Education), and in the report to the Board of Inquiry chaired by Judge Southwell, September 1971. He presented his vision for education in 'Forces for continuity in Australian education' an address to the 1970 ACE conference entitled 'Continuity and change in education'. (Shears' personal papers).
548 *Interchange*, no. 14, November 1972, p. 5.
549 ibid.
550 I Mathews, *The Age*, November 1972.
551 Conversation between Shears and the author, 2009.
552 Shears, oral history interview conducted by the author, 2007.
553 M Ryan, *The Age*, 21 March 1973.
554 *Sun*, 21 March 1973, p. 11; *The Australian*, 21 March 1973, p. 5.
555 Shears, oral history interview conducted by the author, 2007.
556 R Goodman, Whither the College or where do we go from here?, address to the weekend conference of the Victorian Chapter of the Australian College of Education, 19 April 1969.
557 ibid.
558 J Kirner, letter published in *The Australian*, 22 September 1972.
559 L Shears, 22 September 1972, letter in personal files.
560 Anecdotal evidence.
561 Letter in Shears' personal file.

## Chapter 14

562 Shears, oral history interview conducted by Tony Ryan, archivist for the Australian College of Educators, 2005; Selleck 1982, p. 262; 'Little God Almighty' – term used by Selleck in the John Smyth Memorial Lecture, 1982; L Shears, 35th Frank Tate Memorial Lecture, 'Reflections of an optimist: a future for education', *VIER Bulletin,* Issue 55, 1985, p. 2 (underlining in text).
563 F Watts, letter of congratulations to Shears, 1973.
564 Press release dated 3.5.1973 and stamped 'Not to be released until 5 pm Saturday the 5.5.1973'; views reiterated in *Interchange*, no. 20, May 1973.
565 Shears, 1985, Reflections of an optimist: A future for education, p. 2.
566 'Which way the teacher?', undated paper from Shears' personal file believed to have been delivered during the celebrations for the centenary of State education in 1972.
567 From 'Schools in Australia: Report of the Interim Committee for the Australian Schools Commission', cited in 'The Schools Commission: A Review', presented by Professor Ken McKinnon at the University of Melbourne, 3 September 2010.
568 *The Age*, 19 June 1973.
569 *The Age*, 19 June 1973.
570 Shears, oral history interview conducted by Tony Ryan, archivist for the Australian College of Educators, 2004; *News Exchange* no. 5 1973; Shears presented similar views at the Primary Principals' Conference, 2 July 1973, held at the Southern Cross Hotel, Melbourne.

571 Shears, oral history interview conducted by Tony Ryan, archivist for the Australian College of Educators, 2005.

572 The Commission had twelve members – four were full time and five had served on the Interim Committee. Commission members included Peter Tannock (Dean, University of Western Australia), Jean Blackburn (Jean Muir from Shears' UHS days), Alby Jones (DGE, SA), Joan Kirner (Victorian involved in parent and community organisations), Tony McNamara (representative of Catholic parents), Ray Costello (representing unions), Barry McGaw (Head of the Research and Curriculum Branch, Department of Education, Queensland) and Don Edgar (Reader in Sociology, La Trobe University).

573 L Shears, address at a conference of technical teachers from the Bendigo region held at White Hills Technical School, 9 August 1973, Shears' personal file.

574 *The Age*, 15 November 1973; Mathews was the Chairman of the House of Representatives Select Committee on Specific Learning Difficulties (1974–75). He was a student at Toorak TC during Shears' lectureship tenure; Shears, oral history interview conducted by Tony Ryan, archivist for the Australian College of Educators, 2005.

575 AEC Standing Committee Debate, April 1975, p. 15, detailed in Spaull, 1987, p. 201.

576 *Interchange*, no. 28, February 1974, pp. 6, 7; no. 29, March 1974, p. 2; no. 32, June 1974, pp. 4, 5.

577 J Pascoe, oral history interview conducted by the author, 2007.

578 Alan Hunt's perception expressed in an interview with the author, 2009.

579 Commonwealth Year Book, 1974, p. 665, The Department regulated four-fifths of Victoria's schools, employed four-fifths of its teachers and educated four-fifths of its students; 'The Schools Commission: a review', presented by Professor Ken McKinnon at the University of Melbourne, 3 September 2010; Shears, oral history interview conducted by Tony Ryan, archivist for the Australian College of Educators 2004; Shears, oral history interview conducted by the author, 2007.

580 Terms and conditions as stated in the *Education Act* 1958 (No. 6240); the term Director-General replaced Director as in the 1958 Act under the *Education and Teaching Service Amendment Act* 1967 (No 7533), 17 March 1967.

581 Office of the Director-General of Education, *Structure at the State level: departmental guidelines for the future*, Paper 1, a paper for discussion and debate by interested groups from the Office of the Director-General of Education, Education Department of Victoria, Melbourne, 1975; Branches listed in *Interchange*, no. 28, February 1974, p. 3: Accounts, Buildings, Estates, Examinations, General Correspondence, Inspection, Papers, Post Primary, Primary Teachers, Secretariat, Stores, Teacher Education and Transport.

582 'About the Bland Report', *Interchange*, no. 41, April 1975, p. 1; Shears, Qualities of an administrator, speech delivered in Hobart 24 June 1961.

583 L Shears, Some forces leading to continuity in Australian education – how they might be reinforced, weakened or changed, paper presented to the ACE Conference, Canberra, May 1970.

584 L Shears, address to the Primary Principals' Conference, 2 July 1973, Southern Cross Hotel, Melbourne; Shears, oral history interview conducted by Tony Ryan, archivist for the Australian College of Educators, 2005; Shears, oral history interview conducted by the author, 2007.

585 E Peeler, Imaginations of an educator: An historic account of a leader's inspirations and innovations, paper presented to the annual conference of the Australian College of Educators, Hobart, May 2008.

586 Shears, Qualities of an administrator.

587 Letter of congratulations from Tom Moore.

588 Shears, address to the Primary Principals' Conference, 2 July 1973, Southern Cross Hotel, Melbourne.

589 Office of the Director-General of Education, *Structure at the State level: departmental guidelines for the future*, Paper 1, Education Department of Victoria, Melbourne, 1975; figures frequently presented in later life when he considered the enormity of the task.

590 Shears, Secondary education for the seventies, Lecture 3: The supply of teachers – with some digressions, presented in the Secondary Education Lecture Series of the Victorian Institute for Educational Research, 20 September 1971; in 1954, 8 per cent of students beginning Form 1 completed Form 6 but by 1971 the figure had risen to 34 per cent.

591 Shears, oral history interview conducted by the author, 2007.

592 From Friday evening until Sunday afternoon (21–23 February 1975). By invitation the media attended the Saturday session and the Minister addressed the group.

593 *News Exchange*, no. 10, 26 June 1974.

594 *Education (Administration) Act* 1975 (No. 8768) passed 25 November 1975.

595 *News Exchange*, no. 20, 22 November 1974; 61 applicants applied for positions as ADGE, 18 from overseas, *News Exchange*, no. 6, 24 April 1974.

596 Office of the Director-General of Education, *Structure at the regional level*, Paper 3, Education Department of Victoria, Melbourne, revised July 1975, p. 9.

597 *Interchange* no. 28, February 1974.

598 Residential seminar for inspectors held at Mannix College, February 1975.

599 Pascoe, oral history interview conducted by the author, 2007.

600 Senior administrators comprised the Director-General, his deputy and assistants, regional and divisional directors, and district and staff inspectors; Moyle, oral history interview conducted by the author, 2007.

601 *Interchange* no. 28, February 1974.

602 Office of the Director-General of Education, *Structure at the regional level*, Paper 3, Education Department of Victoria, Melbourne, revised July 1975, p. 9.

603 J Rich, *Innovations in Education: reformers and their critics*, Allyn & Bacon, Boston, 1992, p. 23; http://en.wikipedia.org/wiki/William_Wirt_(educator).

604 E Peeler, 'Communicating communities', paper presented at the Australian Association for Research in Education, Brisbane, 30 November–4 December 2008.

605 Shears, seminar for technical school principals in the Bendigo Region, White Hills Technical School, 9 August 1973; Shears identified $8.5 million to target school councils and school communities for the current year.

606 L Shears, Director-General's papers, T.73/725 (DG) Memorandum issued to Principals and Staffs of All Schools, 9 November 1973.

607 *The Age*, 13 November 1973.

608 Ideas presented by S Mahood, C Moyle and K Murray, 'The control of education – the role of parents and the community', proceedings of a seminar held at St Mary's College, University of Melbourne, 4 May 1973. This seminar occurred one day prior to Shears' appointment as Director-General, indicating that the concept was already mooted and that Shears went to battle where the swords of some were already drawn.

609 *News Exchange* no. 20, 22 November 1974.

610 Office of the Director-General of Education, *The school and the community*, Paper 4,

Education Department of Victoria, Melbourne, 1975.

611 J Kirner, oral history interview conducted by the author, 2007; Kirner, letter to *The Age*, 20 November 1973.

612 G Reid, *The Age*, 20 November 1973; Shears, oral history interview conducted by the author, 2009.

613 *The Age*, 2 October 1973.

614 Corr, oral history interview conducted by the author, 2007.

615 Shears, oral history interview conducted by the author, 2008; *News Exchange*, no. 11, 9 July 1975; *Interchange*, no. 44, July 1975.

616 L Shears, Memorandum for Interested Persons and Groups, 19 July 1974.

617 Shears, oral history interview conducted by the author, 2007.

618 B Henderson, oral history interview conducted by the author, 2007.

619 Pascoe, oral history interview conducted by the author, 2007.

620 Office of the Director-General of Education, *The teacher and the school administrator*, Paper 5, a paper for discussion and debate by interested groups, Education Department of Victoria, Melbourne, 1975.

621 ibid.

622 From 1963–64 to 1985–86, 22 Australians received a scholarship or fellowship at the University of Alberta. Australia had no training of educational administrators though the matter received consideration in the 1960s.

623 *Interchange*, no. 33 July 1974, p. 2.

624 N Barwick, oral history interview conducted by the author, 2007.

625 ibid.

626 *The Age*, 10 October 1974; Conference in Paris, 17 October–23 November 1974.

627 Recommendations: http://www.unesco.org/education/nfsunesco/pdf/Peace_e.pdf

628 UNESCO's Tensions Project (1949–53); http://unesdoc.unesco.org/images/0017/001793/179399eb.pdf; the result of research by James and Tenen was the publication *The Teacher Was Black*. See note 27, chapter 8.

629 L Shears, 'What education means to me', address to the Association of Catholic Teachers' Impact Series 25 July 1963, Education Week, St Michael's Church of England School, 21 August 1966; Thompson, 1969, pp. 4–5.

630 UNESCO, Records of the General Conference, 18th Session, Paris, 17 October to 23 November 1975; Resolutions.

631 Universal Declaration of Human Rights, Article 26 (2).

632 Letter to Shears from Hedley Beare, Director, Northern Territory Education, 25 September 1974, Shears' personal file. Hedley Beare – 1967: Harkness scholar, Harvard University; 1971: regional director, South Australian Education Department; 1972: established Northern Territory's integrated public school system; 1974: oversaw evacuation of Darwin after Cyclone Tracy; 1975: created new school system and final-year certificate for ACT; 1981: Melbourne University's first professor of educational administration. www.austcolled.com./notepad/article/emeritus-professor-hedley-beare-am-face-tribute

633 Letters from R Senior dated 23 July, 3 September 1975, Shears' personal file.

## Chapter 15

634 'Education – whose responsibility?' Script of an ABC talk given on Thursday 22 August 1963, during Education Week, and repeated in revised form in Wilson Hall to the Parents and Friends Federation of Victoria, an organisation established in 1959 by a group of Catholic school parents concerned with the lack of government support for Catholic schools. Within a short time a groundswell of support from parents led to the Victorian Parents Council extending its interests to independent schools also. See http://www.vicparentscouncil.vic.edu.au/index.php/about-us/history.

635 J Steinle tribute to Alby Jones and his service to education in South Australia, cited in Connell, 1993, p. 203.

636 B Hill, *The Age*, 4 March 1974.

637 Bessant and Spaull, 1976, p. 181.

638 Memorandum, 12 March 1975, Shears' personal files.

639 Hird, chapter 10, pp. 100–06.

640 Hird, p. 103; D Holloway, oral history interview conducted by the author, 2007.

641 ibid.; senior officers were aware of Moore's deep disappointment at being second in place to Shears.

642 Hill, *The Age*, 4 March 1974; perceptions often conveyed by Shears, reinforced during discussions with the author 25 February 2012, regarding this period of his term as Director-General.

643 Pascoe, oral history interview conducted by the author 2007.

644 Hill, *The Age*, 4 March 1975.

645 L Shears 'Education', in *Australia 2025: fifteen leading Australians examine the changed face of their country fifty years from now*, Electrolux, Melbourne, 1975, p. 90.

646 ibid., pp. 92–5.

647 L Shears, address to those attending the 16 residential conference for senior administrators at Somers school camp, 28 August 1975.

648 *Interchange*, no. 39, February 1975, p. 3, comments made by ADTE Noel Watkins.

649 *News Exchange*, no. 1, 13 February 1974; The Council met five times annually, held public meetings and workshops and published a journal and newsletters.

650 At its second conference, held at the University Sains in Malaysia, 27 August–3 September 1975 the Commonwealth Council for Educational Administration discussed issues regarding the role of the school principal.

651 Structures and priorities within the Education Department, Seminar No 2, Thursday, 29–Saturday 31 May 1975.

652 R Brown, DI Camberwell, *Interchange*, no. 41, April 1975, p. 5.

653 Office of the Director-General of Education, *The teacher and the school administrator*, Paper 5, a paper for discussion and debate by interested groups, Education Department of Victoria, Melbourne, 1975.

654 ibid.

655 Moyle, oral history interview conducted by the author, 2007; Professor James Lipham was well known and had published prolifically in educational administration.

656 K Andrews, A study of a leadership training program conducted by the Institute of Educational Administration utilising a naturalist paradigm, unpublished doctoral thesis, University of Nebraska, Lincoln, 1983, p. 76.

657 Education Department of Victoria, Report of the Minister of Education 1978–79, Government Printer, Melbourne, Victoria, introduction by Dr L W Shears, Director-General of Education, p. 7.

658 *News Exchange*, no. 20, 23 November 1979.

659 *Geelong Lands Act* 1981 (No. 9538)

660 *Institute of Education Act* 1980 (No. 9465), assented to on 16 December 1980, established a Body Corporate under the name of the Institute of Educational Administration, and for other purposes.

661 Andrews, 1983.

662 *Geelong Advertiser*, 5 February 1982.

663 Moyle, oral history interview conducted by the author, 2007.

664 Education Minister Robert Fordham reported on this in 1982 and identified his intent to develop the School Improvement Plan in 1983.

665 Initial moves by the Whitlam Government in 1973; formalised by the Fraser Liberal Government in 1978.

666 An Act relating to the entry into, and presence in, Australia of aliens, and the departure or deportation from Australia of aliens and certain other persons.

667 An Act relating to the provision of certain courses of instruction for immigrants and certain other persons.

668 Connell, 1993, p. 465.

669 Connell, 1993, chapter 10 gives a detailed account of policy shifts from assimilation through integration to multiculturalism; statistics re Victoria, p. 460; and details of the CMEP, p. 462.

670 L'Ecole Française de Melbourne began at Lauriston Girls School in 1968 and moved to Glamorgan in 1972. The 'primary' section, known as 'Petite Ecole', shifted to Auburn South Primary School in 1985 and moved to Camberwell Primary School in 1990. In 1992 it merged with the secondary section at John Gardiner High School (Hawthorn Secondary College). It is now based at Caulfield Junior College, a government school in North Caulfield.

671 D Whitton, 'Constant pressure "to be one of us"', *The Age*, 6 March 1979.

672 G Maslen, 'Guide to class war', *The Age*, 9 April 1979.

673 *The Age*, 7 December 1978.

674 *The Age*, 12 August 1978.

675 Shears' recruitment campaign included representation at the 19 UNESCO Conference 26 November 1976 that stressed the development of adult education; http://unesdoc.unesco.org/images/0011/001140/114038e.pdf; http://www.unesco.org/education/pdf/NAIROB_E.PDF; Shears, oral history interview with author 2009.

676 Shears, oral history interview with author 2009.

677 *The Age*, 11 January 1977.

678 A Wilcox, oral history interview conducted by the author, 2007.

679 http://www.go8.edu.au/university-staff/go8-policy-_and_-analysis/2009/50-year-old-report-on-the-role-of-australian-universities

680 Martin Report, vol. 1, August 1964.

681 Concepts presented by Connell 1993, who describes the development of TAFE, pp. 324–70; D McKenzie and C Wilkins (eds), *The TAFE Papers*, Macmillan, Melbourne,

1979, p. 5, cited in Connell, 1993, p. 330.
682 Spaull, 1987, pp. 206–7; Professor (later Sir) Bruce Williams, president of the Committee of Enquiry into Education and Training (1976–79), position held during his term as Vice Chancellor of the University of Sydney.
683 Born in Ireland, James Auchmuty CBE taught in his home country then lectured at Farouk University, Egypt, until 1952 when he moved to Australia. He held professorial positions at Newcastle University College and upon the foundation of the University of Newcastle was appointed Vice Chancellor.
684 Thomas B Swanson was Chairman of the Australian Commission on Advanced Education (1971–76). In this position he chaired the Swanson Committee's Inquiry into Teacher Education, 1973–75, which produced 'Teacher education, 1973–1975: report of the Special Committee on Teacher Education' (Cohen Report), authored by the Australian Commission on Advanced Education and T Swanson and S Cohen, Australian Government Printing Service, Canberra, Australia, 1973.
685 J Auchmuty, Report of the National Inquiry into Teacher Education, Canberra, 1980; J Carrick, Statement by the Minister for Education Senator Hon. J L Carrick, Canberra: Commonwealth of Australia, 1979; J Knight, B Lingard and L Bartlett, Reforming Teacher Education Policy under Labour Governments in Australia 1983–93, *British Journal of Sociology of Education*, 1994, 15(4), pp. 451–66, cited in M Dyson 'Australian Teacher Education: Although Reviewed to the Eyeball is there Evidence of Significant Change and Where to now?', *Australian Journal of Teacher Education*, vol. 30, no. 1, February, 2005; http://ro.ecu.edu.au/cgi/viewcontent.cgi?article=1394&context=ajte.
686 J Auchmuty, Report of the National Inquiry into Teacher Education, Canberra, 1980.
687 Teacher Education in Victoria, Interim Report of the Committee of the Victorian Enquiry into Teacher Education, February 1980, pp. 64, 65; Shears in *Australia 2025*.
688 ibid., pp. 90, 91.
689 *News Exchange* no. 14, 19 August 1980.
690 *News Exchange* no. 21, 25 November 1980; Connell 1993, gives insight into the Auchmuty Report, pp. 392–94 – he identified 53,000 full-time pre-service enrolments in 1976 and predicted a decline to about 35,000 by the mid 1980s; In *The Age*, 29 September 1980, 'Teachers a pet subject for committee', Geoff Maslen alleged 70 institutions prepared 50,000 trainees nationwide. Four-year training was essential but only half of Victoria's 50,000 teachers met these criteria.
691 Education Department of Victoria, Report of the Minister of Education 1978–79.
692 L Shears, address to the Annual Conference of the Technical Schools Association of Victoria, 23 October 1975.
693 L Shears, Schools' new role in society, *Herald*, 9 March 1978.
694 Post Secondary Education Act, gazetted on 10 December 1978.
695 P Roberts, *The Age*, 30 September 1978.
696 *Interchange*, no. 99, March 1980.
697 *News Exchange*, no. 3, 18 March 1980; W Johnson, *Technical to Post Primary: a history of the School Councils Association, Victoria (1914–1990)*, Association of Councils of Post Primary Institutions in Victoria, Box Hill, 1992, argued that Ministers Hunt and Lacy supported the autonomy of TAFE colleges. Johnson claimed Minister Thompson's reticence to take this step was due to Director-General Shears' firm views to maintain them within the Education Department's fold, pp. 113–43.
698 *Interchange*, no. 111, March 1981; *Interchange*, no. 118, October 1981 lists the 16 TAFE colleges at the time of separation and identifies the forthcoming inclusion of Whitehorse Technical College by November; *Interchange*, no. 117, September 1981 p.

4.

699 *Interchange*, No. 114, June 1981 p. 4.

700 G Tickell, oral history interview conducted by the author, 2007; Tickell, a union supporter, was instrumental in the community school movement.

701 Letter to the Editor, *The Age*, 17 July 1975.

702 R Jenkin, who later served as President of the VSTA, was appointed Principal of Box Hill High School in 1985. bob Jenkin, oral history interview with the author, 2008.

703 Pascoe, oral history interview conducted by the author, 2007.

704 A Hird (ADGE Personnel) and R Francis (DSE) conducted the survey. Responses came from 6 Australian States, 14 States in the USA (20 replies), 6 Canadian provinces (13 replies) and 7 local education authorities in the UK (7 replies); Statement in *The Age*, 27 December 1974.

705 *The Age*, 27 December 1974.

706 'Confidential. A Without Prejudice Statement – The Working Conditions of Teachers in Secondary Schools: An Analysis of National and International Practices', 22 July 1974, pp. 1–5, in Shears' personal files.

707 The Working Conditions of Teachers in Secondary Schools, pp. 1–5.

708 Views expressed by Shears in an oral history interview conducted by the author, 2008.

709 The Working Conditions of Teachers in Secondary Schools, p. 5.

710 Kirner, oral history interview conducted by the author, 2007.

711 Henderson and Kirner, oral history interviews conducted by the author 2007; Hannan, p. 319.

712 T Pankhurst, *The Age*, 4 March 1977

713 *The Age*, 13 August 1977.

714 *The Age*, 22 March 1977; Shears' personal files contain documents pertaining to procedures when similar concerns were raised at a later date. They include letters of advice to the Minister regarding actions, details of meetings with union representatives, press releases, actions taken and comment.

715 Hannan, p. 319.

716 ibid.

717 *The Age*, 24 February 1977.

718 Papers from Shears' personal files.

719 N Brand, 'Education job is heavy burden to bear – but he carries it well', *City of Preston Post-Times*, 8 February 1980.

## Chapter 16

720 D Ballantyne, 'People I meet', The Age, 24 June 1979; J Crawford, oral history interview conducted by the author, 2008.

721 L Shears, confidential paper, 23 March, 1979.

722 L Shears, Victorian Government Board of Review into Parliamentary Salaries: Hearing before Sir Andrew Grimwade, 15 September 1980.

723 Shears, Victorian Government Board of Review into Parliamentary Salaries, 1980.

724 ibid.

725 Farewell to 'Alice', Sunday, 23 March 1980, Osborne Street Campus Garden, Bendigo.

726 Shears, Reflections of an optimist – a future for education, 32nd Frank Tate Memorial Lecture, printed in VIER Bulletin, 1985.

727 L Foster, oral history interview conducted by the author, 2008.

728 ibid.

729 Ballantyne, The Age, 24 June, 1979; Crawford, oral history interview conducted by the author, 2007.

730 A Hunt, oral history interview conducted by the author, 2009.

731 Ballantyne, The Age, 24 June, 1979.

732 Hunt, oral history interview conducted by the author, 2009.

733 ibid.

734 ibid.

735 Hunt, 'A government thrusts towards change'. In M Frazer, J Dunstan & P Creed (eds), Perspectives in Organisational Change: lessons from education, Longman Cheshire, Melbourne, 1985, p. 15.

736 N Lacy, 'Implementing change'. In Frazer et al., 1985, p. 38.

737 T Moore, 'Change process from inside'. In Frazer et al., 1985, p. 301–2.

738 Moore, 1985, p. 301–2.

739 N Curry, 'Difficulties and achievements in implementing organisational change'. In Frazer et al., 1985, p. 408.

740 J Dunstan, 'The location of decision-making responsibility in the new structure'. In Frazer et al., 1985, p. 258.

741 J Kirner, 'Organisational change: parent line'. In Frazer et al., 1985, pp. 343–63.

742 Kirner, oral history interview conducted by the author, 2007.

743 Formed by Shears, this committee of 16 members had met regularly on Tuesdays to determine policy. Hird says that it consisted of Assistant Directors-General and divisional directors but it 'was not a vehicle for effective policy making' as under existing legislation it 'lacked necessary powers', p. 162. Hird also says that guided (or stirred) by one divisional director, the divisional directors established their own routine of meetings to determine policy prior to the Policy Committee meeting, p. 103.

744 R Bates, 'The socio-political context of administrative change'. In Frazer et al., 1985, p. 290.

745 Hird, p. 179.

746 Kirner, 1985, p. 347–8.

747 Maslen, 'Big shake-up in education', *The Age*, 2 August 1979.

748 Holloway, pp. 496–97; Holloway, oral history interview conducted by the author, 2007.

749 Kirner, 1985, p. 348; Frazer et al. Appendix III lists members of the Ministerial Review Committee, Organisations Reference Group, Implementation Steering Committee, Implementation Task Force and some Education Department personnel.

750 Kirner, 1985, p. 349.

751 L Shears, Controversial issues: a further paper, September 1979; Maslen, 'Bell rings for big debate', *The Age*, 3 August 1979.

752 L Shears, correspondence with Hunt, 24 April 1980.

753 A Hunt, in Frazer, et al., 1985, pp. 13–32.

754 Hunt, oral history interview conducted by the author, 2009.

755 Curry, pp. 31–55.

756 L Shears, 'Implementing change'. In Frazer et al., 1985, pp. 74–103.

757 Hunt, oral history interview conducted by the author, 2009.

758 G Harman, 'Planned organisational change'. In Frazer et al., 1985, pp 155–188.

759 L Shears, Letter to senior staff, 13 April 1981.

760 Hird, p. 165.

761 Shears, correspondence, 1981.

762 ibid.

763 Murfett, oral history interview conducted by the author, 2007.

764 Barwick maintained his position on the Australian Schools Commission Buildings Committee. He became Director-General of Youth, Sport and Recreation, a position he held until 1984. Morton was seconded to the position ADGE (Buildings) from the VIC; Barwick considered the shifts in educational provision and an increasing trend towards coordination with other community services; *Interchange*, no. 100, April 1980, p. 1.

765 Shears, correspondence, 1981.

766 The Corporate Management Group (CMG) was proposed in the *White Paper on Strategies and Structures for Education in Victorian Government Schools*, presented to Parliament in December 1980. It was to be an executive group, 'a group of managers of which the Minister was one' to replace the Permanent Head of the Education Department (p. 35 of the White Paper). In practice it consisted of two Ministers, the Director-General and the five Assistant Directors-General. The CMG reviewed recommendations of the Implementation Steering Committee.

767 Shears, correspondence, 8 May 1981.

768 Bates, pp. 288–9.

769 Kirner, 1985, pp. 343–63.

770 Maslen, *The Age*, 29 August 1981.

771 Kirner, oral history interview by the author, 2007.

772 Kirner, 1985, pp. 343–63; personal papers.

773 Brouwer, *Sun*, 14 October 1981.

774 ibid.; Bolt, *The Age*, 16 October 1981; Maslen, *The Age*, 20 August, 1981.

775 Maslen, *The Age*, 20 August 1981.

776 *The Age*, Letter to the Editor, 10 November 1981.

777 ibid.

778 Sargeant, Letter to the Editor of *The Age*, 13 November 1981. The editor noted support from members of the VIER and Melbourne University's Faculty of Education.

779 Unpublished letter to the Editor of *The Age*, 11 November 1981.

# Chapter 17

780 G Maslen, 'Double hurdle for Shears', *The Age*, 16 November 1981.

781 L Shears, letter to Hunt, 16 November 1981.

782 P Chubb, 'Shears gets new job as education coordinator-general', *The Age*, 17 November 1981.

783 S Green, 'New Shears job to cost $¼ m.', *Herald*, 17 November 1981.

784 S Green, 'Old guard loses out in shake-up', *The Age*, 31 December 1981; *Interchange*, No. 122, February 1982, p. 1.

785 J McKenzie, letter to *The Age*, 13 January 1982.

786 S Green, '$40,000 a year for six without official positions', *The Age*, 23 January 1982; *Interchange*, No. 122, February 1982, p. 1.

787 *Interchange*, no. 121, January 1982, p. 3; Hird, p. 191.

788 Hird, pp. 188–9; Hird claimed he had previously seen the proposal for Coordinator-General as offered to Shears, prepared for Director-General Brooks by a 'gentleman seeking a place in the sun'.

789 S Green, 'Education chief: I'm in charge', *The Age*, 6 February 1982.

790 Shears, oral history interview conducted by Tony Ryan, archivist for the Australian College of Educators, 2004.

791 Maslen, 'Libs stumble in first round of election fight', *The Age*, 10 March 1982; Maslen's thoughts produced in *The Age* February–April 1982 detail debates and events.

792 Henderson, oral history interview conducted by the author, 2007.

793 Education Policy Statement, Australian Labor Party (Victoria), 1976, pp. iv, v.

794 Maslen, 'Fordham confident on eve of changes', *The Age*, 17 August 1982, p. 12; 'Some new education posts to be axed', 17 April 1982.

795 R Fordham, oral history interview conducted by the author, 2007.

796 Minister of Education, *Decision making in Victorian education*, Ministerial Paper 1, Education Department of Victoria, Melbourne, Victoria, 1983.

797 Minister of Education, *The School Improvement Plan,* Ministerial Paper 2, Education Department of Victoria, Melbourne, Victoria, 1983, p. 2.2.

798 Minister of Education, *The State Board of Education,* Ministerial Paper 3, Education Department of Victoria, Melbourne, Victoria, 1983.

799 *The Age,* editorial, 21 October 1982.

800 Minister of Education, *School councils,* Ministerial Paper 4, Education Department of Victoria, Melbourne, Victoria, 1983.

801 Minister of Education, *Curriculum development and planning in Victoria,* Ministerial Paper 6, Education Department of Victoria, Melbourne, Victoria, 1984.

802 Henderson, oral history interview conducted by the author, 2007.

803 E Dale, oral history interview conducted by the author, 2007.

804 R Batties, 'Report urges new style youth centres', *The Age,* 15 February 1983.

805 L Shears and J Matthews, *Youth Policies,* Office of the Coordinator-General, Education Department of Victoria, Education Department, Melbourne, Victoria, 1983.

806 Shears and Matthews, 1983.

807 L Shears and J Matthews, *Curriculum: an international perspective,* Office of the Co-ordinator-General, Education Department of Victoria, Education Department, Melbourne, Victoria, 1984, p. 129.

808 L Shears, Administrative Structures in Education, Office of the Coordinator-General, Education Department of Victoria, 1984.

809 ibid.

810 Maslen, 'Education chief slams youth policy', *The Age,* 4 March 1983.

811 Maslen, 'Pity the poor teenager', *The Age,* 16 June 1983. Maslen gives a detailed account of the report and the background to it.

812 A Wright, former member of the Ballarat Transition Task Force, *The Age*, letter to the editor, 10 March 1983.

813 Crawford, oral history interview conducted by the author, 2007.

814 Holloway, oral history interview conducted by the author, 2007.

815 Moyle, oral history interview conducted by the author, 2007.

816 Murfett, oral history interview conducted by the author, 2007.

817 D Murray (ed.), Reports from Victorian Fellows, International Teaching Fellowship Program, 1981.

818 Maslen, 'Education chief stepping down after pursuing hobby for 45 years', *The Age*, 28 May 1984.

819 Maslen, *The Age*, 29 May 1984.

820 *A Memento of L W Shears*, 1984.

821 L Shears, retirement speech, 3 August, 1984.

## Chapter 18

822 W Churchill, a speech at the Lord Mayor's Day luncheon at the Mansion House, London, 9 November 1942. Rommel's forces turned back at El Alamein, thus won The Battle of Egypt.

823 Jean Blackburn, formerly Jean Muir, from Shears' University High School days.

824 L Shears, 4th National Conference, Australian Association for Community Education, opening address, 1984.

825 Shears, 'Reflections of an optimist – a future for education', 32nd Frank Tate memorial lecture, 1975.

826 C Carroll, Victorian representative, Council of Education Centres, *The Age*, letter to the editor, 1 October 1986.

827 Shears, Commonwealth sponsored education centres: report of Committee of Review to Commonwealth Schools Commission December, 1984, p. 2; Dr Peter Tannock was a member of the Australian Schools Commission from 1974 to 1979 and served as Chairman between 1980 and 1984; views expressed by Shears in conversation with the author.

828 C Carroll, 1986.

829 R E Ross Trust, n.d.; Shears, Commonwealth Sponsored Education Centres, 1984.

830 Spaull, 1987; Dr Alby Jones, Director-General in South Australia (1970–77), Dr Ron Browne, AEC Secretary since 1978, Dr Peter Tannock, Chairman, Schools Commission (1980–84), Dr Andrew Spaull, Senior Lecturer and Reader, Faculty of Education, Monash University (1969–2003).

831 A concept cultivated Brian Dixon and the Education Department in 1975, it became a Commonwealth responsibility but when funds were withdrawn in 1978 it was run as a community organisation in 1981. It joined forces with the National Heart Foundation of Australia and continued for a time before it went into hibernation. It was revived in 2000 in Victoria and South Australia and still runs in South Australia.

832 L Shears, *Computers and schools*, ACER, Melbourne, Victoria, 1995, preface.

833 L Shears, 1995. Thoughts expressed by Barry McGaw, Chairman, ACER, introduction.

834 Tickell, oral history interview conducted by the author, 2007.

835 Kirner, oral history interview conducted by the author, 2008.

836 Kirner, oral history interview conducted by the author, 2007.

837 W Shakespeare, *Hamlet* Act 1, Scene 3, Advice from Polonius to Laertes.

# SELECT BIBLIOGRAPHY

This select bibliography is presented in five sections.
- **Section 1** contains papers, both personal and professional, and publications by Lawrence Shears, listed in date order from the award of his Merit certificate in 1934 to the present. Particular thanks are due to archivists from Deakin University, Institute of Education (London), University of Melbourne, Wayne State University (Michigan) for their assistance.
- **Section 2** lists all printed materials, alphabetically by author where possible, or by publication (e.g. newspapers) or sometimes by title.
- **Section 3** lists relevant legislation in date order, separated into Victorian and Commonwealth.
- **Section 4** lists oral history interviews and conversations.
- **Section 5** lists web sites accessed during the writing of the book.

## 1. Shears

Shears, L. Merit Certificate No. 259572, Education Department of Victoria.
— 1939–84, Teaching record of Lawrence William Shears, Education Department of Victoria, Melbourne.
— 1949a, *A Short Course in Farm Bookkeeping*, Bellmain Bros Pty Ltd, Melbourne Victoria.
— 1949b, The educational needs of adults in rural areas, Bachelor of Education thesis, University of Melbourne.
— 1952, The dynamics of leadership in adolescent school groups, doctoral thesis, Institute of Education, University of London.
— 1952b, A report to the Imperial Relations Trustees: an account of activity under the Award of the Imperial Relations Trust Fellowship

1950–1951, Institute of Education, University of London.
— 1953, *A Short Course in Farm Bookkeeping*, 2nd ed. revised, Robertson and Mullens, Melbourne.
— 1958a, 'The training of teachers for primary schools', *Australian Journal of Education, 2* (3).
— 1958b, Application for Harkness Fellowship. The Shears file, containing the application and all letters, memos and reports, is at the Rockefeller Foundation, USA, and the National Library of Australia, ACT, nla.gov.au/nla.ms-ms9258. Full reference for materials attained from Rockefeller Archive Centre: Commonwealth Fund, Series 20.2, Harkness Fellowships, Box 192, Folder 1549.
— 1959–2013, personal letters and correspondence.
— 1959, 1969, 1972, 1981, curricula vitae.
— 1959–60, First report to the Commonwealth Trust of New York. Harkness Fellowship File.
— 1960, 'My American diary', *Teachers' Journal* (monthly publication of the Victorian Teachers Union), July and August.
— 1961a, 'Qualities of an administrator' speech delivered in Hobart, 24 June.
— 1961b, submission by Shears to the Committee for the development of tertiary education in Victoria, 29 September 1961.
— 1962, 'Educational administration in California and Victoria', presentation to the Martin Committee (see detail in list below under *Tertiary Education in Australia*), duplicated and circulated by the Committee on the Future of Tertiary Education, Australian Universities Commission, February.
— 1963a, 'What education means to me', address to the Association of Catholic Teachers' Impact Series 25 July.
— 1963b, 'Education—whose responsibility?' Script of an ABC talk given 22 August during Education Week.
— 1965, 'Tertiary Education—Can we provide it more economically?' Unpublished article submitted to *The Australian*, 19 March, filed with letter of apology from the Editor.
— 1966, 'What education means to me', address during Education Week at St Michael's Church of England School, 21 August.
— 1969, paper presented to the Australian Association of Teachers'

College Principals in Brisbane 18 January.
— 1970, 'Some forces leading to continuity in Australian education— how they might be reinforced, weakened or changed', address to the Australian College of Education Conference entitled 'Continuity and change in education', in Canberra, in May.
— 1971, Secondary education for the seventies, Lecture 3: 'The supply of teachers—with some digressions', presented in the Secondary Education Today Lecture Series of the Victorian Institute for Educational Research, 20 September.
— 1971–72, 'The supply of teachers in various Western countries and Victoria, with some digressions', an address given in various forms in various places, including:
  - McKinnon High School Parents and Teachers' Association, 1971, March
  - College of Nursing Australia, 1971, June
  - Rotary clubs of Horsham and Stawell, 1971, October
  - Malvern Principals' Fraternal, 1972, July.
— 1972a, 'Which way the teacher?', address to Beaumaris Women's Group, June.
— 1972b, letter in personal files on support for teachers in government schools, 22 September.
— 1973a, opening remarks at a meeting of the Council of Teachers' College Staff Association Victoria entitled 'The origins, progress and future of the State College of Victoria', 6 April, Melbourne Teachers College.
— 1973b, press release dated, 3.5.1973 and stamped 'Not to be released until 5 pm Saturday the 5.5.1973'.
— 1973c, 'Critical look at school', *The Age*, 19 June.
— 1973d, address to the Primary Principals' Conference held at the Southern Cross Hotel, Melbourne, 2 July.
— 1973e, 'Technical education: school and working life', address at a conference of technical teachers from the Bendigo region held at White Hills Technical School, Bendigo, 9 August.
— 1974a, Memorandum for interested persons and groups, 19 July.
— 1974b, Confidential. A Without Prejudice Statement—The Working Conditions of Teachers in Secondary Schools: An Analysis of

National and International Practices, 22 July.
- 1975a, address to a residential seminar for inspectors, February.
- 1975b, letter to the editor, *The Age*, 17 July.
- 1975c, address to those attending the 16th residential conference for senior administrators at Somers school camp, 28 August.
- 1975d, address to the Annual Conference of the Technical Schools Association of Victoria, 23 October.
- 1975e, address at the Australian College of Education Conference entitled 'Learning throughout life—Lifelong learning—Learning through living', Hobart.
- 1975f, 'Education' in *Australia 2025: fifteen leading Australians examine the changed face of their country fifty years from now*, Electrolux, Melbourne, Victoria, pp. 89–98.
- 1975g, memorandum, 12 March.
- 1977, 'Who should run our schools?', *The Age*, 13 August.
- 1978, 'Schools' new role in society', *Herald*, 9 March.
- 1978–79, Introduction, annual report of the Education Department, Education Department of Victoria, Melbourne.
- 1979a, confidential paper, 23 March.
- 1979b, *Controversial Issues: A Further Paper*, September.
- 1980a, Farewell to 'Alice', Osborne Street Campus Garden, Bendigo, 23 March.
- 1980b, correspondence with Minister Hunt, 24 April.
- 1980c, Victorian Government Board of Review into Parliamentary Salaries: Hearing before Sir Andrew Grimwade, 15 September.
- 1981a, letter addressed to senior staff, 13 April.
- 1981b, unpublished letter to *The Age*, 11 November.
- 1984a, *Administrative Structures in Education*. Office of the Coordinator-General, Education Department of Victoria, Melbourne.
- 1984b, 'In appreciation', retirement speech given at retirement dinner, Camberwell Civic Centre, Melbourne, 3 August.
- 1984c, *Review of Commonwealth Sponsored Education Centres*, Australian Schools Commission. Canberra.
- 1984d, opening address, 4th National Conference, Australian Association for Community Education, Frankston, 2 December.

— 1985a, Reflections of an optimist: A future for education, 35th Frank Tate Memorial Lecture, printed in *VIER Bulletin* (55), pp. 1–30.
— 1985b, 'The fragmentation of power', in M. Frazer, J. Dunstan & P. Creed (Eds.), *Perspectives in Organisational Change: Lessons from Education*, Longman Cheshire, Melbourne, pp. 74–103.
— 1995, *Computers and Schools*, ACER, Melbourne, preface.
— 2004–06, Oral history interviews for the Australian College of Educators, Melbourne (Tony Ryan, ACE archivist, interviewer).
— 2006–10, Oral history interviews. (E. Hemphill Peeler, interviewer).
— 2009, Memoir of Lou Barberis written at the request of Alan Gregory for forthcoming publication by Melbourne High School.
Shears, L. & Dale, E. 1983, *Computers in Education*. Office of the Coordinator-General, Education Department of Victoria, Melbourne.
Shears, L. & Matthews, J. 1983, *Youth Policies*, Office of the Coordinator-General, Education Department of Victoria, Melbourne.
Shears, L., & Matthews, J. 1984, *Curriculum: An international perspective*, Office of the Coordinator-General, Education Department of Victoria, Melbourne.

## 2. Printed materials
These articles are all from *The Age*.
28 May 1946, 'Farm training for ex-servicemen: Eight weeks' course at Dookie planned'
16 August 1948, size of land for schools
24 September 1969, 'Two get top posts in education.'
24 September 1969, Education Department's executive team
15 February 1971, 'Visiting teachers welcomed'
5 May 1973, 'The new Director-General of Education takes over.'
8 May 1973, 'Shears profile'
2 October 1973 'Catholics join in education inquiry'
13 November 1973, 'New community rules for running of schools'
15 November 1973, 'Victoria is spending without authority: Mathews'
10 October 1974, 'Dr Shears to attend UN conference'
27 December 1974, 'Class size "no longer criterion" '
11 January 1977, 'Teacher swap proposed with Russia'

24 February 1977, 'Anarchy warning by school heads'
22 March 1977, 'Skating over unrest'
14 April 1977, 'State ends import of teachers'
12 August 1978, 'Schools survey: Dr Shears hits migrant findings'
7 December 1978, 'Gross ignorance of migrant needs'
Aldrich, R. 2002, *The Institute of Education 1902–2002: A Centenary History*, Institute of Education, London.
Aldridge, R.. 1986, *Dookie College: The First 100 Years*, Victorian College of Agriculture and Horticulture, Melbourne, Victoria.
Allen, G. 1960, *Social Studies in the Primary School*, Macmillan, Melbourne.
Andrews, K. 1983, A study of a leadership training program conducted by the Institute of Educational Administration utilising a naturalist paradigm, unpublished doctoral thesis, University of Nebraska, Lincoln.
Annear, R. 1995, *Bearbrass: Imagining Early Melbourne*, Vintage, Milson's Point, NSW.
Auchmuty Report, *see* National Inquiry into Teacher Education.
*The Australian*, 21 March 1973, announcing the new Director-General
— 5 May 1973, 'The new Director-General of Education takes over'
Australian Bureau of Statistics 1974, *Official Year Book of Australia No. 60, 1974*, Cat. No. 1301.0, ABS, Canberra.
Australian College of Education 1968, 'Teachers in Australian Schools', Australian College of Education, Melbourne.
Australian Commission on Advanced Education and T. Swanson and S. Cohen 1973, 'Teacher education, 1973–1975: Report of the Special Committee on Teacher Education' (Cohen Report), Australian Government Printing Service, Canberra.
Australian Council for Educational Research 1956, 'The Shire of Ferntree Gully and its educational future: A report compiled in collaboration by officers of the Australian Council for Educational Research, University of Melbourne Faculty of Education, Victorian Education Department ... at the request of the Combined State Schools' Committees' Conference of the Shire of Ferntree Gully', ACER, Melbourne.
*Bairnsdale Advertiser*, 1943–45

Ballantyne, D. 1979, 'People I meet', *The Age*, 24 June.

Bassett, G. 1980, *Teachers in Australian Schools 1979*, Australian College of Education, Melbourne.

Bates, R. 1985 'The socio-political context of administrative change', in M. Frazer, J. Dunstan & P. Creed (eds), *Perspectives in Organisational Change: Lessons from Education*, Longman Cheshire, Melbourne, pp. 283–300.

Batrouney, T. 1973, Tertiary education in Victoria from the Murray Report and the State College of Victoria Act manuscript: an analysis of the changing definitions of tertiary education in Victoria and the educational ideologies which underline them, unpublished Master of Education thesis, Monash University.

Batties, R. 1983, 'Report urges new style youth centres', *The Age*, 15 February.

Bertaut, J. (ed.) 1916, *Napoleon in His Own Words*, trans. H. Law and C. Rhodes, A. C. McClurg and Co., Chicago.

Bessant, B. and Spaull, A. 1976, *Politics of Schooling*, Pitman Pacific, Carlton.

Bessant, B. and Holbrook, A. 1995, *Reflections on Educational Research in Australia: a history of the Australian Association for Research in Education*, AARE, Coldstream.

Blake, L. and Lovett, K. 1962, *Wimmera Shire Centenary: An Historical Account*, Shire of Wimmera, Horsham, Victoria.

Blake, L. (ed.) 1973, *Vision and Realisation: A Centenary History of State Education in Victoria*, 3 vols, Education Department of Victoria, Melbourne.

Bland Report, 1974, *see* Victoria, Board of Inquiry into the Victorian Public Service.

Bloomfield, J. 1967, Address, *Teachers Journal*, March.

Bolt, A. 1981, 'Hunt denies ALP claim of personal motive', *Sun* 16 October.

Boyce, M. 1992, *A Perspective of the VIER: A View of the First Sixty Years of the Victorian Institute of Educational Research 1929–1989*, Victorian Institute of Educational Research, Malvern, Victoria.

Brand, N. 1980, 'Education job is heavy burden to bear—but he carries it well', *City of Preston Post-Times*, 8 February.

Brickman, W. 1958, Educational developments in the United States during 1956, *International Review of Education*, 4 (1).

Broome, R. 1980, *The Victorians: Arriving*, Fairfax, Syme & Weldon Associates, Melbourne.

Brouwer, A. 1981, 'New law hits Shears' post', *Sun* 14 October.

Browne, G. 1958, letter of support for Shears' application for a Harkness Fellowship. *See above*, Shears 1958b.

Browning, R. 1864, Confessions, *Dramatis Personae*, Chapman and Hall, London.

Burchell, L. 1980, *Victorian Schools: A History of Government Architecture, 1837–1900*, Melbourne University Press, Melbourne.

Burwood Teachers College 1954–69, *Parabo*, college magazine, Burwood TC, Melbourne.

Butts, R. 1955, *Assumptions underlying Australian Education*, ACER, Melbourne.

Carrick, J. 1979, Statement by the Minister for Education Senator Hon. JL Carrick, Commonwealth of Australia, Canberra

Carroll, B. 1995, *A Decade of Achievement: Phillip Institute of Technology*, RMIT Press, Mebourne.

Carroll, C. 1986, 'Education cuts to centres are shortsighted', *The Age*, 1 October.

Catrice, A. 2009, Foundations of Burwood and Toorak Teachers Colleges, *Glenbervian*, May.

Chubb, P 1981, 'Shears gets new job as education coordinator-general', *The Age*, 17 November.

Churchill, W. 1942, A Speech at the Lord Mayor's Day Luncheon at the Mansion House, London, 9 November, from Churchill, W. 1943, *The End of the Beginning*, Cassell, London.

Clark, J., Murray, G., Bowles, G., Barr, T., Barberis, L., and Eldens, J. 1981, letter to the editor, *The Age*, 10 November.

Clyne, M. 1991, *Community languages: the Australian experience*, Cambridge University Press, Cambridge.

Cochrane, P. 2006, *Colonial Ambition: Foundations of Australian Democracy*, Melbourne University Press, Melbourne.

Cohen Report, *see* Australian Commission on Advanced Education.

Committee on State Education in Victoria 1960, Report of the

Committee on State Education in Victoria (A Ramsay, Chairman), Goverment Printer, Melbourne.

Connell, W. 1971, letter to L. Shears, 9 November.

— 1993, *Reshaping Australian Education 1960–1985*, ACER, Melbourne.

Conway, B. 1972, letter to *The Age*, 23 March.

Curry, N. 1985, 'Difficulties and achievements in implementing organisational change' in M. Frazer, J. Dunstan & P. Creed (eds), *Perspectives in Organisational Change: Lessons from Education*, Longman Cheshire, Melbourne, pp. 391–409.

*Cygnet*, magazine of Bairnsdale High School 1944–46.

Darling, J. 1943, report of the Educational Reform Association meeting at the Melbourne Town Hall, *The Age*, 19 May.

Dimmack, M. 1958, *Modern Art Education in the Primary School*, Macmillan, Melbourne.

Dingle, A. 1984, *The Victorians: Settling*, Fairfax, Syme & Weldon Associates, McMahons Point, NSW.

Docherty, J. 1981, *The Emily Mac: The Story of the Emily McPherson College, 1906–1979*, Ormond Book and Educational Supplies Pty Ltd, Melbourne.

*Dookie Collegian*, magazine of Dookie Agricultural College 1946–50.

Duerdoth, P. and Vlahogiannis, N. 1992, *More than a School: Glendonald School for the Deaf 1951-1991*, Victoria College Press, Melbourne.

Dunstan, J. 1985, 'The location of decision-making responsibility in the new structure, in M. Frazer, J. Dunstan & P. Creed (eds), *Perspectives in Organisational Change: Lessons from Education*, Longman Cheshire, Melbourne, pp. 255–80.

Dyson, M. 2005, 'Australian teacher education: although reviewed to the eyeball is there evidence of significant change and where to now?' *Australian Journal of Teacher Education*, vol. 30, no. 1, February.

Education Department of Victoria, 1930–84, *Education Gazette and Teachers' Aid*, Education Department, Melbourne.

— 1928–30, *The Victorian Readers*, Books 1–8, Government Printer, Melbourne.

— 1971–84, *Interchange*, Publications Branch, Education Department, Melbourne.

— 1973–84, *News Exchange*, Publications Branch, Education Department, Melbourne.

— 1984, *A Memento of L. W. Shears*, Education Department, Melbourne, 3 August.

Eliot, T. 1910–11, 'Preludes'.

*Every Week*, W Heath in Bairnsdale, 1944–45.

Fleming, W. 1967, 'Educational research in tomorrow's society', *VIER Bulletin*, no. 17.

Ford Foundation 1953, *New Directions in Teacher Education: An Interim Report of the Work of the Fund for the Advancement of Teacher Education and Recruitment*. Ford Foundation, New York.

Fourth University Committee Victoria 1972, Report for the Hon. LHS Thompson, Minister of Education/Victorian Fourth University Committee; Chairman: Sir Thomas Ramsay, Goverment Printer, Melbourne.

Frazer, M. Dunstan, J. and Creed, P. (eds) 1985, *Perspectives in Organisational Change: Lessons from Education*, Longman Cheshire, Melbourne.

Friedman, M. 2002, *Martin Buber—The Life of Dialogue*, Harper & Row, New York, chapter 27.

Gallagher, H. 2003, *We Got a Fair Go: A History of the Commonwealth Reconstruction Training Scheme 1945–1952*, Hector Gallagher, Melbourne.

Garden, D. 1982, *The Melbourne Teacher Training Colleges: From Training Institution to Melbourne State College 1870-1982*, Heinemann Educational Australia, Richmond, Victoria.

Garfield, S. 2004, *Our Hidden Lives*, Random House, London.

*Geelong Advertiser* 1982, Institute of Educational Administration, 5 February.

Gibran, K. 1923, *The Prophet*, Alfred A. Knopf, New York.

Gladman, F. 1877, *School Method*, Jarrod and Sons, London.

Goodman, R. 1969, 'Whither the College or where do we go from here?', address to the weekend conference Victorian Chapter of the Australian College of Education, 19 April.

Green, S. 1981a, 'New Shears job to cost $1/4 m.', *Herald*, 17 November.
— 1981b, 'Old guard loses out in shake-up', *The Age*, 31 December.
— 1982a, '$40,000 a year for six without official positions', *The Age*, 23 January.
— 1982b, 'Education chief: I'm in charge', *The Age*, 6 February 6.
Hannan, W. 2009, *The best of times: the story of the great secondary schooling expansion*, Lexis, Northcote, Victoria.
Harman, G. 1985, 'The White Paper and planned organisational change', in M. Frazer, J. Dunstan & P. Creed (eds), *Perspectives in Organisational Change: Lessons from Education*, Longman Cheshire, Melbourne, pp. 155–88.
*Herald* 1973, 'The new Director-General of Education takes over', 5 May.
Higgins, F. 1964, *Music in the Primary School*, Macmillan, South Melbourne.
Hill, B. 1974, Shears' leadership style, *The Age*, 4 March.
Hird, A. 1985, *Limited Tenure: personal memoirs*, self-published, Melbourne.
Hirst, P. 1998, 'Philosophy of education: the evolution of a discipline', in G. Haydon (ed.), *50 Years of Philosophy of Education: Progress and prospects*, Institute of Education, London.
Holloway, D. 2000, *The Inspectors: An Account of the Inspectorate of the State Schools of Victoria 1851–1983*, The Institute of Senior Officer of the Victorian Education Services Incorporated, Melbourne.
Hoy, A. 1958, letter of support for Shears' application for a Harkness Fellowship. *See above*, Shears 1958b.
— 1961, *A City Built to Music: the History of University High School, Melbourne, 1910 to 1960*, University High School, Melbourne, Victoria.
Hughes, P. 1969, *VIER Bulletin*, no. 20.
Hunt, A. 1985, 'A government thrusts towards change', in M. Frazer, J. Dunstan & P. Creed (eds), *Perspectives in Organisational Change: Lessons from Education*, Longman Cheshire, Melbourne, pp. 13–32.
Hustvedt, S. 2011, *The Summer without Men*, Sceptre, London.
Institute of Educational Administration 1978, *Handbook of Educational Leadership*, Programs 1 and 2, August–October, IEA, Geelong.

James HEO and Tenan, C. 1953, *The Teacher Was Black: an experiment in international understanding*, sponsored by UNESCO, Heinemann, London.

Jersild, A. 1955, *When Teachers Face Themselves*, Teachers' College Press, New York.

Johnson, W. 1992, *Technical to Post Primary: a history of the School Councils Association, Victoria (1914–1990)*, Association of Councils of Post Primary Institutions in Victoria, Box Hill, Victoria.

*Journal of Education 1954–56*, VIER, Melbourne.

Karmel, P. 1962, 'Some economic aspects of education', the Buntine Oration delivered at the 3rd Annual Conference the Australian College of Education, 18 May.

Karmel Report, 1973, Schools in Australia: Report of the Interim Committee for the Australian Schools Commission, AGPS, Canberra.

Kiernan, M. (ed.) 1985, *The Essayes or Counsels, Civill and Morall*, Clarendon Press, Oxford, vol. 15 of The Oxford Francis Bacon.

Kirner, J. 1972, letter on the independent–government school divide, *The Australian*, 22 September.

— 1973, 'What about the role of parents?' *The Age*, 20 November.

— 1985, 'Organisational change in education: the parent line', in M. Frazer, J. Dunstan & P. Creed (eds), *Perspectives in Organisational Change: Lessons from Education*, Longman Cheshire, Melbourne, pp. 343–63.

Knight, J., Lingard, B. and Bartlett, L. 1994, 'Reforming teacher education policy under Labour governments in Australia 1983–93', *British Journal of Sociology of Education*, 15, pp. 451–66.

Lacy, N. 1985, 'Implementing change: a personal view', in M. Frazer, J. Dunstan & P. Creed (eds), *Perspectives in Organisational Change: Lessons from Education*, Longman Cheshire, Melbourne, pp. 33–55.

Law, A. 1940, *Modern Teaching*, Robertson & Mullins, Melbourne.

Law, P. 1967, lecture presented to the Victorian Institute of Educational Research, 10 March, *VIER Bulletin*, no. 17.

Law Suart, W. 2001, *Golden Morning: An Australian Childhood*, Dingo Books, Bordon, Hampshire.

Madgwick, R. 1960, 'Education—a challenge to Australia!', printed in the report of the National Education Conference held at the Leichhardt Stadium, Sydney: Saturday, 21 May, 1960, published by the Australian Council of School Organisations and the Australian Teachers' Federation, Sydney.

Mahood, S., Moyle, C. and Murray, K. 1973, 'The control of education—the role of parents and the community', proceedings of seminar held at St Mary's College, University of Melbourne, 4 May.

Martin, F. 1973, Benefits of sharing facilities, *The Age*, 2 October.

Martin Report, 1964–65, *see 'Tertiary Education in Australia'*.

Maslen, G. 1979a, 'Guide to class war', *The Age*, 9 April.

— 1979b, 'Big Shake up in Education', *The Age*, 2 August.

— 1979c, 'Bell rings for big debate' *The Age*, 3 August.

— 1980, 'Teachers a pet subject for committee', *The Age*, 29 September

— 1981a, 'A Bill passed, an Act amended, a man dumped', *The Age*, 20 Ocober

— 1981b, 'Start of a new empire', *The Age*, 29 August.

— 1981c, 'Double hurdle for Shears', *The Age*, 16 November.

— 1982a, 'Talking shop', *The Age*, 23 February.

— 1982b, 'Libs stumble in first round of election fight', *The Age*, 10 March.

— 1982c, 'System faces a Fordham shake-up', *The Age*, 6 April.

— 1982d, 'Some new education posts to be axed', *The Age*, 17 April.

— 1982e, 'Schools to be the focus' ban on corporal punishment from 1983', *The Age*, 21 May.

— 1982f, 'Fordham confident on eve of changes', *The Age*, 17 August, p. 12.

— 1982g, 'A sting in the tail for the tribunal', *The Age*, 21 September.

— 1982h, 'A quiet revolution in State education' *The Age*, 3 December.

— 1983a, 'Education chief slams youth policy', *The Age*, 4 March.

— 1983b, 'Pity the poor teenager', *The Age*, 16 June.

— 1984a, 'Education chief stepping down after pursuing hobby for 45 years', *The Age*, 28 May.

— 1984b, 'Lawrie Shears: end of the road for a pace setter', *The Age*, 29 May.

Mathews I. 1972, 'Going—a $22,500 job', *The Age*, 9 October.

— 1973, 'Victoria is spending without authority', *The Age*, 15 November.

McCrae, C. 1929, *Psychology and Education*, Whitcombe and Tombs, Melbourne.

McCrae H. (ed.) 1934, 1966, *Georgiana's Journal: Melbourne 1841–1865*, Angus and Robertson, Melbourne.

McDonnell R. 1956, *Review of Education in Australia 1948–1954*, Australian Council for Educational Research, Melbourne.

McKenzie, D. and Wilkins, C. (eds) 1979, *The TAFE Papers*, Macmillan, Melbourne.

McKenzie, J. 1982, letter, *The Age*, 13 January.

McKinnon, K. 2010, 'The Schools Commission: A review', presented at a Schools Commission Seminar at the University of Melbourne, 3 September.

McNair Report 1944, Teachers and Youth Leaders Report of the Committee appointed by the President of the Board of Education to consider the Supply, Recruitment and Training of Teachers and Youth Leaders London: His Majesty's Stationery Office.

Menzies-Smith, H. 1966, 'Desirable training of teachers', in P. Partridge, *Teachers in Australian Schools: An Appraisal, including the 1966 Buntine Oration*, papers presented at the Seventh Annual Conference of the Australian College of Education, held at the University of Sydney, published by Cheshire for the Australian College of Education, Melbourne.

Minister of Education 1983–84, 4 policy papers, Education Department of Victoria, Melbourne.

Paper 1. *Decision making in Victorian education*.

Paper 2. *The School Improvement Plan*.

Paper 3. *The State Board of Education*.

Paper 4. *School councils*.

Minister of Education 1985, Policy papers 1–6, collected ed., Education Department of Victoria, Melbourne.

Papers 1–4 as above.

Paper 5. *Regional boards of education*.

Paper 6. *Curriculum development and planning in Victoria*.

Ministry of Education (Schools Division) 1986, *The Victorian Readers*, Books 1–8, Facsimile Reprint, Melbourne, Victoria.

Moore, T. 1985, 'The change process from the inside' in M. Frazer, J.

Dunstan & P. Creed (eds), *Perspectives in Organisational Change: Lessons from Education*, Longman Cheshire, Melbourne, pp. 301–14.

Murray, D. (ed.) 1981, Reports from Victorian Fellows, International Teaching Fellowship Program 1981.

National Inquiry into Teacher Education (Australia) 1980, *Report of the National Inquiry into Teacher Education*, AGPS, Canberra. (Auchmuty Report).

Office of the Director-General of Education, 1975, 5 papers for discussion and debate by interested groups, from the Office of the Director-General of Education, Education Department of Victoria, Melbourne.

Paper 1. *Structure at the State level: departmental guidelines for the future.*

Paper 2. *Planning Services Division.*

Paper 3. *Structure at the regional level.*

Paper 4. *The school and the community.*

Paper 5. *The teacher and the school administrator.*

Pankhurst, T. 1977, 'School union "plays games"', *The Age*, 4 March.

Peeler, E. 2005, Changing culture, changing practice: Immigrant teachers in search of self, unpublished Doctor of Education thesis, Monash University.

— 2008a, Imaginations of an educator: An historic account of a leader's inspirations and innovations, paper presented to the annual conference of the Australian College of Educators, Hobart, May.

— 2008b, 'Communicating communities', paper presented at the Australian Association for Research in Education, Brisbane, 30 November–4 December.

J Polesel, J. and Teese, R. 1998, *The 'colleges': growth and diversity in the non-university tertiary studies sector (1965–75)*, Department of Education, Training and Youth Affairs (Evaluations and Investigations Programme), Canberra.

*Port Phillip Gazette*, 12 December 1841.

Radford, W. 1939, *The Educational Needs of a Rural Community*, Melbourne University Press in conjunction with Oxford University Press, Melbourne.

Ramsay, A. 1958, letter of support for Shears' application for a Harkness Fellowship. *See above*, Shears 1958b.

Ramsay Report 1960, *see* Committee on State Education in Victoria 1960.

Ramsay Report 1972 *see* Fourth University Committee, Victoria.

*Record* 1935–38, University High School, Melbourne, Victoria.

Reed, R. 1967, 'The organisation of secondary education', 14th Frank Tate Memorial Lecture, 27 June 1967, *VIER Bulletin*, no. 17.

Reid, G. 1973, 'Bolt from blue for teachers', *Education Age*, 20 November.

Reports by the Minister of Public Instruction 1936–37 to 1947–48.

Reports of the Minister of Education 1948–49 to 1983–84.

Rich, J. 1992, *Innovations in Education: Reformers and Their Critics*, Allyn & Bacon, Boston.

Roberts, P. 1978, Dr Shears on the TAFE Council, *The Age*, 30 September 1978.

Robertson, K. 1973, *Myrtleford: Gateway to the Australian Alps*, Rigby, Adelaide.

Robertson, T. 1968, 'Educational research in Australia', 15th Frank Tate Memorial Lecture, *VIER Bulletin*, no. 19.

Rodgers, R and Hammerstein, O. 1959, 'Do-Re-Mi', song from *The Sound of Music*.

Ryan, M. 1973, 'Travel broadens the teachers' scope, says education's top rover', 21 March.

Sargeant, K. 1981, letter to the editor—'Dr Shears we need you', *The Age*, 13 November. The editor noted support from members of the VIER and Melbourne University's Faculty of Education.

Saunders, A. 1957, in Keyes, R. 2007, *The Quote Verifier: Who said what, where, and when*, St Martin's Press/Macmillan Publishing, London.

Schiegel, N. 2005, *Larnook—our thoughts to thee will fly: a book of memories 1952-1983*, Berri Publishing, Glen Iris, Victoria.

Selleck, R. 1972, 'The Hadow report: a study in ambiguity', *Melbourne Studies in Education* (R. Selleck, ed.), Melbourne University Press, Carlton, pp. 180–1.

— 1982, *Frank Tate: A Biography*, Melbourne University Press, Carlton.

— 2003, *The Shop: the University of Melbourne 1850–1939*, Melbourne University Press, Carlton.

Shakespeare, W. *Hamlet*, Act 1, Scene 3.

Smallwood, R. 1992, *Hard To Go Bung: World War II Soldier Settlement in Victoria 1945–1962*, Hyland House, Melbourne.

Smith, R. 1999, *In Pursuit of Nursing Excellence: A History of the Royal College of Nursing Australia 1949–99*, Oxford University Press, Melbourne.

Spaulding, W. and Meindl, G. 1960, 'The institutional recommendation for certification', *Journal of Teacher Education*, vol. 11, June.

Spaull, A. 1987, *A History of the Australian Education Council 1936–1986*, Allen & Unwin, Sydney.

St Ellen, J and Shears, L. 1954, 'An experimental course in education for teachers' colleges', *The Forum of Education*, vol. XII, no. 3, April.

*Stock and Land*, 31 August 1949, 'Soldier settlers: training at Dookie is successful'.

*Sun* 22 September 1948, 'Record number graduate at Dookie College'

— 21 March 1973, 'Our new top teacher'.

— 5 May 1973, 'The new Director-General of Education takes over'.

*Sydney Gazette*, 12 August 1815, capture of *Frances and Eliza* by an American privateer, *Warrior*.

Tate, F. 1904, Report of the Director of Education upon some aspects of education in New Zealand.

Teacher Education in Victoria 1980, Interim Report of the Committee of the Victorian Enquiry into Teacher Education, February.

Teachers in Australian Schools, a report by the Australian College of Education, 1967.

*Tertiary Education in Australia*: report of the Committee on the Future of Tertiary Education in Australia to the Australian Universities Commission, 1964–65, (L. Martin, chairman), Government Printer, Canberra.

Thompson, L. 1969, *Looking Ahead in Education*. Education Department of Victoria, Melbourne.

— 1989, *I Remember: an autobiography*, Hyland House, South Yarra, Victoria.

Tinning, R. 2008, 'From Dr Fritz Duraz to the cult of the body and the obesity crisis: Observations of the evolution of Human Movement Studies as an academic field', Inaugural Fritz Duraz lecture, Dean's Lecture, Melbourne Graduate School of Education, the University of Melbourne, 9 September.

*Trainee* 1939–43, annual magazine of Melbourne Teachers College.

Victoria, Board of Inquiry into the Victorian Public Service 1974, First report of the Board of Inquiry into the Victorian Public Service (H. Bland, chairman), Government Printer, Melbourne.

Victorian Teachers Union 1960–84, *Teachers Journal: journal of the Victorian Teachers' Union*, Melbourne.

Waddington, D., Radford, W. and Keats, J. 1950, *Review of Education in Australia 1940–48*, Melbourne University Press, Melbourne.

Waller, D. 1957, Principal's address, *Parabo*.

Watts, F. 1973, letter of congratulations to Shears.

Whiteley, R. 1980, Donald Clark, the first chief inspector of technical schools, unpublished Master of Education thesis, University of Melbourne.

Whitton, D. 1979, 'Constant pressure "to be one of us"', *The Age*, 6 March.

Williams, B. 1994, *Education with Its Eyes Open: A Biography of Dr K.S. Cunningham*, Australian Council for Educational Research, Melbourne.

Woodgate, G. 1955, August, reference for Lawrence Shears.

Wright, A. 1983, 'Give community more say on youth', *The Age*, 10 March.

*Yabba*, the twice-yearly student magazine of Burwood Teachers College.

*Yakkity High*, magazine of Ringwood High School.

## 3. Legislation (listed in date order)
### Victorian

*Land Sales Act* 1860 (Nicholson Act) (No. CXVII)
*Land Act* 1862 (Duffy Act) (No. CXLV
*The Common Schools Act* 1862 (No. 149)
*Amending Land Act* 1865 (First Grant Act)
*Land Act* 1869 (Second Grant Act)
*The Education Act* 1872 (No. 447)

*Education Act* 1901 (No. 1777)
*University of Melbourne Act* 1904 (No. 1926)
*Education Act* 1905 (No. 2005)
*Teachers Act* 1905 (No. 2006)
*Registration of Teachers and Schools Act* 1905 (No. 2013)
*Education Act* 1910 (No. 2301)
*Teachers Act* 1933 (No. 4205)
*Education (Fees) Act* 1933 (No. 4207)
*Teaching Service (Married Women) Act* 1956 (No. 6030)
*Education Act* 1958 (No. 6240)
*Victoria Institute of Colleges Act* 1965 (No. 7291)
*Education and Teaching Service (Amendment) Act* 1967 (No. 7533)
*Victoria Institute of Colleges Act* 1967 (No. 7644)
*State College of Victoria Act* 1972 (No. 8736)
*Youth, Sport and Recreation (State Schools Premises) Act* 1973 (No. 8499).
*Education (Administration) Act* 1975 (No. 8768)
*Education (School Councils) Act* 1975 (No. 8799)
*Post-Secondary Education Act* 1978 (No. 9145)
*Institute of Education Act* 1980 (No. 9465)
*Geelong Lands Act* 1981 (No. 9538)
*Education (Amendment) Act* 1981 (No. 9582)
*Victorian Post Secondary Education (Amendment) Act* 1981 (No. 9711)

**Commonwealth**
*Migration Act* 1958.
*Australian Universities Commission Act* 1959.
*Immigration (Education) Act* 1971.

## 4. Oral history interviews and conversations

Over the period 2006–09, the author, Eleanor Hemphill Peeler, conducted interviews with a number of people. The list follows in alphabetical order by family name. Entries marked 'in conversation' were not recorded.

Formal interviews with Shears were recorded over the same period but there were also many unrecorded conversations.

Tony Ryan, archivist with the Australian College of Educators, conducted three interviews with Shears between 2004 and 2006. Recordings and transcripts of these interviews will be held in the National Library of Australia.

Anderson, E. 2008.
Barwick, N. 2007.
Bell, L. 2007.
Boyce, M. 2008.
Cameron, A. 2009.
Collins, J. 2007.
Collins, K. 2007.
Corr, G. 2007.
Crawford, J. 2007.
Creed, P. 2008.
Cullen, R. 2007.
Curry, N. 2007.
Dale, E. 2007.
Dimmack, M. 2008.
Fisher, R. 2008.
Fordham, R. 2007.
Foster, L. 2008.
Gallagher, H. 2007.
Gleeson, B. (in conversation).
Greenberg, H. 2008.
Greenwood, A. (in conversation).
Gregory, A. (in conversation).
Gunstone, R. 2009.
Henderson, B. 2007.
Hess, F. 2007.
Holloway, D. 2007.
Hunt, A. 2009.
Izard, J. (in conversation).
Jackman, F. (in conversation).
Jeffrey, P. (in conversation).
Jenkin, R. 2008.
Kelleher, M. 2007.
Kirner, J. 2007.

Law, P. 2007.
Limb, C. 2007.
McKinty, W. 2007.
Moyle, C. 2008.
Murfett, R. 2007.
Newman, P. 2007.
Nixon, H. 2007.
Pascoe, J. 2007.
Reeves, D. 2007.
Ring, B. (in conversation).
Selleck, R. (in conversation).
Shears, Mark 2007.
Thompson, L. 2007.
Tickell, G. 2007.
Towns, D. (in conversation).
Waugh, M. 2007.
Whiteley, R. 2007.
Wilcox, A. 2007.

Significant assistance has been given by a wide range of people who have known Shears through the years in his various capacities. Some names have been included in the list above with an 'in conversation' note. Many tales have been told over meals or at reunions. The insights of such people have been invaluable. The following list is indicative of such assistance.

- Ex-servicemen who attended the rural training centre have attended reunions at Dookie Agricultural College (now part of the University of Melbourne) to which both Shears and Peeler have been invited, as a result of which a DVD entitled *Rural Training Centre: Lest we forget* was made by eep (Eleanor Peeler Productions) in 2009.
- Photographs and anecdotes that enriched the story came from such people as Keith Brownbill, Denis Cunningham, Peter Gemmell, Denis Gill, Graham Scott and Graham Stewart.
- Former students and staff of Burwoood TC have shared memories.
- Archivists from Deakin University, Institute of Education

(London), University of Melbourne, Wayne State University (Michigan).
- Members of the Shears family have offered unique insights.

## 5. Web sites

Adam-Smith, P., *Clapp, Sir Harold Winthrop (1875–1952)*, Australian Dictionary of Biography, National Centre of Biography, Australian National University, http://adb.anu.edu.au/biography/clapp-sir-harold-winthrop-5657/text9549, accessed 16 December 2013.

*A Master Plan for Higher Education in California, 1960–1975*, http://content.cdlib.org/ark:/13030/hb9c6008sn/, accessed 16 December 2013.

Australian Labor Party (Victoria) 1976, *Education Policy Statement*, February, https://www.google.com.au/search?q=Australian+Labor+Party+%28Victoria%29+1976,+Education+Policy+Statement,+&ie=utf-8&oe=utf-8&rls=org.mozilla:en-US:official&client=firefox-a&gws_rd=cr&ei=g2OuUp2XMcL9oASU9oKYBg, accessed 16 December 2013

*a2zPsychology.com*. 2002–2010, www.a2zpsychology.com/great_psychologists/hans_j_eysenck.php, accessed 16 December 2013

*Byaduk pioneers*, http://www.swvic.org/byaduk/byaduk_pioneers.htm, accessed 16 December 2013

Calisphere, University of California 2011, *A Master Plan for Higher Education in California, 1960–1975*, http://content.cdlib.org/view?docId=hb9c6008sn&chunk.id=div00072&brand=calisphere&doc.view=entire_text

Churchill, W. 1940, *We Shall Fight on the Beaches*, speech delivered to the House of Commons of the Parliament of the United Kingdom, 4 June, http://en.wikipedia.org/wiki/We_shall_fight_on_the_beaches, accessed 20 December 2013

Clarke, Sir Fred, Papers, http://www.ioe.ac.uk/services/617.html, accessed 19 December 2013

Collins Street, 1840, *Streets and Roads*, City of Melbourne, www.melbourne.vic.gov.au/AboutMelbourne/History/Pages/Streetsandroads.aspx, accessed 16 December 2013

Commonwealth Fund: http://www.commonwealthfund.org/About-Us/Foundation-History.aspx, accessed 16 December 2013.

Connell, W. Browne, *George Stephenson (1890–1970)*, Australian Dictionary of Biography, National Centre of Biography, Australian National University, http://adb.anu.edu.au/biography/browne-george-stephenson-9604/text16933, accessed 16 December 2013.

Death of King George VI, *On This Day 1950-2005*, (BBC News, Producer), http://news.bbc.co.uk/onthisday/hi/dates/stories/february/6/newsid_2711000/2711265.stm, accessed 21 December 2013.

Dyson, M. 2005, Australian Teacher Education: Although reviewed to the eyeball is there and where to now? *Australian Journal of Teacher Education*, vol. 30, no. 1, http://dx.doi.org/10.14221/ajte.2005v30n1.4, accessed 16 December 2013

Finster, M. http://www.adf-serials.com.au/2a20b.htm, accessed 16 December 2013

Ford Foundation 1962, http://www.fordfound.org/archives/item/1962/text/20, accessed 13 January 2010. (NB In 2012, the Ford Foundation transferred its archives to the Rockefeller Archive Centre, http://www.rockarch.org/collections/ford/)

German settlers, http://www.germanaustralia.com/e/chron/chron3.htm, accessed 16 December 2013

Gervasoni, C. 2006, *William Frank Lord*, Federation University of Australia (formerly University of Ballarat) Honour Roll, www.ballarat.edu.au/centres/art-and-historical-collection/ub-honour-roll/l/william-frank-lord-1969, accessed 16 December 2013

Gillard, D. 'The Hadow Reports: an introduction', *the encyclopaedia of informal education*, www.infed.org/schooling/hadow_reports.htm, accessed 16 December 2013

— *Education in England: a brief history*, 2007, www.educationengland.org.uk/history, accessed 16 December 2013

Glenlyon town name: http://www.ballaratgenealogy.org.au/art/loddon.htm#SQUAT, accessed 16 December 2013

Gold Street Primary School, Clifton Hill, school history, 'The design of the building was a reflection of the times' http://www.cliftonhillps.vic.edu.au/sub/about/history.html#submenu3, accessed 18 December 2013

Hannah, W. *Fink, Theodore (1855–1942)*, Australian Dictionary of Biography, National Centre of Biography, Australian National

University, http://adb.anu.edu.au/biography/fink-theodore-6171/text10601, accessed 18 December 2013

*History of the Army Staff College 2012*, (mrsite.com), Fort Queenscliffe Army Staff College: http://www.fortqueenscliff.com.au/page11.htm, accessed 16 December 2013

Institute of Education London, www.ioe.ac.uk/about/761.html, accessed 13 August 2013

*James Leslie Provan, Principal, Dookie Agricultural College, Vic.* 2010, Australia's Postal History and Social Philately,Pandora Australias Web Archive, www.auspostalhistory.com/articles/1616.shtml, accessed 18 December 2013

James, W. 1890, *Talks to Teachers on Psychology*, http://ebooks.adelaide.edu.au/j/james/william/talks/chapter8.html, accessed 18 December 2013

Jones, the Hon. Dr Barry 2007, 'Our education failures', Dean's Lecture, the Faculty of Education, The University of Melbourne, 30 May, www.theage.com.au/news/opinion/our-education-failures/2007/05/29/1180205246158.html, accessed 18 December 2013

Karmel, P. Dr WA Jones Oration: *The Greatest Educational Statesman of the Century: The unification of South Australian secondary education, 1970–1977*, http://www.lythrumpress.com.au/vision/261.html, accessed 18 December 2013.

Kerin, S. and Spaull, A. 2002, *Vroland, Anton William Rutherford (1874–1957)*, Australian Dictionary of Biography, National Centre of Biography, Australian National University, http://adb.anu.edu.au/biography/vroland-anton-william-rutherford-11928/text21371, accessed 19 December 2013

*Letters from Abroad: Replanning Teacher Education in Victoria.* (1950, February). (G. H. Fitzwater, Producer) Retrieved January 1, 2012, from http://www.ascd.org/ASCD/pdf/journals/ed_lead/el_195002_pryor.pdf, accessed 19 December 2013

McNair Report 1944, *Teachers and Youth Leaders*, Report of the Committee appointed by the President of the Board of Education to consider the Supply, Recruitment and Training of Teachers and Youth Leaders, His Majesty's Stationery Office, London, www.educationengland.org.uk/documents/mcnair/mcnair19.html, accessed 16

December 2013

Menzies, Robert, Declaration of War, http://www.menziesvirtualmuseum.org.au/1930s/1939.html, accessed 20 December 2013

Murray Report on Australian universities, 1957, Group of Eight Ltd, Australia, http://www.go8.edu.au/university-staff/go8-policy-_and_-analysis/2009/50-year-old-report-on-the-role-of-australian-universities, accessed 19 December 2013

National Archives of Australia. (n.d.). *Your story, our history*, enlistment document of Donald Maine Waller 1915, National Archives of Australia. Retrieved from http://naa12.naa.gov.au/scripts/imagine.asp?B=8399914&1SE=1, accessed 19 December 2013

(n.d.) (Melbourne Business School) From http://www.mbs.edu/go/about/mbs/about-our-school/history

(n.d.) (UNESCO, Producer) Retrieved 2012 from http://unescodoc.unesco.org/images/0017/001793cb.pdf

Peeler, E. and Shears, L. 2010, *A Tribute to Paul McKeown*, Australian College of Educators, http://austcolled.com.au/notepad/article/tribute-paul-mckeown, accessed 19 December 2013

Register of ships arriving in Port Phillip in 1841 details the captain, crew and passengers. http://search.slv.vic.gov.au/primo_library/libweb/action/dlDisplay.do?vid=MAIN&reset_config=true&docId=SLV_VOYAGER1635770, accessed 19 December 2013

*RE Ross Trust*, see http://www.rosstrust.org.au/about-us/roy-everard-ross/, accessed 19 December 2013

RMIT, 16 December 2013, *History of the Royal Melbourne Institute of Technology*, http://en.wikipedia.org/wiki/History_of_the_Royal_Melbourne_Institute_of_Technology, accessed 19 December 2013

Selleck, R. 1990, *Tate, Frank (1864–1939)*, Australian Dictionary of Biography, National Centre of Biography, Australian National University, http://adb.anu.edu.au/biography/tate-frank-8748/text15325, accessed 19 December 2013

Spaull, A., *McRae, James (1871–1939)*, Australian Dictionary of Biography, National Centre of Biography, Australian National University, http://adb.anu.edu.au/biography/mcrae-james-7443/text12959, accessed 16 December 2013

— *Smyth, John (1864–1927)*, Australian Dictionary of Biography,

National Centre of Biography, Australian National University, http://adb.anu.edu.au/biography/smyth-john-8566/text14951, accessed 19 December 2013

Standing Conference of Ministers of Education and Cultural Affairs 1971, *Educational Organization and Development in the Federal Republic of Germany in 1970/71*. Prepared for the XXXIIIrd International Conference on Education, received in September, http://www.ibe.unesco.org/National_Reports/Germany/nr_mf_gw_1971_ef.pdf, accessed 4 February 2013.

*Stonington Mansion*, 2013, 15 June, retrieved 16 August 16 2013, from Wikipedia, http://en.wikipedia.org/wiki/Stonington_mansion, accessed 19 December 2013

UNESCO, 1953, 20 August, Department of Social Sciences, Statement concerning the UNESCO Tensions Project (1949–1953): http://unesdoc.unesco.org/images/0017/001793/179399eb.pdf, accessed 19 December 2013

— 1974, Recommendation concerning education for international understanding, co-operation and peace and education relating to human rights and fundamental freedoms adopted by the General Conference at its eighteenth session, Paris, 19 November 1974, (UNESCO, Producer) Retrieved September 17, 2013 from http://www.unesco.org/education/nfsunesco/pdf/Peace_c.pdf, accessed 19 December 2013

— 1976 stressed the development of adult education; http://unesdoc.unesco.org/images/0011/001140/114038e.pdf, both accessed 19 December 2013

— (n.d.), *The Organization's History*, Retrieved 13 August 2013, from www.unesco.org/new/en/unesco/about-us/who-we-are/history/, accessed 19 December 2013

University of California, Berkeley 2010, *The History and Future of the California Master Plan for Higher Education* (J. Douglas, T. Greenspan, Producers, and Centre for Studies in Higher Education, Bancroft Library, Institute of Government Studies at UC Berkeley), retrieved 19 August 2013, http://sunsite.berkeley.edu/uchistory/archives_exhibits/masterplan/1960.html, accessed 19 December 2013

Victoria's population 1841: http://home.vicnet.net.au/~pioneers/

pppg5bl.httm, accessed 19 December 2013

Visit of the Duke of Gloucester to Melbourne 1934: http://australianscreen.com.au/titles/centenary-celebrations/clip1/, accessed 19 December 2013

*Windham* recapture 6 October 2013, http://en.wikipedia.org/wiki/Battle_of_Grand_Port, accessed 19 December 2013

Wirt, W. 22 September 2013, (Wikipedia) Retrieved 19 September 2013 from http://en.wikipedia.org/wiki/William_Wirt_(educator), accessed 19 December 2013

Woodhouse, F. 2008, *Still Learning*. Retrieved August 15, 2013, from Monash University books.publishing.monash.edu/apps/bookworm/view/Still+Learning/143/xhtml/chapter02.html, accessed 19 December 2013

# INDEX

## A

Acts of Parliament
  Australian Universities Commission
    (1959) 91, 232
  Common Schools Act
    (1862) 394
  Education
    (1872) 21, 22, 23, 27, 28, 252
    (1901) 35
    (1905) 35, 107
    (1910) 35, 81
    (1944) 117
    (1958) 153
  Education (Amendment)
    (1975) 257
    (1981) 336, 345, 363
  Education (Fees)
    (1933) 397
  Education (School Councils) 263
    (1975) 263, 352
  Education and Teaching Service
    (Amendment)
    (1967) 415
  Immigration (Education)
    (1971) 286
  Institute of Education Act
    (1980) 281
  Land Acts
    Land Sales, Nicholson (1860) 17
    Duffy (1962) 17
    First Grant (1865) 17
    Second Grant (1869) 17
    Geelong Lands (1981) 418
  Migration
    (1958) 286
  Post-Secondary Education
    (1978) 296
  Post-Secondary Education
    (Amendment)
    (1981) 298
  Registration of Teachers and Schools
    (1905) 42, 107
  State Board of Education Act
    (1983) 352
  State College of Victoria
    (1972) *236*
  Teachers Act
    (1905) 107
    (1933) 54
  Teaching Service (Married Women)
    (1956) 153
  University of Melbourne
    (1904) 42
  Victoria Institute of Colleges
    (1965) 413
    (1967) 411
  Victorian Post Secondary Education
    (Amendment) Act
    (1981) 298, 336, 345, 363
  Youth, Sport and Recreation (State
    School Premises)
    (1973) 264
Adamson, Hugh M 320
Advisory Committees
  School Broadcasts 248
  Mothers' Club and Parents'
    Association 45
  Research and Development in
    Education 207
  Teacher Training 154
  Tertiary Education 315
*Age, The* 218, 236, 238, 240, 249, 261, 269, 275, 289, 300, 304, 335, 337, 343, 344, 365, 369, 386, 387, 400, 405, 410, 411, 412, 414, 416, 417, 418, 419, 420, 421, 422, 423
Agent-General's Office 185, 224, 226
Agribusiness 384
Aims and objectives for education 197, 206, 317, 318, 325, 361
Ainley, Mary 339
Alberta Mafia 268

Albert Park State School, High School 67, 288
Albury, Albury-Wodonga 15, 248, 298
Alexandra 101, 264, 384
Allen, Graham 245, 298, 306, 337, 367, 376
Allowances
    Studentship / trainee 53, 57, 74, 132, 133, 155, 157, 158, 162, 200, 230
    Repatriation 92
    Living 157, 225
    Travel / Equipment 175, 176, 225
Alternative schools 287, 352
Alvin Purple 273
Andrews, Keith C 278, 280, 283
Angelou, Maya 141
Angus, Ruby 154
Armstrong-Grant, Patricia 280, 283
Asche, KJ Austin 293, 294, 295
Ashridge House 144
Associations
    American Teachers' Association 177
    Association for Health, Physical Education and Recreation 182
    Association of Pre-School Teachers 226
    Association of Secondary Teachers in Victoria 42
    Australian and New Zealand Student Services Association 356
    Australian Association for Community Education 380
    Australian Medical Association 303
    Bairnsdale Junior Football Association 86
    California Teachers' Association 180, 182, 188
    California Association of School Administrators 180
    East Gippsland Football Association 86
    Educational Reform Association 82
    Girls' Winter Sports Association 85
    Health, Physical Education and Recreation 182
    Modern Teaching Methods Association 314
    Mothers' Club and Parents' Association 45
    National Association for Supervision and Curriculum Development 175
    National Education Association 175, 179
    Old Pupils' Association 48
    Parent Teacher Association 118
    Pre-School Teachers 226
    Primary Principals' Association 314
    Primary Teachers' College Principals' Association 195
    State Schools Amateur Athletics Association 39
    Victorian Football Association 86
Auchmuty, James J 293, 295
*Australian, The* 240
Australian Administrative Staff College 267, 278, 283, 318, 340
Australian Broadcasting Commission/ Corporation (ABC) 78, 222, 273, 360
    Concerts at Bairnsdale
    Thomas, John Charles 86–7
    Scott, Babe 87
    Wallace, George 87
    Commonwealth Conference (1975) 307
    Watts, Frank 244
    Radio 31, 61, 78, 128, 206, 217, 269, 273, 287, 359
    Floyd, AE 83
    Federal School Broadcasts Advisory Committee 247
    State Advisory Committee (School Broadcasts) 247
    Television 168, 176, 179, 184, 217, 269, 273, 287, 359, 360
Australian College of Education/ Educators (ACE) 169, 173, 204–6, 208, 217, 232, 241, 265, 280, 306, 386
    Buntine Oration 190
    Sorrento Conference (Whitehall Guesthouse) 206, 241, 280
    Teachers in Australia 202, 205, 404, 410
Australian Education Council (AEC) 216, 227, 228, 235, 238, 245, 261, 264, 283, 284, 293, 316, 335, 337, 342, 356, 359, 383
AEC Standing Committee 227, 245, 251,

316, 342, 351
Australian Schools' Commission 248, 249, 250, 251, 258, 272, 278, 292, 299, 340, 349, 365, 367, 382
Australian Youth Olympic Program 384

# B

Badger, Colin R 100, 101
Bacon, Francis 59
Bagge, J 27
Bairnsdale
   Apex Club 82, 85
   *Bairnsdale Advertiser* 82, 85
   *Every Week* 82, 85
   High School 80-5, 173
   School of Mines (North Gippsland / Bairnsdale and District) 80, 81, 233
   Technical School 80, 81
   Victorian Football League (VFL) 86
Baker, John G 170
Ballarat 12, 14, 42
   Region 167, 258, 260
   School of Mines 233
   Teachers College 53, 125, 126, 131, 135, 152, 155, 156, 161, 164
Baranduda 383, 384
Barberis, Lou 70, 72, 75, 79, 84, 87, 176, 246, 337, 385, 387, 388
Barko, Ivan p 226
Barwick, Neville 257, 268, 269, 275, 284, 333, 356, 371
Bastow, Herbert R 23
Bastyan, Cedric M 204
Bates, Richard 321, 333
Batman, John 10
Beare, Hedley 271, 272, 283
Beaurepaire, Francis JE (Frank) 39
Beazley, Kim E 248, 269, 274, 292
Beeby, Clarence E 108
Beechworth 32, 33
Bell, Laurence M (Laurie) 129, 130, 237, 372
Benalla 98, 99, 101, 103, 260, 319
Bendigo 12, 42, 175, 80, 90, 314, 399, 421
   Region 258, 259, 261, 343
   Senior Secondary College 361
   Teachers College 53, 125, 131, 135, 144, 152, 154, 155, 156, 160, 161, 164, 167

Technical School 415, 416
Bennettswood State School, No 4693 131, 195, 199, 200
Bennett, Ian 383
Bennett, JR 148
Beruldsen, E 100
Blackburn 162, 219, 291
Blackburn, Jean E (nee Muir) 46, 379, 397
Blackman, Allan R 156, 159, 161
Blake, Leslie J 22, 24, 162, 244
Bloomfield, John S 143, 147, 153, 156, 191, 215, 274
Board of Inspectors of Secondary Schools (BISS) 77, 84, 144, 164, 219, 224, 260
Boards of Enquiry/Inquiry *see* Enquiries/Inquiries
Bodi, Leslie 226
Bolte, Henry E 143, 163, 225, 239, 252
Bonaparte, Napoleon 244
Bonython Hall 204
Books on Wheels 311
Boort 75, 79
Boronia / Boronia High School 133, 150
Bounty scheme 9
Bouverie Street Theatre 305
Boyce, Max W 339, 366
Bornstein, David 251
Bradshaw, George D 54, 207, 339
Bristol huts 131, 135, 158
Brooks, Frederick H 3, 199, 215, 237-8, 239, 274, 327, 371, 376
Browne, George S 29, 30, 54, 60-4, 78, 82, 103, 109, 136, 137, 145, 151, 161, 167-9, 173, 174, 367, 376, 380
Browne Prize 151, 367
Browne, Ron 283, 284, 383
Brownell, William 178, 186
Browning, Robert 341
Bruce, Stanley M 30
Buber, Martin 198, 375
Burkhardt, Richard W 182, 187
Burridge, Winifred 97
Burt, Cyril L 108, 111
Burton, Rongomai G (Ron) 127, 210, 246, 372
Burwood Teachers College pp 189-212
   'Animum, Cultum, Parabo' 134, 162, 198, 211
   Burwood Model 197

Burwood Statement 189, 197, 372
Camps and tours 199, 200–1
Golden years 3, 189–211, 210, 372
Oxford Hall 132, 133, 134
*Parabo* 134, 162, 198
Bush, George W 290
Butts, R Freeman 141-2, 179, 186, 193, 206
Byaduk 8, 17, 18, 20

# C

Cain Labor government 143, 284
Callandar, Ron 102
Camp Balook 313
Campbell, James DL / Campbellfield 11
Canada 172, 182, 183, 331
    Computers 359, 360
    Curriculum 362
    ITF /Teacher recruitment 224, 225, 226, 289, 368
    Teaching conditions 301, 302, 303
Canadian Education Department 291
Canberra Grammar School 204, 205, 272
Cannon, John G 154
Carlton State School, Faraday Street No. 112 69
Carlton State School, Rathdowne, Rathdowne Rural 68
Carlton North State School, Lee Street 64, 67
Carnegie Corporation 178 Fellowship 144 Foundation 111 Phonograph 63 Scholar / Fellow 158, 164 United Kingdom Trust 108
Carrick, John L 274, 293
Castlemaine 11, 12, 42
Catholic schools 25, 150, 250
    Education Office (CEO) 264, 276, 279, 282, 307
Central classes 75, 76, 101, 147, 149
Central Highlands 8, 9, 11, 12, 13
Central schools 149
Certificates, school
    Certificate of Competence 24–5
    Intermediate 83, 84
    Leaving 47, 58, 83, 84
    Leaving Honours 46
    Matriculation 83, 191, 195, 197, 201, 210

Merit 35, 40, 41, 67, 101, 157
Proficiency 76
Qualifying 35
Certificates, teachers college
    Certificate of Competency in Physical Education 39
    Trained Homecrafts Teachers Certificate 160
    Trained Infant Teachers Certificate (TITC) 154
    Trained Primary Teachers Certificate (TPTC) 59, 63, 64, 70, 75, 103, 127, 154, 160, 238
    Trained Secondary Teachers Certificate (TSTC) 154, 158, 159, 160
        Art and Crafts 160
        Domestic Arts 160
Chapman, Robin 268, 278, 321, 323, 326, 328, 343
Charter of the United Nations 271
Cheltenham 18, 133
Cheltenham Primary School No 84 314
Chifley, Joseph B (Ben) 90
Child-centred 216, 174
China 248, 356
    Computers 359
    Curriculum 361, 362
    International Teaching Fellowship 291, 331, 332, 356
    Ministerial/Priministerial tour 248, 331
    Youth policies 358
Chomley, Patricia D (Pat) 209
Chrishall 18
Croatia 332, 368
Churchill, Winston L 121, 379
Clark, Donald 80–2
Clarke, Dudley B 219
Clarke, Frederick (Sir Fred) 108, 111–12
Clark, J 337
Class size 36, 64, 216, 222, 232, 301, 303
Classified Roll 55, 75, 80, 107, 197
Clyne, Michael 17, 334
Coates, Thomas (Tom) H 109, 136, 168, 170, 207, 380
Cobb and Co 156
Coburg East State School 64, 66
Coburg Teachers College 155, 157, 162,

195, 245, 268, 299
Coburn, June 77, 79
Cockpit theatre 305
Cohen (Freda) Prize 103
   College of Nursing Australia (CNA) 208-9, 217, 219, 241, 243, 245, 306, 372, 377
Collins, M Kevin 320, 323, 326, 343, 355, 390
Committee of Classifiers 107, 230, 266, 279
   Commonwealth and Education 31, 190, 216, 248-51, 265, 268, 278, 291, 282, 293, 347, 349, 382, 291
   Finances, support 151, 228, 232-6, 241, 248, 251, 255, 286, 296, 297, 345, 354, 370, 383
   Inroads 227, 241, 249, 250, 262, 263, 276, 277, 315
   Office of Education 207
Commonwealth Council of Educational Administration (CCEA) 268, 278
   Defence Technical Training Scheme 90, 401
   Department of Supply and Development 90 Fund 172, 174, 175, 178, 180, 184
   Reconstruction Training Scheme (CRTS) 89, 90, 159, 220, 238
   Relations Trust 172
   Sponsored Education Centres 382
   Tertiary Education Commission 292, 325
Community Wednesday 61, 63
Connell, William F (Bill) 168, 189, 202, 241, 296, 333
Consolidation 63, 76, 82, 101, 120, 152
Controversial issues 324, 325, 333
Coordinating council 181, 240, 243
Copland, Douglas B 267
Corporate Management Group 321, 322, 323, 328
Corr, Graham 196
Council on Teacher Education, California 182, 188
Country Party 343 Roads Board (CRB) 316
Cowan, Edith D 31
Cox, May 39

Cranley, Hilma 245, 371
Creed, Phillip 283, 294, 324
Cullen, Ronald 321, 340
Curry, Norman G 166, 220, 245, 319, 342, 343, 344, 346, 349, 350, 352, 355, 356, 367, 371, 376
Cunningham, Kenneth S 30, 53, 54, 108, 144
Cyclone Tracy 248, 268

# D

Dalton Plan 30, 35, 61, 68, 78, 83, 260
Darling, James R 141, 169, 322
Darwin 248, 268
Davidson, Bruce 102
Davies, E Salter 108
Dawson, Harry E 320
Daylesford 11, 12
Deakin University 215, 299, 334
De Brunner, Emil 108
Decentralisation 78, 117, 137, 143, 168, 227, 237, 238, 262, 282, 327
Decini, Terrence 148
Deeley, Michael 321
Dellbridge, Arthur 219
Delves, A (Tony) 367
Denton, CP (Perc) 92, 97, 98, 102
Department of Agriculture 91, 94, 99, 145, 297, 298
   Advanced Studies (IOE) 113
   Education (Sacramento) 178
   Education and Early Childhood Development 389
   Housing and Construction, Canberra 268
   Human Movement Studies, University of Melbourne 283, 284
   Labour and National Service, Industrial Training Division 90
   Soil Conservation 121
   Supply and Development 90
Depression
   1890s 1, 8, 12, 17, 25, 27
   Great Depression 37, 43, 46, 53, 55, 60, 74, 91, 125, 151
Dewey, John 30, 61, 108, 182, 187, 260, 270
Dimmack, Max C 130, 133, 134, 135, 137, 183, 203

Diploma courses
  Diploma of Domestic Arts  160
  Diploma of Education  42, 43, 93, 157, 159, 210
  Diploma of Nurse Education  209
  Diploma of Nursing Administration  209
  Diploma of Nursing Education (Midwifery)  209
  Diploma of Physical Education  39
  Diploma of Teaching  210
  Dookie Diploma of Agriculture (DDA)  92, 94, 96, 102
Diploma Twenty  42, 59
Divisions of the Victorian Education Department
  Building Operations  297
  Personnel  229, 230, 253, 255, 257, 268, 275, 324, 343,
  Planning Services  3, 255, 256, 275, 276, 318, 321, 323, 324
  Special Services  124, 222, 230, 255, 297, 318, 320, 324
  Curriculum and Research  165, 230, 355
  Teacher Education  230, 255
  Teaching Divisions  146, 165, 229, 244, 253, 259, 313, 318, 319, 321, 325, 327, 330, 367
    Primary  259, 268, 319, 320
    Secondary  84, 93, 230, 259, 319
    Technical  159, 230, 258, 259, 278, 297, 319
Dixon, Brian J  264, 272, 383
Dixon, Owen  172
Dobell, Robert J (Bob)  260, 329, 352
Dookie *see* Rural Training Centre (RTC)
Dow, Kwong Lee  333, 337, 340, 341
Downward, Alice  134, 218, 314
Doyle, Thomas  352
Drama Resource Centre  305, 306, 375
Dudley Flats  126
Duke of Edinburgh's Awards  247, 307, 377, 385, 390, 391
Duke of Gloucester  39
Duncan, Don  102, 103
Dunolly  12, 14
Dunstan, Jeffrey F  245, 260, 319, 323
Duras, Fritz  39
Dylan, Bob  209

# E

Education Department Travelling Scholarship  103, 107, 109
Education Department's War Relief Organisation  16
*Education Gazette and Teachers' Aid*  57, 144, 149, 165, 166, 167, 336
*Educational Administration Quarterly* (EAQ)  268
Educational media
  0/28, SBS  287
  ABV2  287
  Channel 7  311
  *You, me and education*  311
Educational research
  American Educational Research Association (AERA)  207
  Australian Association for Research in Education (AARE)  206-7, 241, 306, 391
  Australian Council for Educational Research (ACER)  54, 108, 136, 149, 168, 169, 174, 203, 207, 217, 232, 294, 306, 372, 384, 388, 397, 405, 407
  *Australian Journal of Education*  168, 174, 203, 206, 241, 243, 372
  Canadian Education Research Association  207
  Commonwealth Office of Education, research arm  207
  Educational Research and Development Centre  243
  Foundation for Educational Research  111
  International Bureau of Education, Geneva  108
  National Bureau of Education, South Africa  108
  Scottish Council for Research in Education  108
  Victorian Institute of Educational Research (VIER)  53, 136, 137, 145, 167, 168, 169, 173, 174, 202, 203, 205, 206, 207, 217, 241, 269, 306, 316, 339, 342, 366, 367, 372, 377, 381, 3 85, 391

Frank Tate Memorial Lecture 137, 203, 366, 380
*Journal of Education* 108, 136, 168, 174, 372
*Primary Education Today* 203, 306
Regional groups 203, 306
*Secondary Education Today* 203
*VIER Bulletin* 203, 391
Young Turks 136, 205
Education in England 117–19
11-plus examination 185, 362
Educators, USA
    Albright, D 188
    Brownell, W 178, 186
    Burkhardt, Richard 182, 187
    Eurich, Alvin 175, 178, 186
    Goodlad, John 187
    Hile, F 187
    Keppel, Francis 193, 197, 204
    Konold, Ewing 188
    McIntosh, C 188
    Melbo, Irving 188
    Moon, A 187
    Rehage, Kenneth 186
    Romine, Stephen 187
    Smith, Elmer 185
    Smith, Robert 187
    Stiles, Lindley J 179, 182, 187
    Wattenberg, W 187
    Wennerberg, W 187, 186
Edward, Prince of Wales 31
Einstein, Albert 171
Eisenhower, Dwight D 177
Eliot, TS 79, 112, 391
Ellerker, William H 23
Ellwood, William H 124, 161
Elsternwick 16, 31, 34, 37, 38, 40, 41, 44, 48, 55, 71, 72, 87, 374, 338
Elsternwick State School 37, 38, 374
Eltham, Ernest 90
Elwood 47
Elwood Central School 37
Emerson, Ralph W 89
Emerson, TLW (Les) 230
English as a Second Language (ESL) 286, 287
Enquiries/Inquiries
    Bland Board of Inquiry into the Victorian Public Service 252, 253, 329
    Committee of Enquiry into Education and Training (Williams Committee) 292
    Curriculum Services Enquiry 329, 361, 366
    Fink Royal Commission 26
    Kangan Committee 292, 296
    National Inquiry into Teacher Education (Auchmuty Inquiry) 293–5
    Quality of Education in Australia Review Committee 379
    Swanson Committee of Inquiry into Teacher Education 292
    Victorian Enquiry into Teacher Education (Asche Enquiry) 293–5, 329
Ensor, Beatrice 108
Erskine House, Lorne 278
Essendon 87, 98, 177
    High School 347
Ethical code 128
Eunson, Warwick 56, 157, 161, 162, 195
Eurich, Alvin C 175, 178, 186
Euroa 95, 101
Everage, Edna 273
Ex-servicemen / personnel 16, 90–5, 97, 98, 99, 102, 110, 113, 173
Exhibition Building 48
Exhibition (qualification) 53, 71, 220
Extension of teacher training 39, 54, 70, 75, 124
    courses 154, 160, 183, 238
    schooling 42, 160, 176
Eysenck, Hans J 112, 113, 270

# F

Falk, Leonard (Len) A 259, 260, 329, 386
Farr, Jack 102
Faure Report (Learning to Be) 289
Faust, Clarence 175
Fawkner, John 10
Fawns, Roderick 339
Federal Government 250, 269, 273, 312, 298, 356, 364, 366
Federal funding 209, 249, 251, 327, 371

Federal Minister for/of Education 250, 269
Federal Office of Education 179
   Republic of Germany 226, 227, 270
Fensham, Peter J 352
Ferntree Gully 34, 49, 63
   Ferntree Gully survey 149–51
Festival of Britain 121
Fife, Wallace C (Wal) 274
Finley 15
Finster, Mervyn N 46, 47, 48
Fisher, Reginald H 260, 323
Fisherman's Bend 90
Fitzgerald, Ronald T (Ron) 282, 333
Fitzroy State School (Miller Street) 49, 53, 55–8, 246, 370, 374
Fleming, Charlotte 111, 112, 270
Flinders Rangers 201
Flinders Street 10, 41, 44, 55, 145
Flinders University 202, 228
Footscray 16, 192
   North State School 347
Ford Foundation 175, 178, 186
Fordham, Robert
   Shadow Minister of Education 282, 297, 335, 336, 337
   Minister of Education 346, 347–50
   Profile 346–7
   Policy Papers
      Paper 1: *Decision making in Victorian education* (1983) 350
      Paper 2: *The School Improvement Plan* (1983) 351
      Paper 3: *The State Board of Education* (1983) 351–2
      Paper 4: *School councils* (1983) 352–3
      Paper 5: *Regional boards of education* (1984) 353–4
      Paper 6: *Curriculum development and planning in Victoria* (1984) 354–5
Forster, HC (Carl) 172, 272
France 108, 120, 226
Computers 359–60
Curriculum 361–2
Five-year planning 226, 240
International teaching Fellowship 291, 332, 369
UNESCO Conference 269–71
Youth Policies 358
Franklin, Benjamin 189
Frankston (*see also* Frankston Teachers College) 87, 93, 260
Fraser, John Malcolm 235, 236, 274, 365,
Frederick, Wilfred H 54, 204, 245, 380
Froebel, Frederick WA 28
Fulbright Scholar, Grant 141, 176, 179

## G

Gallagher, Hector H 322, 323, 371
Garden, Don 23, 124, 152
Gardenvale 41, 44
Garfield Junior High 177
Geelong 14, 42, 75
   Grammar School 141, 169, 232
   Institute of Educational Administration 266, 280–5, 294, 306, 331, 341, 356, 365, 367, 368, 369, 373
   Travelodge 281, 284
Gelman, Manuel 158
Germany, 16, 28, 29, 85, 120, 226, 227, 250, 372
   Ancestry, Shears 8
   Computers 359
   Five-year Planning 240
   International Teaching Fellowship 226, 291
   UNESCO 270
Gibbs, Dora 111, 121
Gibbs, William D (Headmaster, Bairnsdale HS) 80, 81
Gibran, Kahlil 215
Gill, Denis 306
Gill, Norman 219, 224, 268
Gillard, Miss J 69
Ginger, Ronald H 210, 260, 375, 385
Gippsland 87, 203, 332
   Region 258, 259
Gladman, Frederick J 28, 161
   Gladman prize 29, 144
Gladstone bag 37, 44
Glendonald, School for the Deaf 131, 160, 161
Goldman, Ronald 244, 367, 376
Goodlad, John I 179, 187

Goodman, Rupert D 241
Goold, James A 22
Goorambat 99
Gorton, John G 235
Goulburn Valley 13, 14, 20, 203
 Goulburn Region 101, 119, 150
Government / non-government school 242, 343, 344
Graduate Diploma in Leadership 268
Grasby, Albert J 294
Green Paper 317, 325, 326
Grey, Thomas (Headmaster, Windsor SS) 36
*Griffin* 72
Guilfoyle, Margaret GC 274
Gunstone, Richard (Dick) 153, 163

# H

Hall, John 219
 Kevin 339
 Peter R 386
Halls of residence (*see also* Hostels) 162, 226
Hamer, Rupert 252, 274, 316
Hamilton 16, 17, 18, 20
Hamley, Herbert R 53, 111
Hammerstein (II), Oscar 7
Hamono, Prue 54, 64
Hannah, Wilma 158
Hannan, William (Bill) 300, 305
Harkness, Anna M 172
 Fellow 3, 171–88, 218, 389
Fellowship 165, 170, 204, 240, 272, 279
Harman, Grant S 327-8, 367
Harris, Arthur L 260
 Rolf 274
 Sir John 74
Harrison, Captain 19
Harvard University 175, 179, 180, 186, 187
Harvey, Gil 102
Hawthorn 47, 161
 Institute of Education 346, 383
 Patterson Street Hostel 162, 199
 State College of Victoria 278, 284
Health Department 156, 160
 education 188, 383, 385
 and recreation camp 164
Heffron, Robert J 190

Henderson, Brian 346, 356
Herbartian approach 28
Higher elementary schools 74, 75, 144, 147, 149, 152, 157, 282
High schools 28, 41, 43, 47, 74, 81, 147, 150, 151, 157, 224, 229, 238, 360, 361
Hill, Barry 275, 276
 James (Mac) 236, 296
Hird, Allan T 257, 268, 275, 276, 322, 324, 330, 343, 344
Hobbs, Halbert S 320
Holloway, David C 320
Holy Spark 198, 363, 375, 389
Hone, Brian W 169
Horsham 13, 17, 260, 313
Howard, cousin 39
Howard, Jack 166
Howe, Freddie 70, 72
 Jackie 36, 49
Hoy, Alice 29, 42, 54, 55, 64, 136, 145, 158, 159, 161, 167, 169, 173, 193, 207, 246
Huffam huts 97
Hughes, Phillip 216, 284
Hunt, Alan J 274, 281, 319
 Vision for education 296, 297, 315, 316, 317, 318, 320
 Tactics 321, 322, 323, 325, 326, 327, 328, 330, 332, 333, 334, 342, 349
 Attitudes to reform 336, 341, 343, 344, 346, 353, 363, 370
 Reflections on Shears 337
 Shears' stance 340, 342, 348
Hustvedt, Siri 273

# I

Immigrant 1, 8, 9, 12, 13, 18, 125, 151, 157, 286, 288, 347
Immigration 31, 91, 143, 286, 362, 368
Imperial League of Australia, Returned Sailors' and Soldiers' (RSSILA / RSL) 91, 95
Imperial Relations Trust 103, 109, 116, 117
Implementation Steering Committee 321, 323, 324, 328, 330, 333
 Task Force 321, 323, 324, 326, 328, 329, 333, 356
Inchbold, Percival 143, 146

Industrial and reformatory schools  14
Inner London Education Authority  224, 369
Inspectors  2, 14, 24, 26, 27, 28, 38, 49, 60, 75, 77, 79, 93, 109, 143, 149, 174, 245, 258, 259, 266, 267, 268, 279, 311, 313, 323, 324
    Assistant Chief Inspector of Secondary Schools (*see* Gill, N, McDonell, A, Moore, W, Russell, W)
    Board of Inspectors of Secondary Schools (BISS)  84, 144, 164, 165
    Chief Inspector of Primary Schools (*see also* Ellwood, Cannon)  156
    Chief Inspector of Technical Schools (*see* Clark, Eltham)
    Inspector-General  21
    Caldwell, James  77
    Embling, Doris G  234
    Heathcote, Norman C  58
    Jobling, Ian HT  234
    Ottaway, Leslie, V  84
    Phillips, Oliver C  77
    Shearer, Norman J  234
    Sinclair, Donald A  234
    Whelpton, F  84
Inspectorate  62, 77, 118, 217, 238, 259, 269, 311, 351, 367
    Living away from home  77
Institute of Early Childhood Development  343, 346
    of Education, University of London  2, 108, 109, 111–12, 120, 145, 167, 172, 182, 270, 282, 342, 383, 388
    of Educational Administration (IEA)  266, 280, 281–4, 285, 331, 341, 373
        Business administration  267, 278, 282
        Sultan of Brunei  385, 368
*Interchange*  237, 238, 260
International Teaching Fellowship (ITF)  233, 255, 227, 237, 247, 286, 312, 331, 369, 337, 370, 387, 389
Izard, J  294

## J

Jackman, Leon  196
James, Harold EO  112, 121, 145, 270

Japan  28, 108, 332, 356
    Wartime activity  71, 75, 78
    Computers  359
    Curriculum  361, 362
    Educational Budget  204
    International Teaching Fellowship  290, 356
    Japanese school  287, 288
    Tokyo  109, 331
    Youth Policies  358
Jeffery, George B  112
Jenkin, George A  162
Jenkin, Robert (Bob)  300
Jerilderie  14, 15
Jersild, Arthur  198
John Gardiner High School  287
Jones, Albert W (Alby)  166, 245, 283
    Barry O  22, 273
Joy, Barry  343, 344
Junior college  177
Junior technical schools/classes  80, 81, 147, 149, 152

## K

Kandel, Isaac L  108
    Karmel, Peter H  190, 228, 248, 249–51, 261, 263, 264, 278, 382
Keillerup, Fred  81, 84
Kellogg Foundation  178, 331
Kennedy, Jack  209
Kennedy, John F  176, 177
Kennedy, Graham  274
Kent, Mick  102, 103, 108, 246
Kew State School, No. 1075  162
King Farouk  123
    George VI  121
King, Martin Luther  177, 311
Knight, Pauline  55, 56, 370
Korong Vale  75–9, 93, 112, 119, 195, 246, 388
    Scully's hotel  76, 77
Korong Vale State School No. 1800  75
Korowa Church of England Girls Grammar School  185, 240, 243, 385
Krongold Centre, Monash University  315

La Trobe Teachers' College  162
    La Trobe University  215, 218, 232, 244–5, 356, 367

La Trobe Valley  287
Labor Government / Party  53, 143, 248, 284, 330, 335, 337, 346, 347, 364, 365, 387
Lacy, Norman  274, 316, 346, 348, 363, 370
   Vision for education  296, 315, 317, 326
      Tactics  318, 320, 321, 323, 325, 328, 330, 333, 335, 337
      Reflections on Shears  336, 349
Lady Godiva  126
Languages Other Than English (LOTE)  17, 286, 287, 288
Law, Arthur J  30, 61, 62, 64, 67, 71, 78, 124, 161
   Phillip G  55, 233, 234, 245, 316, 357, 357, 387, 388
Leach, John A  38
Leggatt, William W  143, 274
Liefman, Charles E (Ted)  48, 246, 387
Len Falk Memorial Lecture  386
Liberal Party / Government / policy  143, 318, 325, 327, 248, 252, 292, 318, 327, 330, 339, 340, 345, 346, 348, 363
Licence to Teach  25, 27
Life. Be In It.  383
Lifelong Learning  277, 291, 296
Limb, Chris  133, 134, 196, 197, 200
Lipham, James (Jim)  280, 283
Lismer, Arthur A  107
Literacy  25, 346, 347, 356, 360, 384
Little, Stewart (Headmaster, Miller Street)  55, 56, 57, 59
Little God Almighty  244
Loader, Harold E  65, 66, 70
Lo Bianco, Joseph (Jo)  352
Local Education Authorities (LEAs)  118, 185, 225, 260, 301
Longerenong Agricultural College  93
Lord, William F (Frank)  125, 126, 127, 131, 161, 372
Lord Mayor  48, 204
Lowndes, Ida  157, 162, 195, 245
Luck, Peter  287

# M

Macedonia  369
MacRobertson Girls' High School  338

Madgwick, Robert B  190, 191
Malvern Central School (Spring Road) No. 1604  220
Mander-Jones, Evan  274
Mannix College  257, 278
Manpower, Directorate of  72, 75, 87
Maribyrnong  90, 229
Martin Report  232, 234, 235, 291
Martin, Father Frank  264
Maslen, Geoff  332, 334, 337, 365, 370
Master Plan for higher education in California  180, 181, 231
Matheson, JA Louis  239
Mathews, C Race T  250
   Iola  238, 239
McCloskey, Bertram  156
McCrae, Georgiana  9
McDonell, Alexander (Alex)  54, 93, 94, 96, 136, 167, 191, 192, 199, 200, 215
   Douglas M  158, 161, 235, 236
McGaw, Barry  384
McKeown, Paul  204–5, 272
McKinnon, Kenneth R (Ken)  245, 250, 340, 352, 376
McKinty, W (Bill)  165, 186
McLaren, Ian F  199
McLellan, Robert  149, 150
McLeod, Robert A  320
McMillan, Allan  67, 70, 85, 86, 98
McPherson, William M  160
McRae, Christopher R (Chris)  30, 54, 107, 168
   James  56, 59–60, 62, 76, 78
Meccano  34
Melba Hall  44, 63
Melbourne Club  10, 248, 307, 386
   Cricket Ground  39, 135
   High School  25, 40, 47, 54, 93, 142, 144, 220, 338, 342, 338
   Teachers College  56, 58, 59, 109, 123, 159, 161, 164
      Shears' experience  59–73
   Teacher Training College  28, 53
   Technical College  90, 131, 159, 161
   Town Hall  46, 48, 109
Mellow, Charles  64, 160
Menzies, Robert G  57, 204, 232
Migration  9, 142, 286, 348
Miller Keith T  40

Millikan, Ross H 339
Ministerial Consultative Committee 321, 323
Ministry for Post-War Reconstruction 89
Montague Special School 385
Montessori philosophies 35
Moorabbin Technical College 315
Mooroopna 20, 100
Moorhouse, Charles E 169, 232
Morwell 287, 288, 386
Morton, Stewart F 177, 218, 224, 237, 257, 268, 333, 343
Moyle, Colin RJ 259, 260, 269, 280, 283, 285, 294, 329, 337, 373, 385
Mt Buffalo 32, 33
Mt Major 98, 386
Murfett, Rex S 153, 290, 332, 368
Murphy, Leo J 160, 161
Murray River 14, 15, 75
Myer 49, 160, 229, 331
Myrtleford 73, 87, 130, 170
   High School 314

# N

National Bureau of Education, South Africa 108
   Commission on Teacher Education and Professional Standards, San Diego 182
   Education Association (USA) 175, 179
   Education Conference 190
   Survey of Teachers in Australia 202, 205, 364
   Theatre Company 63
Nattrass, Peter 339
Neale, Marie 315
Nietzsche, Friedrich 124
New Education / Fellowship 1, 26, 30, 53, 82, 108, 206, 240, 260, 296
Newman, 240
Newton, Burt 274
New York 108, 175, 178, 180, 182, 183, 184, 186, 223, 290, 291, 331, 362
New Zealand 28, 47, 107, 108, 109, 116, 127, 172, 290, 356
*News Exchange* 237, 260, 297, 366
Nixon, Harold A 320
Nongovernment/independent schools 28, 41, 42, 47, 117, 118, 119, 216, 240, 242, 243, 250, 256, 265, 281, 311, 328, 346, 352, 368
Non-government School Registration Board 344
North Gippsland School of Mines 80
North Melbourne State School (Errol Street) No. 1402 49, 69
Norway
   Computers 359, 360
   Curriculum 362
Numurkah 14
Nunn, Sir Percy 108

# O

Office of the Director-General 255, 275, 320, 344, 355, 386
   of the Coordinator-General 345
   of Education, Commonwealth / Federal 179, 207
   of Education US 175
   of the Agent-General, London 185, 224, 226
Old Model School 41
Operation Upgrade 249
Organisation for Economic Cooperation and Development (OECD) 331
Organisations Reference Group 321
Osmond, HS (Bert) 165, 335
Oversea Students 111
Oxford Travelling Scholarship 29

# P

PA Consulting Australia 328
Palmer, Imelda 339
Parliamentary Liberal Party Education Committee 318
Penny, H Harry 155
Penshurst 20, 87, 94
Pharmacy College 234
Philanthropic investment 175, 178
Phillip Institute 157, 299, 366
Piaget, Jean 108
Plain English Speaking Award 313, 331
Platoon system 54, 134, 198
Policy Committee 333, 376
Port Phillip Bay / District 8, 9, 10, 12, 130, 142
Portland 8, 13, 16, 17, 18, 20
Portland State College (USA) 183
Post-secondary schooling 196, 215, 256,

292, 295, 296, 298, 312, 316, 325, 337, 343, 360, 361, 362, 364, 367
Prahran 33, 233, 260, 299
Predl, Ian 297, 298
Prefabricated buildings 98, 125, 135, 146, 148
Prictor, John B 65, 66
Primary schools 35, 61, 117, 120, 124, 127, 129, 147, 150, 152, 154, 156, 268, 320, 361, 362
Prince Albert, Duke of York 31
Princes Bridge 14, 33, 72
Pederson, Clare 224
Project Method 61
Provan, James L 91, 100
Pryor, Leonard J (Len) 124, 125, 143, 144, 146, 154, 161, 164, 165, 195, 196, 230
Psychology 2, 56, 59, 77, 112, 127, 128, 129, 133, 143, 182, 188, 207, 270, 283, 388
Psychology and Guidance Branch 143, 230
Public
 interest 178, 273, 276, 339
 Lecture Theatre 61
 Service Board 252, 253, 268, 321, 340, 341, 345
 transport 156, 199
 Works Department (PWD) 147, 155, 218, 237, 251, 257, 269
Punt Road 33, 162, 163
Pupil teacher 24, 26, 27, 62

## Q

Queen competition 85
Queen Elizabeth II (Princess Elizabeth) 121, 135, 331
Queen Elizabeth (Queen Mother) 121
Queenscliffe 164, 267
Queensland 201, 207, 241, 330, 337, 364

## R

Radford, William C (Bill) 84, 150, 167, 169, 170, 173, 207, 232, 244
Radley (*see* Shears)
Radio 31, 61, 78, 83, 128, 206, 217, 269, 273, 287, 359
Rafferty, Chips 117
 Joseph A 226
Ramsay, Alan H 54, 55, 127, 133, 142–3, 144, 145, 146, 148, 154, 157, 159, 163, 167, 168, 170, 172, 173, 191, 192, 202, 208, 215
Ramsay, Thomas M 232
Rathdowne Street Rural 68
Rayner, SA 203
RE Ross Fellowship Program 382, 383
Recession 25, 224, 357
Red Cross 45, 65, 85, 87, 156
 Australian Red Cross National Committee for International Humanitarian Law 385
Redman (*see* Shears)
Reed, Ronald A 192, 372
Regional development 255, 258
 director(s) 260, 319, 334, 352
 discussion groups 164–5
 network 258
 offices 259, 276, 282, 294, 353, 354
 structure 3, 177, 237, 254, 259, 276, 319, 320, 350, 354, 386
Reid, Arnaud 112
Reid, Geoffrey A 263, 300
Renwick, William L 290, 291
Repatriation Commission 90
Reports (using shortened names where possible)
 Asche Report (Interim) (1980) 294
 Asche Report (Final) (1981) 295
 Auchmuty/NITE Report (1978) 294, 295
 Blackburn Report (1985) 379
 Bland Report 1 (1974) 252, 253, 329
 Cohen Report (1973) 103
 Faure Report (1972) 289
 Fourth University Report (Victoria) 1972 232
 Galbally Report (1978) 287
 Hadow Report(s) (United Kingdom) (1923–33) 82
 Kangan Report (1974) 293, 296
 Karmel Report (1973) 248, 249, 250, 251, 261, 263, 264, 278, 382
 McNair Report (United Kingdom) (1944) 112, 119, 144, 231, 389
 Martin Report (1964) 232, 234, 235, 291
 Murray Report on Australian Universities (1957) 232, 291, 292

PA Report (1980) 340
Pike Report (1929) 91
Plowden Report (United Kingdom) (1967) 216, 263
Ramsay (Alan) Report (1960) 191, 329
Ramsay (Thomas) Report (1972) 232
Report on Educational Organization and Development (Germany) (1972) 227
Report on Educational Reform and Development in Victoria by the Council of Public Education Victoria (1945) 398
Robbins Report (United Kingdom) (1963) 185, 389
Scott Report (1973) 230, 238
Southwell Report (1971) 229, 329
Strayer Report (California) (1947) 231
Williams Report (1979) 293
Residential seminars / groups 144, 164–7, 206, 241, 257, 267, 278, 280, 281, 324
Returned Sailors' and Soldiers' Imperial League of Australia (RSSILA or RSL) 91, 95
RG Wilson Scholarship 144
Richardson, Millicent (Shears) 170
Ring, Barry 148
Ringwood High School 148
Road Safety and Traffic Authority 315
Robinvale 77
Robertson, Thomas L 202, 203, 204, 216, 235
Robertson and Mullens 137
Rockefeller Foundation 178
Roscholler, John N 260, 343
Ross-Edwards, Peter 336
Rossiter, John F 216
Rotary Club of Melbourne 248, 306, 313, 337, 367, 385
Royal Children's Hospital 383
Rugg, Harold 108
Rural Reconstruction Committee 91
Rural Training Centre (RTC) 2, 89–104, 246
Russia
    International Teaching Fellowship 289, 290, 356

Technological advance 120, 177, 179
Russell, Lillian (Shears) 87
Russell, William B (Bill) 215–16, 217, 219
Ruwolt, Charles E 125
Ryan, Anthony (Tony) 205

## S

Salter, Davies E 108
Sampson, William E (Bill) 269
San Francisco 174, 177, 187, 226, 239
Sargeant, Harold B 158, 162
    Kenneth D (Ken), Joy 201, 246, 338, 372, 385
Satchell, David V 144, 146, 162, 164
Saturday School of Languages 288
Saunders, Allen 74
Scandinavian Air System (SAS) 184
Scantling timber 130
Scarff, Charles F 74
School architecture / design
    Buninyong model 23
    Light timber construction (LTC) 148, 155
    Masonry veneer 155, 347
School review 266, 285
    PAAP 266
    SAAP 266
    Senior Teacher Class 266
School and the community
    Heidelberg model 261, 383
    (see Director-General's Paper 4) 260
School within a school
    Greek Orthodox 287
    La petite école 287
    Japanese school 287, 288
Schools of mines 80, 81, 233
Schruhm, Albert E (Bert) 224, 245
Scotch College 44, 210
Scotland 8, 9, 28, 117, 153, 185, 226, 360
SCV Rusden 283, 284, 294, 299
Seaford–Carrum High School 323
Searle, Barney 40
Secondary schools 28, 82, 147, 150, 152, 153, 154, 164, 187, 190, 200, 216, 223, 239, 242, 297, 302, 303, 328, 331, 359, 360, 363
Secondary Teachers College 54, 153, 158, 161, 169, 191, 220, 224, 235, 342

Seconded / secondment  75, 90, 94, 205, 207, 217, 224, 256, 320, 323, 326, 328, 352, 382
Seitz, John Arnold  55, 57, 74, 76, 107
Selby-Smith, Richard  210, 232, 242, 245, 366, 376
Senate House  111
Senior, Roy L (Lloyd)  272
Seymour  95, 101
Sharman, Mathew Stanton  29, 43, 44, 45, 73, 374
Shaw, George B  35
Sloane, Herbert VF  320

...

**Shears, Lawrence William (Lawrie)**
**Section 1.** *The first section of entries for Shears is presented chronologically rather than alphabetically.*
Birth and boyhood (childhood)
  Birth  7
  Beechworth  32, 33
  Crystal set  34
  Southern Naturalists Club  41
  Sunday School  34
Schooldays
  Elsternwick State School  38–41
  University High School  41–9
  Windsor State School  35–7
Home
  Head Street  37, 48
  Newry Street  33, 36, 37
  Pakington Street  37
Student teacher
  Miller Street  55–8
Trainee teacher, Melbourne TC  59–73
  College life  61, 62, 63
  Curriculum  61, 63, 64, 70
  Friendships  70, 71, 72
  Sporting activities  63, 71
  Teaching experience  64–70
University studies  71, 79, 87, 100, 103
Country teacher
  Bairnsdale  80–5
  Community contributions  78, 84–8
  Inspection  77, 84, 85
  Korong Vale  75–9
Rural Training Centre
  Life at  94–100
  Outcomes  102–3

Situation  91–3
Thesis  100–2, 121
Marriage  98
Doctoral studies  109–23
  Institute of Education  111–13
  Thesis (Dynamics of Leadership) 113–16
  Lecture tours  116–7
  Bedales School  113, 117
  Dorking County Grammar School 113
  Education in Britain  118–19
  Education in Sweden  120
College lecturer
  The Little Doctor  2, 123, 126, 129, 267, 372
  Toorak TC  125–30
  'Aims of Education'  128–9
  Burwood TC  131–5
Survey and planning officer
  Educational scene  141–3, 146–7
  Survey and Planning, the position 143–5
  School buildings  148
  Educational expansion  149, 151–5
  Ferntree Gully Case  149–50
  Primary teacher education  151–7
  Secondary teacher education  157–9
  Technical and special teacher education  159–61
Harkness Experience
Harkness Fellow  171–88
  Study program  174–5
  Educational scene  176–7
  Observations in the USA  177–9, 180–2
  Commonwealth Fund authorities' response  180, 183–4
  State College System (California) 175, 180–1
College principal
  Burwood Statement  189, 197–8
  Burwood model  197
  College life  196, 198–202
  Golden years  210, 372
  Philosophies of teaching  193–4, 196–8, 198–9
  Monash connections  210
  Professional standards  235–6

Assistant Director-General
   Educational scene 215-16
   Appointment 216-18
   Professional and public support 218-20
   Profile of the Minister: Thompson 220-2
   National educational crisis
      Growth 227-8, 230
      Commonwealth stance 228
      Pressure groups 229
      Accountability 229, 232-3
Director-General
   Professional and public support 244-6
   National scene 248-51, 273
   Shears' scene 249-53, 274
   Vision (see Policy Papers) 240, 247, 253
   Policy papers
      Paper 1: *Structure at the State level: departmental guidelines for the future* 255-6
      Paper 2: *Planning Services Division* 256-8
      Paper 3: *Structure at the regional level* 258-60
      Paper 4: *The school and the community* 260-5
      Paper 5: *The teacher and the school administrator* 265-9
   Australian Education Council Standing Committee 227, 245, 251, 316, 342, 351
   Five-year planning 240, 253
   Working with unions
Coordinator-General
   Office of Coordinator-General 341-78
      Establishing the role 344-5
      Liberal pickle 340, 345-7
      Fordham's platform 347-9
      Footprints on Fordham's policy papers 349-55
   Ministerial reports
      Youth policies (1983) 357-9
      Computers (1983) 359-61
      Curriculum (1984) 361-3
      Administration (1984) 363-4

Retirement 371
   Reflections 371
   Response 374-82
   Post retirement
   RE Ross Trust 382-3
   Commonwealth Education Centres 382
   Computers in Education 384
   Duke of Edinburgh 385
   Agribusiness 384

**Shears, Lawrence William (Lawrie)**
**Section 2. Other endeavours**

Research activity
   Australian College of Education 169-70, 204-6, 208, 217, 241-2, 265, 280, 306
   Australian Association for Research in Education 206-7, 241
   Victorian Institute of Educational Research 33, 136-7, 167-9, 217, 241
Other activity
   College of Nursing Australia 208-9, 217, 219, 241, 243, 245, 306, 372, 377
   Other professional, personal links 240, 241
   ANZAAS Conference address 242
   UNESCO 227, 269-71, 289, 356
   Teacher shortage (see ITF, VTSP)
   Promotion of teacher education 210, 231-3,
      Victoria Institute of Colleges 215, 233-4, 254, 373,
      State College system 234-7, 247, 284, 293, 319, 342,
      Fourth University Committee 232, 236-7, 239, 253
Teacher- child relationship 117, 128, 261, 262
Ministerial relationship
   Thompson 220, 239-40, 269, 276, 316, 322, 346
   Fordham 348, 376
   Hunt 315, 316, 317, 320, 322-3, 330, 332, 346
   Lacy 315, 317, 323, 328, 330, 333, 336, 337, 349

**Shears, Lawrence William (Lawrie)**
**Section 3. Family**
Shears line
  Babbington, Richard 12
  Halden, Mary (Craig) (Great-great grandmother) 8–11
    Robert (Great-great grandfather) 8–12
  Shears, Robert William (Grandfather) 13, 14
    Ernest William (Ernie) / Poppa (Father) 7, 15, 16, 20, 31–4, 37, 41, 44, 47, 48, 73, 75, 87, 110, 123, 130, 170, 240
    Stephen Thomas (Great grandfather) 8, 12, 13
    Mary / Young Mary (Halden) (Great-grandmother) 10, 11, 12
    Edna Anderson (Aunt) 15
    Aunt Lil 48
    Cousin Howard 39
    Cousin Ellis 37, 47
  Leithoff, Charles Frederick (Great grandfather) 6, 14
    Annie (Elizabeth) (Grandmother) 6, 7, 8, 14, 15, 16, 31, 34
    Mary Charlotte (Higham) (Great grandmother) 6, 14
Brand line
  Brand, Frederick Charles (Great grandfather) 6, 7
    Rebecca (Cook) (Great grandmother) 6, 18
    Josiah (Grandfather) 6, 8, 16, 18, 20, 34, 37,
    Victoria Madeline (Radley) (Grandmother) 6, 8, 16, 18, 20, 34, 37
    Dorothy Irene (Mother) 6, 7, 8, 16, 18, 20, 31, 32, 34, 37, 47
  Radley, John 6, 20
    Mary Anne (Hooley) (Great grandmother) 6, 20
    Suzanne (Patching) (Great-great grandmother) 6, 20
    William (Great-great-great grandfather) 18, 19
    Catherine (Cavanagh) (Great-great-great grandfather) 18
Mavis's family
  Redman, Mavis Margaret
    Young woman 85, 87, 88, 93
    Wife 97, 98, 101, 109, 110, 130, 131, 145, 176–7, 201, 227, 271, 285, 289, 374, 375, 386, 391
    Mother 98, 99, 135, 170, 184, 185, 306
    Independent woman 116, 121, 195, 240, 314
  Fred (Mavis's father) 87, 110, 123, 240
  Ethel (Mavis's mother) 240
  Betty (Mavis's sister) 87, 385
  Radley connection (unidentified link) Sir Gordon 116, 184
    Lady Dorothy 184
    Jennifer 184
Immediate family
  Christine M 98, 99, 109, 110, 116, 121, 123, 135, 170, 177, 184, 185, 240, 246, 389
  Mark L 121, 135, 170, 177, 184, 185, 389
  Paul W 170, 177, 184, 185, 385
  Meredith J 170, 184, 185, 240, 246, 382, 389
  Anne 170
  Barbara Brand 390
...
Shepparton 16, 20, 42, 49, 87, 92, 99, 281, 282
  Football league 99
  Preserving Company (SPC) 20, 99, 103
Ships
  *Alan Kerr* 9
  *Argyle* 9
  *Canada* 19
  *Ceylan* 18
  *Dominion Monarch* 185
  *Frances and Eliza* 19
  *HMS Windham* 18
  *SS Mariposa* 177
  *SS Moreton Bay* 110
  *SS Otranto* 123

Ulysses 19
Warrior 19
Shrine of Remembrance 44
Slater, Patricia V (Pat) 208, 209, 219, 372, 373
Sloyd 36, 76
Smith, Elmer 186
Smyth, John 28, 29, 62, 109, 161
   John and Eric Smyth Travelling Scholarship 103
   John Smyth Memorial Lecture 63, 109, 203, 367
Snook, Harold 86
Social Studies 77, 83, 84, 108, 129, 132, 134, 166
Socrates 21
Slomons campaign 78
Solomon Islands 382
Southwell, Alec J / Report 229, 238, 329
Spaull, Andrew D 383
Spearman, Charles 108
Special Committee for Appointments to Professional Positions in Teachers Colleges 154
Sputnik 177, 179
St Andrew's church, Bairnsdale 85, 86, 98
St Ellen, Joseph J (Joe) 127, 136, 161, 372
St John Ambulance Marketing Committee 385
St John's, Footscray 16
St John's, Toorak / vestry 240, 307, 323, 335, 367, 377
St Margaret's School 156
State Advisory Council on Tertiary Education 235
   Board of Education 349, 350, 351–2, 353, 354
   College of Victoria (SCV) 234–7, 247, 284, 293, 342
   Council for Technical Education 297
   Colleges, USA 175, 180–1, 183, 187–8
   Library 48
   Planning Council 247
   Rivers and Water Supply Commission 100, 103
   Savings Bank 87, 248
   schools 21, 35–6, 37–8, 42, 49, 53, 55, 64, 66, 67, 68, 69, 75, 93, 131, 135, 155, 161, 162, 195, 242, 347, 370, 374, 388
Statement of Aims and Objectives for Education in Victoria 325
Stewart, Alexander 27
Stephen, James Wilberforce 21
Stephenson, Jack 72
Stevens, H Geoffrey (Geoff) 48, 69, 385, 387
Story Street, Parkville 41, 43, 44
Streader, D Clive 103, 149, 150, 260
Street, Anthony A (Tony) 330
Studentship 54, 74, 132, 133, 155, 157, 162, 200, 230
Suart, Wendy Law 44
Surrey 13, 133
Survey and Planning Officer
   of needs 145, 180, 227
   of Needs, California (1948) 227, 231
Swanson Committee on Teacher Education (1973) 292, 293
Sweden 117, 120
   Computers 359, 360
   Curriculum 362
   Youth Policies 358
Swinburne College of Advanced Education 205
Swinburne University of Technology 229
Sydney 33, 177, 204, 205, 249, 287, 306
   Cove 8, 18
   Gazette 19
   Road 43, 157, 162
   Teachers College 29
   University of 91, 168, 202, 241, 296

# T

TAFE 256, 276, 286, 291, 292–3, 296–8, 316, 358, 361, 364, 376
Tannock, Peter D 365, 367, 382, 383
Tasmania 18, 19, 63, 98, 201, 218, 364
   Tate, Frank 26–8, 41, 59–60, 76, 77, 107, 108, 137, 161, 162, 107, 173, 176, 179, 181–2, 183–4, 186, 187, 197, 202, 205, 210, 230, 232–3, 235–7, 245, 255, 260, 270, 313, 366, 370
   Building, Melbourne TC 59, 68
   House 162
   Memorial Lecture (see VIER)

Tate (Headmaster, Coburg East State School) 64
Taylors College 47
Teacher education 53, 55, 61, 111, 113, 134, 142, 154, 161, 215, 235, 236, 245, 286, 291–2, 293–5, 299, 329
(*see also* Fourth University, Murray Report, National Inquiry into teacher Education, Special Services, State College of Victoria, Swanson Committee, Victoria Institute of Colleges, Victorian Enquiry into Teacher Education)
  education (Burwood TC) 197, 202, 205, 210
  education (California) 174, 175, 176, 179, 181, 182, 183, 184
  education (Primary) 155
  education (Secondary) 157
  education (Superintendent) (*see* Pryor)
  shortage 151, 158, 222, 239, 305
  supply 25, 112, 124, 152, 216, 223, 237, 253, 256
  training 3, 26, 28, 53, 55, 62, 70, 124, 125, 144, 154, 158, 160, 161, 162, 170, 172, 174, 175, 176, 179, 181, 183, 187, 193, 195, 196, 197
  unions 288, 319, 325, 335
Technical Teachers' Association of Victoria (TTAV) 229
Victorian Secondary Teachers' Association (VSTA) 192, 229, 259, 263, 266, 299, 300, 303, 304, 305, 342, 346, 349, 370
Victorian Teachers' Union (VTU) 74, 192, 166, 229, 245, 333, 399
Teachers College, Columbia University 108, 179, 186
Teachers college hostels 144, 146, 158, 162, 163, 164, 167
Teachers colleges (Victoria)
  Adelaide 155
  Armidale 219
  Ballarat 53, 125, 126, 131, 135, 152, 155, 156, 161
  Bendigo 53, 125, 131, 135, 144, 152, 154, 155, 156, 161, 164
  Burwood 131–57, 161, 162, 164, 189–212, 299, 314, 375, 385
  Coburg 155, 157, 162, 195, 245, 268
    Pentridge 157
  Emily McPherson College of Domestic Economy (Emily Mac) 160, 407
  Frankston 156, 162, 195, 260, 299
    Struan 155, 156, 162
  Geelong 125, 131, 135, 155, 161
    Lunan House 155, 161
  Glendonald School for the Deaf 131, 160, 161, 162
  Larnook 160, 161
  La Trobe 162
  Melbourne 29, 53, 56, 58, 59–73, 107, 109, 123, 159, 161, 164
    Teacher Training Institute 28, 30
  Monash 159, 162, 191
  Secondary 54, 153, 154, 158, 159, 161, 169, 220, 220, 224, 235, 342
  Toorak 123, 125, 134, 161, 218, 372, 195
    Claymore 125, 156,
    Glenbervie 125, 126, 155, 160
    Lady Godiva / Topper 126
    Stonington 156, 160, 161
Teachers Tribunal 229, 230, 253, 269, 325, 341, 346, 349
Technical and Further Education (*see* TAFE)
  Administrative Committee 297
Technical Schools 56, 150, 162, 250, 260, 261
  Bairnsdale 80, 81, 82
  Schools Division 159, 259, 258, 278, 297
  Training Scheme 90
Technological advance 31, 128, 141, 190, 215, 227, 279, 254, 360, 371, 379
Temporary lecturer / assistant 55, 126, 131
  premises 134, 155
  teacher / assistant 75, 78, 79, 153, 158, 223, 349
Tertiary Education Assistance Scheme (TEAS) 248
Thailand
  Computers 359
  Curriculum 361, 362

Leadership Training 285
Youth Policies 358
*The Ritz* 60
*The School Paper* 31, 38, 57, 58, 78
*The Sun* 240
*The Trainee* 60, 62, 63, 70, 71, 72
*The Victorian Readers* 31, 38
Thompson, Lindsay HS
    Profile 220-2, 228
    International Teaching Fellowship 225
    Minister of Education 199, 215, 220, 228, 229, 239, 250, 251, 252, 253, 258, 269, 270, 272, 315, 316, 317, 320, 322, 370
    Premier 272, 335, 337, 346, 355, 356, 373, 374
    Relationship with Shears (*see* Shears)
Thorndike, Edward 108
Tickell, Gerry 299, 352
Timpson, Tom H 169
Tocumwal 15
Topp, Charles A 25
Tovell, Raymond W 143
Towns, Deborah 384
    Trainee teacher 1, 24, 29, 42, 53, 54, 58-65, 67-70, 74, 75, 109, 124-9, 131-5, 144, 146, 155, 156, 160, 163, 171, 177, 182, 187, 193, 195, 107, 221, 224, 233, 235
Tweedledee 276
Tweedledum 276
Tylee, AF (Tom) 205

# U

UK
    Computers 359
    Curriculum 361, 362
    Doctoral Studies 109
    Knowledge Exchange 103, 108, 144, 148, 158, 173, 175, 184, 193, 195, 237, 268, 270
    Teacher Recruitment 223, 224, 240, 289, 331
    Teacher Work Conditions 301, 302, 303
    Youth Policies 119, 358
UNESCO 107, 144, 227, 289, 291, 296, 334
    18th General Conference, Paris 1974 269-71
    19th General Conference, Nairobi 1976 356, 357
United Nations
    Charter of the United Nations Act 271
    Day 287
    International Schools (UNIS) 290, 306
    Universal Declaration of Human Rights 270, 271
University High School 1, 29, 41-8
University of Adelaide 190
    of Alberta 224, 238, 268, 284
    of British Columbia 183
    of California 178, 179, 181, 186, 223
    of Cape Town 111
    of Chicago (Illinois) 183, 187
    of Colorado (Boulder) 187
    Dijon 107
    Edinburgh 109
    of Hawaii 284
    of Heidelberg 109
    of London 107, 111, 172, 342, 397
    of Melbourne 25, 29, 39, 41, 43, 54, 61, 80, 93, 103, 127, 137, 144, 149, 159, 161, 172, 174, 204, 206, 220, 224, 232, 242, 245, 267, 282, 283, 284, 299, 327, 337, 339, 342, 343, 346, 347
    Michigan (Ann Arbor) 182, 187
    of New England 190, 267, 279, 283, 284
    of New South Wales 189
    of New York 186
    of Oregon 268
    of Pittsburg 367
    of Queensland 367
    of Southern California 188
    Sydney 168, 202, 241, 296
    of Technology, Swinburne 299
    of Washington 179
    of Wisconsin (Madison) 141, 179, 183, 280, 283
    Wayne State 182, 187, 187, 270
    Practicing School 43
Upwey Higher Elementary School 75
USA

Computers 360
Curriculum 362
Educational Budget 204, 218
Educational Scene, 1950s 176-7, 178, 183, 195
International Teaching Fellowship 225, 289
Knowledge Exchange 29, 30, 107, 108, 109, 136-7, 158, 172, 173, 193, 238-9, 332
Philosophies of Education 186, 187
Teacher Recruitment 179, 223-5, 226
Work Conditions 301, 302, 303
Youth Policies 358
Usher-Smith, Kathleen 111

## V

Valley Sawmills 130
VE Day 85
Vernon, Philip 112
Victoria College 299
    Gardens 34
    Institute of Colleges (VIC) 215, 233-4 236, 245, 247, 253, 270, 273, 298, 315, 357, 388
Victorian Enquiry into Teacher Education (1981) 293-5, 329
    Federation of State Schools Mothers Clubs 242, 246, 282, 230
    In-service Education Committee 251
    Post-Secondary Education Commission (1978) 298, 316, 337
    Primary Principals' Association 314
    Railways 32, 160
    Teacher Selection Program (VTSP) 223, 224, 237, 253, 289, 389
Vietnam War 177, 273
Vincent, Frank R 156
Violet Town 95, 101
Virtue, Rosalie 39
Vroland, Anton WR 38, 374

## W

Wagner, John 156
Wainwright, Gwendoline M (Gwen) 64, 158, 244
Wales 116, 117, 226, 360
Walker, Evan H 335
    William G (Bill) 267, 279, 282, 321, 340, 367
Wallace, Robert S 90
Waller, Donald M 131-5, 161, 194, 196
Wanganui District (NZ) 28, 109
Warburton 49, 220, 325, 326, 328
War effort
    Industry 30, 90
    Schools 45, 58, 72, 78, 85
Warrnambool 18, 42
Warrnambool Technical College 233
Washington DC 180, 226, 239
Watkins, A Noel 323, 343, 385
Watson, William C (Bill) 134, 136, 158, 162
Wattenberg, W 182, 187, 270
Wattle Park Teachers College (SA) 155
WD Scott & Co 229, 230, 238, 327, 329
Wedderburn 76, 78, 79
Wesley College 44, 283, 284
Westall High School 313
Westbrook, Eric 199, 331
Western District (Victoria) 10, 20, 94
Westminster system 316, 324, 334, 349, 381
Whitehead, Graham J 297, 306, 324, 366
White Hills Technical School 250, 261
Whitehorse Technical College 278
Whiteoak, Leonard G (Len) 64, 68, 125, 161, 195
White Paper 317, 325-6, 328-9, 333, 334-5
Whittier Elementary School 177
Whiting, Milton S 336
Whitlam Labor government 248, 252, 274, 292, 347, 348
Wickman, EK 175-6, 178, 180, 183, 184
Wilcox, Alan 290, 390
Williams Committee (1976-79) 293
    Lorna 245
Williamstown 90, 389
Willis, Eric A 272
Wilson Hall 72
Wimmera 13, 203, 313
Windsor (see also Windsor State School) 33
Windsor Hotel 306
    State School No. 1896 35, 36, 37, 69, 374, 388

Winneke, Henry A  281
Winnetka Plan  30, 35, 83, 108, 260
Wirt, William A  260
Wodonga  248, 298, 383
Woodgate, George B  93, 94–5, 96, 102, 103, 145
Wordsworth, William  95
World War I (Great War)  16, 17, 30, 58, 85, 91, 132
World War II  71, 78, 273
Wrigley, Leslie J  43, 44, 62, 63, 136, 161
Wyeth, Ezra R  149, 150

Wyndham, Harold S  137, 168, 169, 235

# Y–Z

Yalca  7, 16, 41
Yarra Park State School No. 1406  93
You Yangs  63, 71
Yugoslavia, Computers  359
    International Teaching Fellowship  291, 332, 356, 368
    Youth Policies  358
Zilliacus, Laurin  108

www.ingramcontent.com/pod-product-compliance
Lightning Source LLC
Chambersburg PA
CBHW032027150426
43194CB00006B/184